HISTORICAL RHETORIC

An Annotated Bibliography
of Selected Sources in English

A
Reference
Publication
in
Literature

HISTORICAL RHETORIC

An Annotated Bibliography
of Selected Sources in English

Edited by

WINIFRED BRYAN HORNER

G.K.HALL &CO.

70 LINCOLN STREET, BOSTON, MASS.

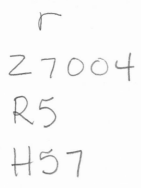

Library of Congress Cataloging in Publication Data
Main entry under title:

Historical rhetoric.

   Includes index.
   1. Rhetoric—Bibliography. I. Horner, Winifred
Bryan.
Z7004.R5H57   [PN187]   016.808   80-21947
ISBN 0-8161-8191-8

This publication is printed on permanent/durable acid-free paper
MANUFACTURED IN THE UNITED STATES OF AMERICA

Contents

Contents

General Introduction

This study is an attempt to trace the tradition of rhetoric through its long history from ancient Greece to its evolution within the English-speaking world. Modern scholars are inclined to forget the long intertwining of the roots of such disciplines as philosophy, psychology, grammar, rhetoric, poetics, logic, aesthetics, and literary criticism, but the roots are buried deep in the intellectual soil of Western civilization, and a study of any one of these disciplines must finally include some knowledge of the others.

Rhetoric can never be successfully or neatly removed for study from other areas of intellectual endeavor, any more than those areas can be fully comprehended without some knowledge of historical rhetoric. The anatomy student who studies the heart in isolation from the circulatory system and from the rest of the body must temporarily ignore the rest of the body in order to probe the single organ, but an understanding of the separate organ will eventually enhance the understanding of the whole. Similarly, though rhetoric may be presented here cut off from other disciplines, its life ultimately depends on its interconnection with other areas of human knowledge. All thought takes form in language, and language, in turn, produces and generates new intellectual currents. Historically, rhetoric has been concerned with the discovery of ideas and their proliferation through oral and written discourse. Thus, the great philosophers of all ages have recognized that rhetoric stands at the center of all intellectual endeavor.

If this bibliography here and there conjoins other disciplines, the reason is that the separation and excision can never be neat or clear. The authors grant, willingly, that separating rhetoric from other disciplines is always difficult--sometimes impossible--and admittedly reductive, but this work represents an effort to separate the roots of rhetoric in order to better understand that single and singular tradition.

Rhetoric can be defined only within a cultural context, and the point at which rhetoric is rhetoric, and not a number of other things, is difficult to determine at any time. As men discover their world, define their realities, and interact with each other through the medium of discourse, the practice of rhetoric is born. From the practice comes theory, a statement of the ethical and linguistic concerns governing human interaction. The study of such concerns is the province of rhetoric, and this bibliography deals with that theory as it has altered and has been altered by the changing intellectual climate of each era. Scholars of rhetoric have traditionally focused on three aspects of language: the creative act, the linguistic text, and the effect of the text on the reader or the hearer. Although it is difficult to separate those aspects, rhetoric's historical concern has been with the creative act as that act seeks to gain the attention and conviction of an audience. That concern shaped and focused the selections included in this bibliography.

The range and diversity of historical rhetoric poses problems for any single researcher in any single field. Such diversity became obvious to the authors of this study as they pursued call numbers in unfamiliar parts of the library (or in unfamiliar libraries) and explored journals in disciplines other than their own. The scholars represented in the secondary works come from the fields of history, classics, philology, philosophy, speech, psychology, linguistics, English letters, and intellectual history. Such diversity, while suggesting an extraordinary richness of source materials, poses a problem for those people who are primarily, or only secondarily, interested in rhetoric since they must search through the literature of many disciplines. The bibliographers who compiled this study, each a specialist in a particular period of rhetoric, have attempted to draw together within a single work what they consider to be the basic studies of rhetoric from all periods and from many disciplines.

This select bibliography is designed to serve a number of purposes. First, it furnishes a list of important primary works for those persons who know these works only through secondary sources. Second, it provides a basis for a new focus for scholarship in English letters. Third, it suggests reliable translations of classical texts and indicates where they may be readily obtained by the student who may not have a reading knowledge of Greek or Latin. Finally, it allows scholars of rhetoric in any one historical period to see their work not only within the context of ancient doctrine, but also in the light of what immediately precedes or follows that one period.

The bibliography is divided into five sections that cover the following periods of history: the Classical period, the Middle Ages, the Renaissance, the eighteenth century, and the nineteenth century. Each section contains a list of primary works arranged in chronological order by date of publication, and a list of secondary studies arranged alphabetically by last name of author. The chronological arrangement of primary works is intended to give the reader a picture of rhetoric as it evolved in time. For the convenience of the reader, in all cases the most recent, or useful, or readily available edition is cited in preference to the editio princeps. The secondary sources include materials of three kinds: works about the primary works, works about the rhetorical concerns of the primary authors, and works about important rhetorical issues of the period. Page numbers are inclusive; that is, prefaces, introductions, indexes, and other materials are considered to be part of the total page count of each work cited. No attempt has been made to list all editions. A primary concern has been to inform the reader where a work may be easily obtained. Thus, if editions are available in facsimile or micro-reproduction, such information appears in the citation or annotation. Within this framework, each bibliographer has made adjustments on the basis of the particular problems posed by the period, which are covered by the authors in their introductions. Items that were not available for examination by the authors are designated by an asterisk preceding the entry number.

Finally, the bibliography is not intended to be complete, so that some scholars will look in vain for one, two, or three citations that they are convinced _must_ be included in such a work. All the bibliographers have attempted to present, through their introductions, selections, and annotations, a picture of the rhetoric of a period. The works listed are only meant to indicate trends and to suggest directions for anyone who wishes to go further.

There are a number of general studies that the scholar of historical rhetoric may find useful. The Province of Rhetoric, edited by Joseph Schwartz and John A. Rycenga (New York: The Ronald Press, 1965, 568 pp.) contains several articles on the early development of rhetorical theory. Two anthologies, Historical Studies of Rhetoric and Rhetoricians, edited by Raymond F. Howes (Ithaca, N.Y.: Cornell University Press, 1961, 460 pp.) and Readings in Rhetoric, edited by Lionel Crocker and Paul A. Carmack (Springfield, Ill.: Charles C. Thomas, 1965, 612 pp.), trace the tradition from early Greece to the modern "new rhetoric" of Kenneth Burke and I. A. Richards. In the eighteenth and nineteenth centuries, however, these two works emphasize primarily public speaking. All three anthologies are cited often in this bibliography since they contain reprints of many important secondary articles for all periods.

Richard Lanham's A Handlist of Rhetorical Terms: A Guide for Students of English Literature (Berkeley: University of California Press, 1969, 160 pp.) is an excellent dictionary of rhetorical terminology derived chiefly from classical sources. He provides pronunciation, examples, and definitions of the terms. Finally, James J. Murphy's Doctoral Dissertations on Rhetoric and Rhetorical Criticism (Ann Arbor, Mich.: University Microfilms International, n.d., 32 pp.) provides a list of more than 400 dissertations on the subject of rhetoric available from University Microfilms.

WINIFRED BRYAN HORNER
University of Missouri–Columbia
General Editor

Abbreviations

ABR	American Benedictine Review
AJP	American Journal of Philology
Archiv	Archiv für das Studium der Neueren Sprachen und Literaturen
BCRE	British and Continental Rhetoric and Elocution Microfilms. Ann Arbor, Mich.: 1953
C&M	Classica et Mediaevalia
CCC	College Composition and Communication
CE	College English
CF	Classical Folia: Studies in the Christian Perpetration of the Classics
CJ	Classical Journal
CM	Communication Monographs (formerly Speech Monographs)
CP	Classical Philology
CSSJ	Central States Speech Journal
EAI	Early American Imprints, 1639–1800. Edited by Clifford K. Shipton. Published for the American Antiquarian Society. Worcester, Mass.: Readex Corporation, 1969.
Ed	Education
EJ	English Journal
ELH	Journal of English Literary History
HLQ	Huntington Library Quarterly
HSCP	Harvard Studies in Classical Philology
JEGP	Journal of English and Germanic Philology
JHI	Journal of the History of Ideas
JMRS	Journal of Medieval and Renaissance Studies
MAE	Medium AEvum
M&H	Medievalia et Humanistica: Studies in Medieval and Renaissance Culture
MKNAL	Mededelingen der Koninklijke Nederlandse Akademie, Afdeling Letterkunde
MLN	Modern Language Notes
MLR	Modern Language Review
MP	Modern Philology
MS	Mediaeval Studies
NEQ	New England Quarterly
NUC	National Union Catalog
PAPS	Proceedings of the American Philosophical Society
PBA	Proceedings of the British Academy
PMLA	Publications of the Modern Language Association of America
PQ	Philological Quarterly
PR	Philosophy and Rhetoric
QJS	Quarterly Journal of Speech
RES	Review of English Studies
RQ	Renaissance Quarterly
RUO	Revue de l'Université d'Ottawa
SM	Speech Monographs (see CM, Communications Monographs)
SMC	Studies in Medieval Culture

Abbreviations

SMed	Studi Medievali
SP	Studies in Philology
SQ	Shakespeare Quarterly
SRen	Studies in the Renaissance
SSJ	Southern Speech Communication Journal (formerly SSB, Southern Speech Bulletin)
ST	Speech Teacher
TAPA	Transactions and Proceedings of the American Philological Association
TCBS	Transactions of the Cambridge Bibliographical Association
TS	Today's Speech (now Communication Quarterly)
TSLL	Texas Studies in Literature and Language
UTQ	University of Toronto Quarterly
WMQ	William and Mary Quarterly
WS	Western Speech

Part 1
The Classical Period
RICHARD LEO ENOS

Introduction

As the subsequent sections of this work will demonstrate, the history of rhetoric is rooted in its classical origins. This section attempts to synthesize, for the reader of English, a collection of works that will make apparent the important contributions of Greek and Roman rhetoric. In order to facilitate an understanding of this collection, certain general presumptions about the study of classical rhetoric need to be made clear.

The study of classical rhetoric is commonly divided into two major categories: Greek and Roman. The establishment of rhetoric as a formal discipline is popularly credited to Corax and Tisias, two Sicilians who, in approximately the first quarter of the fifth century B.C., are believed to have developed the first systematic methods for effective discourse in public situations. Of course, techniques for the composition of oral and written literature were already being developed by such improvisators as Homeric bards and rhapsodes, lyric poets, Pre-Socratic philosophers and historians. As the readings of this collection illustrate, these individuals also contributed to the subsequent development and refinement of rhetoric. In fact, the close relationship of rhetoric to such disciplines as philosophy, history, and poetry is clearly established in the early years of rhetoric.

The classical period of fifth-century B.C. Athens witnessed the popularization of rhetoric and its subsequent spread throughout the Greek-speaking world. As rhetoric flourished, so did the theories and individuals who contributed to it, and some of the greatest minds of Western civilization, such as Plato and Aristotle, spent considerable time examining its nature and province.

Out of the Hellenic period, and with the spread of Greek culture throughout the known world in the Hellenistic age which followed, evolved the major traditions of rhetoric. These "traditions," as they have been characterized by such contemporary historians of rhetoric as James J. Murphy, can be distinguished on the basis of four major differences in emphasis. The Sophistic tradition, represented by such individuals as Gorgias of Leontini and Protagoras,

3

emphasized, usually in ornate style, notions of relativism and proba-
bility. This fifth-century B.C. phenomenon was revised in the second
century A.D. and called the "Second Sophistic," which was popularized
by Greek sophists who traveled throughout the Roman Empire teaching
rhetoric.

Next came the philosophical and grammatical traditions of rhetoric. The philosophical tradition arose with Plato, Aristotle, and
other thinkers who examined the philosophical and epistemological
presumptions of rhetoric--frequently in contrast to sophistic thought
and practice. The grammatical tradition, often considered a discipline in its own right, coexisted with or was subsumed by rhetoric
but persisted throughout the Greek world. All three traditions
flourished to varying degrees throughout the Greek world and subsequently, with the rise of the Roman Republic and the establishment
of the Empire, spread to the West and were often assimilated into
Roman culture.

Although these traditions are apparent in Latin works of
rhetoric, the Roman world was dominated by the Ciceronian tradition
of rhetoric. The rhetorical treatises of Marcus Tullius Cicero and
his deliberative and forensic orations became the standard for rhetoric in the Latin-speaking world. Virtually every subsequent Latin
rhetorician, such as Quintilian, Seneca, and Augustine, openly acknowledged his debt to Cicero. In fact, it is commonly believed that
even in the Middle Ages the study of rhetoric was based upon the
Rhetorica ad Herennium, thought to have been written by Cicero, and
his De Inventione. Ironically, although Cicero was a student of
Greek rhetoric, his writings had virtually no impact on the Greek
world.

This brief overview indicates the main presumptions on which the
history of classical rhetoric is based: specifically, that there
were two major geographical and cultural divisions, the Greek-
speaking East and the Latin-speaking West; and that these two divisions were influenced by major traditions of rhetoric.

One other major presumption which the contemporary reader should
be aware of is that virtually all ancient literature, oral and written, was intended to be read aloud. In fact, there is clear evidence
to indicate that very few ancient readers mastered the technique of
reading silently--all reading was meant to be oral. Therefore, it
should be understood that works discussing rhetoric in antiquity pertain to both oral and written discourse.

Finally, certain aspects of the format here should be noted.
This collection is composed of two major sections, primary and
secondary works. The primary sources, with translations, are dated
in order to provide a general idea of their chronology. The purpose
of this study is not to "fix" dates to works of rhetoric, but to
illustrate their general place in the progress of the discipline.

Introduction

It should be obvious that dating of these earlier treatises is almost always uncertain and never completely agreed upon. In those cases where even a remote date of the treatise was unavailable, the dates of the author's life or the century are listed.

The vast majority of the secondary works, which are presented in alphabetical order, are also intended for the reader of English. This collection should not be considered definitive or comprehensive; in fact, editing of several works, such as treatises of grammar, was necessary in order to meet the scope of the project. The goal of this undertaking is to draw together relevant readings for those interested in the general history of classical rhetoric. If the reader understands these presumptions and believes the collection to be a helpful starting point for a more detailed examination, then the objective of this work will have been attained.

This contribution would not have been possible without the support and encouragement of Jane E. Helppie of The University of Michigan and Richard E. Young of Carnegie-Mellon University. Special appreciation is extended to Otis M. Walter of the University of Pittsburgh for his careful reading and helpful criticism of the manuscript. Finally, recognition is due to the faculty, staff, and students at Carnegie-Mellon University, who do so much to encourage such research projects in rhetoric.

RICHARD LEO ENOS
Carnegie-Mellon University

Primary Works

1.1 Pre-Homeric to c̲. Peloponnesian War. <u>Die Fragmente der Vorsokratiker</u>. Edited by Herman Diels and Walter Kranz. 2 vols. Dublin: Weidmann, 1972, 1603 pp.

A comprehensive collection of fragments of Pre-Socratic thinkers. Many references to the theory and practice of rhetoric, particularly by sophists. The fragments are in the original Greek and contain some Latin references. Commentary in German.

1.1a FREEMAN, KATHLEEN. <u>Ancilla to the Pre-Socratic Philosophers</u>. Oxford: Basil Blackwell, 1971, 172 pp.

Presents a synopsis and translation of the fragments in <u>Die Fragmente der Vorsokratiker</u>. Philosophical and sophistic views of rhetoric are documented.

1.1b FREEMAN, KATHLEEN. <u>The Pre-Socratic Philosophers: A Companion to Diels, Fragmente der Vorsokratiker</u>. 2nd ed. Oxford: Basil Blackwell, 1966, 499 pp.

This work, along with the <u>Ancilla</u>, is intended to provide the reader with a thorough knowledge of the fragments of Pre-Socratic thinkers.

1.2 c̲. 387-385 B.C. PLATO. <u>Gorgias</u>.

In this dialogue, Socrates questions the claim that rhetoric ought to be considered a serious discipline and examines the nature and role of rhetoric in Hellenic Greece. Often considered to be required reading for anyone interested in the history of rhetoric.

1.2a <u>Plato: Gorgias--A Revised Text with Introduction and Commentary</u>. Edited by E. R. Dodds. Oxford: At the Clarendon Press, 1959, 413 pp.

No English translation accompanies the Greek text, but the introduction and commentary provide a detailed explanation of many points of debate in the <u>Gorgias</u>.

1.2b <u>Lysias--Symposium--Gorgias</u>. Translated by W. R. M. Lamb. The Loeb Classical Library. Cambridge: Harvard University Press, 1925, 556 pp.

The Loeb series provides the Greek texts and English translations of Plato's dialogues. An introduction and explanation of the text are included.

1.3 <u>c</u>. 370 B.C. PLATO. <u>Phaedrus</u>.
This dialogue by Plato, commonly considered to be written after the <u>Gorgias</u>, examines the possibility of an ideal rhetoric and its relationship to philosophy, and evaluates contemporary logography as practiced by Lysias.

1.3a <u>Plato's Phaedrus: Translated with an Introduction and Commentary</u>. Translated by R. Hackforth. Cambridge: The University Press, 1972, 182 pp.
Provides detailed biographical information on Plato and the dialogue-characters, background information on the period, and an explanation of many of the central issues of the dialogue.

1.3b <u>Euthyphro--Apology--Crito--Phaedo--Phaedrus</u>. Translated by H. N. Fowler. The Loeb Classical Library. Cambridge: Harvard University Press, 1914, 603 pp.
The Loeb series provides the Greek texts and English translations of Plato's dialogues. An introduction and explanation of the text are included.

1.4 <u>c</u>. 340 B.C. ANAXIMENES. <u>Rhetorica ad Alexandrum</u>.
Long thought to be the work of Aristotle, the <u>Rhetorica ad Alexandrum</u> is considered to be the oldest extant manual of rhetoric. The treatise contains numerous technical rhetorical figures and schemes.

1.4a <u>Problems, Books XXII-XXXVIII</u>. Translated by W. S. Hett. <u>Rhetorica ad Alexandrum</u>. Translated by H. Rackham. The Loeb Classical Library. Cambridge: Harvard University Press, 1937, 462 pp.
The Loeb edition places the <u>Rhetorica ad Alexandrum</u> in the corpus of Aristotelian works. An introduction and outline of the treatise are provided along with the Greek text and an English translation.

1.5 <u>c</u>. 335-330 B.C. ARISTOTLE. <u>Rhetorica</u>.
Long considered to be the most well-known treatment of rhetoric. Aristotle outlines the discipline in three books. Emphasis is placed on the rhetor, the audience, and the composition of discourse.

1.5a <u>The "Art" of Rhetoric</u>. Translated by J. H. Freese. The Loeb Classical Library. Cambridge: Harvard University Press, 1926, 539 pp.
This edition of the <u>Rhetorica</u> provides both the Greek text and an English translation, which enables key terms to be interpreted. The introductory pages present a

Isocrates?

synopsis of the early history of rhetoric, relevant information on Aristotle's life, and the province of the Rhetorica
in his thought.

1.5b   Rhetoric and Poetics of Aristotle. Translated by W. Rhys
Roberts and Ingram Bywater. Introduction and notes by
Friedrich Solmsen. New York: Modern Library, 1954,
311 pp.
     This edition of the Rhetorica is considered by many to
be one of the most lucid translations. The introduction by
Solmsen provides an explanation of the views of Plato and
Aristotle on rhetoric.

1.5c   The Rhetoric of Aristotle. Translated by Lane Cooper.
New York: Appleton-Century-Crofts, Inc., 1960, 307 pp.
     One of the most widely read editions of Aristotle's
Rhetorica. Cooper provides a detailed synopsis of the
Rhetorica, which permits an overview of the work prior to
the reading.

1.6 c. 86-82 B.C. [CICERO]. Rhetorica ad Herennium.
     Considered to be the earliest manual of rhetoric in the
Latin West. The Rhetorica ad Herennium, long thought to be
the work of Cicero, provides a detailed list of rhetorical
figures and serves as an illustration of the Roman notion
of technical rhetoric.

1.6a   Ad C. Herennium de Ratione Dicendi (Rhetorica ad
Herennium). Translated by Harry Caplan. The Loeb Classical Library. Cambridge: Harvard University Press, 1954,
491 pp.
     A comprehensive treatment of the Rhetorica ad Herennium.
The Caplan edition provides the Latin text with an English
translation, as well as an introduction, a bibliography of
works on rhetoric, and an analysis of the text.

1.6b   NADEAU, RAY. "Rhetorica ad Herennium, Commentary and
Translation of Book I." SM, 16 (August 1949), 57-68.
     Provides a guide for the reading of the first section
of the Rhetorica ad Herennium. The translation offers an
alternative edition to the Caplan translation.

1.7 86 B.C. CICERO. De Inventione.
     The earliest rhetorical manual known to have been writ-
ten by Cicero, De Inventione was one of the primary works
of rhetoric in the Latin West throughout the Middle Ages.
The treatise contains extensive analysis on the discovery
and arrangement of discourse.

1.7a   De Inventione--De Optimo Genere Oratorum--Topica.
Translated by H. M. Hubbell. The Loeb Classical Library.
Cambridge: Harvard University Press, 1949, 484 pp.
     Includes the Latin text and an English translation along
with an introduction and bibliography.

1.8 55 B.C. CICERO. De Oratore.
     Considered to be Cicero's most polished, complete state-
     ment of rhetoric. In the three books that comprise the De
     Oratore, Cicero surveys the nature and requirements of rhet-
     oric and oratory in the Roman Republic.

1.8a   De Oratore. Books I-II. Translated by E. W. Sutton and
     H. Rackham. The Loeb Classical Library. Cambridge: Har-
     vard University Press, 1942, revised 1948, 503 pp. De
     Oratore. Book III. De Fato--Paradoxa Stoicorum--De
     Partitione Oratoria. Translated by H. Rackham. The Loeb
     Classical Library. Cambridge: Harvard University Press,
     1942, 445 pp.
         These two volumes provide the Latin text of De Oratore
     with an English translation. The work also includes an
     introduction stressing relevant background information and
     a synopsis of the treatise.
1.8b   Cicero on Oratory and Orators. Translated by J. S.
     Watson. Edited by Ralph A. Micken. Carbondale: Southern
     Illinois University Press, 1970, 430 pp.
         This translation of Cicero's treatise served for years
     as a standard reference. The edition includes an introduc-
     tion by Micken and a foreword by David Potter.

1.9 c. 50 B.C. CICERO. Partitiones Oratoriae.
     Cicero's brief treatise on the compositional structure
     and arrangement of discourse. An illustration of Cicero's
     later view on the canon of rhetoric.

1.9a   De Oratore. Book III. De Fato--Paradoxa Stoicorum--De
     Partitione Oratoria. Translated by H. Rackham. The Loeb
     Classical Library. Cambridge: Harvard University Press,
     1942, 445 pp.
         Includes the Latin text with an English translation as
     well as an introduction and synopsis of the treatise.

1.10 46 B.C. CICERO. De Optimo Genera Oratorum.
     Originally intended to serve as an introduction to
     Cicero's Latin translation of Demosthenes' On the Crown
     and Aeschines' Against Ctesiphon. This brief rhetorical
     treatise discusses the qualifications of the best type of
     orator.

1.10a   De Inventione--De Optimo Genere Oratorum--Topica.
     Translated by H. M. Hubbell. The Loeb Classical Library.
     Cambridge: Harvard University Press, 1949, 484 pp.
         Includes the Latin text with an English translation. A
     brief introduction comparing the work with some of Cicero's
     other rhetorical treatises is also included.

1.11   46 B.C.   CICERO.   <u>Brutus</u>.
       Cicero's treatise provides a history of Roman orators,
many of whom would be unknown except for this work.   In
describing the qualities of outstanding orators, Cicero
reveals his own cultural standards for eloquence.

1.11a   <u>Brutus</u>.   Translated by G. L. Hendrickson.   <u>Orator</u>.
Translated by H. M. Hubbell.   The Loeb Classical Library.
Cambridge: Harvard University Press, 1952, 543 pp.
       Includes the Latin text with an English translation.
A general introduction and a summary of the contents are
also provided.

1.12   46 B.C.   CICERO.   <u>Orator</u>.
       Written after <u>De Oratore</u>, the <u>Orator</u> is a continued ex-
amination of the qualifications of the ideal orator.   References are made to prominent models, such as Demosthenes, as
well as to various traits and qualifications of effective
orators.

1.12a   <u>Brutus</u>.   Translated by G. L. Hendrickson.   <u>Orator</u>.
Translated by H. M. Hubbell.   The Loeb Classical Library.
Cambridge: Harvard University Press, 1952, 543 pp.
       Includes the Latin text with an English translation.
A brief introduction to the <u>Orator</u> is provided which com-
pares the work, in part, with the <u>Brutus</u>.

1.13   44 B.C.   CICERO.   <u>Topica</u>.
       Although more properly regarded as a treatise for the
study of argument, Cicero reveals his belief in the relationship between rhetoric and philosophy.   Also provides
information on the nature of commonplaces and <u>topoi</u>.

1.13a   <u>De Inventione--De Optimo Genere Oratorum--Topica</u>.
Translated by H. M. Hubbell.   The Loeb Classical Library.
Cambridge: Harvard University Press, 1949, 484 pp.
       Provides the Latin text with an English translation.
The introduction stresses Cicero's adaptation of Aris-
totle's <u>Topica</u> and the work's function as a treatise on
invention and other areas of rhetoric.

1.14   <u>c</u>. 43 B.C.   VARRO.   <u>De Lingua Latina</u>.
       Discusses philological and linguistic concepts concern-
ing the nature of the Latin language.

1.14a   <u>De Lingua Latina</u>.   Translated by Roland G. Kent.   2 vols.
The Loeb Classical Library.   Cambridge: Harvard University
Press, 1951, 728 pp.
       Contains the Latin text with an English translation.   An
introduction is provided for those interested in relevant
information on grammar and syntax.

1.15 [First Century A.D.]. DEMETRIUS. <u>On Style</u>.
Provides an example of the emphasis on style in discourse by drawing examples from poets, historians, and such orators as Demosthenes. Also includes a discussion of letter writing.

1.15a   <u>(Aristotle), The Poetics and Longinus, On the Sublime</u>. Translated by W. Hamilton Fyfe. <u>Demetrius, On Style</u>. Translated by W. Rhys Roberts. The Loeb Classical Library. Cambridge: Harvard University Press, 1932 (revised), 521 pp.
Provides the Greek text with an English translation. The collection enables the reader to draw comparisons from three works on criticism.

1.15b   <u>Aristotle's Poetics, Demetrius on Style, Longinus on the Sublime</u>. Introduction by John Warrington. Translated by John Warrington, T. A. Moxon, and H. L. Havell. London and New York: Everyman's Library, 1963, 222 pp.
A lucid translation of the most famous works on style and criticism in antiquity.

1.16 <u>c</u>. 37 A.D. SENECA (The Elder). <u>Oratorum Sententiae Divisiones Colores</u>.
Seneca's life spans the transition of the Roman state from the late Republic to the early Empire. Provides numerous examples of exercises in declamation from that period. Illustrates how themes were composed and the use of rhetorical exercises in higher education.

1.16a   <u>Controversiae, I-VI</u>. Translated by Michael Winterbottom. Vol. 1. The Loeb Classical Library. Cambridge: Harvard University Press, 1974, 555 pp.
Not only provides the Latin text with an English translation but also includes a brief introduction which discusses the place of declamations in the Silver Age of Latin literature.

1.16b   <u>Controversiae, VII-X. Suasoriae</u>. Translated by Michael Winterbottom. Vol. 2. The Loeb Classical Library. Cambridge: Harvard University Press, 1974, 645 pp.
Winterbottom continues Seneca's <u>Controversiae</u> in this volume and, with the <u>Suasoriae</u>, provides both forensic and deliberative examples of declamations.

1.17 <u>c</u>. 40 A.D. LONGINUS. <u>On the Sublime</u>.
This work provides a comprehensive analysis of eloquence and has come to be regarded as a standard of literary criticism. Longinus departs from the rhetorical tradition of pedantic exercises and examines the nature of literary excellence. For translated editions of <u>On the Sublime</u> <u>see</u>: 1.15a, b.

1.18 c. 50-120 A.D. PLUTARCH. Vitae Parallelae: Demosthenes.
Cicero.
Plutarch wrote short biographies of distinguished states-
men, two of whom were Demosthenes and Cicero. In comparing
their abilities, Plutarch provides important historical information and reveals his own views on eloquence.

1.18a   Parallel Lives. Demosthenes and Cicero--Alexander and
Caesar. Translated by B. Perrin. The Loeb Classical
Library. Cambridge: Harvard University Press, 1919,
632 pp.
Provides the Greek text and an English translation.
Background information is also included.

1.19 c. 50-120 A.D. [PLUTARCH]. Vitae decem oratorum.
The ten Attic orators were "canonized" hundreds of
years after their existence. The lives of these orators,
although discovered in Plutarch's Moralia, were probably
not recorded by him. The manuscript, however, does provide
valuable information on the rhetorical qualities of the most
popular orators of ancient Greece.

1.19a   Moralia: [Lives of the Ten Orators]. Translated by
H. N. Fowler. Vol. 10. The Loeb Classical Library.
Cambridge: Harvard University Press, 1936, 503 pp.
Provides the Greek text with an English translation.
A short introduction discusses the formulation of the Canon
of the Ten Attic Orators and the nature of the text.

1.20 c. 84-85 A.D. TACITUS. Dialogus.
This famous historian of the Roman Empire writes on the
decay of eloquence in Rome and the resulting transformation
of rhetoric from a source of political power to a pedantic
educational exercise. Includes observations on Cicero.

1.20a   Agricola. Translated by M. Hutton, revised by R. M.
Ogilvie. Germania. Translated by M. Hutton, revised by
E. H. Warmington. Dialogus. Translated by Wm. Peterson,
revised by M. Winterbottom. The Loeb Classical Library.
Cambridge: Harvard University Press, 1970, 372 pp.
Includes the Latin text and an English translation.
The introduction to the Dialogus discusses the characters
who appear in the dialogue.

1.21 c. 94-95 A.D. QUINTILIAN. Institutio oratoria.
Quintilian's twelve books of rhetoric reveal his belief
in the importance of rhetoric to the moral education of
youth and the resulting obligations of the orator in civic
affairs. Quintilian's writings provide information about
the history of rhetoric, both in Rome and Greece.

1.21a   The Institutio oratoria of Quintilian. Translated by
         H. E. Butler. 4 vols. The Loeb Classical Library.
         Cambridge: Harvard University Press, 1920-22, 2254 pp.
             Provides the Latin text with an English translation. A
         synopsis of the books in each of the respective volumes is
         included. The first volume summarizes the life of
         Quintilian and contains a letter to his publisher, Trypho.

1.22 [Second Century A.D.] MINUCIAN. On Epicheiremes.
             Rhetoric in the second century after Christ was a highly
         systematic discipline. Minucian wrote on the methodology
         of argument and persuasion. He is also known for writing
         a commentary on Demosthenes.

1.22a   MEADOR, JR., PRENTICE A. "Minucian, On Epicheiremes:
         An Introduction and a Translation." SM, 31 (March 1964),
         54-63.
             The epicheireme was an important method of argument and
         invention in ancient rhetoric. This article discusses its
         use by an ancient author who was influenced by Aristotle
         and Theodorus. Provides one of the few translations on the
         subject.

1.23 c. 106-113 A.D. SUETONIUS. De Rhetoribus.
             As an antiquarian and historian of Rome, Suetonius's
         treatise on rhetoricians illustrates the way rhetoric was
         regarded in the Republic and some views about prominent
         rhetoricians.

1.23a   The Lives of the Caesars (continued), The Lives of
         Illustrious Men. Translated by J. C. Rolfe. The Loeb
         Classical Library. Cambridge: Harvard University Press,
         1914, 563 pp.
             Provides the Latin text with an English translation but
         with limited commentary.
1.23b   ENOS, RICHARD LEO. "When Rhetoric Was Outlawed in Rome:
         A Translation and Commentary of Suetonius's Treatise on
         Early Roman Rhetoricians." SM, 39 (March 1972), 37-45.
             A translation of De Rhetoribus with detailed commentary
         and an introduction discussing Suetonius and his period.

1.24 [Second Century A.D., fl. c. 150 A.D.]. HERMOGENES. On Stasis.
             Hermogenes of Tarsus is considered by many to be the most
         influential rhetorician of his period. His writing on the
         process of invention and argument is a detailed statement
         of methodology.

1.24a   NADEAU, RAY. "Hermogenes' On Stasis: A Translation
         with an Introduction and Notes." SM, 31 (November 1964),
         361-424.

A translation of Hermogenes' writings with emphasis on the discovery and structuring of points at issue.

1.25 c. 230-238 A.D. PHILOSTRATUS. Vitae Sophistarum.
This Second Sophistic writer offers important information both on sophists of ancient Greece, such as Gorgias, and also on the role of rhetoric in sophistic education.

1.25a   Philostratus, Lives of the Sophists. Eunapius, Lives of the Philosophers and Sophists. Translated by Wilmer C. Wright. The Loeb Classical Library. Cambridge: Harvard University Press, 1921, 639 pp.
Includes a Greek text with an English translation. The introduction supplies important information on the history of rhetoric and additional information about sophists unknown to Philostratus.

1.26 c. 396 A.D. EUNAPIUS. Vitae Sophistarum.
Eunapius, a writer and Greek sophist of the Empire, supplies information on the sophists of antiquity and reveals the educational role of the sophists within the Empire. Much of his writing illustrates the importance of declamation and comes from firsthand information. Includes informative reading on fourth-century Neoplatonists.

1.26a   Philostratus, Lives of the Sophists. Eunapius, Lives of the Philosophers and Sophists. Translated by Wilmer C. Wright. The Loeb Classical Library. Cambridge: Harvard University Press, 1921, 639 pp.
Similar to the section on Philostratus mentioned earlier, the Loeb edition provides the Greek text and an English translation, and supplements the historical information of Eunapius with factual material in the introduction.

Secondary Works

1.27 ALLEN, W. SIDNEY. <u>Accent and Rhythm--Prosodic Features of Latin and Greek: A Study in Theory and Reconstruction</u>. Cambridge, England: Cambridge University Press, 1973, 408 pp.

    Examines the linguistic features of Greek and Latin and complements studies that emphasize the relationship between rhetorical figures and the structure of language.

1.28 ANDERSON, FLOYD DOUGLAS. "Aristotle's Doctrine of the Mean and Its Relationship to Rhetoric." <u>SSJ</u>, 34 (Winter 1968), 100-107.

    Aristotle's doctrine of the mean is examined in relation to such concepts as rhetorical invention, virtue and justice, style and arrangement.

1.29 AVOTINS, I. "The Holders of the Chairs of Rhetoric at Athens." <u>HSCP</u>, 79 (1975), 313-24.

    Traces the endowments and the process by which municipal and imperial chairs of rhetoric were established and maintained at Athens. Provides an explanation of the nature and role of formal rhetorical education in Athens during the Roman Empire.

1.30 AYERS, DONALD MURRAY. "Cato's Speech Against Murena." <u>CJ</u>, 49 (1953-54), 245-53.

    Based on Ayers's dissertation, this article examines Cato's opposing arguments to Cicero. Contrasts Cicero's <u>Pro Murena</u> with the techniques of another highly respected Roman advocate and statesman.

1.31 AYERS, DONALD MURRAY. "The Speeches of Cicero's Opponents: Studies in <u>Pro Roscio Amerino</u>, <u>In Verrem</u>, and <u>Pro Murena</u>." Ph.D. dissertation, Princeton University, 1950, 157 pp.

    Examines the strategies of the forensic oratory of Cicero's opponents. Deals with both prosecution and defense topics and offers a detailed examination of important Roman cases.

1.32 BACKES, JAMES C. "Aristotle's Theory of <u>Stasis</u> in Forensic
      and Deliberative Speech in the <u>Rhetoric</u>." <u>CSSJ</u>, 12
      (Autumn 1960), 6-8.
          The concept of <u>stasis</u>, or the examination and discovery
      of critical points of issue in a dispute, is treated. Em-
      phasis on Aristotle's views.

1.33 BAHN, EUGENE. "Interpretative Reading in Ancient Greece."
      <u>QJS</u>, 18 (June 1932), 432-40.
          Describes the role of oral interpretation in Greek
      literature. Stresses the part that bards and rhapsodes
      played in the transmission of ancient literature.

1.34 BAHN, EUGENE and MARGARET L. BAHN. <u>A History of Oral Interpre-</u>
      <u>tation</u>. Minneapolis: Burgess, 1970, 192 pp.
          Outlines the history of the oral interpretation of lit-
      erature. Pages 1-46 treat the role of interpreters in
      Greece and Rome. Makes apparent the importance of oral
      discourse and its relationship to the written word.

1.35 BALDWIN, CHARLES SEARS. <u>Ancient Rhetoric and Poetic</u>.
      Gloucester, Mass.: Peter Smith, 1959, 275 pp.
          One of the first works in English to provide a history
      of ancient rhetoric. Discusses rhetoric primarily by
      digesting and summarizing the writings of authors such as
      Aristotle and Cicero. Also examines poetic in ancient
      drama and narrative, as well as rhetoric in the criticism
      of poetic.

1.36 BEASEY, MARY FOWLER. "It's What You Don't Say: <u>Omissio</u> in
      Cicero's Speeches." <u>SSJ</u>, 39 (Fall 1973), 11-20.
          A treatment of the concept of <u>omissio</u>, or the conscious
      omission of various arguments in a piece of discourse.
      Examines the significance of such a strategy in Ciceronian
      rhetorical theory, including such forms of <u>omissio</u> as
      <u>reticentia</u>.

1.37 BENSON, T. W. and M. H. PROSSER. <u>Readings in Classical Rhet-</u>
      <u>oric</u>. Boston: Allyn & Bacon, 1969, 351 pp.
          A collection of readings from ancient authors that
      examines the nature of rhetoric and the five canons of
      rhetoric. Includes a chronology of classical rhetoric
      and a selected bibliography.

1.38 BITZER, LLOYD. "Aristotle's Enthymeme Revisited." <u>QJS</u>, 45
      (December 1959), 399-408.
          Since the writings of Aristotle, the enthymeme has been
      regarded as a critical component of rhetorical argument and
      invention. Bitzer examines Aristotle's discussion of the
      enthymeme and stresses the audience's role in completing
      the thought implied in the enthymeme articulated, in part,
      by the rhetor.

1.39   BLACK, EDWIN. "Plato's View of Rhetoric." QJS, 44
       (December 1958), 361-74.
            Plato's view of rhetoric, evident throughout several
       dialogues, is synthesized and discussed by Black. Readers
       will find this essay complements the Gorgias and the
       Phaedrus. Black's claim that Plato "was seeking a series
       of true propositions about an existential class" (p. 365)
       when he examined the nature of rhetoric does not agree with
       traditional interpretations. Of particular interest is
       Black's interpretation that the Gorgias is not an attack
       on rhetoric but an attempt to understand its true form, and
       that Plato may have been closer to the sophists than Aris-
       totle in his view of the relationship between morality and
       rhetoric.

1.40   BLACK, EDWIN. Rhetorical Criticism: A Study in Method. New
       York: The Macmillan Co., 1966, 186 pp.
            Included in this work on contemporary rhetorical criti-
       cism is a chapter entitled, "Aristotle and Rhetorical Criti-
       cism," which provides a synopsis of Aristotle's views on
       the subject and an explication of many issues in the
       Rhetorica. Also included in this chapter is a discussion
       of the enthymeme.

1.41   BONNER, ROBERT J. Evidence in Athenian Courts. Chicago: The
       University of Chicago Press, 1905, 98 pp.
            Based on Bonner's Ph.D. dissertation from the University
       of Chicago, this book examines the notions of argument and
       proof in Hellenic forensic oratory. In the initial pas-
       sages of the Rhetorica, Aristotle expressed his concern
       for the process of legal proof; this work describes such
       concepts of rhetoric.

1.42   BONNER, ROBERT J. Lawyers and Litigants in Ancient Athens:
       The Genesis of the Legal Profession. Chicago: The Uni-
       versity of Chicago Press, 1927, 287 pp.
            Provides a synoptic view of the Attic orators, forensic
       oratory, and the nature of Athenian litigation. Furnishes
       background information on the conceptual basis of legal
       argument in ancient Greece, particularly the presumptions
       of legal procedure.

1.43   BONNER, S. F. Roman Declamation in the Late Republic and
       Early Empire. Liverpool: University Press, 1949, 185 pp.
            A comprehensive collection of various exercises of
       declamation in the Roman Republic and Roman Empire that
       serve to illustrate that declamation ought to be con-
       sidered a serious method of instruction in Roman delibera-
       tive and forensic rhetoric.

Secondary Works

1.44 BOWERSOCK, G. W. <u>Greek Sophists in the Roman Empire</u>. Oxford: At the Clarendon Press, 1969, 150 pp.
    Examines the role of the Greek sophist in the Roman Empire, particularly the sponsorship of Roman emperors and patrons who endowed sophistic instruction. Supplies information on the social forces operating during the Second Sophistic.

1.45 BRAKE, ROBERT J. "A Reconstruction of Aristotle's Concept of Topics." <u>CSSJ</u>, 16 (May 1965), 106-12.
    Examines Aristotle's concept of <u>topoi</u>, or "seats of argument," and takes exception to earlier interpretations of Aristotle's system of topics, particularly the view of Richard C. Huseman (1.105).

1.46 BRANDES, PAUL D. "Evidence in Aristotle's <u>Rhetoric</u>." <u>SM</u>, 28 (March 1961), 21-28.
    Examines the notion of proof in Aristotle's <u>Rhetorica</u> and explicates the concepts presented in the primary source. Philological interpretations are discussed and explained in detail.

1.47 BROCKRIEDE, WAYNE E. "Toward a Contemporary Aristotelian Theory of Rhetoric." <u>QJS</u>, 52 (February 1966), 33-40.
    Discusses the application of Aristotelian views of rhetoric in contemporary society, and also provides a general summary of Aristotle's writing on the subject and discusses Aristotle's cultural perspectives.

1.48 BRYANT, DONALD C., ROBERT W. SMITH, PETER D. ARNOTT, ERLING B. HOLTSMARK, and GALEN O. ROWE. <u>Ancient Greek and Roman Rhetoricians: A Bibliographical Dictionary</u>. Columbia, Missouri: The Artcraft Press, 1968, 104 pp.
    A handlist of ancient rhetoricians with short, authoritative entries. The description of Plato presented by Everett Lee Hunt, for example, is a concise treatment of Plato's views and a condensation of Hunt's own writings. A substantial amount of compilation was done by Robert W. Smith.

1.49 CALHOUN, GEORGE MILLER. "Oral and Written Pleading in Athenian Courts." <u>TAPA</u>, 50 (1919), 177-93.
    Stresses the close association between oral and written literature in the law courts of the ancient world and discusses the implications of that relationship for litigation.

1.50 CAPLAN, HARRY. "Classical Rhetoric and the Medieval Theory of Preaching." <u>CP</u>, 28 (April 1933), 73-96. Revised and reprinted in <u>Historical Studies of Rhetoric and Rhetoricians</u>. Edited by Raymond F. Howes. Ithaca, N.Y.: Cornell University Press, 1965, pp. 71-89, 387-91.

Although the major emphasis of the essay is on medieval pulpit eloquence, Caplan discusses the classical concepts that influenced medieval rhetoric. Deals with several ancient authors and provides a statement of the bridge between the ancient and medieval world.

1.51 CAPLAN, HARRY. "The Decay of Eloquence at Rome in the First Century," in Studies in Speech and Drama in Honor of Alexander M. Drummond. Edited by Herbert A. Wichelns. Ithaca, N.Y.: Cornell University Press, 1944, pp. 295-325.
Examines the political changes that occurred in the transformation of Rome from a Republic to an Empire. Presents the views of prominent writers of the Imperial period along with a discussion of the role of declamation, epideictic oratory, and debased educational practices.

1.52 CAPLAN, HARRY. "The Latin Panegyrics of the Empire." QJS, 10 (February 1924), 41-52.
Examines the role of declamation within the empire and stresses the Roman panegyric, the presentation of a eulogy to a living individual. Such orations were usually composed for, and delivered to, emperors.

1.53 CHURCH, DAVID A. and ROBERT S. CATHCART. "Some Concepts of the Epicheireme in Greek and Roman Rhetoric." WS, 29 (Summer 1965), 140-47.
The epicheireme, or an extended rhetorical syllogism, was a method of argument and analysis in the ancient world. This study examines and explains interpretations of this process in Greece and Rome.

1.54 CLARK, DONALD LEMEN. Rhetoric in Greco-Roman Education. New York: Columbia University Press, 1957, 298 pp.
Examines the nature of rhetoric, particularly its function in school and society. Provides a general overview of rhetoric and is often used as an introduction to the study of ancient rhetoric.

1.55 CLARKE, MARTIN L. Rhetoric at Rome. London: Cohen & West, 1953, 203 pp.
One of the first modern treatments of Roman rhetoric in English. Detailed notes thoroughly documented from primary sources.

1.56 COPE, EDWARD M. An Introduction to Aristotle's Rhetoric: With Analysis, Notes and Appendices. London: The Macmillan Co., 1867, 480 pp.
Considered by many to be the most comprehensive explanation of Aristotle's Rhetorica written in English. Also includes a discussion of the Rhetorica ad Alexandrum.

21

1.57   COPE, EDWARD M. and JOHN EDWIN SANDYS. <u>The Rhetoric of</u>
       <u>Aristotle</u>. 3 vols. Cambridge, England: Cambridge
       University Press, 1877, 933 pp.
           This edition of the Greek text includes extensive com-
       mentary and explanation for the reader of English. Each
       passage is accompanied by analysis, which requires little
       or no knowledge of the primary language.

1.58   CORBETT, EDWARD P. J. <u>Classical Rhetoric for the Modern Stu-</u>
       <u>dent</u>. New York: Oxford University Press, 1965, 671 pp.
           The contemporary application of classical principles of
       rhetoric is presented throughout the book. Of particular
       relevance, however, is the section entitled "A Survey of
       Rhetoric" (pp. 535-68), which includes an overview of
       classical rhetorics.

1.59   COWLES, FRANK HERWITT. "Gaius Verres: An Historical Study."
       <u>Cornell Studies in Classical Philology</u>. Vol. 20. Ithaca,
       New York: Press of Andrus & Church, 1917, 207 pp.
           A thorough examination of the rhetorical situation which
       leads up to, and took place during, Cicero's <u>In Verrem</u>.
       Although the study does not itself deal with rhetoric, the
       implicit relevance to understanding Cicero's argument is
       made apparent in the reading. Readers may also wish to
       see: Frank Herwitt Cowles, "Cicero's Debut as a Prosecutor."
       <u>CJ</u>, 24 (March 1929), 429-48.

1.60   CRONKHITE, GARY. "The Enthymeme as Deductive Rhetorical
       Argument." <u>WS</u>, 30 (Spring 1966), 129-34.
           The enthymeme is regarded as a major component in
       rhetorical argument and invention. Cronkhite examines
       the implications of the process as a deductive method.

1.61   D'ALTON, J. F. <u>Roman Literary Theory and Criticism</u>. New
       York: Russell and Russell, 1962, 616 pp.
           Discusses literary and rhetorical movements in Rome and
       provides information on the various intellectual positions
       advanced on style. A treatment of the Roman view of
       Atticism is included.

1.62   DEARIN, RAY D. "The Fourth <u>Stasis</u> in Greek Rhetoric," in
       <u>Rhetoric and Communication</u>. Edited by Jane Blankenship
       and Hermann G. Stelzner. Urbana: University of Illinois
       Press, pp. 3-16.
           Analyzes four forms of <u>stases</u> and discusses how the
       fourth <u>stasis</u>, or "quality," was conceived for the law
       courts. Detailed notes also serve as a survey of earlier
       research on the subject.

1.63   de ROMILLY, JACQUELINE. <u>Magic and Rhetoric in Ancient Greece</u>.
       Cambridge: Harvard University Press, 1975, 113 pp.

Devotes four chapters, originally presented as lectures, to the role of rhetoric as an emotive, magical force and as a formal discipline. Individuals such as Gorgias, Plato, and Aristotle are discussed.

1.64 DICK, R. C. "Topoi: An Approach to Inventing Arguments." ST, 13 (November 1964), 313-19.

Provides an overview of the Aristotelian notion of topics and explains how Aristotle's views on topoi served as a basis for the Roman use of topics. A general synthesis of major ideas on the subject, both by contemporary and ancient authors.

1.65 DIETER, OTTO A. L. "Stasis." SM, 17 (August 1950), 345-69.

A detailed and thorough explanation of the concept of stasis derived from the writings of ancient authors. Uses illustrations to explain the concepts and the various methods of determining the point of issue in a dispute.

1.66 DiLORENZO, RAYMOND. "The Critique of Socrates in Cicero's De Oratore: Ornatus and the Nature of Wisdom." PR, 11 (Fall 1978), 247-61.

The concept of ornatus, traditionally taken to mean rhetorical ornamentation, is discussed as a concept with philosophical implications. DiLorenzo illustrates how the dialogue-character Crassus uses this concept in De Oratore when he discusses Socrates.

1.67 DOBSON, J. F. The Greek Orators. Freeport, N.Y.: Books for Libraries Press, 1971, 328 pp.

Presents biographical information and stylistic traits of the Attic orators. A discussion of the beginning and decline of oratory is also included.

1.68 DORTER, KENNETH. "The Significance and Interconnection of the Speeches in Plato's Symposium." PR, 2 (Fall 1969), 215-34.

Argues that Plato's structuring of speeches in the Symposium was a manipulated attempt to establish a progression of thought and the implication of this structure upon the meaning of Eros will increase an understanding of the dialogue.

1.69 DORTER, KENNETH. "Socrates' Refutation of Thrasymachus and Treatment of Virtue." PR, 7 (Winter 1974), 25-46.

Students of rhetoric usually observe the ability of the dialogue-character Socrates in argument only in the Gorgias and Phaedrus. Examines Socrates' use of argument and treatment of virtue, particularly in the Republic. A relationship between rhetorical and philosophical argument is discussed.

1.70 DUFF, J. WRIGHT. <u>A Literary History of Rome: From the</u>
<u>Origins to the Close of the Golden Age</u>. Edited by A. M.
Duff. London: Ernest Benn Ltd., 1967, 535 pp.
Examines the social and intellectual role of literature
in Rome up to the age of Augustus. Rhetoric is discussed
throughout the book and is frequently mentioned through the
commentary of prominent authors.

1.71 DUFF, J. WRIGHT. <u>A Literary History of Rome in the Silver Age:</u>
<u>From Tiberius to Hadrian</u>. Edited by A. M. Duff. 3rd ed.
London: Ernest Benn Ltd., 1964, 599 pp.
Complements Duff's <u>A Literary History of Rome: From the</u>
<u>Origins to the Close of the Golden Age</u>. Duff examines the
writings of authors from Tiberius to Hadrian with references to rhetoric throughout the work.

1.72 EHNINGER, DOUGLAS W. "The Classical Doctrine of Invention."
<u>Gavel</u>, 39 (March 1957), 59-62, 70.
A brief survey of ideas on the process of discovering
lines of argument for a piece of discourse.

1.73 EHNINGER, DOUGLAS W. "On Systems of Rhetoric." <u>PR</u>, 1
(Summer 1968), 131-44.
A broad view of the various systems of rhetoric that
operated in the course of Western civilization's development. Characterizes the rhetoric of the classical period
as essentially "grammatical" and compares this view of
rhetoric with subsequent systems.

1.74 ENGNELL, RICHARD A. "Implications for Communication of the
Rhetorical Epistemology of Gorgias of Leontini." <u>WS</u>, 37
(Summer 1973), 175-84.
Draws together the views and epistemology of Gorgias of
Leontini and makes the claim that many of the issues that
concerned Gorgias and his notion of communication remain
concerns for contemporary researchers.

1.75 ENOS, RICHARD LEO and JEANNE L. McCLARAN. "Audience and
Image in Ciceronian Rome: Creation and Constraints of the
<u>Vir Bonus</u> Personality." <u>CSSJ</u>, 29 (Summer 1978), 98-106.
Examines the nature and notion of the audience with
emphasis on how orators such as Cicero attempted to present
an image of morality to listeners. In this respect, the
impact of the appearance of morality became an effective
force in suasory discourse.

1.76 ENOS, RICHARD LEO. "Cicero's Forensic Oratory: The Manifestation of Power in the Roman Republic." <u>SSJ</u>, 40
(Summer 1975), 377-94.
Discusses how Cicero used his rhetorical ability as a
source of power in Roman society by examining Cicero's

career and his ability to establish patrons and supporters
for political favors through his expertise as an advocate.

1.77 ENOS, RICHARD LEO. "The Effects of Imperial Patronage on the
Rhetorical Tradition of the Athenian Second Sophistic."
Communication Quarterly, 25 (Spring 1977), 3-10.
Stresses the relationship between Roman patronage and
the sponsorship of rhetoric, both through endowments to
individual sophists and through cultural building programs
in Athens until the decline and fall of the Roman Empire.

1.78 ENOS, RICHARD LEO. "The Epistemological Foundation for
Cicero's Litigation Strategies." CSSJ, 26 (Summer 1975),
207-14.
Discusses Cicero's views on the value of conjoining
philosophy and rhetoric in litigation. Specific attention
is paid to principles of ethics and the process of dialectic
in Roman litigation.

1.79 ENOS, RICHARD LEO. "The Epistemology of Gorgias's Rhetoric:
A Re-examination." SSJ, 42 (Fall 1976), 35-51.
Advances the claim that Gorgias was a serious thinker
on the nature of rhetoric and based his views of the discipline of rhetoric on epistemological grounds that were
antithetical to Platonic thought.

1.80 ENOS, RICHARD LEO. "The Forensic Oratory of Marcus Tullius
Cicero: The Development and Application of a Practical
Rhetoric." Ph.D. dissertation, Indiana University, 1973,
255 pp.
Compares Cicero's views on effective forensic rhetoric
with his actual strategies as revealed in his legal oratory.
The synthesis of his position is derived from the corpus of
his work.

1.81 ENOS, RICHARD LEO. "The Hellenic Rhapsode." WS, 42
(Spring 1978), 134-43.
Prior to the creation of a formal discipline of rhetoric,
Greek bards and rhapsodes were developing techniques of
communication that enabled them to transmit oral literature effectively. Examines the history of this transmission
and posits an explanation for its decline.

1.82 ENOS, RICHARD LEO. "A Rhetorical Analysis of Cicero's Prosecution of Gaius Verres." Master's thesis, Indiana University, 1970, 145 pp.
Examines Cicero's prosecution of Gaius Verres and provides
rhetorical criticism based upon Cicero's own tenets as articulated in his works dealing with rhetorical theory.

1.83 ENOS, RICHARD LEO. "Rhetorical Intent in Ancient Historiography: Herodotus and the Battle of Marathon." Communication
 Quarterly, 24 (Winter 1976), 24-31.
   Herodutus's account of the Battle of Marathon is examined
 as a piece of rhetoric. Argues that Herodotus's intent was
 to persuade his listeners to adopt a certain view rather
 than to provide a factual account of the battle.

1.84 ERICKSON, KEITH V. Aristotle's Rhetoric: Five Centuries of
 Philological Research. Metuchen, N.J.: The Scarecrow
 Press, Inc., 1975, 195 pp.
   A brief history of Aristotle's Rhetorica and an exten-
 sive bibliography of research on Aristotle's treatise.
 This study, based on Erickson's doctoral dissertation at
 The University of Michigan, lists 1,563 citations in the
 major collection plus references in an addendum.

1.85 ERICKSON, KEITH V., ed. Aristotle: The Classical Heritage of
 Rhetoric. Metuchen, N.J.: The Scarecrow Press, 1974,
 323 pp.
   A collection of seventeen essays on ancient rhetoric
 with emphasis on the contributions of Aristotle. Historical
 information on Aristotle's study of and lectures about rhetoric complement specific studies dealing with the enthymeme,
 example, topics, metaphor, delivery, and stasis. An index
 is provided.

1.86 ERICKSON, KEITH V. "The Lost Rhetorics of Aristotle." SM,
 43 (August 1976), 229-37.
   Claims that present-day knowledge of Aristotle's views
 on rhetoric are limited. In this essay, Erickson provides
 information about the lost works of rhetoric written by
 Aristotle and their possible influence on his views of
 rhetorical discourse.

1.87 FLEMMING, EDWIN G. "A Comparison of Cicero and Aristotle on
 Style." QJS, 4 (January 1918), 61-71.
   Although the article is dated, Flemming compares the two
 famous commentators of rhetoric and concludes that while
 both Aristotle and Cicero agree that style is an essential
 component of rhetoric, their interpretations of what appropriate style can mean are different.

1.88 FREEMAN, KATHLEEN. The Murder of Herodes and Other Trials
 from the Athenian Law Courts. New York: W. W. Norton,
 1963, 236 pp.
   Provides translations of Greek forensic orations and an
 introduction to Athenian legal procedure and the nature
 of forensic rhetoric. Brief comments and observations
 about the individual speeches are provided.

1.89 GOMPERZ, HEINRICH. Sophistik und Rhetorik. Stuttgart: B. G. Teubner Verlagsgesellschaft, 1965, 297 pp.
Written in German, this work provides a comprehensive statement of sophistic influence in the history of rhetoric. More recent studies in English have elaborated on Gomperz's contributions, but the work persists as a standard reference on the subject.

1.90 GRIMALDI, WILLIAM M. A., S.J. "Rhetoric and Truth: A Note on Aristotle, Rhetoric 1355a." PR, 11 (Summer 1978), 173-77.
Aristotle claims in his Rhetorica that rhetoric can make truth apparent. Grimaldi analyzes the implications of Aristotle's observation by examining the philological and philosophical relationship between rhetoric and truth expressed in the passage.

1.91 GRIMALDI, WILLIAM M. A., S.J. "Studies in the Philosophy of Aristotle's Rhetoric." Hermes: Zeitschrift für klassische Philologie, 25 (1972), 1-151.
This comprehensive essay examines the unity of the Rhetorica and provides an extensive treatment of the enthymeme, including its centrality to rhetoric, its function as a method of rhetorical argumentation, and its function as a source of rhetorical argumentation. For related reading see: Grimaldi, William M. A., S.J. "A Note on the Pisteis in Aristotle's Rhetoric 1354-56." AJP, 78 (1957), 188-92.

1.92 GRONBECK, BRUCE E. "Gorgias on Rhetoric and Poetic: A Rehabilitation." SSJ, 38 (Fall 1972), 27-38.
Gronbeck isolates and identifies the major tenets of Gorgias's thought concerning rhetoric. Posits that present-day views of Gorgias ought to be reexamined in light of his contributions to rhetorical theory.

1.93 GUTHRIE, W. K. C. Socrates. Cambridge, England: Cambridge University Press, 1971, 207 pp.
Examines the sources that treat the life of Socrates as well as his character and philosophical significance. Guthrie's treatment of Socrates provides the opportunity to study an interpretation of Socrates that can be compared with Plato's views.

1.94 GUTHRIE, W. K. C. The Sophists. Cambridge, England: Cambridge University Press, 1971, 354 pp.
Presents a lucid explanation of the primary tenets of sophists and discusses their respective philosophical views. Readers will find the chapter "Rhetoric and Philosophy" an aid in understanding sophistic epistemology.

1.95 GWYNN, AUBREY. Roman Education from Cicero to Quintilian.
Oxford: University Press, 1926, 260 pp.
Considered to be a classic text on ancient education.
Examines the role of education in Rome from the republic
into the Empire with a treatment of rhetoric as a major
educational force.

1.96 HAMMOND, N. G. L. and H. H. SCULLARD, eds. The Oxford Classical Dictionary. 2nd ed. Oxford: At the Clarendon Press,
1970, 1198 pp.
A comprehensive guide to subjects and individuals in
antiquity. Several concepts of rhetoric are explained, and
prominent rhetoricians and orators are discussed. Of particular interest are the summaries of rhetoric entitled
"Rhetoric, Greek" and "Rhetoric, Latin."

1.97 HARGIS, DONALD E. "The Rhapsode." QJS, 56 (December 1970),
388-97.
Presents a synthesis of ancient commentary on rhapsodes,
who developed techniques for the composition and transmission of ancient literature. Emphasizes Plato's views
on rhapsodes, particularly as articulated in the Ion.

1.98 HARGIS, DONALD E. "Socrates and the Rhapsode: Plato's Ion,"
in Studies in Interpretation. Edited by Esther M. Doyle
and Virginia Hastings Floyd. Amsterdam: Editions Rodopi
N. V., 1977, No. 2, pp. 1-12.
Rhapsodes were ancient oral interpreters and transmit-
ters of literature who developed methods of composition
that were similar to those used by contemporary rhetoricians. Hargis examines Plato's views of these interpreters
and provides an interesting parallel to Plato's views on
rhetoric.

1.99 HAUSER, GERALD A. "The Example in Aristotle's Rhetoric:
Bifurcation or Contradiction?" PR, 1 (Spring 1968),
78-90.
Much research on Aristotle's notion of logical proof in
rhetorical discourse has centered on the enthymeme. Hauser,
however, stresses the importance of understanding the example and how it functions in rhetorical discourse. The
author analyzes and synthesizes Aristotle's views on the
example beyond the Rhetorica and posits definitions for
consideration.

1.100 HAVELOCK, ERIC A. and JACKSON P. HERSHBELL, eds. Communication
Arts in the Ancient World. New York: Hastings House, 1978,
176 pp.
Several authors provide essays on various methods of
communication in the ancient world. The methods of mass
communication and the transmission of discourse in oral,
written, and visual media are emphasized.

Secondary Works

1.101 HINKS, D. A. G. "Tisias and Corax and the Invention of
        Rhetoric." Classical Quarterly, 34 (April 1940), 61-69.
            Examines the creation of rhetoric as a formal discipline
        and stresses the notion of probability as a seminal idea in
        the founding of rhetoric. Claims that studies of rhetoric
        prior to Corax and Tisias are irrelevant to the discipline.

1.102 HOWELL, WILBUR S. "Aristotle and Horace on Rhetoric and
        Poetics." QJS, 54 (December 1968), 325-39.
            A lucid explanation of the province of rhetoric and
        poetic in ancient literature. Howell establishes the
        difference between literature of symbol and literature of
        statement in these two basic disciplines.

1.103 HUBBELL, H. M. The Influence of Isocrates on Cicero, Dionysius
        and Aristides. New Haven: Yale University Press, 1913,
        84 pp.
            Based on Hubbell's Ph.D. dissertation, this work ex-
        amines the impact of Isocrates on subsequent rhetoricians.
        As an educator, Isocrates encouraged the study of history
        and rhetoric for the development of statesmanship and pro-
        duced many prominent students during his lifetime. Hubbell
        examines the sustaining influence of Isocrates in the his-
        tory of rhetoric.

1.104 HUNT, EVERETT LEE. "Plato and Aristotle on Rhetoric and
        Rhetoricians." QJS, 6 (June 1920), 35-56.
            Often regarded as a classic article on the views of
        Plato and Aristotle concerning rhetoric. Synthesizes the
        observations of these prominent thinkers and provides a
        detailed statement of sophistic rhetoric as well.

1.105 HUSEMAN, RICHARD C. "Modern Approaches to the Aristotelian
        Concept of the Special Topic." CSSJ, 15 (February 1964),
        21-26.
            Examines Aristotle's concept of the special topic and
        then advances a comparison with modern public-speaking
        texts, which often treat special topics in their
        discussions.

1.106 HYLAND, DREW A. "Why Plato Wrote Dialogues." PR, 1
        (January 1968), 38-50.
            Examines the hermeneutic of Plato's dialogue form and,
        for purposes of illustration, provides an interpretation
        of the structure of Plato's Crito.

1.107 JAEGER, WERNER. Paideia: The Ideals of Greek Culture.
        Translated by Gilbert Highet. 3 vols. New York: Oxford
        University Press, 1945, 1378 pp.
            This comprehensive work examines the notion of intel-
        lectual excellence in Greek thought. Offers views on the

history of Greek rhetoric within the context of intellectual growth and discusses issues of intellectual dispute. Many consider Jaeger's writings to be a standard reference work on Greek rhetoric.

1.108   JEBB, RICHARD C.   The Attic Orators from Antiphon to Isaeos.
2 vols. New York: Russell and Russell, 1962, 949 pp.
A detailed analysis of several orators in the Attic canon. Also provides a cursory history of Greek rhetoric as well as explicating key terms. Examples of orations are cited throughout the work.

1.109   KAUFER, DAVID S.   "The Influence of Plato's Developing Psychology on His Views of Rhetoric." QJS, 64 (February 1978), 63-78.
Claims that Plato's view of rhetoric will be better understood when it is recognized that Plato moved from a cognitive to a conflict psychology. Kaufer uses this viewpoint as a basis for discussing the Gorgias and the Phaedrus.

1.110   KENNEDY, GEORGE.   "The Ancient Dispute Over Rhetoric in Homer."
AJP, 78 (1957), 23-35.
Examines claims by ancient authors concerning the possibility that Homer was aware of formal techniques of rhetoric in his composition of the Iliad and the Odyssey. Provides interesting observations from ancient sources and reveals their perception of Homeric literature.

1.111   KENNEDY, GEORGE.   The Art of Persuasion in Greece.   Princeton,
N.J.: Princeton University Press, 1963, 350 pp.
Generally considered to be required reading for the study of Greek rhetoric. Provides a comprehensive analysis of the origin and development of Greek rhetoric through the Hellenistic period. The numerous references and notes are a helpful guide to a more detailed examination of a particular topic.

1.112   KENNEDY, GEORGE.   The Art of Rhetoric in The Roman World:
300 B.C.--A.D. 300. Princeton, N.J.: Princeton University Press, 1972, 674 pp.
A history of rhetoric from the Roman Republic to the Roman Empire. Treats prominent literary figures and includes a detailed treatment of Cicero's views. Includes numerous sources and documentation for additional reading.

1.113   KENNEDY, GEORGE.   "The Earliest Rhetorical Handbooks." AJP,
80 (1959), 169-78.
A study of the early development of rhetoric and an examination of the earliest manuals. Provides insight into the basic presumptions that initiated the discipline.

1.114   KENNEDY, GEORGE. <u>Quintilian</u>. New York: Twayne Publishers,
        Inc., 1969, 164 pp.
            Provides biographical information on one of the most
        prominent educators of rhetoric in antiquity. Discusses
        Quintilian's views on education, rhetoric, and criticism,
        as well as providing a selected bibliography.

1.115   KENNEDY, GEORGE. "Review Article: The Present State of the
        Study of Ancient Rhetoric." <u>CP</u>, 70 (October 1975), 278-82.
            A detailed account of research in ancient rhetoric,
        listing several sources for reading. Kennedy encourages
        the study of rhetoric in non-Western cultures and
        the cultural modifications of ancient principles.

1.116   KENNEDY, VERNE R. "<u>Auxesis</u>: A Concept of Rhetorical Ampli-
        fication." <u>SSJ</u>, 37 (Fall 1971), 60-72.
            Examines the concept <u>auxesis</u> and, after discussing this
        device of amplification and its meaning in antiquity, com-
        pares it to present-day theory and practice.

1.117   KERFERD, G. B. "Gorgias on Nature or That Which is Not."
        <u>Phronesis</u>, 1 (November 1955), 3-25.
            The presumptions behind Gorgias's view on the nature of
        things are presented and insights into his notion of anti-
        thetical reasoning are provided. Offers a perspective of
        Gorgias that differs from the dialogue-character presented
        by Plato.

1.118   KING, THOMAS R. "The Perfect Orator in <u>Brutus</u>." <u>SSJ</u>, 33
        (Winter 1967), 124-28.
            Examines Cicero's views on the qualities of oratory in
        the <u>Brutus</u>, which is itself a synthesis of the prominent
        orators of Rome. A summary of the qualifications of the
        perfect orator and an outline for reference to the primary
        source are provided.

1.119   KIRK, G. S. <u>Homer and the Oral Tradition</u>. Cambridge,
        England: Cambridge University Press, 1976, 231 pp.
            Examines the nature and transmission of oral literature.
        Emphasizes verse structure and formular language.

1.120   LAUSBERG, HEINRICH. <u>Handbuch der Literarischen Rhetorik</u>.
        2 vols. Munich: Max Huber, 1960, 983 pp.
            Although written in German, this source provides a de-
        tailed guide to rhetorical terms and provides references
        from classical sources that illustrate the use and meaning
        of the terms for the English reader.

1.121   LEEMAN, A. D. <u>Orationis Ratio: The Stylistic Theories and
        Practice of the Roman Orators, Historians and Philosophers</u>.
        2 vols. Amsterdam: Adolf M. Hakkert, 1963, 1043 pp.

A detailed study of the stylistic contributions of Roman orators, historians, and philosophers. The second volume of the work is composed entirely of notes and provides a detailed reference for further research.

1.122 LESKY, ALBIN. <u>A History of Greek Literature</u>. Translated by James Willis and Cornelis de Heer. London: Methuen, 1966, 940 pp.
An articulate statement of the history of Greek literature and the social role of rhetoric. Ancient sources are consistently documented. Many consider Lesky's work to be a lucid and authoritative statement about Greek literature.

1.123 McBURNEY, JAMES A. "The Place of the Enthymeme in Rhetorical Theory." <u>SM</u>, 3 (1936), 49-74.
This article is an abstract of McBurney's dissertation done at The University of Michigan. The concept of the enthymeme, particularly Aristotle's views, are discussed in detail, and diagrams are provided throughout the essay to help explain the place of the enthymeme in demonstration, dialectic, and rhetoric, as well as the relationship between the enthymeme and topics.

1.124 McNALLY, J. RICHARD. "Comments on Rhetoric and Oratory in Cicero's Letters." <u>SSJ</u>, 39 (Fall 1973), 21-32.
Although Cicero's views on rhetoric are taken directly from his treatises on the subject, his informal comments on rhetoric discussed throughout his numerous letters provide additional information. McNally's study synthesizes Cicero's comments on rhetoric and oratory.

1.125 MARROU, H. I. <u>A History of Education in Antiquity</u>. Translated by George Lamb. New York: New American Library, 1964, 600 pp.
Provides a broad examination of the role of education in antiquity and the social force of rhetoric. Although somewhat dated, the translated edition cited above offers a lucid and thorough understanding of the subject.

1.126 MARTIN, JOSEF. <u>Antike Rhetorik: Technik und Methode</u>. München: C. H. Beck'sche Verlagsbuchhandlung, 1974, 431 pp.
This German treatise examines such technical concepts as <u>stasis</u>, types of discourse, and figures and tropes of rhetoric. The work contains numerous citations from primary sources.

1.127 MEADOR, JR., PRENTICE A. "The Classical Epicheireme: A Re-Examination." <u>WS</u>, 30 (Summer 1966), 151-55.
Claims that the epicheireme has its roots in early Peripatetic theories of logic. Examines contemporary

views on the subject and provides a diagram to illustrate this process of reasoning.

1.128 MEADOR, JR., PRENTICE A. "Rhetoric and Humanism in Cicero."
       PR, 3 (Winter 1970), 1-12.
           Examines Cicero's commitment to humanism and the impli-
       cations of his philosophical position on his view toward
       rhetoric as articulated in De Oratore.

1.129 MEADOR, JR., PRENTICE A. "Skeptic Theory of Perception: A
       Philosophical Antecedent of Ciceronian Probability." QJS,
       54 (December 1968), 340-51.
           Advances the claim that Cicero's view of probability is
       better understood as an outgrowth of a philosophical rather
       than a rhetorical tradition. Also treats its relationship
       with skeptic philosophy and its centrality to Ciceronian
       rhetoric in the process of establishing credibility.

1.130 MICHEL, ALAIN. Rhétorique et Philosophie chez Cicéron: Essai
       sur les Fondements Philosophiques de l'Art de Persuader.
       Paris: Presses Universitaires de France, 1960, 752 pp.
           Cicero believed strongly in the unity of rhetoric and
       philosophy. This study written in French provides a de-
       tailed examination of Cicero's views of this relationship.
       Many students of Roman rhetoric regard Michel's work as
       one of the most comprehensive statements on the subject.

1.131 MUDD, CHARLES. "The Enthymeme and Logical Validity." QJS,
       45 (December 1959), 409-14.
           Argues that Aristotle's notion of the enthymeme is not
       fully understood or correctly treated in contemporary texts
       on communication. Attempts to clarify Aristotle's position
       on the enthymeme and point out shortcomings in contemporary
       treatment of the subject.

1.132 MURPHY, JAMES J. "Cicero's Rhetoric in the Middle Ages."
       QJS, 53 (December 1967), 334-41.
           Although this essay examines the place of rhetoric in
       the Middle Ages, the dominance of Cicero's works in the
       Latin West is clear. Provides an insight into his sus-
       tained influence and contributions. Murphy reminds the
       reader that Cicero's reputation as a "master of eloquence"
       in the Middle Ages is deserved, but that it is also based
       largely upon the De Inventione and Rhetorica ad Herennium.

1.133 MURPHY, JAMES J., ed. Demosthenes' On the Crown. New York:
       Random House, 1967, 217 pp.
           On the Crown has long been considered a model of rhetor-
       ical eloquence and Murphy provides a detailed examination
       of the oration and background information. A translation
       of On the Crown by John J. Keaney is included along with
       essays by other contributors.

1.134 MURPHY, JAMES J., ed. <u>A Synoptic History of Classical Rhetoric</u>.
Berkeley: University of California Press, 1972, 207 pp.
   Contributions from several authors provide general over-
views of prominent theories of classical rhetoric. The
text is intended to serve as an undergraduate introduction
and to complement primary sources. Forbes Hill treats
Aristotelian rhetoric and Donovan J. Ochs summarizes the
major rhetorical theories of Cicero. Includes select bibliography compiled by Michael Leff.

1.135 NADEAU, RAY. "Classical Systems of <u>Stases</u> in Greek:
Hermagoras to Hermogenes." <u>Greek, Roman and Byzantine</u>
<u>Studies</u>, 2 (January 1959), 51-71.
   A survey of the views of prominent rhetoricians on the
concept of <u>stasis</u> from approximately the second century
B.C. to the second century A.D. It was during this period
that the concept of <u>stasis</u> received great currency, particularly among the authors listed in the title.

1.136 NADEAU, RAY. "Delivery in Ancient Times: Homer to Quintilian."
<u>QJS</u>, 50 (February 1964), 53-60.
   Although an established canon of rhetoric, delivery has
not been thoroughly examined by contemporary writers.
Nadeau provides an overview of the canon and, in the
process, synthesizes some of the prominent notions on
the subject. Stresses the psychological connection between the orator's feelings and the arousal of the audience's emotions. Also draws implications on the "literary"
process of composing discourse.

1.137 NADEAU, RAY. "Hermogenes on 'Stock Issues' in Deliberative
Speaking." <u>SM</u>, 25 (March 1958), 59-66.
   Provides a commentary and explanation of the second-
century rhetorician's views on stock issues. The essay
makes available writings that are normally in Greek or in
German translations. In addition to a translation of
Hermogenes' views on stock issues, Nadeau presents a
diagram that illustrates the stock issues examined by
prominent rhetoricians throughout antiquity.

1.138 NADEAU, RAY. "Some Aristotelian and Stoic Influences on the
Theory of <u>Stasis</u>." <u>SM</u>, 26 (November 1959), 248-54.
   Offers varying interpretations on the complex process of
discerning issues in rhetorical discourse. Claims that the
analytical methodology of rhetorical <u>stases</u> used by ancient
rhetoricians reflects the Aristotelian predictables of
genus, definition, property, and coincident, along with
the Stoic categories of a body of a particular kind, state,
and relation. A table summarizing the conclusions is
provided.

1.139   NISBET, R. G. M. "The Speeches," in <u>Cicero</u>. Edited by T. A.
        Dorey. New York: Basic Books, Inc., Publishers, 1965,
        pp. 47-79.
            A general overview of the stylistic qualities of Cicero's
        speeches. A useful introduction for those who desire a
        broad perspective of Cicero's oratorical career.

1.140   NORDEN, EDUARD. <u>Die Antike Kunstprosa</u>. 2 vols. Stuttgart:
        B. G. Teubner, 1974, 1014 pp.
            A detailed account of writings on prose-rhythm in both
        Greek and Roman rhetoric. Examines the establishment of
        these traditions up into the Renaissance. Written in
        German but provides a clear and systematic treatment.

1.141   NORTH, HELEN. "Poetry in the Education of the Ancient Orators."
        <u>TAPA</u>, 80 (1949), 430.
            Although rhetoric and poetry were often seen as discrete
        disciplines they were related in the education of ancient
        orators. North examines this relationship and provides
        insights into the educational process that incorporated
        these disciplines. The citation listed above is a one-
        page abstract of North's paper.

1.142   OCHS, DONOVAN J. "Aristotle's Concept of Formal Topics." <u>SM</u>,
        36 (November 1969), 419-25.
            The notion of topics is an important aspect of classical
        rhetoric, both for the discovery of ideas and the structure
        of discourse. This essay, which is based on Ochs's disser-
        tation, examines Aristotle's views on the subject. Advances
        the position that Aristotle's use of topics is a process of
        establishing relationships among terms, propositions, and
        events. A time-line and diagram are provided to illustrate
        these concepts. For a more detailed statement on the sub-
        ject <u>see</u>: Ochs, Donovan J. "The Tradition of the Classical
        Doctrines of Rhetorical <u>Topoi</u>." Ph.D. dissertation, The
        State University of Iowa, 1966, 221 pp.

1.143   ORAVEC, CHRISTINE. "'Observation' in Aristotle's Theory of
        Epideictic." <u>PR</u>, 9 (Summer 1976), 162-74.
            Claims that scholars of rhetoric, such as Lane Cooper
        and E. M. Cope, have come to consider epideictic rhetoric
        as merely a form of entertainment. Advances the argument
        that there are judicial and educative functions of
        epideictic discourse.

1.144   PARRY, ADAM, ed. <u>The Making of Homeric Verse: The Collected
        Papers of Milman Parry</u>. Oxford: At the Clarendon Press,
        1971, 545 pp.
            Posits the claim that Homeric literature was composed
        with the idea of being read aloud. The papers of Parry
        offer studies in formulaic composition of literature and
        make apparent the close relationship of oral and written
        discourse in ancient Greece.

1.145 PARRY, MILMAN. "Studies in the Epic Technique of Oral Verse-
       Making, II. The Homeric Language as the Language of Oral
       Poetry." HSCP, 43 (1932), 1-50.
           Considered by many to be a classic essay in the field,
       this work indicates the close relationship between oral and
       written literature. The study has direct relevance to com-
       positional structure by poets and techniques of logography
       by rhetoricians. For related reading on the impact of
       logography see: Enos, Richard Leo. "The Persuasive and
       Social Force of Logography in Ancient Greece." CSSJ, 25
       (Spring 1974), 4-10.

1.146 PATZER, HARALD. "Ῥαψῳδός." Hermes, 80 (1952), 314-25.
           Examines the philological origin and development of the
       term "rhapsode." The study is intended only for those who
       have a strong interest in detailed issues of etymology and
       philology, and who have a knowledge of German.

1.147 PAVESE, CAROLO ODO. Studi Sulla Tradizione Epica Rapsodica.
       Roma: Edizioni dell'Ateneo, 1974, 175 pp.
           A lengthy study of the epic tradition of rhapsodic dis-
       course. The emphasis is on philological issues of composi-
       tion. Does not stress the historical evolution of the
       rhapsodic tradition. Written in Italian and no English
       translation is known.

1.148 PEABODY, BERKLEY. The Winged Word: A Study in the Technique
       of Ancient Greek Oral Composition as Seen Principally
       through Hesiod's Works and Days. Albany: State University
       of New York Press, 1975, 578 pp.
           An extensive explanation of the techniques of oral trans-
       mission and the formulae used by Hesiod. The text is
       accompanied by detailed notes. The opening chapter on the
       general nature of oral literature is a helpful introduction.

1.149 PFEIFFER, RUDOLF. History of Classical Scholarship from the
       Beginnings to the End of the Hellenistic Age. Oxford: At
       the Clarendon Press, 1968, 328 pp.
           Pfeiffer's work provides the reader with the opportunity
       to examine ancient scholarship about classical literature.
       Much of Pfeiffer's writings deal directly with the theory
       and development of rhetoric. The study is documented
       thoroughly and in detail.

1.150 PLATNAUER, MAURICE, ed. Fifty Years (and Twelve) of Classical
       Scholarship. 2nd ed. Oxford: Basil Blackwell, 1968,
       538 pp.
           Documents research on classical scholarship. The respec-
       tive sections devoted to Greek and Latin rhetoric and ora-
       tory are of particular interest to those who desire a

review of classical research. Much of the research cited
comes from England and Europe.

1.151 RAMAGE, EDWIN S. "Cicero on Extra-Roman Speech." TAPA, 92
(1961), 481-94.
Concentrating on Cicero, Ramage discusses the concept of
urbanity and the cultural refinement of eloquence in Roman
rhetoric.

1.152 RAYMENT, CHARLES S. "A Current Survey of Ancient Rhetoric."
The Classical World, 52 (December 1958), 75-91.
Although somewhat dated, this essay provides a helpful
survey of scholarship on classical rhetoric.

1.153 REYNOLDS, L. D. and N. E. WILSON. Scribes and Scholars: A
Guide to the Transmission of Greek and Latin Literature.
London: Oxford University Press, 1968, 193 pp.
Treats the transmission of classical works by the recording and preservation of manuscripts. Although the subject
is more appropriate to the Middle Ages, the writings of
Reynolds and Wilson reveal the manner in which classical
works of rhetoric were transmitted from generation to
generation.

1.154 ROBERTS, W. RHYS. Greek Rhetoric and Literary Criticism.
New York: Longmans, Green & Company, 1928, 171 pp.
Provides a survey of rhetoric as a discipline and examines its history in ancient Greece. The study is often
regarded as a standard reference on the subject.

1.155 ROBERTS, W. RHYS. "The New Rhetorical Fragment (Oxyrhynchus
Papyri, Part III, pp. 27-30) in Relation to the Sicilian
Rhetoric of Corax and Tisias." Classical Review, 18
(February 1904), 18-21.
Presents a brief but clear explanation of the relationship of Corax, Tisias, and Gorgias, as well as the founding
of the discipline of rhetoric and the popularization of
rhetoric in Athens. Much of the information is from papyri
discovered in the twentieth century.

1.156 SAINTSBURY, GEORGE. A History of Criticism and Literary Taste
in Europe: From the Earliest Texts to the Present Day.
Vol. 1. Edinburgh and London: William Blackwood and Sons,
1900, 514 pp.
This volume provides an overview of classical and medieval criticism. Although dated, the work provides a synthesis of views of prominent Greek and Roman rhetoricians.
Of particular interest is the chapter entitled "Byzantine
Criticism," which examines a period and topic in the history of rhetoric that is rarely treated.

1.157 SATTLER, WILLIAM M. "Conceptions of Ethos in Ancient Rhetoric."
SM, 14 (1947), 55-65.
Ethos, or the artistic creation of a favorable character
in the minds of the audience within a piece of discourse,
was considered a major force in classical rhetoric. Sattler
examines this notion and provides insight into varying interpretations. A diagram is presented that attempts to
synthesize Aristotle's doctrine of ethos. For a more detailed discussion of the topic see: Sattler, William M.
"Conceptions of Ethos in Rhetoric." Ph.D. dissertation,
Northwestern University, 1941, 357 pp.

1.158 SATTLER, WILLIAM M. "Some Platonic Influences in the Rhetorical Works of Cicero." QJS, 35 (April 1949), 164-69.
Claims that although much of Cicero's view on rhetoric
is influenced by Aristotle, Isocrates, and Stoic writing,
he nonetheless clearly reveals a Platonic influence. References to Plato occur throughout Cicero's writings and
Sattler attempts to draw these references together.

1.159 SEGAL, C. P. "Gorgias and the Psychology of the Logos."
HSCP, 66 (1962), 99-155.
Presents a detailed account of Gorgias's view of logos
and advances the claim that Gorgias should be considered a
serious thinker who established detailed, sophisticated
theories of knowledge and human behavior. The comprehensive notes provide thorough references to additional reading.

1.160 SHIPP, G. P. Studies in the Language of Homer. 2nd ed.
Cambridge, England: Cambridge University Press, 1972,
392 pp.
Examines the structure of Homeric language including
such features as vocabulary, metrical technique, and other
related topics. Discusses early language composition prior
to the canonization of rhetoric.

1.161 SIDER, ROBERT DICK. Ancient Rhetoric and the Art of Tertullian.
Oxford: University Press, 1971, 153 pp.
Discusses the rhetorical background of Tertullian and
the structure of his treatises. Sections of the work are
also devoted to a clarification of issues, topics, and
themes in Tertullian's works. Includes a bibliography and
index of references to Tertullian's works.

1.162 SMITH, BROMLEY. "Gorgias: A Study in Oratorical Style."
QJS, 7 (November 1921), 335-59.
Provides a general outline of the stylistic qualities
of Gorgias while encouraging readers to be aware that
Gorgias was "a participant in the philosophical contro-
versies of his time." Considerable research has followed
Smith's pioneer essay, but the work provides a lucid intro-
ductory reading.

1.163　SMITH, ROBERT W. The Art of Rhetoric in Alexandria: Its Theory and Practice in the Ancient World. The Hague: Martinus Nijhoff, 1974, 180 pp.

　　　　A treatment of ancient rhetoric in Greco-Roman Egypt. Stresses the role of classical rhetoric in Alexandria from 300 B.C. to 400 A.D., emphasizing the cultural climate, education, and Christian preaching.

1.164　SOCHATOFF, A. F. "Basic Rhetorical Theories of the Elder Seneca." CJ, 34 (March 1939), 345-54.

　　　　The Elder Seneca was a noted rhetorician of the late Roman Republic and early Roman Empire. Sochatoff synthesizes the rhetorical theories of Seneca and provides information important to those interested in the declamation of this period.

1.165　SOLMSEN, F. "The Aristotelian Tradition in Ancient Rhetoric." AJP, 62 (1941), 35-50, 169-90.

　　　　Examines the Aristotelian, or Peripatetic influence on later theories of rhetoric and attempts to clarify those factors of Aristotelian rhetoric that are unique contributions to rhetorical theory. Provides a comprehensive explanation of many technical terms found in Aristotle's writings.

1.166　SOLMSEN, F. "Cicero's First Speeches: A Rhetorical Analysis." TAPA, 69 (1938), 542-56.

　　　　With the exception of De Inventione, Cicero wrote his treatises on rhetoric after he initiated his career as a distinguished orator. This study provides readers with the opportunity to examine Cicero's early techniques and strategies.

1.167　SPITZER, ADELE. "The Self-Reference of the Gorgias." PR, 8 (Winter 1975), 1-22.

　　　　Claims that the dialogue Gorgias is itself an illustration of the defects of rhetoric, both through its argument and the words and actions of the dialogue-characters. Further posits that Plato meant to illustrate that philosophy was the only true form of justice and the only true form of statesmanship or politics. In this respect, Socrates himself is seen as the philosopher-king.

1.168　STANFORD, W. B. The Sound of Greek: Studies in the Greek Theory and Practice of Euphony. Berkeley: University of California Press, 1967, 183 pp., and phonodisc.

　　　　Discusses the oral nature of ancient Greek. Of particular interest to students of rhetoric are the first two chapters, "The Primacy of the Spoken Word" and "Speech and Music." A record is included with the text in which Stanford attempts to duplicate the sounds of ancient Greek.

1.169 TEJERA, V. "Irony and Allegory in the Phaedrus." PR, 8
        (Spring 1975), 71-87.
            Claims that the Phaedrus, long considered to be a
        standard primary source in the history of rhetoric, is
        a dialogue that cannot be understood without recognizing
        Socrates' use of irony.

1.170 THOMPSON, WAYNE N. "Stasis in Aristotle's Rhetoric." QJS,
        58 (April 1972), 134-41.
            Claims that a thorough study of Aristotle's view of
        stasis requires an examination of the Rhetorica. Asserts
        that although Aristotle's views on the subject lack the
        precision of Hermagoras, it is clear that the two authors
        differ in their treatment of stasis.

1.171 UNTERSTEINER, MARIO. The Sophists. Translated by Kathleen
        Freeman. New York: Philosophical Library, 1954, 384 pp.
            Considered by many to be the most authoritative state-
        ment on sophistic thought in ancient Greece. Provides in-
        sights to sophistic philosophy and rhetoric with detailed
        references for additional reading. There are, for example,
        six chapters devoted to Gorgias and an entire chapter deal-
        ing with Gorgias's view of rhetoric.

1.172 VOLPE, MICHAEL. "The Persuasive Force of Humor: Cicero's
        Defense of Caelius." QJS, 63 (October 1977), 311-23.
            Examines Cicero's ability to understand the nature of
        his audience and to use humor to adapt to the psychological
        needs of the rhetorical situation present in the Pro Caelio.

1.173 WILKINS, AUGUSTUS S. M. Tulli Ciceronis De Oratore Libri Tres.
        Hildesheim: Georg Olms Verlagsbuchhandlung, 1965, pp. 1-71.
            Although this edition of Cicero's De Oratore is limited
        to the Latin text, Wilkins provides an introduction con-
        taining important background information on the history of
        rhetoric as well as information concerning De Oratore.
        The text includes extended commentary on critical points
        throughout Cicero's treatise. An analysis of the Rhetorica
        ad Herennium is also provided.

1.174 WILKINSON, L. P. Golden Latin Artistry. Cambridge, England:
        Cambridge University Press, 1963, 296 pp.
            Wilkinson's treatment of the development of the Latin
        language provides students of rhetoric with a comprehensive
        statement of literary and philological issues that comple-
        ment the writings of ancient authors concerned with the
        notion of eloquence. The work is often considered to be
        helpful in providing an explanation of prose rhythm and
        balance.

1.175 YATES, FRANCIS AMELIA. <u>The Art of Memory</u>. London & Chicago: Routledge and University of Chicago Press, 1966, 415 pp.
　　　　Treats the history of memory throughout Western civilization. Those interested in classical rhetoric will find that the early section of the book provides a synthesis of the ancient views of this canon of rhetoric.

Part 2

The Middle Ages

LUKE REINSMA

Introduction

In tracing the intellectual lines of influence--the Sophistic,
Platonic, Aristotelian, and Ciceronian--binding classical and medieval studies of rhetoric, scholars have reminded us that medieval
studies of language stand securely on the shoulders of the past. We
cannot fully understand Augustine's De doctrina christiana IV unless
we see that it is not only a response to his church but also to his
heritage--to Plato ("Should . . . the defenders of truth speak so
that they tire their listeners. . . ?" [2.2a, 4.2.3]); and to Cicero
("'Eloquence without wisdom is often extremely injurious and profits
no one'" [4.5.7]). It is important that we trace, too, the history
of Aristotle's organon in Boethius's De differentiis topicis and
John of Salisbury's Metalogicon; or the sophists' love of language
in the early De praeexercitamentis rhetoricis of Priscian, in Bede's
Liber de schematibus et tropis, and, later, in the ars poetica.

   Still, such an approach to medieval rhetorical treatises harbors
several disadvantages. First, as Richard J. Schoeck points out in
response to James J. Murphy on Chaucer's intellectual heritage
(2.149), a dogged insistence on clear-cut lines of influence tends
to turn the useful art of classification into arbitrary legislation
(2.181). Too many of the treatises considered here simply refuse
conventional labels: not just the grammars of Priscian, Alexander
of Villedieu, and Eberhard of Béthune, and the treatise on topics of
Boethius, but such intriguing approaches to the uses of language as
Alcuin's politically motivated Disputatio, Eberhard the German's
satirical Laborintus, Henri of Andeli's allegorical Bataille des Sept
Arts, and Dante's apologia for a vernacular, De vulgari eloquentia.
Once we attempt to account for the fundamental rhetorical traditions
of the twelfth century and those traditions that followed--the ars
dictaminis, the ars poetica, and ars praedicandi, and the lesser arts
of metrics and rhythm, and the speculative grammars of the modistae--
we are forced to concede that medieval students of language, while
recognizing their debt to the past, recognized their responsibility
to the present even more.

Introduction

Of Notker Labeo, Otto Dieter writes: "He . . . realized that
rhetoric, founded on the past, had to keep in close contact with life
in the living present" (2.78, p. 33). Notker Labeo's attention to--
his response to--the needs of the present appears to have been a
central concern of the medieval rhetoricians. Nowhere is that concern illuminated more clearly than in several studies of the ars
dictaminis included in this bibliography of medieval rhetoric.
William D. Patt, for instance, persuasively demonstrates that treatises on the art of letter writing grew not so much out of the intellectual springs of Bologna as they did in response to cultural
developments that swept throughout much of Europe (2.161). Charles H.
Haskins on medieval students and their letters (2.98), Ernst H.
Kantorowicz on Guido Faba (2.113), and I. S. Robinson on the investiture contest (2.172) all make, in their own distinguished ways, the
same point: The ars dictaminis grew out of the peculiar and lively
need of scholars and clerics, students and kings. Jacques Fontaine's
study of Isidore's culture (2.85), Luitpold Wallach on the via regia
in Alcuin's Disputatio (2.191), Maartje Draak on the painstaking
Irish glosses in the St. Gall Priscian (2.80), and Gian C. Garfagnini
on the political context of John of Salisbury's Metalogicon and
Policraticus (2.91)--these scholars and others remind us, too, that
not just the ars dictaminis but every rhetorical and grammatical and
logical treatise comes to us first in acknowledgement, not of the
past, but of the present.

The medieval students of language confronted two such fundamental
needs: the need to understand the arts of language--grammar, rhetoric, logic--within an intellectual context; and, second, the need
to apply those arts to practical human concerns. So we begin with
the encyclopedias of Capella, Cassiodorus, Isidore, and, later, of
Hugh of St. Victor, John of Salisbury, Brunetto Latini, and Giles of
Rome. Most of these encyclopedists sought to place rhetoric within
the trivium and quadrivium; all sought to weigh the relative merits,
effects, and purposes of rhetoric and the related sciences of grammar,
logic, ethics, and politics.

But the medieval rhetoricians knew that classification and analysis are never enough. What were the purposes of a study and an understanding of the ars rhetorica? It is this question that unlocks the
doors of the medieval rhetorical tradition. In the early Middle Ages
the standard for correct writing was Priscian; later it became
Alexander of Villedieu and Eberhard of Béthune. In the early Middle
Ages the treatises of Priscian and Bede taught one how to write well;
after the twelfth century one would have turned to the manuals on
letter writing of Alberic of Monte Cassino, Hugh of Bologna, Guido
Faba, Boncompagno, and their successors; or (if his subjects were
fiction rather than fact) to Mathew of Vendôme's Ars versificatoria,
Geoffrey of Vinsauf's Poetria nova, and John of Garland's Parisiana
poetria. If the preacher wished to speak well--if, in Cicero and
Augustine's words, he wished to teach, to entertain, and to persuade--
then he could turn to manuals of preaching, ranging from Augustine's

46

Introduction

fifth-century De doctrina to Alain of Lille's De arte praedicatoria, written at the close of the twelfth century, to any one of dozens of later treatises on the university sermon. If he wished to think sharply and clearly and argue well, there were treatises on the arts of logic and disputation for that purpose, too. These, then, are the needs and traditions reflected in this bibliography of medieval rhetoric.

Since this bibliography spans eleven centuries, from c. 400-c. 1500 A.D., it is, of necessity, select: 235 primary and secondary sources are represented in these 200 entries. In selecting primary works, I have attempted to represent the manifold interests of the medieval student of language. Each of these works is fundamental to an understanding of medieval rhetoric; most of them have been translated. The secondary studies provide sound, general introductions to various aspects of the rhetorical tradition. Emphasis has been placed on more recent publications (approximately 30 per cent of the secondary scholarship was published after 1970) and, secondly, on liberally documented texts and articles, so that if a particular author or treatise or topic catches the student's eye, he might be directed toward a broad range of earlier studies. Students of English literature will find, too, that I have paid some, although not inordinate, attention to the influence of rhetorical studies on literary works: to Jackson J. Campbell for Old English literature; to John M. Manly, James J. Murphy, Robert O. Payne, and Richard J. Schoeck for Chaucer; and to Erich Auerbach, Ernst R. Curtius, and Aldo Scaglione for medieval Latin literature. Since this bibliography is intended to introduce rather than to conclude the study of medieval rhetoric, more specialized studies of meter, rhythm, grammar, logic, disputation, and memory have received less than just attention.

Any student of medieval rhetoric will recognize my considerable debt to James J. Murphy's fundamental survey, Rhetoric in the Middle Ages, and to his Medieval Rhetoric: A Select Bibliography as well. A bibliography of this limited scope must of necessity duplicate many of the entries in his. Nevertheless, nearly half the citations in this select bibliography are not in Murphy's; I trust that my annotations will usefully complement those that are.

The alphabetical list of secondary sources has its obvious advantages, but it does not permit, of course, a grouping of sources beneath convenient heads: ars grammatica, ars poetica, ars dictaminis, ars praedicandi, and so on. The index that accompanies this text, however, cross-listing both primary and secondary sources under each of these and further headings, will provide the student with a convenient guide to these and related rhetorical traditions.

Consistency of entries has been a greater difficulty. Whenever possible and reasonable, I have anglicized medieval names so that, for example, Alanus de Insulis is consistently referred to in the annotations as Alain of Lille; Evrardus Allemanus, as Eberhard the

German, and so on. As a result, several scholars cited here will find their subjects cited in the annotations with a spelling that differs from theirs. The index cross-lists both anglicized and latinate spellings. Editors of the primary sources are not cited in the index; all authors of secondary scholarship are. Wherever possible, modern authors are referred to by full first name, middle initial, and last name. Church titles have been dropped. And, except for the first key word, Latin titles are generally printed in lower case.

Clark Malcolm at the University of Michigan and Ted Leinbaugh at Harvard checked several of the entries in this bibliography; I owe them my thanks. But I owe a special debt to Traugott Lawler, Aldo Scaglione, and Robert O. Payne for having read portions or the whole of the manuscript and for having provided a good number of useful emendations, notes of caution, and further suggestions. Whatever egregious omissions and discrepancies may remain in the bibliography are, of course, of my own making; for whatever merits and usefulness this select bibliography harbors, I offer these readers my especial thanks.

LUKE M. REINSMA
Gustavus Adolphus College

Primary Works

2.1 c. 405. AUGUSTINE OF HIPPO (Saint Aurelius). De catechizandis rudibus.

    Like his De doctrina (2.2), an educational treatise that marks Augustine's break with the rhetoric of the Second Sophistic. Let the rhetoricians know, writes Augustine, "that there is no voice to reach the ears of God save the emotion of the heart . . ." (2.1a, p. 45). Adapted in the works of Cassiodorus (2.7), Isidore (2.8), Bede, Alcuin, and Rabanus Maurus (2.11).

2.1a   S. Avreli Avgvstini Hipponiensis Episcopi, De catechizandis rvdibvs liber vnvs; Translated with an Intro-duction and Commentary. Edited and translated by Joseph P. Christopher. The Catholic University of America Patristic Studies, No. 8. Washington, D.C.: The Catholic University of America, 1926, 386 pp.

    Bibliography, pp. xiii-xxi; introduction, pp. 1-13; and notes, pp. 122-336. Translation reprinted in 2.1b.

2.1b   St. Augustine, The First Catechetical Instruction [De catechizandis rudibus]. Translated by Joseph P. Christopher. Ancient Christian Writers: The Works of the Fathers in Translation, No. 2. Westminster, Md.: The Newman Press; London: Longmans, Green and Co., 1946. Reprinted: 1952, 169 pp.

    Reprint of translation in 2.1a.

2.2 396-426. AUGUSTINE OF HIPPO (Saint Aurelius). De doctrina christiana.

    A response to what James J. Murphy calls "the 'Platonic rhetorical heresy'" (2.139, p. 60)--the notion that truth in the hands of a good man is enough. Following three books on the material of the sermon, Book 4 argues, as Cicero had, that rhetoric should teach, delight, and per-suade. The levels of style (plain, middle, and grand) are treated as well. Adapted by Rabanus Maurus (2.11), Alain of Lille (2.18), Humbert of Romans (2.28), and Robert of Basevorn (2.33).

2.2a   On Christian Doctrine; Translated, with an Introduction.
Translated by Durant W. Robertson, Jr. The Library of
Liberal Arts, No. 80. Indianapolis and New York: The
Bobbs-Merrill Company, Inc., Liberal Arts Press, 1958,
191 pp.
           A standard translation of the four books of De doctrina.
2.2b   S. Avreli Avgvstini Hipponiensis Episcopi, De doctrina
christiana, liber qvartvs; A Commentary, with a Revised
Text, Introduction, and Translation. Edited and translated
by Thérèse Sullivan. The Catholic University of America
Patristic Studies, No. 23. Washington, D.C.: The Catholic
University of America, 1930, 219 pp.
           Text and translation of Book 4 alone. Bibliography,
pp. ix-xiv. Introduction (pp. 1-42) includes consideration
of text and manuscripts, date and occasion of composition,
analysis of contents, sources and parallels, Biblical quotations, style, and influence of the text.
2.2c   De doctrina christiana libri qvattvor. Edited by
Guilelmus M. Green. Sancti Avreli Avgvstini Opera, Sect. 6,
Pars 6. Corpvs Scriptorvm Ecclesiasticorvm Latinorvm,
No. 80. Vindobonae: Hoelder-Pichler-Tempsky, 1963,
234 pp.
           An edition of the entire treatise.

2.3 c. 410-39. MARTIANUS CAPELLA. De nuptiis Philologiae et
Mercurii.
           The first standard codification of the seven liberal
arts. Two books of flamboyant allegory are followed by
more conventional reviews of grammar, dialectic, rhetoric,
geometry, mathematics, astronomy, and music. De rhetorica
(Book 5) emphasizes invention, disposition, and the
Ciceronian status.

2.3a   "De nuptiis Philologiae et Mercurii, V: 'The Book of
Rhetoric.'" Translated by Joseph M. Miller. In Readings
in Medieval Rhetoric. Edited by Joseph M. Miller,
Michael H. Prosser, and Thomas W. Benson. Bloomington and
London: Indiana University Press, 1973, pp. 2-5.
           A readily available translation of Book 5, De rhetorica.
2.3b   Martianus Capella and the Seven Liberal Arts. Vol. 2:
The Marriage of Philology and Mercury. Translated by
William H. Stahl, Richard Johnson, and E. L. Burge.
Columbia University Records of Civilization, Sources and
Studies, No. 84. New York: Columbia University Press,
1977, 389 pp.
           Includes a translation of the trivium. Book 5,
"Rhetoric," is translated in pp. 155-214. For vol. 1,
see Stahl, 2.185.
2.3c   "XIII. Martiani Minnei Felicis Capellae, Liber de arte
rhetorica," in Rhetores Latini Minores: Ex Codicibus
Maximam Partem Primum Adhibitis. Edited by Carolus F. Halm.

Leipzig: B. G. Teubneri, 1863. Reprinted: Frankfurt:
Minerva, 1964; Dubuque, Iowa: Wm. C. Brown Reprint Library,
n.d., pp. 451-92.
   Still a standard edition of Book 5.

2.3d   Martianus Capella. Edited by Adolfus Dick. Bibliotheca
Scriptorvm Graecorvm et Romanorvm Tevbneriana. Leipzig:
B. G. Teubneri, 1925. Revised by Jean Préaux. Stuttgart:
B. G. Teubneri, 1969, 614 pp.
   Complete edition of De nuptiis. Includes bibliography,
pp. xxxi-xxxiii, in the 1925 edition.

2.4 c. 510. PRISCIAN. De praeexercitamentis rhetoricis.
   Partly translates, partly adapts Hermogenes' second-
century Progymnasmata. A series of school exercises in
constructing the fable, narrative, anecdote, sentence, refutation, commonplace, encomium, comparison, characterization,
description, thesis, and presentation of a legal brief.

2.4a   "Fundamentals Adapted from Hermogenes." Translated by
Joseph M. Miller. In Readings in Medieval Rhetoric.
Edited by Joseph M. Miller, Michael H. Prosser, and
Thomas W. Benson. Bloomington and London: Indiana Uni-
versity Press, 1973, pp. 52-68.

2.4b   "XVII. Praeexercitamina Prisciani Grammatici ex
Hermogene versa," in Rhetores Latini Minores: Ex Codicibus
Maximam Partem Primum Adhibitis. Edited by Carolus F. Halm.
Leipzig: B. G. Teubneri, 1863. Reprinted: Frankfurt:
Minerva, 1964; Dubuque, Iowa: Wm. C. Brown Reprint Library,
n.d., pp. 551-60.

2.5 c. 510. PRISCIAN. Institutio grammatica.
   A lengthy, sophisticated examination of grammar—according to R. H. Robins, "the culmination of late Latin grammatical scholarship" (2.171, p. 64). Includes an
examination of letters, syllables, comparatives and super-
latives, nouns, verbs, participles, pronouns, prepositions,
adverbs, and conjunctions. More than a thousand manuscript
copies exist today. Still untranslated.

2.5a   Prisciani Grammatici Caesariensis Institvtionvm
grammaticarvm libri XVIII. Edited by Martin Hertz. In
Grammatici Latini. Vols. 2 and 3. Edited by Heinrich
Keil. Leipzig: B. G. Teubner, 1857-80. Reprinted:
Hildesheim: G. Olms, 1961, pp. 1-384.

2.6 c. 520. BOETHIUS, ANICIUS MANLIUS SEVERINUS. De differentiis
topicis (Topica Boetii).
   Books 1-3 introduce the invention of dialectical topics;
they would become a standard twelfth-century text in the
so-called old logic. Book 4 distinguishes rhetoric (arguments based on fact, an uninterrupted discourse designed to

move a judge) and dialectic (hypothetical arguments lodged against an adversary, proceeding by question and answer) and subordinates the former to the latter.

2.6a   Boethius's De topicis differentiis; Translated, with Notes and Essays on the Text. Translated by Eleonore A. Stump. Ithaca, N.Y., and London: Cornell University Press, 1978, 287 pp.
     Introduction, pp. 13-26; text, pp. 29-95; notes, pp. 97-155. For supplementary essays, see Stump, 2.187.

2.6b   "An. Manl. Sev. Boetii, De differentiis topicis libri quatuor," in Patrologiae Cursus Completus, Series Latina. Vol. 64. Edited by Jacques P. Migne. Paris: Garnier Fratres, 1844-1864, cols. 1173-216.

2.7 c. 551-62. CASSIODORUS, M. A. (Senator). Institutiones divinarum et saecularium litterarum.
     An encyclopedic introduction to divine and secular studies for the monks at Vivarium. Book 2 provides a sketchy treatment of the liberal arts. Defined as "expertness in discourse on civil questions" (2.7a, p. 148), rhetoric is divided into its five traditional parts (invention, disposition, style, memory, and delivery), but the emphasis is on legal positions (constitutiones) and modes of argument.

2.7a   An Introduction to Divine and Human Readings by Cassiodorus Senator; Translated with an Introduction and Notes. Translated by Leslie W. Jones. Columbia University Records of Civilization, Sources and Studies, No. 40. New York: Columbia University Press, 1946. Reprinted: New York: W. W. Norton & Company, Inc., 1969, 250 pp.
     Book 2, ii, "On Rhetoric," is translated in pp. 148-58. For the introduction, see Jones, 2.111.

2.7b   "XIV. Ex Cassiodorii, Humanarum institutionum pars quae De arte rhetorica agit," in Rhetores Latini Minores: Ex Codicibus Maximam Partem Primum Adhibitis. Edited by Carolus F. Halm. Leipzig: B. G. Teubneri, 1863. Reprinted: Frankfurt: Minerva, 1964; Dubuque, Iowa: Wm. C. Brown Reprint Library, n.d., pp. 495-504.
     Still a standard edition of Book 2, ii, "De rhetorica."

2.7c   Cassiodori Senatoris Institutiones. Edited by Roger A. B. Mynors. Oxford: At the Clarendon Press, 1937. Reprinted: 1963, 249 pp.
     An edition of the entire text. The introduction is largely concerned with the manuscripts of Institutiones.

2.8 c. 600. ISIDORE OF SEVILLE. Etymologia (Origines).
     Perhaps the most widely known and influential encyclopedia of the Middle Ages. A review of human knowledge, beginning with studies of grammar, rhetoric, and dialectic

as a preliminary step to medical, legal, Biblical, historical, astronomical, and other lore. James J. Murphy suggests that Isidore departs from Boethius in distinguishing
rhetoric from dialectic and in allying it with grammar
(2.139, p. 73). Isidore's brief discussion of rhetoric
(parts of rhetoric, the status, figures of speech, etc.)
is adapted largely from Cassiodorus (2.7).

*2.8a   "The Rhetoric and Dialectic of Isidorus of Seville: A
Translation and Commentary." Translated by Dorothy V.
Cerino. Master's thesis, Brooklyn College, 1938.
           Cerino's translation of Book 2, i-xv, "De rhetorica,"
is reprinted in Miller, Prosser, and Benson, eds., 2.45,
pp. 80-95, as "The Etymologies, II.1-15: 'Concerning
Rhetoric.'" The thesis is cited in Murphy, 2.142, No. T76.

2.8b   "XV. Ex Isidori Originum libro secundo capita quae sunt
De rhetorica," in Rhetores Latini Minores: Ex Codicibus
Maximam Partem Primum Adhibitis. Edited by Carolus F. Halm.
Leipzig: B. G. Teubneri, 1863. Reprinted: Frankfurt:
Minerva, 1964; Dubuque, Iowa: Wm. C. Brown Reprint Library,
n.d., pp. 507-22.
           Still a standard edition of "De rhetorica."

2.8c   Isidori Hispalensis Episcopi Etymologiarvm sive originvm
libri XX. Edited by Wallace M. Lindsay. 2 vols.
Scriptorum Classicorum Bibliotheca Oxoniensis. Oxford:
At the Clarendon Press, 1911. Reprinted: 1971.

2.9   701-702. BEDE (the Venerable). Liber de schematibus et tropis.
           The first rhetorical treatise written in England. Bede's
De schematibus perhaps anticipates England's later tendency
to equate rhetoric and stylistic flourish. Although this
collection of seventeen schemes and twenty-eight tropes
follows the format of Donatus's Barbarismus, Bede follows
Augustine's lead in providing--with three exceptions--
Scriptural examples of the figures of speech.

2.9a   "Bede's De schematibus et tropis--A Translation."
Translated by Gussie H. Tannenhaus. QJS, 48 (1962), 237-53.
           Reprinted without the introduction (pp. 237-40) in
Miller, Prosser, and Benson, eds., 2.45, pp. 97-122, as
"Concerning Figures and Tropes."

2.9b   "XXIIII. Bedae Venerabilis Liber de schematibus et
tropis," in Rhetores Latini Minores: Ex Codicibus Maximam
Partem Primum Adhibitis. Edited by Carolus F. Halm.
Leipzig: B. G. Teubneri, 1863. Reprinted: Frankfurt:
Minerva, 1964; Dubuque, Iowa: Wm. C. Brown Reprint Library,
n.d., pp. 607-18.
           Long a standard edition of De schematibus, although
not as authoritative as 2.9c.

2.9c   De arte metrica et De schematibvs et tropis. Edited by
Calvin B. Kendall. In Bedae Venerabilis Opera, Pars I:

Opera didascalica. Edited by Ch. W. Jones. Corpus
Christianorum, Series Latina, No. 123A. Turnhout:
Brepols Editores Pontificii, 1975, pp. 60-171.
 Introduction, pp. 60-79; De arte metrica, pp. 80-141;
De schematibus et tropis, pp. 142-71.

2.10 794. ALCUIN. Disputatio de rhetorica et de virtutibus.
 A dialogue between the magister Alcuin and Charlemagne,
thoroughly Ciceronian in character: the matter of invention is adapted from the De inventione; the four remaining
parts of rhetoric, from Julius Victor's late fourth-century
Ars rhetorica. Questions of the status and of basic rhetorical terminology are aimed at defining a rhetoric that is
both secular in character and political in orientation.

2.10a The Rhetoric of Alcuin & Charlemagne; a Translation,
with an Introduction, the Latin Text, and Notes. Edited
and translated by Wilbur S. Howell. Princeton, N.J.:
Princeton University Press, 1941. Reprinted: New York:
Russell & Russell, 1965, 184 pp.
 For the introduction, see Howell, 2.102.

2.11 819. RABANUS MAURUS. De institutione clericorum.
 Following two books on priestly duties, Rabanus Maurus
devotes Book 3 to the matter of speaking, choosing not
Cicero but Augustine as his guide. Following a brief discussion of the quadrivium, De institutione touches on the
levels of style, tasks of the speaker, and so forth, adopt-
ing--often verbatim--passages from De doctrina 4 (2.2).
"The assimilation of classical rhetoric into Christian
methodology is here almost complete," writes James J.
Murphy (2.139, p. 82).

2.11a "On the Training of the Clergy, III.19." Translated by
Joseph M. Miller. In Readings in Medieval Rhetoric.
Edited by Joseph M. Miller, Michael H. Prosser, and
Thomas W. Benson. Bloomington and London: Indiana
University Press, 1973, pp. 125-27.

2.11b Beati Rabani Mauri Fuldensis Abbatis et Moguntini
Archiepiscopi, De clericorum institutione ad Heistulphum
Archiepiscopum libri tres (Anno 819). Vol. 107.
Patrologiae Cursus Completus, Series Latina. Edited by
Jacques P. Migne. Paris: Garnier Fratres, 1844-1864,
cols. 293-420.
 Not an entirely reliable edition. See also 2.11c.

2.11c Rabani Mauri De institutione clericorum libri tres.
Edited by Aloisius Knoepfler. Veröffentlichungen aus dem
Kirchenhistorischen Seminar München, No. 5. Munich:
J. J. Lentner'schen Buchhandlung, 1900, 329 pp.
 Knoepfler's introduction briefly touches on Rabanus's
life and on manuscripts of De institutione (pp. ix-xxix).

2.12 <u>c</u>. 1087. ALBERIC OF MONTE CASSINO. <u>Dictaminum radii (Flores
rhetorici)</u>.

Often hailed as the father of the <u>ars dictaminis</u>--the
application of rhetorical principles to the composing of
letters--Alberic takes the important step of distinguishing
the <u>salutatio</u> and exordium of the letter and of dividing
the letter into its parts: the exordium, narration, argument, and conclusion. Much of the <u>Dictaminum radii</u> is
devoted to a review of the figures and tropes.

2.12a   "Flowers of Rhetoric." Translated by Joseph M. Miller.
In <u>Readings in Medieval Rhetoric</u>. Edited by Joseph M.
Miller, Michael H. Prosser, and Thomas W. Benson.
Bloomington and London: Indiana University Press, 1973,
pp. 132-61.

2.12b   <u>Alberici Casinensis Flores rhetorici</u>. Edited by D. M.
Inguanez and Henry M. Willard. Miscellanea Cassinese,
No. 14. Montecassino: Arti Grafiche e Fotomeccaniche
Sansaini, 1938, 59 pp.
Introduction, pp. 9-30; text, pp. 33-59.

2.12c   HAGENDAHL, HARALD. "Le Manuel de Rhétorique d'Albericus
Casinensis." <u>C&M</u>, 17 (1956), 63-70.
Emendations and corrections to Inguanez and Willard,
eds., 2.12b.

2.13 1119-24. HUGH OF BOLOGNA. <u>Rationes dictandi prosaice</u>.

Hugh of Bologna's <u>Rationes</u> devotes a considerable amount
of its attention to an elaborate codification of salutations, pairing grammatical constructions with the social
rank of pope, king, bishop, friend, and so on. Following
an analysis of the four-part letter (<u>salutatio</u>, exordium,
narration, and conclusion), the treatise concludes with
seventy model salutations and another seventeen model let-
ters--"not really coordinated with the theoretical section,"
writes Carol D. Lanham (2.122, p. 100). Still untranslated.

2.13a   "Rationes dictandi prosaice," in <u>Briefsteller und
Formelbücher des eilften bis vierzehnten Jahrhunderts</u>.
Edited by Ludwig Rockinger. 2 vols. Quellen und
Erörterungen zur bayerischen und deutschen Geschichte,
No. 9, 1-2. Munich: Georg Franz, 1863-64. Reprinted
with continuous pagination, Burt Franklin Research &
Source Works Series, No. 10. New York: Burt Franklin,
1961, pp. 53-94.

2.14 <u>c</u>. 1127. HUGH OF ST. VICTOR. <u>Didascalicon</u>.

Although not a rhetorical treatise, Hugh of St. Victor's
well-known, encyclopedic treatment of human knowledge provides an important measure of the triumph of logic over
rhetoric in the twelfth century. He divides philosophy
into theoretical, practical, mechanical and logical wisdom;

logical wisdom, into demonstration, probable argument, and
sophistic; probable argument, into dialectic and rhetoric.
The key to man's success, he argues, is his ability to
think clearly and logically and to speak with eloquence.

2.14a   The Didascalicon of Hugh of St. Victor: A Medieval Guide
to the Arts; Translated from the Latin with an Introduction
and Notes. Translated by Jerome Taylor. Columbia University Records of Civilization, Sources and Studies, No. 64.
New York and London: Columbia University Press, 1961,
266 pp.
          Introduction discusses nature and date of the
Didascalicon; the theoretical, practical, mechanical, and
logical arts; sources, and the author (pp. 3-39). Bibliography, pp. 229-36.

2.14b   Hugonis de Sancto Victore Didascalicon de Studio Legendi;
A Critical Text. Edited by Charles H. Buttimer. The
Catholic University of America, Studies in Medieval and
Renaissance Latin, No. 10. Washington, D.C.: The Catholic
University Press, 1939, 212 pp.
          An extensive introduction classifies some thirty manu-
scripts and lists twelve earlier editions of the Didascalicon
(pp. vii-lii). Includes indexes to classical sources,
names, subjects, and words.

2.15 c. 1135. ANONYMOUS OF BOLOGNA. Rationes dictandi.
          It is quite clear from the tone of the Rationes dictandi
that the ars dictaminis was securely established in the
University of Bologna during the early twelfth century.
The longest of the thirteen sections of the Rationes is
devoted to the salutatio; further sections discuss methods
of securing good will, narration, petition, conclusion,
the shortening of a letter, grammatical constructions, and
the variation of a letter.

2.15a   The Principles of Letter-Writing (Rationes dictandi).
Translated by James J. Murphy. In Three Medieval Rhetorical
Arts. Edited by James J. Murphy. Berkeley, Los Angeles,
and London: University of California Press, 1971, pp. 5-25.
          In some respects, an inadequate translation of the first
of two books of the Rationes dictandi (for which see
Traugott Lawler's review in Speculum, 48 [1973], 388-94).

2.15b   "Rationes dictandi," in Briefsteller und Formelbücher
des eilften bis vierzehnten Jahrhunderts. Edited by
Ludwig Rockinger. 2 vols. Quellen und Erörterungen zur
bayerischen und deutschen Geschichte, No. 9, 1-2. Munich:
Georg Franz, 1863-64. Reprinted with continuous pagination, Burt Franklin Research & Source Works Series, No. 10.
New York: Burt Franklin, 1961, pp. 9-28.
          An edition of Book 1 of two. Note as well that Rockinger
mistakenly attributes the treatise to Alberic of Monte
Cassino (see Patt, 2.161, p. 137 and footnote 11).

2.16   1159.   JOHN OF SALISBURY.   Metalogicon.
An encyclopedic reexamination of the nature and bounds
of Aristotelian logic, grammar, and rhetoric, relying on
Boethian translations of the Organon.   Seeking out the
rational foundations of discourse, John of Salisbury insists
that rational inquiry and eloquent presentation are the distinguishing characteristics of man as man.   Anticipates the
predominant influence of Aristotle's works in the late Middle Ages and, perhaps, the Ramistic segregation of logic-
invention and rhetoric-eloquence.

2.16a   The Metalogicon of John of Salisbury: A Twelfth-Century
Defense of the Verbal and Logical Arts of the Trivium;
Translated with an Introduction & Notes.   Translated by
Daniel D. McGarry.   Berkeley and Los Angeles: University
of California Press, 1955.   Reprinted: 1971, 332 pp.
Bibliography, pp. 279-94.
2.16b   Ioannis Saresberiensis Episcopi Carnotensis Metalogicon
libri IIII.   Edited by Clemens C. I. Webb.   Oxford: At the
Clarendon Press, 1929, 261 pp.

2.17   c. 1170.   MATTHEW OF VENDÔME.   Ars versificatoria.
One of the earliest of the ars poetica, written for
students of grammar at Orleans.   In his searching out of
topics of invention and description, Matthew betrays his
interest in matters of rhetoric; in his demonstration of
the figures of speech, his interest in grammatical lore.
Gallo (2.17a) divides the treatise into four concerns:
methods of description; diction; figures, tropes, and
colors; and organization and content.

2.17a   "Matthew of Vendôme: Introductory Treatise on the Art
of Poetry."   Translated by Ernest Gallo.   PAPS, 118 (1974),
51-92.
Introduction, pp. 51-61; bibliography, pp. 60-61; text,
pp. 61-92.
2.17b   "Ars versificatoria," in Les Arts Poétiques du XIIe et
du XIIIe Siècle: Recherches et Documents sur la Technique
Littéraire du Moyen Age.   Edited by Edmond Faral.
Bibliothèque de l'Ecole des Hautes Etudes, Sciences
Historiques et Philologiques, No. 238.   Paris: Librarie
Ancienne Honoré Champion, 1924.   Reprinted: 1962,
pp. 109-93.

2.18   c. 1199.   ALAIN OF LILLE (Alanus de Insulis).   De arte
praedicatoria.
According to James J. Murphy, the first attempt to provide a rhetoric of preaching since Saint Augustine's De
doctrina (2.139, p. 306).   Alain follows an initial chapter
defining the nature of preaching with forty-seven exemplary
sermons on such varied topics as the contempt of the world,

against gluttony, and on behalf of obedience; or addressed
to a number of audiences--orators, doctors, princes, widows,
sleepyheads, and so on. Methodical threefold distinctions
throughout anticipate the later predilection of the ars
praedicandi for division and subdivision of themes.

2.18a   "A Compendium on the Art of Preaching, Preface and
         Selected Chapters." Translated by Joseph M. Miller. In
         Readings in Medieval Rhetoric. Edited by Joseph M. Miller,
         Michael H. Prosser, and Thomas W. Benson. Bloomington and
         London: Indiana University Press, 1973, pp. 229-39.
             Translates preface and chapters or excerpts from chap-
         ters 1, 38-39, and 41.

2.18b   Summa Magistri Alani Doctoris Universalis De arte
         praedicatoria. Vol. 210. Patrologiae Cursus Completus,
         Series Latina. Edited by Jacques P. Migne. Paris: Garnier
         Fratres, 1844-1864, cols. 109-98.

2.19 1199. ALEXANDER OF VILLEDIEU. Doctrinale.
         An enormously popular grammatical treatise, the first to
         usurp the popularity of Donatus's grammar. Composed in
         hexameter verse, the Doctrinale emphasizes the "logical"
         or syntactic aspects of grammar rather than the literary,
         and reflects the changes in the Latin language that had
         taken place since Priscian. Consists of three major sec-
         tions: on etymology; on syntax; and on quantity, accent,
         and the figures of speech. Its editor, Reichling, counted
         some 250 extant manuscripts of the treatise extending into
         the sixteenth century, and nearly 300 printed editions.
         Untranslated.

2.19a   Das Doctrinale des Alexander de Villa-Dei: kritisch-
         exegetische Ausgabe mit Einleitung, Verzeichniss der
         Handschriften und Drucke nebst Registern. Edited by
         Dietrich Reichling. Monumenta Germaniae Paedagogica,
         No. 12. Berlin: A. Hofmann & Comp., 1893, 520 pp.
             A comprehensive introduction of over 300 pages includes
         a bibliography, pp. xiii-xxiii.

2.20 c. 1200. GUIBERT de NOGENT. Liber quo ordine sermo fieri
         debeat.
         One of the first systematic manuals of instruction for
         preachers since Augustine's De doctrina (2.2), demonstrat-
         ing not what, but how to preach. This preface to Guibert's
         commentary on Genesis passes over matters of ethos, pathos,
         invention, and delivery, and serves primarily as a defense
         of his fourfold method of interpreting Scripture. Accord-
         ing to Joseph M. Miller, he was "a master of the Aristotelian
         and Ciceronian systems of rhetoric" (2.20a, p. 45).

2.20a   "Guibert DeNogent's Liber quo ordine sermo fieri debeat:
A Translation of the Earliest Modern Speech Textbook."
Translated by Joseph M. Miller. TS, 17, no. 4
(November 1969), 45-56.
       Reprinted with a revised introduction in Miller,
Prosser, and Benson, eds. (2.45, pp. 163-81) as "A Book
about the Way a Sermon Ought to be Given."

2.20b   "Guibert of Nogent: How to Make a Sermon." Translated
by George E. McCracken and Allen Cabaniss, in their Early
Medieval Theology. The Library of Christian Classics,
No. 9. Philadelphia: The Westminster Press, 1957,
pp. 287-99.
       A more literal but, as a result, less readable transla-
tion than 2.20a.

2.20c   "Quo ordine sermo fieri debeat." In Ad Commentarios in
Genesim. Vol. 156. Patrologiae Cursus Completus, Series
Latina. Edited by Jacques P. Migne. Paris: Garnier
Fratres, 1844-1864, cols. 21-32.

2.21 c. 1208-1213. GEOFFREY OF VINSAUF. Poetria nova.
       The best known of the medieval artes poetica, a text-
book used by Chaucer, Geoffrey of Vinsauf's Poetria nova
experienced extraordinary popularity in the Middle Ages.
Indebted especially to the Rhetorica ad Herennium and
Horace's Ars poetica, this verse treatise attends to
matters of disposition, amplification and abbreviation,
figures of speech, memory, and delivery.

2.21a   Poetria nova of Geoffrey of Vinsauf. Translated by
Margaret F. Nims. Toronto: Pontifical Institute of
Mediaeval Studies, 1967, 110 pp.
       Of the three available translations (see also 2.21b
and 2.44), by far the most accurate and readable.

2.21b   The Poetria nova and Its Sources in Early Rhetorical
Doctrine. Edited and translated by Ernest A. Gallo. De
Proprietatibus Litterarum, Series Maior, No. 10. The
Hague and Paris: Mouton, 1971, 241 pp.
       Latin text incorporating emendations suggested by W. B.
Sedgwick (in 2.41) and translation on facing pages
(pp. 14-129). For analysis and sources, see Gallo, 2.89.

2.21c   "Poetria nova," in Les Arts Poétiques du XIIe et du
XIIIe Siècle: Recherches et Documents sur la Technique
Littéraire du Moyen Age. Edited by Edmond Faral.
Bibliothèque de l'École des Hautes Etudes, Sciences
Historiques et Philologiques, No. 238. Paris: Librairie
Ancienne Honoré Champion, 1924. Reprinted: 1962,
pp. 197-262.

2.22 c. 1212. EBERHARD OF BÉTHUNE (Evrard of Béthune).
Graecismus.

Nearly as popular as the Doctrinale (2.19), Eberhard's 4,440-line verse commentary on Donatus's Ars maior begins with a section on schemes and tropes, and then covers matters of etymology, orthography, nouns, pronouns, and Greek derivatives--the latter "a subject," writes Paul Abelson, "quite unknown to the author" (2.46, p. 45). Remains untranslated.

2.22a   Eberhardi Bethuniensis Graecismus ad fidem librorum manu scriptorum recensuit. Edited by Ioh. Wrobel. Corpus Grammaticorum Medii Aevi, No. 1. Wratislava: G. Köbneri, 1887, 339 pp.

2.23   c. 1215. GEOFFREY OF VINSAUF. Documentum de modo et arte dictandi et versificandi.
     Geoffrey covers most of the same ground in his prose Documentum that he had discussed in his Poetria nova, but here the subject is the writing of prose. Treats beginnings, amplification and abbreviation, and methods of ornamentation. Edmond Faral (2.23b) has edited the shorter version of the Documentum; the longer and later version-- extant in at least five manuscripts--remains unedited (for which see Lawler, 2.24a, pp. 327-32).

2.23a   Documentum de modo et arte dictandi et versificandi (Instruction in the Method and Art of Speaking and Versifying). Translated by Roger P. Parr. Mediaeval Philosophical Texts in Translation, No. 17. Milwaukee: Marquette University Press, 1968, 105 pp.
     Translates the short version of Documentum. Introduction reviews the rhetorical tradition in Europe, England, and the vernacular (pp. 3-37).

2.23b   "Documentum de modo et arte dictandi et versificandi," in Les Arts Poétiques du XIIe et du XIIIe Siècle: Recherches et Documents sur la Technique Littéraire du Moyen Age. Edited by Edmond Faral. Bibliothèque de l'Ecole des Hautes Etudes, Sciences Historiques et Philologiques, No. 238. Paris: Librairie Ancienne Honoré Champion, 1924. Reprinted: 1962, pp. 265-320.

2.24   c. 1220. JOHN OF GARLAND (Johannes Anglicus). Parisiana poetria.
     Markedly influenced by the dictaminal tradition, John of Garland attempts to find a common rationale for prose and metrical composition. As a result the treatise is an uneasy amalgam--a cross between an ars poetica and an ars dictaminis. The Parisiana poetria begins with an advertisement of its contents: invention, selection of material, arrangement, parts of the letter, rhetorical ornament (including considerable attention to amplification), examples of letters, and metrical and rhythmical composition.

Traditionally John of Garland's treatise has been called
De arte prosayca, metrica, et rithmica, but Lawler has
restored its original title to the text.

2.24a   The Parisiana Poetria of John of Garland; Edited with
Introduction, Translation, and Notes. Edited and translated by Traugott Lawler. Yale Studies in English, No. 182.
New Haven and London: Yale University Press, 1974, 377 pp.
    Appendixes include evidence of John of Garland's debt
to Geoffrey's prose Documentum (2.23). Bibliography,
pp. 339-43.

2.25 c. 1228-29. GUIDO FABA. Summa dictaminis.
    One of nine dictaminal treatises written by a leading
master at the University of Bologna, largely theoretical
in nature and traditional in content. Untranslated.

2.25a   "Summa dictaminis." Edited by Augustus Gaudenzi.
Il Propugnatore, NS 3 (1890), Fasc. 15, 287-338; Fasc. 18,
345-93.

2.26 1235. BONCOMPAGNO. Rhetorica novissima.
    A sprawling dictaminal treatise by one of the most noto-
rious members of the Bolognese faculty. One of eleven
treatises on letter writing composed by Boncompagno, the
Rhetorica novissima--his culmination of rhetorical lore--
ranges through the sources of law, the parts and nature of
rhetoric, various sorts of discourses, the use of invective
and flattery, and so on. "At once over-divided and ill-
digested," writes Charles S. Baldwin (2.52, p. 212).
Untranslated.

2.26a   Boncompagni Rhetorica novissima. Edited by Augustus
Gaudenzi. In his Bibliotheca Iuridica Medii Aevi. 3 vols.
Scripta Anecdota Glossatorum. Bononiae: In Aedibus Petri
Virano olim Fratrum Treves, 1892-1913. Reprinted: Turin:
Bottega d'Erasmo, 1962, 2, pp. 251-97.
    Imprint varies. Above is the imprint for vol. 2, pub-
lished first in 1892.

2.27 c. 1250. EBERHARD THE GERMAN (Evrardus Allemanus).
Laborintus.
    Very nearly a satire, Eberhard's Laborintus opens with
a complaint about the bitter lot of the school teacher,
briefly reviews the seven liberal arts, devotes nearly a
third of its attention to the figures of speech, provides
a list of recommended texts for school reading (including
2.17, 2.19, 2.21, and 2.22), and concludes with excursions
into the ars metrica and ars rithmica. An intriguing revelation, writes James J. Murphy, of "the ultimate decay of
the preceptive impulse in medieval grammar" (2.139, p. 182).

*2.27a   "The Laborintus of Eberhard rendered into English with
            Introduction and Notes." Translated by Evelyn Carlson.
            Master's thesis, Cornell University, 1930.
               Cited in Murphy, 2.142, No. G24.

2.27b   "Laborintus," in Les Arts Poétiques du XIIe et du XIIIe
            Siècle: Recherches et Documents sur la Technique Littéraire
            du Moyen Age. Edited by Edmond Faral. Bibliothèque de
            l'Ecole des Hautes Etudes, Sciences Historiques et
            Philologiques, No. 238. Paris: Librairie Ancienne Honoré
            Champion, 1924. Reprinted: 1962, pp. 337-77.

2.28   c. 1250. HUMBERT OF ROMANS. De eruditione praedicatorum.
               An unusual contribution to the ars praedicandi, Humbert's
            De eruditione is more of a practical psychology for preach-
            ers than a theoretical manual of preaching. This well-
            known Dominican tract deals with such themes as the
            qualities of the office of preaching, how the preacher
            should enter the task of preaching, what he should know,
            his manner of delivery and use of language, things to avoid
            while traveling, and so on.

*2.28a   Treatise on Preaching by Humbert of Romans. Translated
            by Dominican Students, Province of St. Joseph. Edited by
            Walter M. Conlon. Westminster, Md.: Newman Press, 1951.
            Reprinted: London: Blackfriars Publications, 1955, 173 pp.
               Book 2, viii-ix, reprinted in Miller, Prosser, and
            Benson, eds., 2.45, pp. 245-50, as "Treatise on Preaching,
            II.8-9." James J. Murphy cautions that this English trans-
            lation is taken from a French translation of the Latin text
            (2.139, p. 341, footnote 104). Cited in Miller, Prosser,
            and Benson, eds., 2.45, p. 245, footnote 1; and in Murphy,
            2.142, No. P51.

*2.28b   De instructione praedicatorum. Edited by Margarinus de
            La Bigne. In his Maxima Bibliotheca Veterum Patrum et
            Antiquorum Scriptorum Ecclesiasticorum. 28 vols. Lyons:
            Genoa, 1677, 25, 426-567.
               Cited in Caplan, 2.65, No. 224.

2.29 1259. HENRI OF ANDELI. Bataille des Sept Arts.
               Although not a rhetorical treatise, provides a vivid
            picture of academic life in mid-thirteenth-century Europe.
            This mock-heroic account of the battle of Parisian logic
            against grammar and literature of Orleans is studded with
            references both to the classics--Augustine, Capella,
            Priscian--and to thirteenth-century grammarians and logi-
            cians. Much to Henri's dismay, grammar is soundly trounced;
            "one should destroy the glib student," he protests, "who
            cannot construe his lesson" (2.29a, lines 458-59).

2.29a   The Battle of the Seven Arts: A French Poem by Henri
            d'Andeli, Trouvère of the Thirteenth Century. Edited and

translated by Louis J. Paetow. Memoirs of the University
of California, No. 4, 1. Berkeley: University of California Press, 1914. Reprinted as Part 1 of Paetow's Two
Medieval Satires on the University of Paris. Berkeley:
University of California Press, 1927.

2.30 <u>c</u>. 1260. BRUNETTO LATINI. Li livres dou Tresor.
An encyclopedic prose compendium, the first written in
the vernacular (Old French). Li livres divides knowledge
into three books: theoretical, practical, and logical.
Book 3, however, markedly Ciceronian in spirit and rhetorical in substance, emphasizes oral discourse and the ars
dictaminis, virtually ignoring logical concerns. Translated from the French into Italian by Bono Giambono as Il
Tesoro by 1266.

2.30a   "Book Three of Brunetto Latini's Tresor: An English
Translation and Assessment of its Contribution to Rhetorical
Theory." Translated by James R. East. Ph.D. dissertation,
Stanford University, 1960, 193 pp.
Book 3, pp. lx–lxv, reprinted in Miller, Prosser, and
Benson, eds., 2.45, pp. 253–64, as "Li Livres dou Tresor,
III.60–65."
2.30b   Li livres dou Tresor de Brunetto Latini. Edited by
Francis J. Carmody. University of California Publications
in Modern Philology, No. 22. Berkeley and Los Angeles:
University of California Press, 1948, 515 pp.
Bibliography, pp. lvii–lxii.

2.31 <u>c</u>. 1290. GILES OF ROME (Aegidius Romanus). De differentia
rhetoricae, ethicae, et politicae.
A disciple of Thomas Aquinas, Giles of Rome's scholastic
tract distinguishes rhetoric from the artes morales--those
sciences of human behavior such as ethics and politics--and
allies it with the artes sermocinales, the intellectual
activities. Quoting the opening line of William of
Moerbeke's translation of Aristotle's Rhetoric, Giles
insists that rhetoric is, in fact, "'the handmaiden of
Dialectic'" (2.31a, p. 266).

2.31a   "On the Difference between Rhetoric, Ethics, and Politics, Part 1." Translated by Joseph M. Miller. In Readings in Medieval Rhetoric. Edited by Joseph M. Miller,
Michael H. Prosser, and Thomas W. Benson. Bloomington and
London: Indiana University Press, 1973, pp. 266–68.
2.31b   "The 'De differentia rhetoricae, ethicae et politicae'
of Aegidius Romanus." Edited by Gerardo Bruni. The New
Scholasticism, 6 (1932), 1–18.

2.32 <u>c</u>. 1304. DANTE ALIGHIERI. <u>De vulgari eloquentia</u>.
For any student tracing the development of linguistic
and rhetorical concerns in the vernacular, Dante's apology
for the Italian language is a seminal chapter. Here he
traces the origins of language and demonstrates that
Italian, too, is capable of the low, middle, and grand
styles.

2.32a   <u>De vulgari eloquentia</u>. Translated by Alan G. F. Howell.
In <u>Howell and Philip H. Wicksteed's</u> <u>A Translation of the</u>
<u>Latin Works of Dante Alighieri</u>. London: J. M. Dent and
Co., 1904. Reprint of text, New York: Greenwood Press,
Publishers, 1969, pp. 3-115. Reprint of Howell's transla-
tion of <u>De vulgari</u> in <u>Classical and Medieval Literary Criti-</u>
<u>cism: Translations and Interpretations</u>. Edited by Alex
Preminger, O. B. Hardison, Jr., and Kevin Kerrane. New
York: Frederick Ungar Publishing Co., 1974, pp. 412-46.
Chapter 6 reprinted in Miller, Prosser, and Benson, eds.,
2.45, pp. 270-71.
2.32b   <u>De vulgari eloquentia</u>. Edited by Pier V. Mengaldo.
Vulgares Eloquentes, No. 3. Padua: Antenore, 1968, 184 pp.
Bibliography, pp. cxxii-xxv. Scaglione cites alternate
editions in 2.178, p. 28, footnote 55.

2.33 1322. ROBERT OF BASEVORN. <u>Forma praedicandi</u>.
Following a general discussion of the nature of preaching and a review of the preaching of Christ, St. Paul,
St. Gregory, and St. Bernard, Robert of Basevorn describes
twenty-two ways of ornamenting a sermon: invention, introduction, division, amplification, digression, modulation of
voice, gesture, humor, and so on. James J. Murphy partly
translates, partly summarizes the treatise in 2.139,
pp. 344-55.

2.33a   <u>The Form of Preaching</u> (Forma praedicandi). Translated
by Leopold Krul. In <u>Three Medieval Rhetorical Arts</u>.
Edited by James J. Murphy. Los Angeles and London:
University of California Press, 1971, pp. 114-215.
Not a good translation (for which, <u>see</u> Traugott Lawler's
review in <u>Speculum</u>, 48 [1973], 388-94).
2.33b   <u>Forma praedicandi</u>. In <u>Artes Praedicandi: Contribution</u>
<u>a l'Histoire de la Rhétorique au Moyen Age</u>. Edited by
Thomas M. Charland. Publications de l'Institut d'Etudes
Médiévales d'Ottawa, No. 7. Paris: Libr. Philosophique
J. Vrin; Ottawa: Inst. d'Etudes Médiévales, 1936,
pp. 233-323.

2.34 <u>c</u>. 1349. THOMAS WALEYS. <u>De modo componendi sermones cum</u>
<u>documentis</u>.
A "relentlessly systematic. . . . summary of the modern
mode" of preaching, writes James J. Murphy (2.139, p. 334),

with nine chapters on the so-called modern methods of preaching. Thomas Waleys's key concerns are discovery of the theme, introduction, division, and amplification.

*2.34a   "Thomas Waleys' De modo componendi sermones Rendered into English." Translated by Dorothy E. Grosser. Master's thesis, Cornell University, 1949.
          Cited in Murphy, 2.142, No. P58.

2.34b   De modo componendi sermones cum documentis. In Artes Praedicandi: Contribution a l'Histoire de la Rhétorique au Moyen Age. Edited by Thomas M. Charland. Publications de l'Institut d'Etudes Médiévales d'Ottawa, No. 7. Paris: Libr. Philosophique J. Vrin; Ottawa: Inst. d'Etudes Médiévales, 1936, pp. 327-403.

2.35 c. 1475. "HENRY OF HESSE." Tractatulus de arte praedicandi. There is a mixture of rhetorical and dialectical concerns in this late fifteenth-century Germanic ars praedicandi. "Henry of Hesse's" description of the four-fold interpretation of Scripture is followed by his analysis of four methods of preaching: the oldest (antiquissimus), the old (antiquus), the modern (modernus [theme, protheme, division, and subdivision]), and a combination of all three (subalternus).

2.35a   "'Henry of Hesse' On the Art of Preaching." Edited and translated by Harry Caplan. PMLA, 48 (1933), 340-61. Reprinted in Caplan, 2.43, pp. 135-59.

2.36 c. 1490. PSEUDO-AQUINAS. De arte praedicandi. Like "Henry of Hesse's," this late fifteenth-century treatise on preaching marks the culmination of the university sermon. A description of the parts of the sermon (theme, protheme, division, and subdivision) is followed by an extensive demonstration of ways to amplify subject matter: by use of authority, etymology, analogies, opposites, comparisons, etc. A final analogy of the author's model sermon with the roots, trunk and branches of a tree concludes the treatise. No modern edition of the treatise exists.

2.36a   "A Late Medieval Tractate on Preaching." Translated by Harry Caplan. In Studies in Rhetoric and Public Speaking in Honor of James Albert Winans by Pupils and Colleagues. Edited by Alexander M. Drummond. New York: The Century Co., 1925, pp. 61-90. Reprinted: New York: Russell & Russell, Inc., 1962. Reprint of article in Caplan, 2.43, pp. 40-78.

Primary Works

In 1925 Caplan was unable to discover the illustration of the so-called tree of preaching to which pseudo-Aquinas refers; later he found it in a Munich manuscript and included it in 2.43, p. 76. For the tree of preaching, <u>see also</u> Dieter, 2.77.

Collections of Primary Works

2.37 HALM, CAROLUS F., ed. <u>Rhetores Latini Minores: Ex Codicibus</u>
<u>Maximam Partem Primum Adhibitis</u>. Leipzig: B. G. Teubneri,
1863. Reprinted: Frankfurt: Minerva, 1964; Dubuque,
Iowa: Wm. C. Brown Reprint Library, n.d., 674 pp.
    An indispensable collection of early medieval rhetorical
treatises. Aside from editions of chapters from or the
whole of Nos. 2.3, 2.4, and 2.7-2.10, Halm's edition
includes:
    Rutilius Lupus. <u>Schemata lexeos</u>. Pp. 3-21.
    Aquila Romanus. <u>De figuris sententiarum et elocutionis</u>
<u>liber</u>. Pp. 22-37.
    Rufinus. <u>De figuris sententiarum et elocutionis liber</u>.
Pp. 38-47.
    Fortunatianus. <u>Artis rhetoricae libri III</u>. Pp. 81-134.
    Pseudo-Augustine. <u>De rhetorica</u>. Pp. 137-51.
    Sulpicius Victor. <u>Institutiones oratoriae</u>. Pp. 313-52.
    Julius Victor. <u>Ars rhetorica</u>. Pp. 373-448.

2.38 ROCKINGER, LUDWIG, ed. <u>Briefsteller und Formelbücher des</u>
<u>eilften bis vierzehnten Jahrhunderts</u>. 2 vols. Quellen
und Erörterungen zur bayerischen und deutschen Geschichte,
No. 9, 1-2. Munich: Georg Franz, 1863-64. Reprinted with
continuous pagination, Burt Franklin Research & Source Works
Series, No. 10. New York: Burt Franklin, 1961, 1216 pp.
    A comprehensive collection of dictaminal treatises,
including Nos. 2.13, 2.15 (incorrectly attributed to
Alberic of Monte Cassino), and a summary with excerpts of
2.24. Rockinger's <u>Briefsteller</u> includes complete editions
of:
    Boncompagno. <u>Cedrus</u>. Pp. 121-27.
    Guido Faba. <u>Doctrina ad inueniendas incipiendas et</u>
<u>formandas materias et ad ea que circa huiusmodi requiruntur</u>.
Pp. 185-96.
    Ludolf of Hildesheim. <u>Summa dictaminum</u>. Pp. 359-400.
    Konrad of Mure. <u>Summa de arte prosandi</u>. Pp. 417-82.
    Bernold of Kaisersheim. <u>Summula dictaminis</u>.
Pp. 845-924.

Lawrence of Aquilegia. <u>Practica sive usus dictaminis</u>.
Pp. 956-66.

2.39 KEIL, HEINRICH, ed. <u>Grammatici Latini</u>. 7 vols. Leipzig:
B. G. Teubner, 1857-80. Reprinted: Hildesheim: G. Olms,
1961.
This massive collection of early medieval grammatical
treatises includes an edition of Priscian's <u>Institutio
grammatica</u>; yet another edition of his <u>De praeexercitamentis</u>;
Donatus's <u>Ars minor</u> (vol. 4, 355-66) and <u>Ars maior</u> (vol. 4,
367-402); minor grammatical treatises of Phocas, Eutyches,
Augustine, Asper, and others; and a number of treatises on
metrics (vol. 6) and orthography (vol. 7).

2.40 MIGNE, JACQUES P., ed. <u>Patrologiae Cursus Completus, Series
Latina</u>. 221 vols. Paris: Garnier Fratres, 1844-1864.
An astounding collection of medieval Latin treatises,
especially early patristic and ecclesiastical: homiliaries,
commentaries, works on the liberal arts, letters, ecclesiastical documents, and so on. Whenever possible, Migne
simply reprinted earlier editions; as a result, texts
printed here should be avoided or, at least, used with
caution. Includes an edition of many of Boethius's
treatises on the <u>Organon</u> (vol. 64); Cassiodorus, <u>In
psalterium expositio</u> (vol. 70, cols. 25-1056); and Alcuin,
<u>Ars grammatica</u> (vol. 101, cols. 849-902). Imprint varies.

2.41 FARAL, EDMOND, ed. <u>Les Arts Poétiques du XIIe et du XIIIe
Siècle: Recherches et Documents sur la Technique
Littéraire du Moyen Age</u>. Bibliothèque de l'Ecole des
Hautes Etudes, Sciences Historiques et Philologiques,
No. 238. Paris: Librairie Ancienne Honoré Champion,
1924. Reprinted: 1962, 400 pp.
Long a standard introduction to the <u>ars poetica</u>, Faral's
text is divided into three parts. Part 1 includes bio-
graphical sketches of Matthew of Vendôme, Geoffrey of
Vinsauf, Gervase of Melkley, and Eberhard the German.
Part 2 discusses matters of disposition, amplification,
ornamentation, and sources. Part 3 includes editions
(aside from Nos. 2.17, 2.21, 2.23, 2.27) of Ekkehard IV,
<u>De lege dictamen ornandi</u> (pp. 104-5); Geoffrey of Vinsauf,
<u>Summa de coloribus rhetoricis</u> (pp. 321-27); and summaries
of 2.24 and of Gervase of Melkley's <u>Ars versificaria</u>.
Walter B. Sedgwick has provided "Notes and Emendations on
Faral's <u>Les Arts Poétiques du XIIe et du XIIIe Siècle</u>" in
<u>Speculum</u>, 2 (1927), 331-43.

2.42 CHARLAND, THOMAS M., ed. <u>Artes Praedicandi: Contribution à
l'Histoire de la Rhétorique au Moyen Age</u>. Publications de
l'Institut d'Etudes Médiévales d'Ottawa, No. 7. Paris:
Libr. Philosophique J. Vrin; Ottawa: Inst. d'Etudes
Médiévales, 1936, 421 pp.

An indispensable introduction to the ars praedicandi.
Part 1 (pp. 17-106) provides details on authors and their
manuscripts, including: Pseudo-Bonaventure, William of
Auvergne, "Henry of Hesse" (Henry of Langenstein), Humbert
of Romans, Jacobus of Fusignano, Ranulph Higden, Richard of
Thetford, Robert of Basevorn, Simon Alcock, Pseudo-Aquinas,
and Thomas Waleys. Part 2 (pp. 109-26) discusses the
treatment of theme, protheme, division, development, and
ornamentation in the treatises. Part 3 (pp. 229-403) provides editions of the manuals of Robert of Basevorn (2.33)
and Thomas Waleys (2.34).

2.43 CAPLAN, HARRY. Of Eloquence: Studies in Ancient and Mediaeval
Rhetoric. Edited by Anne King and Helen North. Ithaca and
London: Cornell University Press, 1970, 302 pp.
In addition to reprints of "Henry of Hesse" and Pseudo-
Aquinas's treatises on preaching (2.35, 2.36), includes
reprints of further articles on the ars praedicandi (2.66-
2.68) and another on the Rhetorica ad Herennium (2.64).

2.44 MURPHY, JAMES J., ed. Three Medieval Rhetorical Arts.
Berkeley, Los Angeles, and London: University of California Press, 1971, 258 pp.
Three translations of medieval rhetorical documents:
the dictaminal treatise of Anonymous of Bologna (2.15),
the manual on preaching by Robert of Basevorn (2.33), and
yet another translation of Geoffrey of Vinsauf's Poetria
nova (2.21), this one by Jane Baltzell Kopp. Bibliography,
pp. 233-35.

2.45 MILLER, JOSEPH M., MICHAEL H. PROSSER, and THOMAS W. BENSON,
eds. Readings in Medieval Rhetoric. Bloomington and
London: Indiana University Press, 1973, 316 pp.
In addition to translations of 2.3, 2.4, 2.8, 2.9, 2.11,
2.12, 2.18, 2.20, 2.28, 2.30, 2.31, 2.32 (either the whole
or part), Miller, Prosser and Benson provide translations
that include:
Pseudo-Augustine. De rhetorica. Pp. 7-24.
Fortunatianus. Artis rhetoricae libri III (excerpt
from Book 1). Pp. 25-32.
Rufinus. Comentarii de metris comicorum et de numeris
oratorum (excerpt). Pp. 37-51.
Boethius. Speculatione de rhetorica cognatione.
Pp. 70-76.
Alain of Lille. Anticlaudianus (excerpts). Pp. 223-27.
Thomas of Todi. Ars sermocinandi ac etiam faciendi
collationes (excerpts). Pp. 273-79.
Poggio Bracciolini. Two letters on the discovery of
Quintilian's Institutio oratoria in 1416. Pp. 281-85.

Brief commentaries accompany each of twenty-seven translations; in the case of works with readily available translations, commentary alone is provided. Bibliography, pp. 287-90.

Secondary Works

2.46 ABELSON, PAUL. <u>The Seven Liberal Arts: A Study in Mediaeval Culture</u>. Columbia University Teachers' College Contributions to Education, No. 11. New York: Teachers' College, Columbia University, 1906. Reprinted: New York: AMS Press, 1972, 158 pp.

An early but still useful introduction to the seven liberal arts. Abelson devotes three chapters to the scope, purposes, and texts of the medieval grammatical tradition (pp. 11-51), another chapter to early rhetorical and dictaminal treatises (pp. 52-71), and further chapters to logic, arithmetic, geometry, astronomy, and music. Annotated bibliography, pp. 137-50.

2.47 ALLEN, JUDSON B. "Hermann the German's Averroistic Aristotle and Medieval Poetic Theory." <u>Mosaic</u>, 9 (1976), 67-81.

On Averroes' adaptation of Aristotle's <u>Poetica</u> and Hermann the German's Latin translation of Averroes. Averroes' <u>Commentarium</u> has too long been misunderstood, Allen writes. It is a distinctly and characteristically medieval document: "To classify poetic as a branch of logic is to pay it the high compliment of being one of the arts of valid language; to classify poems under ethics is to recognize that by medieval standards of decorum, ethical behavior partook in fact of the style and intentionality which modern experience has learned to expect only of literature, but never of life" (p. 81).

2.48 ARBUSOW, LEONID H. N. <u>Colores rhetorici: Eine Auswahl rhetorischer Figuren und Gemeinplätze als Hilfsmittel für akademische Übungen an mittelalterlichen Texten</u>. Göttingen: Vandenhoeck & Ruprecht, 1948. Second edition edited by Helmut Peters, 1963, 157 pp. Reprinted: Geneva: Slatkine Reprints, 1974.

More a bibliographical guide than a discussion. Analyzes medieval methods of amplification and abbreviation (pp. 21-33), provides detailed illustrations of the figures and tropes from dozens of medieval treatises (pp. 35-91), and

concludes with a guide to the topics or commonplaces--
those used in exordiums, in manuals of devotion, in epi-
logues, for the locus amoenus, of the puer senex, and so
forth. Accompanied by indexes to words, names, and treatises; and by a bibliography, pp. 124-28.

2.49 ATKINS, JOHN W. H. English Literary Criticism: The Medieval
      Phase. New York: The Macmillan Co.; Cambridge, England:
      The University Press, 1943. Reprinted: London: Methuen;
      New York: Peter Smith, 1952, 220 pp.
         Brief, often uneven, history of the contributions of
      medieval England to literary theory, with especial atten-
      tion to Bede's De schematibus and Alcuin's grammatical and
      rhetorical treatises (pp. 42-58), John of Salisbury's
      Metalogicon (pp. 65-90), and to the ars poetica of Geoffrey
      of Vinsauf, John of Garland, and Matthew of Vendôme
      (pp. 94-118). Further chapters consider the literary
      theory of John of Garland, Robert Grosseteste, Roger Bacon,
      and Richard of Bury; and discuss the literary practice of
      Chaucer and others.

2.50 AUBREY, ANNIE. "An Analysis of the Medieval Artes poetriae
      with a Discussion of Amplification of Character in Chaucer's
      Troilus." Ph.D. dissertation, University of Cincinnati,
      1970, 196 pp.
         Analyzes the assumptions underlying four of the most
      important of the arts of poetry: Matthew of Vendôme's Ars
      versificatoria, Geoffrey of Vinsauf's Poetria nova and
      Documentum, and John of Garland's Parisiana poetria. The
      second part draws lines of correspondence between these
      artes and methods of amplification in Chaucer's Troilus
      and Criseyde. The dissertation is forthcoming in revised
      form as The Organization and Assumptions of the Medieval
      Artes poetriae, to be published by Mouton.

2.51 AUERBACH, ERICH. Literary Language & Its Public in Late Latin
      Antiquity and in the Middle Ages. Translated by Ralph
      Manheim. Bollingen Series, No. 74. New York: Pantheon
      Books; Princeton, N.J.: Princeton University Press, 1965,
      405 pp.
         Essays on the sermo humilis in Augustine, Caesarius,
      Pope Gregory, and Gregory of Tours; on the emergence of
      ornamental, artificial Latin prose in the ninth and tenth
      centuries; and on the rise of the vernacular in the twelfth
      and thirteenth centuries, especially in Dante. Auerbach's
      subject is style and its public, and his concerns brush up
      against rhetorical questions throughout. Bibliography,
      pp. 343-69. Originally published as Literatursprache und
      Publikum in der lateinischen Spätantike und im Mittelalter
      in 1958.

2.52   BALDWIN, CHARLES S.   Medieval Rhetoric and Poetic (to 1400)
       Interpreted from Representative Works.   New York: The
       Macmillan Company, 1928.   Reprinted: Gloucester, Mass.:
       Peter Smith, 1959; St. Clair Shores, Mich.:   Scholarly
       Press, Inc., 1976, 338 pp.
           Long a standard introduction to the history of medieval
       rhetoric, with chapters on the Second Sophistic; Augustine's
       De doctrina 4; rhetoric and poetics between the fifth and
       seventh centuries; grammar, rhetoric, and dialectic during
       the Carolingian period; rhetoric and logic during the
       twelfth and thirteenth centuries; and on the ars poetica,
       ars dictaminis, and ars praedicandi.   Pages 51-73 on
       Augustine reprinted in Joseph Schwartz and John A. Rycenga,
       eds.   The Province of Rhetoric.   New York: The Ronald
       Press Company, 1965, pp. 158-72.

2.53   BANKER, JAMES R.   "The Ars dictaminis and Rhetorical Textbooks
       at the Bolognese University in the Fourteenth Century."
       M&H, NS 5 (1974), 153-68.
           Contends that the "practice of each master writing his
       own dictamen treatise . . . was abandoned after 1325 in
       Bologna when one treatise, Brevis introductio ad dictamen,
       became the standard text and was taught in conjunction with
       lectures upon the pseudo-Ciceronian Rhetorica ad Herennium
       for the remainder of the fourteenth century.   The lectures
       on the two texts were initiated by Giovanni di Bonandrea,
       the author of the dictamen text . . . and were perpetuated
       by Bolognese masters until the end of that century" (p. 154).
       Includes summary and analysis of the treatise.

2.54   BEESON, CHARLES H.   "The Ars grammatica of Julian of Toledo."
       In Miscellanea Francesco Ehrle: Scritti di Storia e
       Paleografia Pubblicati . . . in Occasione dell' Ottantesimo
       Natalizio dell' e.mo Cardinale Francesco Ehrle.   5 vols.
       Studi e Testi, No. 37.   Rome: Biblioteca Apostolica
       Vaticana, 1924, I, 50-70.
           Considers the influence of Donatus and Isidore on the
       seventh-century Ars grammatica, poetica, et rhetorica of
       Julian of Toledo, its use in the writings of Aldhelm and
       Bede, and the relationships of eighth- and ninth-century
       manuscripts.

2.55   BOGGESS, WILLIAM F.   "Hermannus Alemannus's Rhetorical Trans-
       lations."   Viator, 2 (1971), 227-50.
           On Hermann the German's (fl. 1240-56) adaptation of
       Al-Fārābī's commentary on Aristotle's Rhetorica and,
       secondly, his translation of the Rhetorica (with explana-
       tory sections from Averroes and Avicenna).   Includes a sur-
       vey of the scholarship, thorough descriptions of the texts,
       and the Latin prologues to both treatises.

2.56 BOSKOFF, PRISCILLA S. "Quintilian in the Late Middle Ages."
      Speculum, 27 (1952), 71-78.
          Texts and florilegia of Quintilian's Institutio oratoria
      in the hands of Lupus of Ferrières in the ninth century,
      John of Salisbury in the twelfth, and Vincent of Beauvais
      in the thirteenth.

2.57 BREHAUT, ERNEST. An Encyclopedist of the Dark Ages: Isidore
      of Seville. Columbia University Studies in History, Eco-
      nomics, and Public Law, No. 48. New York: Columbia Uni-
      versity; London: P. S. King & Son, 1912. Reprinted:
      Burt Franklin Research & Source Works Series, No. 107,
      New York: B. Franklin, 1964, 274 pp.
          A good introduction to Isidore and his age, with chap-
      ters on Isidore's life and writings, his knowledge of the
      classics, his view of the universe and of secular learning,
      and of his role in education. The emphasis is on Isidore's
      Etymologia: Part 2 provides introduction and analysis and
      translated extracts from each book, including those on
      grammar, rhetoric, and logic (pp. 89-122). Still, no
      substitute for Jacques Fontaine (2.85). Bibliography,
      pp. 270-74.

2.58 BRIDE, MARY. "John of Salisbury's Theory of Rhetoric." SMC,
      2 (1966), 56-62.
          In response to those who assume that John of Salisbury's
      Metalogicon ignores the ars rhetorica, Bride argues that he
      "did have a theory of rhetoric and that this theory con-
      forms in all essential elements to the classical model set
      forth by Aristotle and transmitted by Cicero and
      Quintilian" (p. 62).

2.59 BULLOUGH, DONALD A. "The Educational Tradition in England
      from Alfred to Aelfric: Teaching Utriusque Linguae." La
      Scuola nell' occidente latino dell' alto medioevo:
      Settimane di studio del Centro italiano di studi sull'
      alto medioevo, 19 (1972), 453-94.
          King's Alfred's reestablishment of Latin grammatical
      studies in late ninth-century England, Byrhtferth's Manual,
      Aelfric's adaptation of Priscian's Institutio in his late
      tenth-century Grammatica, and intervening figures. Bullough
      stresses the continued and pragmatic concerns of the Eng-
      lish teacher introducing a foreign tongue to the student.
      Includes a good survey of grammarians known to the tenth-
      century English.

2.60 BURSILL-HALL, G. L. Speculative Grammars of the Middle Ages:
      The Doctrine of Partes orationis of the Modistae.
      Approaches to Semiotics, No. 11. The Hague and Paris:
      Mouton, 1971, 424 pp.

In the thirteenth and early fourteenth centuries a
second generation of grammarians--the so-called modistae--
taught a universal grammar dependent on the structure of
reality rather than of any one language. In their attempt
to conjoin Aristotelian logic and Priscian's grammar,
philosopher-grammarians (particularly Martin of Dacia, De
modis significandi; Siger of Courtrai, Summa modorum
significandi; and Thomas of Erfurt, De modis significandi)
argued that language and its grammar reflect the nature of
reality. Explores and analyzes their elaborate, systematic
linguistic terminology. Bibliography, pp. 400-406.

2.61 CALLUS, DANIEL A. "Introduction of Aristotelian Learning to
      Oxford." PBA, 29 (1943), 229-81.
          With an extended list of teachers of and commentaries on
      the works of Aristotle, Callus seeks to dispel the notion
      that thirteenth-century Oxford played an insignificant role
      in the development of Aristotelian learning. Aristotle was
      firmly entrenched at Oxford by 1209, Callus concludes; by
      the middle of the century Alexander Nequam, John Blund,
      Gundissalinus, Robert Grosseteste, Richard Fishacre, and
      others had surveyed much of the Aristotelian corpus.

2.62 CAMPBELL, A. P. "The Perfection of Ars dictaminis in Guido
      Faba." RUO, 39 (1969), 315-21.
          Dictaminal theory, model letters, wit, and grace in
      Guido Faba's Rota nova (c. 1227).

2.63 CAMPBELL, JACKSON J. "Adaptation of Classical Rhetoric in
      Old English Literature," in Medieval Eloquence: Studies in
      the Theory and Practice of Medieval Rhetoric. Edited by
      James J. Murphy. Berkeley, Los Angeles, and London:
      University of California Press, 1978, pp. 173-97.
          Examines the evidence for the influence of classical
      and early medieval grammar and rhetoric on Old English
      literature: in the work of Aldhelm, Bede, and Alcuin;
      in the homilies of Aelfric and Wulfstan; and in Old Eng-
      lish poetry. Serves as a good introduction to the very
      considerable literature on this subject.

2.64 CAPLAN, HARRY. "A Mediaeval Commentary on the Rhetorica ad
      Herennium," in his Of Eloquence: Studies in Ancient and
      Mediaeval Rhetoric. Edited by Anne King and Helen North.
      Ithaca and London: Cornell University Press, 1970,
      pp. 247-70.
          The twelfth-century commentary of one "Alanus" on the
      Rhetorica ad Herennium. Caplan ranges through nine extant
      manuscripts, noting Alanus's respect for dialectic, his
      frequent references to Cicero's De inventione, his con-
      fident criticism of the Ciceronian texts, his frequent
      etymologizing, references to Peter Helias and Thierry of

Chartres, etc. Reprint of a paper presented at the Fourth
International Congress of Classical Studies in Philadelphia,
1964.

2.65 CAPLAN, HARRY. Mediaeval Artes praedicandi: A Hand-List.
Cornell Studies in Classical Philology, No. 24. Ithaca,
N.Y.: Cornell University Press; London: Oxford University
Press, 1934, 52 pp.
A list of 229 Artes praedicandi, of which Nos. 215-29
were published in 1934. Supplemented in 1936 by Caplan's
Mediaeval Artes praedicandi: A Supplementary Handlist.
Cornell Studies in Classical Philology, No. 25. Ithaca,
N.Y.: Cornell University Press; London: Oxford University
Press, 36 pp.

2.66 CAPLAN, HARRY. "Classical Rhetoric and the Mediaeval Theory
of Preaching." CP, 28 (1933), 73-96. Revised in Historical
Studies of Rhetoric and Rhetoricians, edited by Raymond F.
Howes. Ithaca, N.Y.: Cornell University Press, 1961,
pp. 71-89, 387-91 (notes). Reprinted in Caplan, 2.43,
pp. 105-34.
Despite the medieval distrust of rhetoric as an art of
adornment, the artes praedicandi relied on the classical
and medieval treatises of Aristotle, Cicero, Quintilian,
and Boethius--especially for material on invention. Attend-
ing especially to the manuals of "Henry of Hesse" (2.35),
Pseudo-Aquinas (2.36), St. Bonaventure, and Jacques de
Vitry, Caplan describes the thematic sermon and enumerates
some twenty traditional methods of amplifying a sermon's
theme.

2.67 CAPLAN, HARRY. "The Four Senses of Scriptural Interpretation
and the Mediaeval Theory of Preaching." Speculum, 4 (1929),
282-90. Reprinted in Caplan, 2.43, pp. 93-104.
Both Guibert de Nogent (2.20) and the Pseudo-Aquinas
tractate (2.36) explore the four senses of Scriptural
interpretation (the literal, tropological, allegorical,
and anagogical) as one means of amplifying a sermon.
Caplan discusses the development of this method of exegesis
in both Christian and Jewish doctrine and treatises.

2.68 CAPLAN, HARRY. "Rhetorical Invention in Some Mediaeval
Tractates on Preaching." Speculum, 2 (1927), 284-95.
Reprinted in Caplan, 2.43, pp. 79-92.
Invention and amplification in the treatises of Alain of
Lille (2.18), Humbert of Romans (2.28), Pseudo-Aquinas
(2.36), and William of Auvergne (De faciebus mundi). Caplan
begins by considering the medieval arguments for and against
the use of classical rhetoric and literature in the artes
praedicandi.

2.69 CLARK, ALBERT C. <u>The Cursus in Mediaeval and Vulgar Latin</u>.
Oxford: At the Clarendon Press, 1910, 31 pp.
A useful introductory sketch of the development of the
cursus from its classical conception by Thrasymachus and
Gorgias through the fourteenth century. Includes extracts
from grammarians and rhetoricians throughout its history.

2.70 CLARK, DONALD L. "Rhetoric and the Literature of the English
Middle Ages." <u>QJS</u>, 45 (1959), 19-28. Reprinted in Lionel
Crocker and Paul A. Carmack, eds. <u>Readings in Rhetoric</u>.
Springfield, Illinois: Charles C. Thomas, 1965, pp. 220-34.
Medieval English authors, especially Chaucer, "were
drilled in rhetoric, not only by <u>De inventione</u> and <u>Ad
Herennium</u>, but by the elementary exercises of Priscian. . . .
Rhetoric did teach the poets, as well as the prose writers,
to find arguments and to use an embellished and copious
style, as the allegories attest" (p. 28). Clark concludes
with a summary of Priscian's <u>De praeexercitamentis</u>.

2.71 CONSTABLE, GILES, ed. <u>The Letters of Peter the Venerable</u>.
2 vols. Cambridge: Harvard University Press, 1967.
In the process of demonstrating Peter the Venerable's
independence from the traditional five-part letter and from
the stylistic intricacies of rhythmic prose, Constable provides a thumbnail sketch of medieval letter collections; of
methods of composing, sealing, and sending letters; of the
early history of the <u>ars dictaminis</u>; and of the development
of cursus forms in the twelfth century (vol. 2, 1-44).
Thoroughly documented throughout: for a brief bibliography
of the cursus, see p. 30, footnote 129.

2.72 CREMONA, J. "Dante's Views on Language," in <u>The Mind of Dante</u>.
Edited by Uberto Limentani. Cambridge, England: Cambridge
University Press, 1965, pp. 138-62.
On Dante's argument for a vernacular in <u>De vulgari
eloquentia</u>. A useful introduction to the extensive litera-
ture on the grammatical and rhetorical underpinnings of
Dante's poetry.

2.73 CURTIUS, ERNST R. <u>European Literature and the Latin Middle
Ages</u>. Translated by Willard R. Trask. Bollingen Series,
No. 36. New York: Pantheon Books, 1953. Reprinted with
minor corrections, Princeton, N.J.: Princeton University
Press, 1967, 677 pp.
Argues that one of the common denominators of Mediter-
ranean and Western, early and late medieval literature was
rhetorical studies. Explores the influences of rhetorical
<u>topoi</u>--modes of address, the Goddess of Nature, heroes,
landscapes, the muses, and so on--upon medieval Latin and
vernacular literature, touching especially on Dante.
Curtius's twenty-five "Excursuses" (see especially No. 13,

'Brevity as an Ideal of Style") aptly illustrate the inad-
vertent motto of this fundamental work: "'God is in detail'" (p. 35). Bibliography, pp. 599-602. Originally
published as Europäische Literatur und lateinisches
Mittelalter in 1948.

2.74 DALZELL, ANN. "The Forma dictandi Attributed to Albert of
Morra and Related Texts." MS, 39 (1977), 440-65.
Compares the Forma dictandi of Albert of Morra (d. 1187),
perhaps the earliest treatise on the cursus romanus that we
have, to the De arte dictandi rhetorice of Peter of Blois
and to the Introductiones dictandi of Transmundus. Includes excerpts, commentary, and notes on the treatises.

2.75 DARGAN, EDWIN C. A History of Preaching. 2 vols. New York:
A. C. Armstrong & Son, 1905-1912. Reprinted: Burt
Franklin Research and Source Works Series, No. 177, New
York: Burt Franklin, 1968.
Vol. 1, subtitled From the Apostolic Fathers to the
Great Reformers, includes an extensive account of the
decline of preaching in the seventh and eighth centuries,
the renaissance of interest in the thirteenth, mysticism
and preaching in the fourteenth, and the dawn of the Reformation in the fifteenth (vol. 1, 105-358). Dargan tends to
focus on the social and intellectual milieu and on the
lives and times of the preachers rather than on the ars
praedicandi, but still provides a fascinating backdrop for
the treatises. Bibliography, vol. 1, 565-67; vol. 2,
579-81.

2.76 DENHOLM-YOUNG, NOËL. "The Cursus in England." Oxford Essays
in Medieval History Presented to Herbert Edward Salter.
Oxford: At the Clarendon Press, 1934, pp. 68-103.
Reprinted: Freeport, N.Y.: Books for Libraries Press,
1968. Article reprinted in Denholm-Young. Collected
Papers on Mediaeval Subjects. Oxford: B. Blackwell, 1946,
pp. 26-55. Reprinted with revisions in Denholm-Young,
Collected Papers of N. Denholm-Young. Cardiff: University
of Wales Press, 1969, pp. 42-73.
An essay as useful for its review of English masters
(especially Peter of Blois, Gervase of Melkley, Geoffrey
of Everseley, and John of Garland) who introduced the cursus
to their country in the twelfth and thirteenth centuries,
as for its appendix--a list of extant dictaminal manuscripts,
both foreign and English, in English libraries.

2.77 DIETER, OTTO A. L. "Arbor picta: The Medieval Tree of
Preaching." QJS, 51 (1965), 123-44.
Argues that an elaborate fifteenth-century arbor picta--
a representation of the tree-like divisions and subdivisions
of the thematic sermon--is the work of the Dominican Jacobus

of Fusignano who wrote his <u>Artis praedicationis</u> in the
early fourteenth century. Draws parallels to the pseudo-
Aquinas tractate (2.36).

2.78 DIETER, OTTO A. L. "The Rhetoric of Notker Labeo," in <u>Papers
in Rhetoric</u>. Edited by Donald C. Bryant. St. Louis: 1940.
Reprinted: Iowa City: University of Iowa Press, 1965,
pp. 27-33.
   This brief, general article, based on Dieter's dissertation, analyzes Notker Labeo's early eleventh-century <u>New
Rhetoric</u>: its indebtedness to Cicero, Alcuin, Boethius,
and others; its description of the five parts of rhetorical
lore; and its insistence on a rhetoric relevant to daily,
contemporary concerns. "He was a teacher of rhetoric,"
Dieter concludes, "well versed in rhetorical tradition,
capable of independent thought and purpose, who realized
that rhetoric, founded on the past, had to keep in close
contact with life in the living present" (p. 33).

2.79 DIETER, OTTO A. L. and WILLIAM C. KURTH. "The <u>De rhetorica</u>
of Aurelius Augustine." <u>SM</u>, 35 (1968), 90-108.
   Brief, well-documented introduction (pp. 90-95) attributes the <u>De rhetorica</u> to Augustine and discusses its indebtedness to Hermagoras. Includes a translation of the
treatise (pp. 95-108). Joseph M. Miller attributes the
treatise to a pseudo-Augustine and has translated it again
in Miller, Prosser, and Benson, eds., 2.45, pp. 7-24.

2.80 DRAAK, MAARTJE. "The Higher Teaching of Latin Grammar in
Ireland during the Ninth Century." <u>MKNAL</u>, NS 30 (1967),
109-44.
   Draak's study of the ninth-century Irish glosses to the
St. Gall Priscian concludes that the Irish were more com-
petent grammarians than they have been given credit for.
A continuation of Draak in <u>MKNAL</u>, NS 20 (1957), 261-82.

2.81 EAST, JAMES R. "Brunetto Latini's Rhetoric of Letter Writing."
<u>QJS</u>, 54 (1968), 241-46.
   Provides a useful analysis of Brunetto Latini's <u>Li
livres dou Tresor</u>, III, one of the first vernacular prose
renditions of rhetorical doctrine. "One of Latini's distinct contributions to rhetorical knowledge," East concludes, "is the extent to which he combines the principles
of the classical rhetoric of Cicero with the rhetoric of
<u>ars dictaminis</u>. The result is a rhetoric that is appli-
cable to both oral and written discourse. It is a rhetoric mainly concerned with arrangement" (p. 246).

2.82 ESKRIDGE, JAMES B. <u>The Influence of Cicero Upon Augustine in
the Development of his Oratorical Theory for the Training
of the Ecclesiastical Orator</u>. Menasha, Wis.: The Colle-
giate Press, George Banta Publishing Co., 1912, 58 pp.

Augustine's indebtedness to and adaptation of the
Ciceronian goals of speaking to teach, delight, and persuade, with particular attention to the levels of style.
Eskridge concludes that, unlike Cicero, Augustine taught
that even the temperate or middle style was capable of
moving an audience.

2.83 FAULHABER, CHARLES B. "The Summa dictaminis of Guido Faba,"
in Medieval Eloquence: Studies in the Theory and Practice
of Medieval Rhetoric. Edited by James J. Murphy. Berkeley,
Los Angeles, and London: University of California Press,
1978, pp. 85-111.
Essentially a summary of Guido Faba's Summa dictaminis.
Despite its eclectic nature, writes Faulhaber, the treatise
proved popular because it concentrates on particular points
of difficulty in dictaminal theory; because of its simple,
readable style; because of its liberal use of concrete examples; and because of its "fidelity to the Bolognese school
tradition" (p. 108).

2.84 FAULHABER, CHARLES B. Latin Rhetorical Theory in Thirteenth
and Fourteenth Century Castile. University of California
Publications in Modern Philology, No. 103. Berkeley,
Los Angeles, and London: University of California Press,
1972, 172 pp.
Until the mid-twelfth century, Faulhaber concludes, the
dominant rhetorical texts in Spain were the Ciceronian
De inventione and Rhetorica ad Herennium; thereafter,
dictaminal treatises predominated in the schools. Includes
discussion of the thirteenth- and fourteenth-century treatises of Geoffrey of Everseley (Ars epistolarium ornatus),
Juan Gil de Zamora (Dictaminis epithalamium), and Martin of
Cordoba (Breve compendium artis rethorice). Bibliography,
pp. 151-66.

2.85 FONTAINE, JACQUES. Isidore de Seville et la Culture Classique
dans l'Espagne Wisigothique. 2 vols. Paris: Etudes
Augustiniennes, 1959.
A fundamental study of Isidore's Etymologia. In Parts
1 and 2 Fontaine analyzes Isidore's role as a grammarian
and rhetorician (vol. 1, 211-337). Further chapters discuss his role in mathematics, geometry, music, and astronomy; his philosophy; and the significance of his works
within the context of early medieval Spain. Bibliography,
vol. 2, 889-926.

2.86 FREDBORG, KARIN M. "Petrus Helias on Rhetoric." Université
de Copenhague Cahiers de L'Institut du Moyen-Age Grec et
Latin, 13 (1974), 31-41.
In its handling of the major points of rhetoric--the
theory of argument, of issues, and of rhetorical topics--

Peter Helias's commentary on De inventione (c. 1130-39)
shows a remarkable degree of independence from Cicero.
Relying on the work of his master, Thierry of Chartres,
and to a lesser extent on Boethius and Victorinus, the commentary was carefully studied and adapted by Alain of Lille.

*2.87 FREDBORG, KARIN M. "The Commentary of Thierry of Chartres on
Cicero's De inventione." Université de Copenhague Cahiers
de L'Institut du Moyen-Age Grec et Latin, 7 (1971), 1-36.
Cited in Patt, 2.161, p. 153, footnote 80; and Ward,
2.193, p. 50, footnote 69.

2.88 GALLICK, SUSAN. "Artes Praedicandi: Early Printed Editions."
MS, 39 (1977), 477-89.
Incunabula of thirteen authors of the artes praedicandi,
including: Alain of Lille (2.18), Simon Alcock, Humbert of
Romans (2.28), "Henry of Hesse" (2.35), Pseudo-Aquinas
(2.36), John of Wales, and William of Auvergne.

2.89 GALLO, ERNEST A. The Poetria nova and Its Sources in Early
Rhetorical Doctrine. De Proprietatibus Litterarum, Series
Maior, No. 10. The Hague and Paris: Mouton, 1971, 241 pp.
Gallo's discussion of the sources for Poetria nova and
for its prose rendition, Documentum de modo et arte dictandi
et versificandi (pp. 133-224) demonstrates Geoffrey of
Vinsauf's special debt to the Rhetorica ad Herennium,
Cicero's De inventione, and Horace's Ars poetica. Note,
however, that Gallo's further attempts to link Geoffrey and
Quintilian have been questioned (reviewed by James J.
Murphy in Speculum, 49 [1974], 116-18) and clarified (in
Traugott Lawler's review in Speculum 48 [1973], 750-54).
Gallo analyzes throughout the reworking of classical doc-
trine--especially material on amplification and abbreviation--
into an art of poetry. Bibliography, pp. 237-41.

2.90 GALLO, ERNEST A. "The Poetria nova of Geoffrey of Vinsauf,"
in Medieval Eloquence: Studies in the Theory and Practice
of Medieval Rhetoric. Edited by James J. Murphy. Berkeley,
Los Angeles, and London: University of California Press,
1978, pp. 68-84.
The doctrine of the artificial opening and the processes
of amplification and abbreviation described in Geoffrey of
Vinsauf's Poetria nova, Gallo argues, are not merely poetic
tricks to be searched out in the poetry of the late Middle
Ages. On the contrary, they are habits of mind--marks of
a poetic that is essentially static or "inorganic" in
conception.

2.91 GARFAGNINI, GIAN C. "'Ratio disserendi' e 'ratiocinandi via':
il 'Metalogicon' di Giovanni di Salisbury." SMed, 3rd
Series, 12 (1971), 915-54.

The <u>Metalogicon</u> and <u>Policraticus</u>, Garfagnini argues,
are not erudite works on learning, but specific responses
to the political turmoil of twelfth-century England. Together these works demonstrate the ways in which rational
man must acquire knowledge and in which he must function
within society. Includes some considerations of the treatises in logic that stand behind the <u>Metalogicon</u> and extensive documentation.

2.92 GRABMANN, MARTIN. "Aristoteles im zwoelften Jahrhundert."
      <u>MS</u>, 12 (1950), 123-62.
           Part 1 describes the translations of Aristotelian and
      Boethian logical treatises in the twelfth century; Part 2,
      their use and interpretation by Thierry of Chartres, John
      of Salisbury, and others. Cites numerous unpublished manu-
      scripts throughout.

2.93 GRABMANN, MARTIN. "Eine lateinische Übersetzung der pseudo-
      aristotelischen Rhetorica ad Alexandrum aus dem 13.
      Jahrhundert." <u>Sitzungsberichte der Bayerischen Akademie</u>
      <u>der Wissenschaften</u>, 4 (1931-32), 3-81.
           An edition with introductory notes of a Latin translation
      of the <u>Rhetorica ad Alexandrum</u> (<u>c</u>. 1295), perhaps by
      William of Moerbeke. Text, pp. 26-81.

*2.94 GROSSER, DOROTHY E. E. "Studies in the Influence of <u>Rhetorica</u>
      <u>ad Herennium</u> and Cicero's <u>De inventione</u>." Ph.D. disserta-
      tion, Cornell University, 1954, 185 pp.
           Cited in Arnold H. Trotier and Marian Harman, eds.,
      <u>Doctoral Dissertations Accepted by American Universities,</u>
      <u>1953-54</u>. New York: The H. W. Wilson Company, 1954, 21,
      p. 257. <u>See also</u> Murphy, 2.142, No. R30.

2.95 HARDISON, O. B., JR. "Toward a History of Medieval Literary
      Criticism." <u>M&H</u>, 7 (1976), 1-12.
           "We are only beginning," writes Hardison, "to gain con-
      trol of medieval criticism" (p. 2). Hardison argues this
      premise under four headings: (1) the universality of
      medieval--as opposed to classical or post-medieval--
      culture; (2) the uncertain lines that separate commentaries
      and exegesis from traditional forms of criticism; (3) the
      difficulty of defining the stages of medieval intellectual
      history; and (4) the extent to which classical criticism
      pervades medieval criticism, and medieval criticism per-
      vades that of the Renaissance. Hardison's essay introduces
      six further articles on medieval poetics--articles that
      cross both disciplines (music, literature, history) and
      cultures (Jewish, Arabic, Christian)--presented at the
      Second Biennial Medieval Conference, 1974.

2.96 HASKINS, CHARLES H. "The Early Artes dictandi in Italy," in
his Studies in Mediaeval Culture. New York: Frederick
Ungar Publishing Co.; Oxford: At the Clarendon Press, 1929.
Reprinted: New York: Frederick Ungar Publishing Company,
1965, pp. 170-92.

A good introduction to the scholarship on fifteen authors
of the artes dictandi, among them: Alberic of Monte Cassino
(Breviarium de dictamine), Adalbertus Samaritanus (Praecepta
dictaminum), Henricus Francigena (Aurea gemma), Hugh of
Bologna (2.13), Bernard of Bologna (Introductiones prosaici
dictaminis), and Guido of Bologna (Ars dictandi). This
branch of rhetorical studies apparently began at Monte
Cassino, Haskins writes, but quickly became associated with
the Bolognese masters. But see Patt, 2.161.

2.97 HASKINS, CHARLES H. "An Italian Master Bernard," in Essays
in History Presented to Reginald Lane Poole. Edited by
Henry W. C. Davis. Oxford: At the Clarendon Press, 1927,
pp. 211-26. Reprinted: 1969.

Although the mid-twelfth-century Summa Bernardi is based
on the Rationes dictandi (2.15), Bernard has added an elaborate piece on exordia and amplifies his predecessor's comments on style. Includes considerable discussion of
dictaminal manuscripts in the Bolognese tradition.

2.98 HASKINS, CHARLES H. "The Life of Medieval Students as
Illustrated by their Letters." The American Historical
Review, 3 (1897-98), 203-29. Revised and expanded in his
Studies in Mediaeval Culture. New York: Frederick Ungar
Publishing Co.; Oxford: At the Clarendon Press, 1929.
Reprinted: New York: Frederick Ungar Publishing Co.,
1965, pp. 1-35.

Despite its somewhat whimsical title, Haskins provides a
fascinating look at the students' lot--finances, clothing,
books, and teachers--in twelfth- and thirteenth-century
Paris, Orleans, Bologna, and elsewhere. The article is
introduced by a survey and bibliography of the authors,
treatises, and tradition of the ars dictaminis (see especially p. 2, footnote 2; p. 6, footnote 2).

2.99 HENDLEY, BRIAN P. "John of Salisbury's Defense of the Trivium."
In Arts Libéraux et Philosophie au Moyen Age. Actes du
Quatrième Congrès International de Philosophie Médiévale.
Montreal: Inst. d'Etudes Médiévales; Paris: Libr.
Philosophique J. Vrin, 1969, pp. 753-62.

Hendley contends that John of Salisbury defends "the
arts of the Trivium because they confer the faculty of
appropriate and effective expression. The art of grammar
provides us with rules for clear and comprehensible expression; the art of dialectic (and to a lesser extent, the art
of rhetoric) enables us to persuade others of the likelihood

of our non-trivial assertions about sensible reality"
(p. 761). Demonstrates John of Salisbury's insistence
upon the union of wisdom and eloquence and, in the midst
of a description of the logical method of invention in the
Metalogicon, provides a brief bibliography of the medieval
topical tradition (p. 759, footnote 7).

2.100 HERRICK, MARVIN T. "The Early History of Aristotle's Rhetoric
in England." PQ, 5 (1926), 242-57.
        Provides a useful--although necessarily sketchy--survey
of the history of Aristotle's Rhetoric from Boethius to
1620, and includes works and contributions of Leonard Cox,
Thomas Wilson, John Cheke, Francis Bacon, Philip Sidney,
and others. Concludes that "the Rhetoric seems to have made
little or no impression upon Englishmen of Chaucer's day,
though there is reason for believing that they had access
to it, or at least to some treatment of it" (p. 246).

2.101 HILLGARTH, JOCELYN M. "Visigothic Spain and Early Christian
Ireland." Proceedings of the Royal Irish Academy, 62,
Section C (1962), 167-94.
        On the transmission of manuscripts of Isidore from Spain
to Ireland in the seventh century and later. A continuation
of Hillgarth in Studia Patristica, 4 (1961), 442-56.

2.102 HOWELL, WILBUR S. "Introduction," in his The Rhetoric of
Alcuin & Charlemagne; a Translation, with an Introduction,
the Latin Text, and Notes. Princeton, N.J.: Princeton
University Press, 1941. Reprinted: New York: Russell &
Russell, Inc., 1965, pp. 3-64.
        A superbly done introduction to Alcuin's treatise, with
a dating of the text, review of the manuscripts, history of
the work, sources (especially Cicero's De inventione and
Julius Victor's Ars rhetorica), and a good discussion of the
constitutio and status.

*2.103 HULTZEN, LEE S. "Aristotle's Rhetoric in England to 1600."
Ph.D. dissertation, Cornell University, 1932.
        Cited in Murphy, 2.142, No. R15.

2.104 HUNT, RICHARD W. "The Summa of Petrus Hispanus on Priscianus
Minor." Historiographia Linguistica, 2 (1975), 1-23.
        Describes the so-called Absoluta of Petrus Hispanus, a
commentary on Books 17-18 of Priscian's Institutiones
written in the third quarter of the twelfth century. The
cryptic "P.H." to which several of the fourteen manuscripts
of the text refer is not Peter Helias, but Petrus Hispanus,
Hunt demonstrates, although Petrus Hispanus did rely heavily
on Helias's Summa super Priscianum maior for his own work.
Although he stresses the distinction between grammatical
and dialectical studies, Petrus Hispanus only begins to
erect the elaborate terminological framework of later grammatical treatises.

84

2.105   HUNT, RICHARD W.   "Studies on Priscian in the Twelfth Century:
        II, The School of Ralph of Beauvais." Mediaeval and Renais-
        sance Studies, 2 (1950), 1-56.
            Hunt describes three sets of glosses on Priscian's
        Institutio, written roughly a generation after Peter Helias
        (see Hunt, 2.107), which demonstrate the influence of Ralph
        of Beauvais. These glosses show new emphases in the study
        of grammar, especially the application of logical concerns
        to a study of syntax and a renewed use of illustrative
        quotations. Appendixes list masters and schools cited in
        the glosses (pp. 40-55).

2.106   HUNT, RICHARD W.   "The Introductions to the 'Artes' in the
        Twelfth Century." In Studia Mediaevalia in Honorem Admodum
        Reverendi Patris Raymundi Josephi Martin, Ordinis
        Praedicatorum S. Theologiae Magistri LXXum Natalem Diem
        Agentis. Bruges: Apud Societatem Editricem "De Tempel,"
        1948, pp. 85-112.
            Describes schema for introducing and distinguishing the
        liberal arts and particular works, especially in the twelfth
        century. These elaborate distinctions, derived from
        Boethius's De differentiis topicis (2.6), are demonstrated
        in Thierry of Chartres's Summa super rhetoricam, Peter
        Helias's Summa super Priscianum maior, Gundissalinus's De
        divisione philosophiae, William of Conches's Glosa super
        Priscian, Alain of Lille's Anticlaudianus (2.45), and
        elsewhere.

2.107   HUNT, RICHARD W.   "Studies on Priscian in the Eleventh and
        Twelfth Centuries: I. Petrus Helias and his Predecessors."
        Mediaeval and Renaissance Studies, 1 (1941-43), 194-231.
            On the Summa super Priscianum maior of Petrus Helias
        and two related, earlier sets of glosses on Priscian's
        Institutiones (2.5). Hunt emphasizes the preoccupation
        of the early twelfth-century glossators with questions of
        logic and stresses Peter Helias's attempts to distinguish
        dialectical and grammatical concerns and terminology.

2.108   JANSON, TORE.   Prose Rhythm in Medieval Latin from the 9th
        to the 13th Century. Acta Universitatis Stockholmiensis,
        Studia Latina Stockholmiensia, No. 20. Stockholm: Almqvist
        & Wiskell International, 1975, 133 pp.
            Although Janson is primarily concerned with establishing
        a methodology for measuring the use of the cursus, chapters
        3-5 inadvertently provide a brief history of the develop-
        ment of cursus forms in northern Italy and in Germany and
        France. Touches upon the artes dictandi (pp. 77-79) and
        upon the treatises of Albert of Morra (Pope Gregory VIII),
        Peter of Blois, Bernard of Meung, and Transmundus
        (pp. 92-103). Bibliography, pp. 128-31.

2.109   JENNINGS, MARGARET. "The Ars componendi sermones of Ranulph
        Higden," in Medieval Eloquence: Studies in the Theory and
        Practice of Medieval Rhetoric. Edited by James J. Murphy.
        Berkeley, Los Angeles, and London: University of California
        Press, 1978, pp. 112-126.
            Jennings's analysis of Higden's Ars componendi sermones,
        composed c. 1340, is especially valuable for its comparison
        of Higden's methodical discussion of the thematic sermon
        with the artes praedicandi of John of Wales, Robert of
        Basevorn, Thomas Waleys, "Henry of Hesse," and Pseudo-
        Aquinas. Includes an appendix comparing the organization
        of Higden's treatise to the "typical" manual of preaching
        (pp. 125-26).

2.110   JEUDY, COLETTE. "L'Institutio de nomine, pronomine et verbo
        de Priscien: Manuscrits et Commentaires médiévaux."
        Revue d'Histoire des Textes, 2 (1972), 73-144.
            A catalogue of sixty-nine ninth- through fifteenth-
        century manuscripts of Priscian's Institutio grammatica
        (2.5). Provides a fascinating glimpse of grammatical con-
        cerns throughout the high Middle Ages, for Jeudy offers a
        folio-by-folio analysis of the content of each manuscript.
        Illustrations of seven folios accompany the article.

2.111   JONES, LESLIE W. "Introduction," in his An Introduction to
        Divine and Human Readings by Cassiodorus Senator; Trans-
        lated with an Introduction and Notes. Columbia University
        Records of Civilization, Sources and Studies, No. 40. New
        York: Columbia University Press, 1946. Reprinted: New
        York: W. W. Norton & Company, Inc., 1969, pp. 3-64.
            Chapters on the education and career of Cassiodorus, on
        the library at Vivarium, Cassiodorus's influence, and on
        the manuscripts and printed editions of the Institutio.

2.112   KANTOROWICZ, ERNST H. "Anonymi 'Aurea Gemma.'" M&H, 1
        (1943), 41-57. Reprinted in his Selected Studies. Locust
        Valley, N.Y.: J. J. Augustin Publisher, 1965, pp. 247-63.
            Offers an interesting look at the rationale for the
        artes dictaminis of Adalbertus Samaritanus, Henricus
        Francigena, and of an "anonymous" twelfth-century adapta-
        tion of their treatises, the Aurea gemma. These teachers,
        writes Kantorowicz, "claimed to produce works of truly
        literary value--an endeavor furthered by the insertion of
        letters which were generally acknowledged as 'literature'--
        and accordingly had to provide their manuals with the
        accoutrement of literary works" (p. 48). Includes editions
        of several prefaces to the manuals.

2.113   KANTOROWICZ, ERNST H. "An 'Autobiography' of Guido Faba."
        Mediaeval and Renaissance Studies, 1 (1941-43), 253-80.
        Reprinted in his Selected Studies. Locust Valley, N.Y.:
        J. J. Augustin Publisher, 1965, pp. 194-212.

Describes the early life of Guido Faba, from about 1210 to 1225, as interpreted from the obscure prologue to his Rota nova. Kantorowicz concludes the article with an edition of that prologue (pp. 277-80).

2.114 KANTOROWICZ, ERNST H. "Petrus de Vinea in England." Mitteilungen des Österreichischen Instituts für Geschichtsforschung, 51 (1937), 43-88. Reprinted in his Selected Studies. Locust Valley, N.Y.: J. J. Augustin Publisher, 1965, pp. 213-46.

Following an important review of the dictaminal tradition in twelfth- and thirteenth-century England, Kantorowicz demonstrates the use of Petrus de Vinea's popular collection of model letters in the imperial correspondence of twelfth-century England. Points to the intimate ties between the Roman Curia and the British chancery.

2.115 KAY, RICHARD. "Priscian's Perversity: Natural Grammar and Inferno XV." SMC, 4 (1974), 338-52.

Why did Dante place Donatus in heaven and Priscian in hell? As his De vulgari eloquentia suggests, Dante sought a language that was functional and flexible, and Priscian's Institutio grammatica--fixing a living language into an intricate science of trivial distinctions--refused to meet the poet's needs. For Brunetto Latini in Dante's Inferno, see Kay, "The Sin of Brunetto Latini," MS, 31 (1969), 262-86.

2.116 KELLY, DOUGLAS. "Theory of Composition in Medieval Narrative: Poetry and Geoffrey of Vinsauf's Poetria nova." MS, 31 (1969), 117-48.

In response to arguments such as that of James J. Murphy (2.148, 2.149), Kelly shows "how common Geoffrey's ideas on composition were among writers contemporary with and subsequent to him, and . . . the relevance of this instruction to the interpretation of medieval narrative poetry" (p. 118). Explores Geoffrey's program of invention, disposition, and ornamentation in the Poetria nova, and provides an important checklist of references to the treatise in thirteenth- and fourteenth-century English catalogues (p. 145, footnote 66).

2.117 KELLY, DOUGLAS. "The Scope of the Treatment of Composition in the Twelfth- and Thirteenth-Century Arts of Poetry." Speculum, 41 (1966), 261-78.

"The silence of Matthew of Vendôme and Eberhard the German on invention and disposition is explained by the limited and elementary level of their instruction. . . . as grammarians, [they] confined themselves to versification and ornamentation. But Geoffrey of Vinsauf and John of Garland include all the divisions of rhetoric; thus

inventio and dispositio have a place in their treatises.
Their treatment of these subjects is characterized . . .
by a concern for careful organization of the poem and
the subordination of ornamentation to the plan the author
gives to his poem" (p. 278). Kelly attends particularly
to the adaptation of Horace's Ars poetica in these treatises.

2.118 KOCH, JOSEF, ed. Artes Liberales von der antiken Bildung zur
Wissenschaft des Mittelalters. Studien und Texte zur
Geistesgeschichte des Mittelalters, No. 5. Leiden and
Cologne: E. J. Brill, 1959. Reprinted: 1976, 167 pp.
Includes an abbreviated version of Philippe Delhaye's
article on programs of reading in the ars grammatica
("Grammatica et Ethica au XIIe Siècle," pp. 91-93);
Heinrich Ross on thirteenth-century speculative grammars
("Die Stellung der Grammatik im Lehrbetrieb des 13.
Jahrhunderts," pp. 94-106); and Fritz Schalk on the growth
of the liberal arts program in Germany and Italy ("Zur
Entwicklung der Artes in Frankreich und Italien,"
pp. 137-48).

2.119 KUHN, SHERMAN M. "Cursus in Old English: Rhetorical Ornament
or Linguistic Phenomenon?" Speculum, 47 (1972), 188-206.
An introduction and response to the considerable literature on the cursus and rhythmic prose in Old English. Concludes that "the so-called cursus in Old English literature
is nothing more than a part of the natural rhythm of the
language" (p. 206).

2.120 LAISTNER, MAX L. W. "The Library of the Venerable Bede," in
Bede: His Life, Times, and Writings. Edited by
Alexander H. Thompson. Oxford: At the Clarendon Press,
1935, pp. 237-66.
Considers the sources--classical and patristic--for
Bede's De arte metrica and De schematibus et tropis.
Concludes with a four-page catalogue of authors and works
Bede may have known.

2.121 LAISTNER, MAX L. W. "Bede as a Classical and a Patristic
Scholar." Transactions of the Royal Historical Society,
4th Series, 16 (1933), 69-94.
An oft-quoted study of Bede with some consideration of
the sources of his metrical and rhetorical treatises.

2.122 LANHAM, CAROL D. Salutatio Formulas in Latin Letters to 1200:
Syntax, Style, and Theory. Münchener Beiträge zur
Mediävistik und Renaissance-Forschung, No. 22. Munich:
Bei der Arbeo-Gesellschaft, 1975, 151 pp.
Emphasizes the grammatical and syntactic development of
the salutatio, but Chapter 5, "The Salutatio in Epistolary
Theory" (pp. 89-118), pauses to consider the dictaminal

treatises of Alberic of Monte Cassino (2.12 and <u>Breviarium</u>
<u>de dictamine</u>), Adalbertus Samaritanus (<u>Praecepta dictaminum</u>),
Hugh of Bologna (2.13), Henricus Francigena (<u>Aurea gemma</u>),
and Anonymous of Bologna (2.15). Like Patt (2.161), Lanham
questions Alberic's role as the so-called father of the <u>ars</u>
<u>dictaminis</u> (p. 109). Bibliography, pp. 121-34.

2.123   LAWLER, TRAUGOTT F. "John of Garland and Horace: A Medieval
        Schoolman Faces the <u>Ars poetica</u>." <u>CF</u>, 22 (1968), 3-13.
           Describes John of Garland's use and abuse of Horace's
        <u>Ars poetica</u> in his <u>Parisiana poetria</u>, concentrating on
        John's remarks on verisimilitude and consistency of char-
        acterization. "For the most part," Lawler concludes,
        "John's understanding of Horace was trivial, insensitive,
        even obtuse" (p. 13).

2.124   LEFF, GORDON. <u>Paris and Oxford Universities in the Thirteenth</u>
        <u>and Fourteenth Centuries: An Institutional and Intellectual</u>
        <u>History</u>. New Dimensions in History: Essays in Comparative
        History. New York, London, and Sydney: John Wiley & Sons,
        Inc., 1968. Reprinted: Huntington, N.Y.: R. E. Krieger
        Publishing Co., 1975, 339 pp.
           Provides a fascinating introduction to intellectual life
        at two key universities. Treats the academic program and
        its origins at Paris and Oxford, briefly discusses the
        faltering role of grammar and rhetoric in the face of logic
        and scholasticism (pp. 116-27), and concludes with exten-
        sive consideration of Aristotelianism at Paris and Robert
        Grosseteste at Oxford. Bibliography, pp. 310-15.

2.125   LEFF, MICHAEL C. "Boethius' <u>De differentiis topicis</u>, Book IV,"
        in <u>Medieval Eloquence: Studies in the Theory and Practice</u>
        <u>of Medieval Rhetoric</u>. Edited by James J. Murphy. Berkeley,
        Los Angeles, and London: University of California Press,
        1978, pp. 3-24.
           Breaking from classical tradition, divorcing rhetoric
        from its audience and traditional subject matter, Boethius's
        subordination of rhetoric to dialectic in Book 4 of his <u>De</u>
        <u>differentiis topicis</u> set the stage for the markedly dia-
        lectical cast of many of the late medieval studies in
        rhetoric.

2.126   LEFF, MICHAEL C. "Boethius and the History of Medieval
        Rhetoric." <u>CSSJ</u>, 25 (1974), 135-41.
           Because of the pragmatic and, to some extent, abstract
        concerns of later studies in law and theology, Boethius's
        subordination of rhetoric to the broader concerns of dia-
        lectic in his <u>De differentiis topicis</u> 4 (2.6) was enthusi-
        astically adopted by the medieval universities, resulting
        in "a very narrow and severely rationalistic theory of
        rhetoric" (p. 140).

2.127 LEHMANN, PAUL J. "Die Institutio oratoria des Quintilianus im Mittelalter." Philologus, 89 (1934), 349-83. Reprinted in his Erforschung des Mittelalters; ausgewählte Abhandlungen und Aufsätze. 4 vols. Leipzig: K. W. Hiersemann, 1941-60, vol. 2, 1-28.

    Explores the diffusion of Quintilian's Institutio between the sixth and twelfth centuries. Lehmann suggests that the ninth century may have possessed a complete version of that treatise based on an Anglo-Saxon exemplar, and attributes the flurry of mutilated versions to Lupus of Ferrières.

2.128 LUTZ, CORA E. "The Commentary of Remigius of Auxerre on Martianus Capella." MS, 19 (1957), 137-56.

    Lutz discusses not the content of the Martianus commentaries, but rather questions of authorship--John the Scot or Remigius of Auxerre? In the process, however, she provides a good survey of the extensive scholarship concerning the Carolingian commentaries on Capella's De nuptiis.

2.129 LUTZ, CORA E. "Remigius' Ideas on the Classification of the Seven Liberal Arts." Traditio, 12 (1956), 65-86.

    In a ninth-century commentary on Martianus Capella's De nuptiis, Remigius follows Plato in dividing philosophy or knowledge into physics (the quadrivium), logic (the trivium), and ethics. Especially useful for its review of the development of the concept of the seven liberal arts.

2.130 McGARRY, DANIEL D. "Educational Theory in the Metalogicon of John of Salisbury." Speculum, 23 (1948), 659-75.

    In search of a pedagogy that seeks out correct thinking and effective expression, John of Salisbury subordinates rhetoric to logic, treating it as a subdivision of probable logic. An excellent introduction to the man, and to the sources of and influences upon the Metalogicon: Aristotle alone, McGarry notes, is mentioned by name at least 120 times.

2.131 McKEON, RICHARD. "Poetry and Philosophy in the Twelfth Century: The Renaissance of Rhetoric." MP, 43 (1946), 217-34. Reprinted in Critics and Criticism: Ancient and Modern. Edited by R. S. Crane. Chicago: University of Chicago Press, 1952. Reprinted: 1975, pp. 297-318.

    Explores the Platonic paradox of a poetry capable of effectively presenting truth but just as capable of cloaking lies with elegance; the poets treated are Peter Abelard, Bernard Sylvester, Alain of Lille, John of Salisbury, Hugh of St. Victor, and others. Rhetorical devices and arguments, it seems, played an important role in accommodating the truths of philosophy to the constructions of poetry.

Touches throughout upon the relationship of the liberal
arts--particularly grammar, rhetoric, and logic--to philosophical pursuits.

2.132 McKEON, RICHARD. "Rhetoric in the Middle Ages." Speculum,
17 (1942), 1-32. Reprinted with revisions in Critics and
Criticism: Ancient and Modern. Edited by R. S. Crane.
Chicago: University of Chicago Press, 1952. Reprinted:
1975, pp. 260-96. Reprinted from Crane in Joseph Schwartz
and John A. Rycenga, eds. The Province of Rhetoric. New
York: The Ronald Press Company, 1965, pp. 172-212.
A fundamental introduction to medieval rhetoric, but it
will require close study. McKeon traces three lines of
intellectual influence (the classical, the Augustinian,
and the logical or Aristotelian) and studies the development of medieval dialectic during four periods. Perhaps
excessively emphasizes the influence of dialectic on rhetorical studies.

2.133 MANITIUS, MAX. Geschichte der lateinischen Literatur des
Mittelalters. 3 vols. Handbuch der Altertumswissenschaft,
No. 9, 2, 1-3. Munich: C. H. Beck'sche Verlagsbuchhandlung,
1911-31. Reprinted: 1964-65.
A storehouse of information to which medievalists in
almost any field are inevitably drawn. Manitius provides
a chronological survey of Latin authors and treatises between the Age of Justinian and the twelfth century. Works
are arranged by subject matter, so that we find a substan-
tial treatment of grammatical studies during the sixth and
seventh centuries and during the Carolingian period
(Vol. 1); of the trivium in the tenth century and following (Vol. 2); and of the trivium and dictaminal treatises
through the twelfth century. Entries for authors include
a brief biography, works and editions, and a review of
secondary scholarship.

2.134 MANLY, JOHN M. "Chaucer and the Rhetoricians." Warton Lecture
on English Poetry. PBA, 12 (1926), 95-113. Reprinted in
Chaucer Criticism, The Canterbury Tales: An Anthology.
Edited by Richard J. Schoeck and Jerome Taylor. Notre
Dame: University of Notre Dame Press, 1960, pp. 268-90.
A seminal chapter in the extensive literature on rhetorical influences in Chaucer's poetry. Manly discusses
arrangement, amplification, and figures of speech in
Chaucer's poetry as a demonstration of his debt to the
ars poetica, especially to Geoffrey of Vinsauf's Poetria
nova (2.21, 2.44). For a response, see Murphy, 2.149.

2.135 MARROU, HENRI I. St. Augustine and His Influence Through the
Ages. Translated by Patrick Hepburne-Scott; texts of
St. Augustine translated by Edmund Hill. Men of Wisdom,

No. 2. New York: Harper Torchbooks; London: Longmans,
1957, 191 pp.

Serves as an introduction to St. Augustine's life, works,
and influence in the early Middle Ages, in scholasticism,
and during the Reformation and seventeenth century. Includes translation of excerpts from a large number of his
works (pp. 83-146) and a useful bibliographical guide to
editions of Augustine's writings (pp. 182-86). Bibliography of the scholarship, pp. 187-90. A translation of his
Saint Augustin et l'Augustinisme.

2.136 MARROU, HENRI I. Saint Augustin et la Fin de la Culture
Antique. Bibliothèque des Ecoles Françaises d'Athènes
et de Rome, No. 145. Paris: E. de Boccard, Editeur, 1938,
635 pp.

Provides an important review of Augustine's intellectual
milieu, with a consideration of his grammatical and rhetorical heritage (pp. 3-83) and on Augustine and the liberal
arts (pp. 211-75). The De doctrina and De catechizandis
rudibus are topics throughout, but especially in the two
final chapters, "La Bible et les Lettrés de la Décadence"
and "L'Eloquence Chrétienne" (pp. 469-540). Bibliography,
pp. 587-606.

2.137 MOSHER, JOSEPH A. The Exemplum in the Early Religious and
Didactic Literature of England. Columbia University Studies
in English. New York: The Columbia University Press, 1911.
Reprinted: New York: AMS Press, Inc., 1966, 161 pp.

On the use of exempla, especially in Old English homi-
lies and in Middle English sermons, tracts, and artes
praedicandi. Mosher demonstrates the emergence of the
exemplum as an independent literary genre between the
ninth and fifteenth centuries. Bibliography, pp. 140-46.

2.138 MURPHY, JAMES J., ed. Medieval Eloquence: Studies in the
Theory and Practice of Medieval Rhetoric. Berkeley, Los
Angeles, and London: University of California Press, 1978,
366 pp.

A superb collection of essays on the theory and practice
of medieval rhetoric. In addition to essays annotated here
(Nos. 2.63, 2.83, 2.90, 2.109, 2.125, and 2.193), includes
the following:

M. B. Parkes. "Punctuation, or Pause and Effect."
Pp. 127-42.

Calvin B. Kendall. "Bede's Historia ecclesiastica:
The Rhetoric of Faith." Pp. 145-72.

James J. Murphy. "Rhetoric and Dialectic in The Owl
and the Nightingale." Pp. 198-230.

Douglas Kelly. "Topical Invention in Medieval French
Literature." Pp. 231-51.

Aldo Scaglione. "Dante and the Rhetorical Theory of
Sentence Structure." Pp. 252-69.
Robert O. Payne. "Chaucer's Realization of Himself as
Rhetor." Pp. 270-87.
Samuel Jaffe. "Gottfried von Strassburg and the Rhetoric
of History." Pp. 288-318.
Josef Purkart. "Boncompagno of Signa and The Rhetoric
of Love." Pp. 319-31.

2.139   MURPHY, JAMES J.   Rhetoric in the Middle Ages: A History of
Rhetorical Theory from Saint Augustine to the Renaissance.
Berkeley, Los Angeles, and London: University of California
Press, 1974, 409 pp.
A standard history of medieval rhetoric.   Part 1 begins
with an introductory chapter on classical rhetoric, then a
second on St. Augustine and the early Middle Ages (to 1050),
and a third on the survival of Aristotelian and Ciceronian
traditions of rhetoric in the late Middle Ages.   Part 2
discusses the artes: the ars poetica (Chapter 4), ars
dictaminis (Chapter 5), and ars praedicandi (Chapter 6).
Footnotes provide an extensive bibliography.

2.140   MURPHY, JAMES J.   "Caxton's Two Choices: 'Modern' and
'Medieval' Rhetoric in Traversagni's Nova rhetorica and
the Anonymous Court of Sapience."   M&H, NS 3 (1972),
241-55.
In the late fifteenth century Caxton published two rhetorical treatises, Lorenzo Traversagni's Nova rhetorica
(1479?) and an anonymous The Court of Sapience (1481?)--
both of them, Murphy argues, characteristically medieval
in outlook, relying solely on classical and traditional
sources, ignoring recent advances in Italian scholarship.

2.141   MURPHY, JAMES J.   "Alberic of Monte Cassino: Father of the
Medieval Ars dictaminis."   ABR, 22 (1971), 129-46.
Following a brief survey of the tradition of letters as
witnessed by Julius Victor's commentary on Cicero,
Cassiodorus's Variae, and early formularies, Murphy argues
that Alberic's adaptation of the Ciceronian parts of speech
in his Dictaminum radii and Breviarium de dictamine represents a crucial step in the development of the ars
dictaminis.   But see Patt, 2.161.

2.142   MURPHY, JAMES J.   Medieval Rhetoric: A Select Bibliography.
Toronto Medieval Bibliographies, No. 3.   Toronto and
Buffalo: University of Toronto Press, 1971, 116 pp.
A bibliography of 531 entries--many annotated--with
priority given to primary sources and secondary works "with
good explanatory surveys" (p. xv).   The bibliography is
divided into seven sections: background works, the early
Middle Ages, the survival of classical rhetoric, the ars

grammatica and ars poetica, the ars dictaminis, the ars
praedicandi, and university disputations. An indispensable
guide to rhetorical studies.

2.143 MURPHY, JAMES J. "The Rhetorical Lore of the Boceras in
Byhrtferth's Manual," in Philological Essays: Studies in
Old and Middle English Language and Literature in Honour
of Herbert Dean Merritt. Edited by James L. Rosier. Janua
Linguarum, Series maior, No. 37. The Hague and Paris:
Mouton, 1970, pp. 111-24.
        The grammatical tradition--especially Bede's De
schematibus--behind Byrhtferth's brief review of the
schemata written in 1011.

2.144 MURPHY, JAMES J. "The Scholastic Condemnation of Rhetoric in
the Commentary of Giles of Rome on the Rhetoric of Aristotle," in Arts Libéraux et Philosophie au Moyen Age.
Actes du Quatrième Congrès International de Philosophie
Médiévale. Montreal: Inst. d'Etudes Médiévales; Paris
Libr. Philosophique J. Vrin, 1969, pp. 833-41.
        Giles of Rome's late thirteenth-century commentary on
Aristotle's Rhetorica subordinates the passionate concerns
of rhetoric to the intellectual concerns of dialectic and,
secondly, allies rhetoric with the moral sciences, i.e.,
ethics and politics. Includes comparision with his De
differentia rhetoricae, ethicae, et politicae (2.31).

2.145 MURPHY, JAMES J. "Cicero's Rhetoric in the Middle Ages."
QJS, 53 (1967), 334-41.
        The popularity of Cicero's De inventione and of the Ad
Herennium during the high Middle Ages. Murphy contrasts
their cautious use in Northern Europe to their enthusiastic
endorsement in Italy. A review of early vernacular renditions and of Thierry of Chartres's Heptateuchon and commentaries completes the article. Substantially revised in
Murphy, 2.139, pp. 106-23.

2.146 MURPHY, JAMES J. "Saint Augustine and Rabanus Maurus: The
Genesis of Medieval Rhetoric." WS, 31 (1967), 88-96.
        On the indebtedness of Rabanus Maurus's De institutione
clericorum 3, especially to Augustine's De doctrina 4, but
also to works of Isidore, Cassiodorus, and Alcuin. "He is
the first of many medieval writers," Murphy observes, "to
make a pragmatic choice of only those ideas which are useful to him without swallowing the whole system which gave
birth to the ideas" (p. 91). Substantially revised in
Murphy, 2.139, pp. 82-88.

2.147 MURPHY, JAMES J. "Aristotle's Rhetoric in the Middle Ages."
QJS, 52 (1966), 109-15.
        Despite the fact that nearly 100 manuscripts of Aris-
totle's Rhetorica are extant, the treatise was not widely

used between the eleventh and thirteenth centuries. Murphy
ascribes the treatise's relatively insignificant role,
first, to the triumph of dialectic at the universities and,
more importantly, to the association of the Rhetorica with
Aristotle's Ethica and/or Politica. Substantially revised
in Murphy, 2.139, pp. 89-101.

2.148 MURPHY, JAMES J. "Rhetoric in Fourteenth-Century Oxford."
       MAE, 34 (1965), 1-20.
       The introduction of a sketchy program of rhetorical
       studies into the Oxford curriculum in 1431 is a brief note
       in this useful, encyclopedic review of the rhetorical tradi-
       tions during the classical period (Aristotelian, Ciceronian,
       grammatical, and sophistic), the early Middle Ages
       (Augustine and Rabanus Maurus), and the high Middle Ages
       (the ars dictaminis, ars praedicandi, and ars grammatica).
       Murphy concludes with a survey of several treatises on
       preaching (Robert of Basevorn, 2.33; and Thomas Waleys,
       2.34) and letters (John de Briggis, Thomas Sampson, Thomas
       Merke) written at fourteenth-century Oxford.

2.149 MURPHY, JAMES J. "A New Look at Chaucer and the Rhetoricians."
       RES, NS 15 (1964), 1-20.
       In response to Manly (2.134), Murphy argues that "the
       ubiquity of grammatical texts and the paucity of rhetorical
       texts is so marked in fourteenth-century English records
       that on this ground alone there might be some reason for
       supposing that Chaucer and his contemporaries may have
       participated in a 'grammatical' rather than a 'rhetorical'
       tradition" (p. 4). Eberhard of Béthune's Graecismus was
       perhaps a more likely source of Chaucer's figures of speech
       than Geoffrey of Vinsauf's Poetria nova. But see Schoeck,
       2.181.

2.150 MURPHY, JAMES J. "John Gower's Confessio Amantis and the
       First Discussion of Rhetoric in the English Language."
       PQ, 41 (1962), 401-11.
       "Although [Gower's] vague discussion of 'Rethorique' in
       Confessio Amantis VII is the first known treatment of the
       subject in the English language, the manner in which it is
       derived from Brunetto Latini's Tresor would seem to indicate
       ignorance of the subject rather than knowledge" (p. 411).

2.151 MURPHY, JAMES J. "Saint Augustine and the Debate about a
       Christian Rhetoric." QJS, 46 (1960), 400-410. Reprinted
       in Lionel Crocker and Paul A. Carmack, eds. Readings in
       Rhetoric. Springfield, Illinois: Charles C. Thomas, 1965,
       pp. 203-19.
       Describes the vehement rejection of pagan learning by
       Tertullian and others; its cautious acceptance by Basil,
       St. Ambrose, and St. Jerome; and St. Augustine's outspoken

plea for eloquentia in De doctrina 4. If it was the sin of
the sophist to ignore content, Murphy concludes, it was
often the sin of the early fathers to depend on content
alone--"the Platonic rhetorical heresy." Substantially
revised in Murphy, 2.139, pp. 47-61.

2.152   NIMS, MARGARET F. "Translatio: 'Difficult Statement' in
        Medieval Poetic Theory." UTQ, 43 (1974), 215-30.
        On the development of the concept of translatio or
        metaphor--the semantic extension of words, the symbolic
        extension of things--particularly in the writings of Alain
        of Lille and in Geoffrey of Vinsauf's Poetria nova (2.21)
        and Documentum de modo et arte dictandi et versificandi
        (2.23). Nims touches briefly on Dante's and Chaucer's use
        of metaphor as well.

2.153   NORDEN, EDUARD. Die antike Kunstprosa vom VI. Jahrhundert v.
        Chr. bis in die Zeit der Renaissance. 2 vols. Leipzig:
        B. G. Teubner, 1898. 5th ed. Darmstadt: Wissenschaftliche
        Buchgesellschaft, 1958.
        For the Middle Ages, see vol. 2, with extensive citations
        from original sources on prose styles, on the place of the
        liberal arts in a program of learning, on the conflict of
        classicism and scholasticism, and on Ciceronian influences
        in the prose of the Italian humanists. A richly illustrated
        guide to medieval attitudes toward language and the arts.

2.154   O'DONNELL, J. R. "The Commentary of Giles of Rome on the
        Rhetoric of Aristotle," in Essays in Medieval History Pre-
        sented to Bertie Wilkinson. Edited by Thayron A. Sandquist
        and Michael R. Powicke. Toronto: University of Toronto
        Press, 1969, pp. 139-56.
        A somewhat plodding but still useful summary of Giles's
        commentary on Aristotle's Rhetorica. O'Donnell follows
        Giles in tracing the distinctions between rhetoric and
        dialectic: the goal of rhetoric is to persuade or bend
        our will, whereas dialectic seeks to win the assent of
        reason; rhetoric treats moral questions, whereas dialectic
        considers speculative questions; and rhetoric must regard
        the passions of man, whereas dialectic must ignore them.
        Giles used William of Moerbeke's translation of the
        Rhetorica, and relied heavily on Al-Fārābī and Averroes
        throughout.

2.155   O'DONNELL, J. R. "The Liberal Arts in the Twelfth Century
        with Special Reference to Alexander Nequam (1157-1217),"
        in Arts Libéraux et Philosophie au Moyen Age. Actes du
        Quatriéme Congrès International de Philosophie Médiévale.
        Montreal: Inst. d'Etudes Médiévales; Paris: Libr.
        Philosophique J. Vrin, 1969, pp. 127-35.
        Reviews Alexander of Nequam's commentary on Books 1 and
        2 of Martianus Capella's De nuptiis, taken in part from
        Remigius of Auxerre's earlier commentary.

Secondary Works

2.156 OWST, GERALD R. Literature and Pulpit in Medieval England:
       A Neglected Chapter in the History of English Letters & of
       the English People. Cambridge, England: The University
       Press, 1933. 2nd ed. New York: Barnes & Noble; Oxford:
       Basil Blackwell, 1961. Reprinted: 1966, 614 pp.
            A comprehensive attempt to measure the influence of the
       medieval sermon and the artes praedicandi in England on its
       literature, with chapters on allegory, the exemplum, the
       preaching of satire and complaint, on English drama, and
       on the social gospel in William Langland's Piers Plowman.

2.157 OWST, GERALD R. Preaching in Medieval England: An Introduc-
       tion to Sermon Manuscripts of the Period, c. 1350-1450.
       Cambridge Studies in Medieval Life and Thought. Cambridge,
       England: Cambridge University Press, 1926. Reprinted:
       New York: Russell & Russell, Inc., 1965, 399 pp.
            Owst stresses the sociological context of and human ele-
       ment in the English sermon, with chapters on various preach-
       ers, the audience, and the sermons. Chapter 8,
       "Sermon-Making, or the Theory and Practice of Sacred
       Eloquence," with its analysis of Thomas Waley's ars
       praedicandi, serves as an important reminder that the
       so-called university sermon was only one of several types
       of address delivered from the English pulpit (pp. 309-54).
       The index promises substantive treatment of John Bromyard,
       Ranulph Higden, John Myrc, and Richard Rolle as well.

2.158 PAETOW, LOUIS J. "The Life and Works of John of Garland," in
       his Morale Scolarium of John of Garland (Johannes de
       Garlandia), a Professor in the Universities of Paris and
       Toulouse in the Thirteenth Century; Edited, with an Intro-
       duction on the Life and Works of the Author, together with
       Facsimiles of Four Folios of the Bruges Manuscript. Part 2
       of his Two Medieval Satires on the University of Paris.
       Memoirs of the University of California, No. 4, 2.
       Berkeley: University of California Press, 1927, pp. 77-153.
            A model introduction to John of Garland's life, his
       place in medieval intellectual history, and his more than
       50 works--"an almost unexplored mine of information on
       Latin and the teaching of Latin in the University of Paris"
       (p. 104). Includes a review of his several works on gram-
       mar and rhetoric (pp. 120-28). To be used with caution,
       however; some of Paetow's conclusions are now out of date.

2.159 PAETOW, LOUIS J. The Arts Course at Medieval Universities
       with Special Reference to Grammar and Rhetoric. University
       Studies of the University of Illinois, No. 3, 7. Champaign,
       Ill.: University Press, 1910. Reprinted: Dubuque, Iowa:
       Wm. C. Brown Reprint Library, n.d., 134 pp.
            An oft-cited and just as often disputed study of the
       arts of grammar, rhetoric, and logic in the universities
       of the twelfth through fourteenth centuries. Paetow

describes the flight of the classics from Chartres to
Paris to Orleans; the so-called new grammar of Alexander
of Villedieu and Eberhard of Béthune at the University of
Toulouse; and the triumph of the ars dictaminis and
Boncompagno at the University of Bologna. Annotated bib-
liography, pp. 113-34.

2.160 PALMER, ROBERT B. "Bede as Textbook Writer: A Study of his
De arte metrica." Speculum, 34 (1959), 573-84.
Describes the sources of Bede's treatise on metrics.
Here Bede has achieved, Palmer concludes, "a critical syn-
thesis"--an adaptation of traditional grammars "to the new
Christian vocabulary and metrics" (p. 584).

2.161 PATT, WILLIAM D. "The Early 'Ars dictaminis' as Response to a
Changing Society." Viator, 9 (1978), 133-55.
An introduction to the early artes dictaminis, with a
thorough review of the scholarship. Patt questions the
assumption that several so-called fathers of the ars
(Adalbertus Samaritanus, Henricus Francigena, Hugh of
Bologna, Anonymous of Bologna) were solely responsible for
initiating that program of study: "The ars dictaminis was
not a localized product which spread to the rest of Europe
from individual centers . . . but rather a cultural development which occurred more or less simultaneously in Italy,
France, Germany, and perhaps other parts of Europe as well"
(p. 139).

2.162 PAYNE, ROBERT O. "Chaucer and the Art of Rhetoric," in
Companion to Chaucer Studies. Edited by Beryl Rowland.
Revised edition. Toronto, New York, and London: Oxford
University Press, 1979, pp. 42-64.
Not simply a review of the scholarship, but an evaluation
of the shifting emphases in studies of rhetorical influ-
ences on Chaucer and his poetry since the publication of
Faral's Les Arts Poétiques in 1924. Supplemented by a
bibliography (pp. 61-64), Payne's essay serves as a useful
guide to the considerable literature on the subject.

2.163 PAYNE, ROBERT O. The Key of Remembrance; A Study of Chaucer's
Poetics. New Haven and London: Yale University Press,
1963. Reprinted: Westport, Conn.: Greenwood Press, 1973,
258 pp.
Explores Chaucer's stylistic experiments in The Legend
of Good Women, The Canterbury Tales, Troilus and Criseyde,
and elsewhere in the light of traditional rhetorical conventions. Payne is "not so concerned here with specific
techniques as with the central belief, in rhetorical theory,
that poetry is the art of clothing the already discovered
truth in fitting language" (p. 57). Bibliography,
pp. 233-40.

2.164 PFANDER, HOMER G. "The Mediaeval Friars and Some Alphabetical
        Reference-Books for Sermons." MAE, 3 (1934), 19-29.
          Describes fifteen reference books of thirteenth- through
        fifteenth-century friars, chiefly English, including the
        Speculum laicorum and Bromyard's Summa praedicantium. These
        reference books provided alphabetical lists of Biblical
        allusions, patristic quotations, stories, analogies, and
        references to other sources for literally thousands of
        sermon topics.

2.165 POLHEIM, KARL. Die lateinische Reimprosa. Berlin:
        Weidmannsche Buchhandlung, 1925. Reprinted: 1963, 559 pp.
          Prose style in classical learning and in the treatises
        of Augustine, Isidore, Rabanus Maurus, etc. Although
        Polheim is especially concerned with rhymed prose, he
        includes sections on the cursus as well--and bibliographies
        (pp. 70, 132, 430). Includes extracts from and bibliograph-
        ical guides to medieval theorists and a chronological index
        to editions of the treatises (pp. 460-503).

2.166 POOLE, REGINALD L. Lectures on the History of the Papal Chan-
        cery down to the Time of Innocent III. Cambridge, England:
        Cambridge University Press, 1915, 227 pp.
          See especially Chapter 4, "The Ars Dictandi," on the
        origin and development of the Cursus Curiae Romanae, with
        special attention to Albert of Morra and John of Gaeta's
        dictaminal treatises (pp. 76-97). "The Cursus of the Roman
        Chancery was . . . no new invention," writes Poole, "still
        less a revival based on a misunderstanding of the ancient
        system. Its author . . . adapted [classical] rules to the
        facts of pronunciation of his own day. He thus reflected
        an historical development: accent, not quantity, was the
        one element that could be considered" (p. 93).

2.167 QUAIN, EDWIN A. "The Medieval Accessus ad Auctores." Traditio,
        3 (1945), 215-64.
          Reviews introductory summaries to works in Roman and
        canon law, philosophy, and rhetoric, demonstrating that
        the accessus ad auctores was an interdisciplinary response
        of a writer or a commentator to the work in question.
        Treating questions such as the life of the author, title
        of the work, intention of the author, content of the work,
        and utility, the accessus appears to have stemmed from
        commentators on Greek philosophy and to have been rein-
        forced by the practice of Boethius and, in the twelfth
        century, by the practice of the Bolognese law schools.
        Touches on commentaries on the rhetorics of Theon,
        Hermogenes, and Aphthonius.

2.168 RASHDALL, HASTINGS. The Universities of Europe in the Middle
        Ages. 2 vols. Oxford: At the Clarendon Press, 1895.

2nd ed., revised by F. M. Powicke and A. B. Emden. 3 vols.
Oxford: At the Clarendon Press, 1936.
  Despite his emphasis on details of organization and ad-
ministration, Rashdall provides a valuable introduction to
the intellectual background of medieval rhetorical studies.
Vol. 1: Abelard and the twelfth-century renaissance,
Salerno, Bologna, and Paris. Vol. 2: universities in
Italy, Spain and Portugal, France, Germany, Scandinavia,
and Scotland. Vol. 3: English universities and student
life. Bibliographies accompany most chapters.

2.169 REINSMA, LUKE M. "Rhetoric, Grammar, and Literature in England and Ireland before the Norman Conquest: A Select
Bibliography." The Rhetoric Society Quarterly, 8, no. 1
(1978), 29-48.
  An annotated bibliography of studies in rhetoric and
literature in Anglo-Saxon England and early medieval
Ireland. Includes some consideration of ancillary studies:
education, libraries and catalogues, and monasticism. A
total of 235 entries.

2.170 RICHÉ, PIERRE. Education and Culture in the Barbarian West
from the Sixth through the Eighth Century. 3rd ed.
Translated by John J. Contreni. Columbia, S.C.: University of South Carolina Press, 1978, 594 pp.
  Riché accomplishes for the early Middle Ages what
Rashdall has for education in the medieval universities.
Beginning with the survival and final collapse of classical
education, Riché traces the beginnings of Christian schools
in Italy, Gaul, and Spain. Chapters 8 and 9, of special
interest for our purposes, follow the growth of monastic
and episcopal education in Anglo-Saxon England during the
seventh and eighth centuries. Thoroughly documented, with
an extensive bibliography (pp. 501-16). Originally published as Education et culture dans l'Occident barbare,
6e--8e siècles in 1962.

2.171 ROBINS, R. H. Ancient & Mediaeval Grammatical Theory in
Europe with Particular Reference to Modern Linguistic
Doctrine. London: G. Bell & Sons Ltd., 1951. Reprinted:
Port Washington, N.Y., and London: Kennikat Press, 1971,
111 pp.
  Following chapters on grammatical theory in ancient
Greece and Rome, Robins discusses the linguistic develop-
ments of Donatus and Priscian, of Alexander of Villedieu
in his Doctrinale, of Peter Helias and the beginnings of
speculative grammar, and of the modistae (pp. 69-90).
Bibliography, pp. 100-101.

2.172 ROBINSON, I. S. "The 'Colores Rhetorici' in the Investiture
Contest." Traditio, 32 (1976), 209-38.

A rich, rewarding study of twelfth-century collections
of earlier libelli and epistolae, especially Germanic. The
Codex Udalrici and similar collections, Robinson argues,
were preserved not in order to demonstrate the polemics of
the conflict between King Henry IV and Pope Gregory VII,
but rather to serve as stylistic models. That is ironic,
Robinson continues, for Onulf of Speyer's Colores rhetorici
and similar eleventh-century treatises originally sought to
perfect the figure of speech as "the principal weapon in
the German episcopal propaganda of the early years of the
Investiture Contest" (p. 237).

2.173   ROSS, WOODBURN O. "Introduction," in his Middle English Sermons; Edited from British Museum MS. Royal 18 B. xxiii.
Early English Text Society, OS, No. 209. London: Oxford
University Press, 1940. Reprinted: London, New York, and
Toronto: Oxford University Press, 1960, pp. i-lxvi.
Following a description of this early fifteenth-century
manuscript, Ross outlines the construction of the typical
"modern" sermon--theme, protheme, division, subdivision,
and amplification (pp. xliii-lv). Bibliography, pp. xi-xiii.

2.174   SALMON, PAUL. "Über den Beitrag des grammatischen Unterrichts
zur Poetik des Mittelalters." Archiv, 199 (1962), 65-84.
On the influence of classical and early medieval works
(especially the Rhetorica ad Herennium, Priscian's De
praeexercitamentis and Institutio, and Donatus's
Barbarismus); on the twelfth- and thirteenth-century poetics
of Hugh of St. Victor, John of Salisbury, Guibert de Nogent,
Conrad of Hirsau, etc. Such fundamental training in the
ars poetica, particularly in the figures of speech, was responsible for the commonplace passages of description in
much of medieval Latin poetry.

2.175   SANDYS, JOHN E. A History of Classical Scholarship. Vol. 1:
From the Sixth Century B.C. to the End of the Middle Ages.
Vol. 2: From the Revival of Learning to the End of the
Eighteenth Century. 3rd ed. Cambridge, England:
Cambridge University Press, 1921. Reprinted: New York:
Hafner Publishing Co., 1964.
See especially vol. 1, Book 6, "The Middle Ages in the
West, c. 530-c. 1350 A.D."--a treasure-house of bibliograph-
ical and textual information on Bede, Alcuin, Rabanus
Maurus, John of Salisbury, William of Moerbeke, and many
others; with discussions of the coming of scholasticism,
Aristotelianism, and the triumph of logic in the late Mid-
dle Ages (pp. 443-678). Vol. 2 includes the Italian humanists. Note that more recent scholarship has rendered some
of Sandys's observations out of date; use with a measure
of discretion.

2.176 SANFORD, EVA M. "The Use of Classical Latin Authors in the
       Libri Manuales." TAPA, 55 (1924), 190-248.
           Lists the contents of 414 libri manuales--collections of
       classical authors and treatments of the liberal arts. En-
       tries, dating between the eighth and fifteenth centuries,
       are arranged chronologically, and an index provides a con-
       venient guide to manuscripts preserving the grammatical
       and rhetorical works of Boethius, Cicero, Donatus, Martianus
       Capella, Quintilian, and others.

2.177 SCAGLIONE, ALDO D. The Classical Theory of Composition from
       Its Origins to the Present: A Historical Survey. Univer-
       sity of North Carolina Studies in Comparative Literature,
       No. 53. Chapel Hill, N.C.: The University of North
       Carolina Press, 1972, 447 pp.
           An exploration of literature on style, syntax, and word
       order. Scaglione's treatment of medieval treatises on
       prose style, with special attention to the ars dictaminis
       (pp. 97-125), demonstrates the grammarians' increasing use
       of punctuation, the substitution of cursus forms for clas-
       sical periods, the widening of terminology, and a specula-
       tive, analytical approach to questions of syntax.
       Bibliography, pp. 405-33. Scaglione's The Classical Theory
       is being published in a German translation together with a
       new volume covering German rhetoric and grammar: Die
       klassische Theorie der Prosakomposition von ihren Anfängen
       bis zur Gegenwart. Band I: Stil und Syntax in den
       Romanisch/Westeuropäischen Sprachen; Band 2: Die Theorie
       der Wortstellung im Deutschen (Stuttgart: Klett-Cotta
       Verlag, 1980). A translation of Vol. 2 is tentatively
       scheduled for publication as The Theory of German Word
       Order.

2.178 SCAGLIONE, ALDO D. "The Historical Study of Ars Grammatica:
       A Bibliographic Survey," in his Ars Grammatica: A Biblio-
       graphic Survey, Two Essays on the Grammar of the Latin and
       Italian Subjunctive, and a Note on the Ablative Absolute.
       Janua Linguarum, Series Minor, No. 77. The Hague and Paris:
       Mouton, 1970, pp. 11-43.
           Provides a thoroughly documented account of the consider-
       able number of editions and secondary works published during
       the past century on the medieval ars grammatica. A valuable
       introduction to and review of the scholarship.

2.179 SCHMALE, FRANZ-JOSEF. "Der Briefsteller Bernhards von Meung."
       Mitteilungen des Instituts für österreichische
       Geschichtsforschung, 66 (1958), 1-28.
           On manuscript relationships of some dozen adaptations of
       the Flores dictaminum of Bernard of Meung, late twelfth-
       century master at Orleans. Extensive appendixes (pp. 19-28)
       provide a stemma for the manuscripts and list the incipits
       of nearly 300 letters in Bernard's model collection.

102

2.180   SCHMALE, FRANZ-JOSEF. "Die Bologneser Schule der Ars dictandi."
        Deutsches Archiv für Erforschung des Mittelalters, 13
        (1957), 16-34.
                The indebtedness of several anonymous dictaminal trea-
        tises to the school of Adalbertus Samaritanus and Henricus
        Francigena: an anonymous Aurea Gemma, the Aurea Gemma
        Willehelmi, a De dictamine, and a Lombard tract. Distin-
        guishes the pragmatic concerns of Adalbert from the antique
        interests of Hugh of Bologna.

2.181   SCHOECK, RICHARD J. "On Rhetoric in Fourteenth-Century
        Oxford." MS, 30 (1968), 214-25.
                To call the ars poetica a grammatical tradition, and
        then to question Chaucer's knowledge of rhetorical studies
        on these grounds is to turn classification into legislation,
        argues Schoeck in response to Murphy (2.149). Schoeck fur-
        ther suggests from the evidence of a lively dictaminal tra-
        dition at Oxford, from university statutes, and from the
        intimate relationship of Oxford and continental universi-
        ties that a markedly Ciceronian tradition of rhetoric
        flourished at Oxford throughout the fourteenth century.

2.182   SIRAISI, NANCY G. Arts and Sciences at Padua: The Studium of
        Padua before 1350. Pontifical Institute of Mediaeval
        Studies, Studies and Texts, No. 25. Toronto: Pontifical
        Institute of Mediaeval Studies, 1973, 199 pp.
                Includes chapters on the program of learning at Padua
        and, specifically, on the trivium, the quadrivium, meta-
        physical studies, and medical studies. Siraisi concludes
        that "grammar and rhetoric at Padua were in the thirteenth
        century, under the influence of Boncompagno and Rolandino,
        largely concerned with the professional preparation of
        lawyers and notaries" (p. 55). Literature and the clas-
        sics apparently took a second place to these more pragmatic
        concerns. Bibliography, pp. 177-91.

2.183   SITZMANN, MARION. "Lawrence of Aquileja and the Origins of
        the Business Letter." ABR, 28 (1977), 180-87.
                On the ultimate schematization of the formal letter in
        Lawrence of Aquilegia's Practica sive usus dictaminis:
        "Lawrence's work represents the final state of a mechanical
        tendency which . . . was inherent in ars dictaminis from
        its initial history" (p. 184). Includes a translation of
        Lawrence's first table of alternate salutations, narrations,
        petitions, and conclusions (pp. 186-87).

2.184   SMYTH, CHARLES H. E. The Art of Preaching: A Practical Survey
        of Preaching in the Church of England, 747-1939. London:
        Society for Promoting Christian Knowledge; New York: The
        Macmillan Co., 1940. Reprinted: London: S. P. C. K.,
        1953, 265 pp.

Smyth's analysis of seven precepts in the construction
of the university sermon is based on Robert of Basevorn
(2.33) and Thomas Waleys (2.34). A second chapter on the
medieval period details the use of exempla from the
thirteenth- and fourteenth-century English pulpit. Bibliography, pp. 250-51.

2.185 STAHL, WILLIAM H., RICHARD JOHNSON, and E. L. BURGE.
       Martianus Capella and the Seven Liberal Arts. Vol. 1:
       The Quadrivium of Martianus Capella. Columbia University
       Records of Civilization, Sources and Studies, No. 84.
       New York and London: Columbia University Press, 1971,
       288 pp.
            Stahl's study of the sources for and influence of
       Capella's survey of the quadrivium is followed by Johnson's
       consideration of allegory and the trivium. Remarks on and
       digest of Book 5, De rhetorica, are sketchy (pp. 115-21).
       Bibliography, pp. 253-63.

2.186 STEENBERGHEN, FERNAND van. Aristotle in the West: The Origins
       of Latin Aristotelianism. Revised and translated by Leonard
       Johnston. Louvain: E. Nauwelaerts, Publisher, 1955,
       244 pp.
            A fascinating study of Aristotle at the thirteenth-
       century universities of Paris and Oxford, with special
       attention to the works of Averroes, Avicenna, St. Bonaventure,
       Robert Grosseteste, St. Thomas Aquinas, Siger of Brabant, and
       William of Auvergne. Steenberghen explores the union of and
       conflict between Aristotelianism and Christian thought, cul-
       minating in the Bishop of Paris's condemnation of Aris-
       totelianism in 1277.

2.187 STUMP, ELEONORE A., ed. Boethius's De topicis differentiis:
       Translated, with Notes and Essays on the Text. Ithaca,
       N.Y., and London: Cornell University Press, 1978, 287 pp.
            Includes a series of six clear, useful explorations of
       topics and differentia in the early Middle Ages. An ini-
       tial essay, "Dialectic and Aristotle's Topics," places
       Boethius's De topicis in historical perspective (pp. 159-78);
       a second, "Dialectic and Boethius's De topicis differentiis,"
       studies dialectical rather than rhetorical topics in
       Boethius (pp. 179-204); and a third traces the development
       of the notion of topics from a general strategy of argu-
       mentation to a middle term of the syllogism "Between Aris-
       totle and Boethius" (pp. 205-14). Further essays demon-
       strate later developments in the topics in Peter of Spain's
       Tractatus ("Peter of Spain on the Topics," pp. 215-36) and
       provide analyses of "Differentia and the Porphyrian Tree"
       (pp. 237-47) and of "Differentia" (pp. 248-61). Bibliog-
       raphy, pp. 263-73.

2.188   STUMP, ELEONORE A. "Boethius's Work on the Topics."
        <u>Vivarium</u>, 12 (1974), 77-93.
            Argues against James Shiel's thesis that all of
        Boethius's logical works are translations of Greek scholia
        on Aristotle's <u>Organon</u> (<u>Mediaeval and Renaissance Studies</u>,
        4 [1958], 217-44). The evidence of <u>De differentiis topicis</u>
        and <u>In topica Ciceronis commentariorum</u> suggests that Shiel's
        conclusion is unwarranted; these treatises are original and
        important logical works that attest to Boethius's scholar-
        ship and philosophical acumen.

2.189   THUROT, M. C. <u>Notices et Extraits de Divers Manuscrits Latins</u>
        <u>pour servir à l'Histoire des Doctrines Grammaticales au</u>
        <u>Moyen Age</u>. Notices et Extraits des Manuscrits de la
        Bibliothèque Impériale, No. 22, 2. Paris: Imprimerie
        Impériale, 1868. Reprinted: Frankfurt-am-Main, 1964,
        592 pp.
            Still an indispensable, comprehensive guide to grammat-
        ical masters, treatises, intellectual developments, and
        manuscripts of the high Middle Ages. Includes a century-
        by-century discussion of authors, extracts from the texts,
        and remarks on their significance. Indexes cite manuscripts'
        incipits, authors, and subjects.

2.190   TROUT, JOHN M., III. "Alan of Lille and the Art of Preaching
        in the Twelfth Century." Ph.D. dissertation, Rutgers
        University, 1972, 280 pp.
            Platonism, reason, and natural law are the philosophical
        buttresses of Alain of Lille's <u>De arte praedicatoria</u> and
        <u>Anticlaudianus</u>. Trout particularly attends to Alain's
        views on preaching--the role of the liberal arts in train-
        ing the preacher; the philosophical underpinnings of the
        sermon.

2.191   WALLACH, LUITPOLD. <u>Alcuin and Charlemagne: Studies in</u>
        <u>Carolingian History and Literature</u>. Cornell Studies in
        Classical Philology, No. 32. Ithaca, N.Y.: Cornell Uni-
        versity Press, 1959, 335 pp.
            On the historical and political background of Alcuin's
        <u>Disputatio</u>, with attention paid especially to Alcuin's
        epistolography. Chapters on the <u>littera exhortatia</u>, on
        kingship, and on the legal elements of the <u>Disputatio</u> sup-
        port Wallach's claim that this is as much a tract on king-
        ship or good governing--the <u>via regia</u>--as a rhetorical
        treatise. Bibliography, pp. 277-99. Serves as a useful
        complement to Howell. 2.102.

2.192   WALLACH, LUITPOLD. "Onulf of Speyer: A Humanist of the
        Eleventh Century." <u>M&H</u>, 6 (1950), 35-56.
            On the sources of Onulf of Speyer's mid-eleventh-century
        <u>Colores rhetorici</u>, adapted from the <u>Ad Herennium</u>, indebted

to Horace's Ars poetica and Alcuin's Disputatio as well.
Onulf, Wallach concludes, is "one of the links in the unbroken chain of classical humanism" that connects earlier
centuries with the twelfth-century renaissance (p. 50).
Includes several additional sources for Alcuin's Disputatio
(pp. 54-56).

2.193   WARD, JOHN O.   "From Antiquity to the Renaissance: Glosses
        and Commentaries on Cicero's Rhetorica," in Medieval
        Eloquence: Studies in the Theory and Practice of
        Medieval Rhetoric.   Edited by James J. Murphy.   Berkeley,
        Los Angeles, and London: University of California Press,
        1978, pp. 25-67.
            A richly rewarding survey of the adaptation of commen-
        taries and glosses on the Ad Herennium and Cicero's De
        inventione to time and circumstance. Surges of interest
        in these treatises, especially in the eleventh, twelfth,
        and fifteenth centuries, writes Ward, suggest "a crisis of
        communication: between king and adviser, between opposed
        political or religious parties or factions, between per-
        sonal enemies, . . . between the bearers of Christian truth,
        their opponents, and the bulk of mankind" (p. 65).   The
        essay is based on Ward's survey of nearly 400 texts and
        manuscripts and on his earlier dissertation (Ward, 2.194).

2.194   WARD, JOHN O.   "Artificiosa Eloquentia in the Middle Ages:
        The Study of Cicero's De inventione, the Ad Herennium and
        Quintilian's De institutione oratoria from the early Middle
        Ages to the Thirteenth Century, with special reference to
        the schools of northern France." 2 vols. Ph.D. disserta-
        tion, University of Toronto, 1972.
            Vol. 1 argues that treatises such as the De inventione
        and Ad Herennium were adapted in the works of Isidore,
        Alcuin, John of Salisbury, and others only to the extent
        that classical doctrine was relevant to contemporary
        issues. The ars dictaminis, ars poetica, and ars praedicandi
        are explained similarly--as the adaptation of a rhetorical
        tradition to specific socio-intellectual needs. Vol. 2
        provides a checklist of antique, medieval, and renaissance
        commentaries on and glossed texts of the De inventione and
        Ad Herennium.

2.195   WEISHEIPL, JAMES A.   "The Parisian Faculty of Arts in Mid-
        Thirteenth Century: 1240-1270." ABR, 25 (1974), 200-17.
            A general sketch of the faculty of arts at the University
        of Paris, with special emphasis on the slow growth of Aris-
        totelian studies in the arts program up to the condemnation
        of thirteen Averroist theses by the Bishop of Paris in 1270.
        Weisheipl briefly notes the two key methods of teaching at
        the arts faculty: lectio and disputatio.

2.196 · WEISHEIPL, JAMES A. "Developments in the Arts Curriculum at
      Oxford in the Early Fourteenth Century." MS, 28 (1966),
      151-75.
         By the mid-fourteenth century, Weisheipl argues, studies
      at Oxford were dominated by the libri logicales and the
      libri naturales--by treatises in physics and mathematics.
      Includes a survey of four different types of logical
      treatises--those on terminology, on inferences, on logical
      consistency, and on the so-called liar paradox.

2.197 WEISHEIPL, JAMES A. "Curriculum of the Faculty of Arts at
      Oxford in the early Fourteenth Century." MS, 26 (1964),
      143-85.
         An introduction to the program of studies for under-
      graduates, bachelors, and masters at fourteenth-century
      Oxford. Includes a valuable index of readings in each of
      the liberal arts and in philosophy. For reading assign-
      ments in the trivium, see pp. 168-70.

2.198 WIERUSZOWSKI, HELENE. "Rhetoric and the Classics in Italian
      Education of the Thirteenth Century." Studia Gratiana, 11
      (1967), 169-208. Reprinted in Wieruszowski, Helene, Politics
      and Culture in Medieval Spain and Italy. Storia e
      Letteratura, Raccolta di Studi e Testi, No. 121. Rome:
      Edizioni de Storia e Letteratura, 1971, pp. 589-627.
         Argues against Paetow's thesis (2.159) that thirteenth-
      century Italy witnessed a falling off of Latin studies.
      Despite Boncompagno's notorious war on Cicero, he and
      other rhetoricians (including Guido Faba and Brunetto
      Latini) made extensive use of the classics. Concluding
      with an account of Dante's classical studies at Florence,
      Wieruszowski provides a vigorous, enlightening picture of
      humanism and rhetoric at the leading Italian universities
      of Bologna, Arezzo, Padua, and Florence.

2.199 WIERUSZOWSKI, HELENE. "Arezzo as a Center of Learning and
      Letters in the Thirteenth Century." Traditio, 9 (1953),
      321-91. Reprinted in Wieruszowski, Helene, Politics and
      Culture in Medieval Spain and Italy. Storia e Letteratura,
      Raccolta di Studi e Testi, No. 121. Rome: Edizioni de
      Storia e Letteratura, 1971, pp. 387-474.
         See especially Part 2, "The Liberal Arts Course (Rhetoric)
      and Letters in Arezzo," in which Wieruszowski reviews the
      schools of ars dictaminis and ars notaria in the early
      thirteenth century. Dictaminal treatises of Bonfiglio of
      Arezzo, Mino da Colle, Guittone of Arezzo, and Geri of
      Arezzo demonstrate a return to classical concerns. Edi-
      tions of six letters and fragments from treatises provide
      firsthand evidence of Arezzo's role in rhetorical studies.

2.200 ZINN, GROVER A., JR. "Hugh of Saint Victor and the Art of
       Memory." Viator, 5 (1974), 211-34.
          Describes Hugh of St. Victor's indebtedness to and
       departure from classical rhetorical treatises--Cicero's
       De oratore, Ad Herennium, and Quintilian's Institutio
       oratoria--for the description of mnemonic techniques in
       his preface to the Chronicon, in De arca Noe mystica, and
       in Didascalicon. Inadvertently provides a good introductory
       bibliography to the scholarship on Hugh of St. Victor. For
       further literature on this fourth part of rhetoric, the art
       of memory, see also Frances A. Yates (cited in Murphy,
       2.142, Nos. M15 and M16).

Part 3

The Renaissance

CHARLES STANFORD

Introduction

In 1509, Stephen Hawes presented an allegorical treatment of rhetoric, devoting separate chapters of his The Pastyme of Pleasure to invention, disposition, eloquence, delivery, and memory. Although these terms may change somewhat from author to author, the Renaissance traditionalist believed that all five belonged to rhetoric. In general, he defined invention as the locating and inventing of facts or arguments. Disposition generally meant what is today called organization, and invention and disposition, taken together, constituted what is now called composition. Eloquence, which occupied a large share of the debate over rhetoric during the Renaissance, today has been renamed style. Delivery included gesture and pronunciation, and memory has been replaced today by note cards.

All of the officially sanctioned school books during the entire Renaissance period were in Latin. Erasmus's De duplici copia verborum ac rerum commentari duo (1512, rev. 1514) dealt with amplification, which fell under the headings of both invention and eloquence. Philip Melanchthon's Elementorum Rhetorices (1519) reorganized rhetoric into four divisions, but left eloquence in a central place. Petrus Mosellanus's Tabulae de schematibus et tropia (1529) codified the schemes and tropes--subdivisions of eloquence--and became the standard text in England until it was replaced by Susenbrotus's Epitome troporum ac schematum et rhetoricum (1540). This last work proved so popular that a London edition appeared in 1562.

The vernacular tradition in England followed the Latin model, lagging behind only a few years. In 1530, for example, Leonard Cox published his The Arte or Crafte of Rhetoryke, which closely follows Melanchthon's work and which has the distinction of being the first vernacular rhetoric in English. Twenty years later, Richard Sherry published his A Treatise of Schemes and Tropes (1550), which is an "Englished" version of Susenbrotus. This edition also contains a translation of one of Erasmus's works, although Sherry replaced that work during revision (1555) with a translation of an oration by Cicero.

The first full traditional rhetoric, Thomas Wilson's The Arte of Rhetorique, was published in 1553, just two years after he had

111

published the first full traditional or scholastic logic in English.
These two works by Wilson represent virtually all of what Renaissance
Englishmen understood as traditional rhetoric and logic and they constitute a convenient starting point for a study of the primary material of the period for any scholar with a limited knowledge of the
classical languages.

While the traditionalists were comfortable and secure in England,
Peter Ramus was at work in France. In 1543, he published the second
edition of his Dialectic (the bibliography is complicated--the first
edition also appeared in 1543). Ramism is a complex subject, but it
seems to have three different meanings, depending upon the critic's
viewpoint. First, there is the widely accepted and simplistic view
that Ramism is the separation of logic and rhetoric. Ramus assigned
invention and disposition to logic, and eloquence and delivery to
rhetoric; memory became a part of logic since the Ramist logical
method made retention easier. The second meaning, to oversimplify,
focuses on Ramus's penchant for dividing everything into two. This
dichotomic approach was applied to all subjects, including mathematics and astronomy as well as logic and rhetoric. The third meaning--
irrelevant here--associates Ramism with religious martyrdom. Still,
it cannot be overlooked that his murder as a Protestant convert in a
Catholic country (France) contributed to some extent to his rising
popularity in such Protestant countries as Germany and England.

While the debate over Ramism gathered momentum in Europe, the
traditionalists continued in England. In 1563, Richard Rainolde published his Foundacion of Rhetoric. Ralph Lever carried the scholastic
tradition in the vernacular to its logical conclusion in his The Arte
of Reason, rightly termed, Witcraft (1573). The work is unintention-
ally amusing today, but there was a keen intelligence, although a
dull judgment, behind it.

Ramism finally made its appearance in the English vernacular with
Roland MacIlmaine's translation of Ramus's Logic (1574). Gabriel
Harvey promoted this new approach at Cambridge. His Ciceronianus
(1577) is the story of his own conversion to Ramism, but it was in
Latin. The same year, the vernacular saw the appearance of Henry
Peacham's traditionalist The Garden of Eloquence (1577, rev. 1593).

The rhetoricians were especially active during the 1580s. In
1584, Dudley Fenner published his Logic and Rhetoric in one volume,
and the Rhetoric later appeared in a collection of works by Thomas
Hobbes. Not only was this the first dual edition of a Ramist logic
and rhetoric, but it also marks the most visible early example of a
connection between Ramist rhetoric and religious martyrdom, although
the 1574 translation by MacIlmaine had already advertised Ramus's
martyrdom. In 1586, Angel Day published his The English Secretary,
a traditional "letter writer," which proved more popular than the
Ramist tracts. The year of Fenner's second edition, 1588, also saw
the publication of one of the best-known Ramist rhetorics in English,

Introduction

Abraham Fraunce's <u>The Arcadian Rhetorike</u>. Much of its popularity,
however, was due to its extensive use of Sidney's work as illustration.

From the 1580s on, the traditionalists and Ramists continued to
battle for supremacy. Thomas Farnaby's <u>Index Rhetoricus</u> (1625) was
published as the final salvo in the battle on behalf of traditional
rhetoric. Still, Nadeau (3.161) indicates that Ramism may have had
the better of it since each revision of Farnaby's work became pro-
gressively more Ramist.

By the seventeenth century, however, other forces were at work.
Francis Bacon's <u>Advancement of Learning</u> (1605) emphasized rhetoric
not only as a communicative skill but also as a tool in furthering
knowledge. He also emphasized the relationship between rhetoric and
psychology, an emphasis that had been anticipated in print by Thomas
Wright's <u>On the Passions of the Minde in General</u> (1604). Interest in
pulpit oratory continued as well, although it tended to be Ramist--
Thomas Granger's <u>Divine Logic</u> (1625) is an example.

The year 1660 is extremely problematic as it marks a shift toward
a neoclassical or eighteenth-century attitude; indeed, the year is
often used in literature to mark the beginning of the "Augustan" age.
The Royal Society publications were influenced both by Bacon and the
Port-Royalists, and they aimed at nothing short of a complete restruc-
turing of the language. Sprat (1667) and Wilkins (1668) are representative examples, and Lamy (3.40) illustrates the influence of the
Port-Royalists. Some other authors from this time have been included
in the eighteenth-century portion of this bibliography since both
Professor Horner and I deemed it more appropriate.

The most comprehensive survey of the Renaissance rhetoricians in
England remains Wilbur Samuel Howell's <u>Logic and Rhetoric in England
1500-1700</u> (1956). In it, Howell discusses almost all of the works
included in this bibliography as well as hundreds of others. Although
he limits himself as much as possible to England, he does explore all
the major historical movements in the field.

On the other hand, Walter J. Ong in his <u>Ramus, Method, and the
Decay of Dialogue</u> (1958) limits himself to the subject of Ramism, but
he does include all European authors in his discussion. Ong remains
the major authority in the field, and all later significant works on
the subject are heavily indebted to him. His <u>Ramus and Talon Inven-
tory</u> (1958) is an overwhelming annotated bibliography on Ramism's
primary materials and it contains over 1,100 entries.

T. W. Baldwin's massive (1549 pp.) <u>William Shakespere's Small
Latine and Lesse Greeke</u> (1944) is still extremely valuable, especially
as a repository of translations of excerpts from the standard Latin
works of the day. Sister Miriam Joseph built on his work in a
Herculean attempt to systematize the figures into a variety of subheadings in her <u>Rhetoric in Shakespeare's Time</u> (1947). In the same

year, Rosemond Tuve published her Elizabethan and Metaphysical Imagery which became central in the lively debate over the meaning and
importance of Ramism, a debate ably summarized by Jackson Cope in
1962 (3.70). Two more recent works, Lee Sonnino's A Handbook to
Sixteenth-Century Rhetoric (1968) and Brian Vickers's Classical Rhetoric in English Poetry (1970) continue the work of codifying the
figures in such a way as to be intelligible to modern readers.

Style is a major concern in the seventeenth century scholarship,
and is almost as controversial an area as is Ramism in the sixteenth.
Morris W. Croll is the pioneer in this area, and his work has been
collected by J. Max Patrick and others in "Attic" and Baroque Prose
Style. While Croll concentrates on the role played by classical influences in shaping the style of the period, Richard Foster Jones
explores the effects produced by science--his most impressive work
is The Triumph of the English Language (1953). Although both forces
contributed greatly to the preference for a less ornate style, most
rhetorical scholars lean toward either Croll's or Jones's thesis,
and Croll seems to have the larger following. George Williamson's
The Senecan Amble (1951), for example, accepts Croll's approach.

A classical and continental background is essential for any study
of Renaissance rhetoric. R. R. Bolgar's The Classical Tradition and
its Beneficiaries (1954) is an important source for the study of the
influence of the classics and offers some useful appendixes.
William T. Costello's The Scholastic Curriculum at Early Seventeenth-
Century Cambridge (1958) establishes the pervasiveness of Aristotle's
influence by surveying what was actually taught and read at the universities of the period. Jerrold Seigel's Rhetoric and Philosophy
in Renaissance Humanism (1968) and Nancy Struever's The Language of
History in the Renaissance (1970) are two excellent examples of
studies exploring the relationship between rhetoric and other
disciplines.

Some more specialized studies are available. Sister Joan Marie
Lechner's Renaissance Concepts of the Commonplaces (1962) sorts out
the various meanings of that term while Neal W. Gilbert traces the
meanings of another important term in his Renaissance Concepts of
Method (1960). The more obscure area of memory is explored with
great energy and in detail by Frances A. Yates in her The Art of
Memory (1966), which also theorizes on the architecture of the Globe
Theater.

Many studies focus on a single figure, and Francis Bacon has received the sort of treatment that more prominent rhetoricians such
as Thomas Wilson, Abraham Fraunce, Angel Day, and Joseph Glanville,
to name but a few, still await. Karl R. Wallace's Francis Bacon on
Communication and Rhetoric (1943) is the earliest authoritative full-
length study, and Brian Vickers (1968), Lisa Jardine (1974), and
James Stephens (1975), have all contributed significant studies of
Bacon's theories on rhetoric, communication, or style.

114

Introduction

There are also studies of movements or specialized areas within the traditional field of rhetoric. One of the most visible examples is J. W. Blench's Preaching in England in the Late Fifteenth and Sixteenth Centuries (1964). Another, perhaps even more formidable, work in this vein is A. C. Southern's Elizabethan Recusant Prose, 1559-1582 (1950). Southern includes an extremely valuable annotated bibliography.

I have been as selective as possible in compiling this bibliography. For the primary material, I have included only those works in Latin that are of overwhelming significance. For the English vernacular, I have attempted to include the standard works as well as a representative sampling of some of the undercurrents (Thomas Wright's The Passions of the Minde in General, 1604, is an example). On all the primary material, I have lightly modernized spelling and used a shortened form of the title. I have also given the earliest date of publication and the dates of significant revisions only. I have tried to indicate the popularity of the work in the annotation. I have also tried not to duplicate information contained in Howell (3.114), Ong (3.170, 3.172) or in the introductions to scholarly editions unless it was unavoidable.

In order to limit the secondary material, I have excluded all work prior to 1900, all unpublished dissertations, and all work not in English. I have included, however, Wilfried Barner's Barockrhetoric (1970) in order to give an example of some of the fine work that has been done in other languages and because it contains a bibliography of material written in other languages. A great deal of excellent information still remains in dissertation form as well. For example, Sister Mary Martin McCormick has edited the previously unedited "Sheapeardes Logike" of Abraham Fraunce (St. Louis University, 1968). Thomas Walsh, also at St. Louis University, has edited one of Dudley Fenner's works (1972), and Robert Chandler of the University of Missouri at Columbia has translated Gabriel Harvey's The Rhetor (1978). Anyone interested in rhetoric should also be aware of the microfilm set British and Continental Rhetoric, now distributed by University Microfilms International, and the index of dissertations on rhetoric that James J. Murphy did for them. Murphy is also preparing a short-title catalogue of Renaissance rhetoric for publication by Garland Publishing, Inc., in the near future.

In writing the annotations, I had two major considerations. First, and most important, I have directed them toward the scholar of English literature who may not be familiar with much of the work in question. Second, I have allowed the authors of the secondary material to speak for themselves whenever possible. This was far easier to do in the case of articles than in that of full-length studies. In the case of primary material, I have tried to place the work in its historical perspective.

Introduction

This is not the proper place to discuss the unique problems and considerations of Renaissance bibliography as they pertain to providing an indication of the length of the primary sources. Suffice to say that there is no way at present of indicating with any precision to readers of varying academic backgrounds the exact length of any particular work, and no such pretension is made here. I have, however, attempted to indicate within the annotations the relative length of the work in question if it seemed useful. An accurate indication of length (word count) could be achieved with the help of computers, and one hopes that they eventually will be employed for this purpose.

I owe debts of gratitude greater than I can acknowledge here with facility. Professor Walter J. Ong was extremely generous with his time and expertise throughout this endeavor, and I especially wish to thank him for going over the final draft of the manuscript with me, for making valuable suggestions, and for directing me to the rare book room at Saint Louis University where I was able to see the original editions of many of the primary sources. Professor Wilbur Samuel Howell of Princeton was a great source of encouragement from the earliest stages and helped me properly focus some of the annotations. Catherine Dunn and James J. Murphy sent me useful materials, and I would like to thank the other scholars who responded to my correspondence. Professor William M. Jones of the University of Missouri read the final draft of the manuscript as well. Finally, Professor Winifred B. Horner, the general editor of this work, deserves more thanks than it is possible to extend. Her encouragement, support, and generosity have made this entire project possible from the start.

CHARLES STANFORD
University of Missouri-Columbia

Primary Works

3.1 1509. STEPHEN HAWES. The Pastyme of Pleasure. London:
Wynkyn de Worde, 259 pp. Reprinted: 1517, 1554, 1555.
     Chapters 7-13 of this work are a two-dimensional alle-
gory concerning rhetoric--often cited. Covers the Ciceronian or traditional five parts of rhetoric, but with a
pause (Chapter 9) between invention and disposition to
discuss and attack those who detract from rhetoric's reputation. Places invention first. Images discussed in
memory. Written in rhyme royal stanzas. See Mead, 3.157,
pp. xxix-xli, for information concerning editions.

3.1a   MEAD, WILLIAM EDWARD. The Pastime of Pleasure by
Stephan Hawes. London: Oxford University Press, 1928
(for 1927), 376 pp.
     Annotation based on this edition. Still the standard
edition of this allegory.

3.2 1512. DESIDERIUS ERASMUS. De duplici copia verborum ac rerum
commentari duo, 86 pp. Reprinted: 1514 (rev.), 1526,
1534 (rev.), 1540.
     A lively discussion of amplification through the princi-
ples of variation both of words (Book 1) and thought (Book
2). Subject treated in formulary manner. For example, in
Book 1, Chapter 33, he gives several long examples of ways
to indicate that a person's letter was well received. Often
has a humorous effect. A standard school text.

3.2a   KING, DONALD B. and H. DAVID RIX, trans. Desiderius
Erasmus of Rotterdam, On Copia of Words and Ideas (De
Utraque Verborem ac Rerum Copia). Milwaukee, Wis.:
Marquette University Press, 1963, 119 pp.
     Translation omits chapters 34-94, but introduction gives
a few examples therefrom. Does not lose Erasmus's vitality.

3.3 1519. PHILIP MELANCHTHON. Elementorum Rhetorices, Libri Duo.
Grunenbergii.

Defines eloquence: "<u>Eloquentia</u> facultas est sapienter
et ornate dicendi" (p. 419). Melanchthon was an important
source for, and influence on, Leonard Cox (3.5). Divides
rhetoric into "invention, judgment, arrangement, and style"
(Howell, 3.114, p. 92) in his <u>Institutiones Rhetoricae</u>.
Although Melanchthon is a traditionalist, his division,
which both gives more weight to the logical aspects of
rhetoric and makes it possible to treat eloquence quite
separately, makes his historically important in a study
of Ramism. The <u>Institutiones Rhetoricae</u> is partially reprinted in Carpenter's edition of Cox (3.5a) and discussed
in Carpenter (3.61).

3.4   1526.   PETRUS MOSELLANUS.   <u>Tabulae de schematibus et tropis</u>.
      Cologne.
      A list of schemes and tropes that was a standard text in
      the Tudor grammar schools until it was replaced by the more
      systematic and abundant work of Susenbrotus in the middle
      of the century.

3.5   1530 (?).   LEONARD COX.   <u>The Arte or Crafte of Rhetoryke</u>.
      London.
      Frederic Ives Carpenter dates the first edition at 1530,
      although other dates back to 1524 have been offered (<u>see</u>
      Howell, 3.114, p. 90; and Carpenter, 3.61, p. 10). In any
      case, it is considered to be the first English rhetoric.
      Follows Melanchthon. Lists four essentials to rhetoric:
      Invention, or what an orator can say; Judgment, or whether
      what he can say is to the purpose or relevant; Disposition,
      or the order or organization of the oration; and Eloquence,
      or how it is said (Carpenter, p. 43). Covers only inven-
      tion and judgment. Scholastic or traditional. Uses illus-
      trations from classical authors (chiefly Cicero, but also
      Sallust) to illustrate precepts. Lists figures of inven-
      tion as precepts.

3.5a   CARPENTER, FREDERIC IVES, ed.   <u>Leonard Cox: The Arte or</u>
      <u>Crafte of Rhetoryke</u>. Chicago: The University of Chicago
      Press, 1899, 117 pp.
      Edition of the first English rhetoric. So far as I have
      been able to discover, not supplanted.

3.6   1540.   JOANNES SUSENBROTUS.   <u>Epitome troporum ac schematum et</u>
      <u>grammaticorum et rhetoricorum</u>. Zurich, 1540; London, 1562.
      "Susenbrotus has written his work upon the scheme of
      organization furnished by Melanchthon and as a substitute
      for that of Mosellanus. Into this scheme, he aims system-
      atically to collect, correct, explain, and illustrate in
      detail all the tropes and schemes of both grammar and rhet-
      oric" (Baldwin, 3.47, vol. 2, 140). Claims to have pre-
      sented 132 schemes and tropes, but "this number does not

include the minor divisions and subdivisions" (ibid.).
Sherry (3.9) and Day (3.19) translated it. It is reasonable to assume that most Renaissance authors were quite
familiar with it. Portions have been translated by T. W.
Baldwin (3.47, vol. 2). Although it concentrates on
elocutio, the date alone precludes consideration of it as
a Ramist work. Traditionalist.

3.7 1543. PETER RAMUS. Petri Rami Veromandui Dialecticae
institutiones, ad celeberriman et illustrissimam Lutetiae
Parisiorum Academiam. Paris.
    This is the second of numerous editions, "and the one
cited in the condemnation of Ramus by Francis I" (3.172,
p. 48). Ramus is known for his separation of logic and
rhetoric, and this is his logic ("Dialecticae"), which
was to undergo much revision in several stages. Ramist
logic presents definitions of logical principles exclusive
of fallacies and then follows each principle with several
examples. Milton's logic (3.39) is unique (and Milton
calls attention to this uniqueness) in that it discusses
how these examples illustrate the principles involved. In
general, the Ramist logics without commentaries are much
shorter than the traditional logics (cf. MacIlmaine, 3.14
and Wilson, 3.10). The conclusion that Ramist works were
intended to be a pedagogical tool is inescapable inasmuch
as the connection between precept and example would have
to be explained by a master to the acolyte. For full bibliographical treatment of Ramism see Ong, 3.172, from
which this entry is adapted.

3.8 1548. OMER TALON. Audomari Taleai Rhetorica, ad Carolum
Lotharingum Cardinalem Guisianum. Paris, 108 pp.
    Entry adapted from Walter J. Ong (3.172). Ramist
rhetoric is restricted to elocutio and pronunciatio, with
the overwhelming emphasis on elocutio. Lists tropes and
schemes relating to eloquence (as opposed to logic) with
illustrative examples. Similar to Ramist logic in that
precept is not linked to example through explication.
There is considerable evidence of Ramus's hand in Talon's
publications, and the fact that Ramus never took credit
for his contributions to the rhetorics can be attributed
to his desire to emphasize that logic and rhetoric are two
distinct but supplementary disciplines. For full bibliographical treatment, see Ong, 3.172.

3.9 1550. RICHARD SHERRY. A Treatise of Schemes and Tropes.
London; Revised: 1555. Reprinted in fascimile: Herbert W.
Hildebrant, ed., Gainesville, Fla.: Scholars' Facsimiles
and Reprints, 1961, 248 pp.
    Traditionalist or Ciceronian, but limited to eloquence.
Cites Agricola as an authority for translations. Quintilian

not systematic enough. Cicero lacks precepts. Erasmus
"but a comentarye" (p. 10). Defines eloquence. Treatise
proper (96 pp.) consists of the names of the figures in the
margins next to definitions and examples. Narrow columns
and cramped type. Contains a translation of Erasmus's The
Education of Children. Sparse marginal notes thereto.
Revised in 1555 as Treatise of the Figures of Grammar and
Rhetorike, and replaced Erasmus with an oration by Cicero.
See Howell, 3.114, pp. 125-32.

3.10   1551. THOMAS WILSON. The rule of Reason, conteinying the
       Arte of Logique, set forth in Englishe. London, 270 pp.
            First logic in English vernacular. Ciceronian or Aris-
       totelian, usually referred to as "scholastic." Reason in-
       cludes both logic and dialectic, for example. Terms used
       are clearly defined, discussed, and examples are provided
       in a lively manner. Contains a quotation from Ralph
       Royster Doyster which was not identified as such until the
       nineteenth century. The quotation, in alternate punctua-
       tions, yields two quite distinct meanings. One is highly
       insulting, the other flattering. See Lever, 3.13.

3.10a   SPRAGUE, RICHARD S., ed. The Rule of Reason Conteinying
       The Arte of Logique by Thomas Wilson. Northridge, Calif.:
       San Fernando Valley State College Foundation, 1972, 270 pp.
            Only modern edition of this scholastic logic in English.

3.11   1553. THOMAS WILSON. The Arte of Rhetorique. London: Re-
       printed in facsimile: Robert Hood Bowers, ed. Gaines-
       ville, Fla.: Scholars' Facsimiles and Reprints, 1962.
            The first full traditional rhetoric in English. Treats
       all five of the Ciceronian parts of rhetoric, and includes
       some remarks on memory. Extremely popular as evidenced by
       the many subsequent editions. Well known for its strong
       attack against "inkhorn" terms in English; that attack in-
       cludes a malapropistic parody of highly Latinate epistles.
       Eminently readable. See also Wagner, 3.212.

3.12   1563. RICHARD RAINOLDE. A booke called the Foundacion of
       Rhetorike. London. Reprinted in facsimile: Francis R.
       Johnson, ed. New York: Scholars' Facsimiles and Reprints,
       1945. xiv pp. + lxii fol.
            Formulary. A collection of nineteen orations on sub-
       jects ranging from "howe Semiramis came to bee Queene of
       Babilon" to "the decaie of kingdomes and nobilitie."
       Topical and section headings indicating parts of the ora-
       tion with extensive marginal notes indicating subject mat-
       ter and references. Comparative analysis of orations.
       Includes fables. Contains Zeno's distinction between rhet-
       oric and logic. See Howell, 3.114, pp. 140-42.

3.13 1573. LEVER, RALPHE. The Arte of Reason, rightly termed, Witcraft. London.
> An attempt to construct a logical terminology with a native English vocabulary. "Conclusion" thus becomes "endsay"; "affirmatio," "yeasay"; and "definitio," "say what." Published only twenty-two years after Wilson's Rule of Reason (1551) and the second English logic in the sixteenth century.

3.14 1574. ROLAND MacILMAINE, trans. The Logike of the Moste Excellent Philosopher P. Ramus, Martyr. Reprinted: 1581. Reprinted in facsimile: Leeds, England: The Scholar Press Limited, 1966, 102 pp.
> The first English translation of a Ramist work and done by a Scot. Walter J. Ong's note: "the first English version, from Ramus' text in the stage of the 1569 Basle edition, but with some chapters combined, giving Books I and II respectively 32 and 18 chapters" (Ong, 3.172, p. 196). Introduction admits debt to Aristotle, Cicero, and Quintilian. Is also a paean to Ramism. In the process of "translating," also reorganizes to an extent, chiefly by further subdividing or dichotomizing Ramus's own divisions. One is impressed with the brevity of this logic in comparison with Wilson's "scholastic" version.

3.14a DUNN, CATHERINE M., ed. The Logike of the Moste Excellent Philosopher P. Ramus, Martyr: Translated By Roland MacIlmaine (1574). Northridge, Calif.: San Fernando Valley State College, 1969, 120 pp.
> Only modern edition. See also Dunn, 3.87.

*3.15 1577. GABRIEL HARVEY. Ciceronianus vel Oratio Post Reditum. London.
> Harvey is generally considered the first Ramist in England despite MacIlmaine's earlier translation. Describes his past as a slavish follower of Cicero or as more interested in matters of eloquence and style to the exclusion of substance. Gives account of his discovery of Ramus and his conversion to Ramism. As an index to Harvey it is more reliable than reports of his part in the Harvey-Nash-Greene controversy. See below for translation. Annotation based on Forbes, below.

3.15a FORBES, CLARENCE A., trans. Gabriel Harvey's Ciceronianus, With an Introduction and Notes by Harold S. Wilson. University of Nebraska Studies, November 1945; Studies in the Humanities No. 4. Lincoln, Nebr.: University of Nebraska, 1945, 159 pp.
> A bilingual edition. Only modern edition available.

3.16   1577. HENRY PEACHAM. The Garden of Eloquence. London.
       1593 edition reprinted in facsimile: William G. Crane,
       ed. Gainesville, Fla.: Scholars' Facsimiles and Reprints,
       1954, 204 pp.
            Figurist, after Susenbrotus, Sherry, and Day. In gen-
       eral, the figures are defined and illustrated, and their
       proper use or purpose is described. Finally, a "Caution"
       describes and warns against abuse of particular figures.
       Contains a "Table of the names of all the figures con-
       teined in this booke" (pp. 199-200). Wilbur Samuel Howell
       (3.114, p. 135) puts selections from Peacham and Sherry side
       by side to illustrate how closely Sherry is followed.
       Printing format far superior to that in Sherry's.
       William G. Crane (3.73) discusses the relation between
       this derivative work and that of earlier versions.

3.17   1582. RICHARD MULCASTER. The First Part of the Elementarie.
       London.
            Essentially a grammarian, Mulcaster is also concerned
       with the issue of eloquence as it affects the English
       language. First discusses general conditions needed for
       learning. Strongly committed to the English vernacular;
       defends the language against its detractors. Concerned
       with neologizing, compound words, etc. Concerning his
       "Table," he says "I have gathered togither so manie of
       them both enfranchised and naturall, as maie easilie direct
       our generall writing, either bycause theie be the verie
       most of those words which we commonlie use, or bycause all
       others . . . will conform themselves, to the presidencie
       of these" (3.17a, pp. 184-85). "Elementarie" refers to
       very early schooling, including preschool.

3.17a   CAMPAGNAC, E. T., ed. Mulcaster's Elementarie. Oxford:
       At the Clarendon Press, 1925, 332 pp.
            Edition used by Richard Foster Jones (3.131), and for
       annotation of Mulcaster (3.17).

3.18   1584. DUDLEY FENNER. The Artes of Logike and Rhetorike,
       plainelie set foorth in the Englishe tounge. . . . 1584
       edition reprinted in facsimile: Robert D. Pepper, ed.
       Gainesville, Fla.: Scholars' Facsimiles and Reprints,
       1966, pp. 143-80.
            A translation and adaptation in one volume of a Ramist
       logic and rhetoric. Preface "To the Christian Reader"
       defends translation by arguing that Cicero and Quintilian
       wrote in their own vernacular and not Greek. Logical pre-
       cepts follow Ramus's definitions, but classical examples
       are overwhelmingly ignored and replaced with Biblical
       illustrations. Puts scriptural passages and fables into
       syllogistic form, for example. The adaptation of Talon's
       rhetoric is closer to a study of logical fallacies than to

a discussion of schemes and tropes such as is found in
Sherry (3.9) and Day (3.19). Strong Puritan bias pervades.
See Miller, 3.158, on relation between Ramism and Puritan-
ism. Facsimile edition of the 1584 edition, the first
Ramist logic and rhetoric issued together. Pepper also
includes Sir Thomas Elyot tr., The Education or Bringing VP
of Children (1553); Francis Clement, The Petie Schole with
an English Orthographie (1587); and William Kempe, The
Education of Children in Learning (1588). Introduction
places each work in its historical context and discusses
sources.

3.19   1586. ANGEL DAY. The English Secretary. London. Revised:
       1599. 1599 edition reprinted in facsimile: Robert O.
       Evans, ed. Gainesville, Fla.: Scholars' Facsimiles and
       Reprints, 1967, 308 pp.
           Formulary. Work has three essential parts. The first
       classifies various types of letters, discusses them, and
       then provides examples. Some of the examples are lively
       and have literary merit; especially lively are the
       "Epistle[s] vituperatorie," which provide examples of
       Elizabethan invective. Part 2 is an adaptation of
       Susenbrotus entitled "Tropes, Figures and Schemes" which
       is what led Joseph (3.133) to classify Day as a figurist.
       Part 3 describes the function of a secretary and shows that
       the office carried with it more prestige than in modern
       times.

3.20   1588. ABRAHAM FRAUNCE. The Arcadian Rhetorike. London.
           Ramist rhetoric. Precepts chiefly translated from Talon
       (3.8). Work is most notable for excerpts from Sidney's
       Old Arcadia, but also from the New Arcadia (this before
       the Ms. of the Old Arcadia was discovered at the start of
       the twentieth century). See Seaton, 3.187.

3.20a   The Arcadian Rhetorike by Abraham Fraunce. Edited by
       Ethel Seaton. Oxford: Basil Blackwood, 1950, 191 pp.
           Only modern edition of this Ramist rhetoric. See also
       Seaton, 3.187.

3.21   1588. WILLIAM KEMPE. The Education of Children in Learning.
       London. Reprinted in facsimile in Robert D. Pepper, ed.
       Four Tudor Books on Education. Gainesville, Fla.:
       Scholars' Facsimiles and Reprints, 1966, pp. 181-240.
           Wilbur Samuel Howell (3.114) indicates that this work
       "deserves mention . . . as an account of the way in which
       Ramus's logic and rhetoric were beginning to enter into
       English elementary education during the late sixteenth
       century" (259). Howell may have taken his cue from Baldwin
       who points out that Ramus and Kempe would "have the boys
       begin with the study of inventio, which was the first part

of logic in the Ramist system" (3.47, vol. 2, p. 8). Not
properly a rhetoric, but a treatise on education.

3.22 1589. GEORGE PUTTENHAM. The Arte of English Poesie. London.
       Ciceronian, called "figurist" by Joseph (3.133). The
       rest of the title is descriptive: "Contrived into three
       Bookes" The first of Poets and Poesie, the second of
       Proportion, the third of Ornament." Book 3 is of inter-
       est from a rhetorical standpoint. Discusses high, middle,
       and low styles. Extended discussion of rhetorical figures.
       Discusses language and style in defense of ornamentation of
       figures. His own style is highly figured, especially with
       alliteration. Discussion of decorum, which could be con-
       sidered under the heading of gesture when it deals with the
       proper tone of voice and the appropriate clothing and be-
       havior in certain courtly settings.

3.22a   WILLCOCK, GLADYS DOIDGE and ALICE WALKER, eds. The Arte
       of English Poesie by George Puttenham. Cambridge, England:
       Cambridge University Press, 1936, 469 pp.
           Introduction of 101 pp. See also Willcock, (3.226).
       Appendixes: "Variant Passages," "Textual Corrections,"
       and "The Sources of the Arte." Index. "Index to First
       Lines of Verse Quotations."

3.23 1599 (?). HOSKINS, JOHN. "Directions for Speech and Style."
       Date is conjectured for date of completion. I have
       found no evidence that this work was ever published under
       Hoskins's name until the twentieth century. For history
       of its publication, see Hudson, 3.23a.
           Discussion of figures of "varying," "amplification,"
       and "illustration." Illustrates copiously from Sidney's
       Arcadia. Lists terms and discusses them in depth. Ana-
       lyzes Sidney's use. Also indicates that Hoskins saw a
       copy of the first two books of Aristotle's Rhetoric which
       were "Englished" by Sir Philip Sidney (p. 41), in Hudson,
       3.23a. Work does not betray significant Ramist influence,
       but is extremely eclectic. Hudson indicates Quintilian is
       a major source (p. xxiv).

3.23a   Directions for Speech and Style by John Hoskins.
       Edited by Hoyt Hudson. Princeton, N.J.: Princeton Uni-
       versity Press, 1935, 162 pp.
           Modern spelling edition of the MS. 4604. Contains orig-
       inal and influential introduction (40 pp.) by Hudson who
       discusses the history of Hoskins's work. Pages of it
       appear in Jonson's Timber and were ascribed to Jonson by
       Swinburne and others. The source of Smith's The Mysterie
       of Rhetorique Unvail'd (3.35). Conjectures convincingly
       that the date of composition was 1599 (pp. xiv-xv). Dis-
       cusses sources. Extensive (60 pp.) notes. Appendixes.

124

Index. The most convenient edition yet of Hoskins's work.
Annotation (above) based on this edition.

3.24 1604. THOMAS WRIGHT. The Passions of the Minde in General.
London, 363 pp.
First edition in 1601, but the 1604 edition is extensively revised (see Sloan, 3.189, pp. xlvi-xlix). Perhaps
more relevant to psychology, but Aristotle discusses similar issues in his Rhetoric. Includes subtitles or chapter headings such as "Rashnesse in Speech," and
"Affectation in Speech" (pp. 110-11).

3.24a The Passions of the Minde in Generall by Thomas Wright,
A Reprint Based on the 1604 Edition. Edited by Thomas O.
Sloan. Urbana, Ill.: University of Illinois Press, 1971,
456 pp.
Chiefly a facsimile of the 1630 edition, with edited
material from the 1604 edition. See also Sloan, 3.189.

3.25 1605. FRANCIS BACON. Of the Proficience and Advancement of
Learning. London.
Bacon's remarks on rhetoric, which are scattered
throughout his works, are discussed at length by Wallace
(3.219) and Jardine (3.122). The Advancement, however, is
most frequently cited in this respect, and it is used
heavily by Howell (3.114). Book One is a defense of
learning, and Book Two surveys specific branches of knowledge. On rhetoric he says "notwithstanding, to stir the
earth a little about the roots of this science, as we have
done of the rest: The duty and office of Rhetoric is to
apply Reason to Imagination for the better moving of the
will" (p. 297). James Spedding (3.25a) gives Bacon's
elaboration in a footnote: "'Rhetoric being to the Imagination what Logic is to the Understanding.'--de Aug." (p. 297).
Bacon offers this Aristotelian distinction between logic
and rhetoric: "Logic handleth reason exact and in truth,
and Rhetoric handleth it as it is planted in popular opinions and manners" (p. 300), which may or may not be con-
strued as Ramist. He then turns to Aristotle's "defects"
(p. 301) in the area of rhetorical theory.

3.25a The Advancement of Learning in The Works of Francis
Bacon. Edited by James Spedding, Robert Leslie Ellis, and
Douglas Denon Heath. Vol. 6. Boston: Houghton, Mifflin
and Company; Cambridge: The Riverside Press, 1854-74,
77-412.
Still the standard edition of Bacon's works.

3.26 1614. JOHN RAINOLDS. Oratio in Laudem Artis Poeticae in
D. Johannis Rainoldi . . . Orationes Duodecim. Oxford.

Ringler (3.179) dates this work at 14 July 1572. An oration following the classical pattern until it abruptly ends as Rainolds makes a transition to the "unusual usefulness of poesy" (3.179, p. 61). Argues that "rhetoric is . . . couched in certain rhythms" (p. 49) that are derived from poetry (p. 51). Title is descriptive.

3.26a   Oratio in Laudem Artis Poeticae [Circa 1572] by John Rainolds. Edited by William Ringler and translated by Walter Allen. Princeton Studies in English, 20, edited by G. H. Gerould. Princeton, N.J.: Princeton University Press, 1940, 101 pp.
    Contains text and translation, introduction, commentary, and index.

3.27 1616. THOMAS GAINSFORD. The Secretaries Studie. London.
    A letter writer, similar to Day's (3.19). Lists eighteen types including "Amorous, Morall, and Chiding" (title page). Some fine examples of Renaissance invective included. Differs from Day's work most obviously in that it consists almost exclusively of examples.

3.28 1617. ROBERT ROBINSON. The Art of Pronunciation. London.
    This relatively short (60 pp.) treatise considers pronunciation which would come under the heading of delivery. It emphasizes physiology as it affects speech and pronunciation. (Annotation based on microfilm. BCRE Reel no. 6, Item 65.)

3.29 1620. THOMAS GRANGER. Syntagma Logicum, or The Divine Logic. London.
    A late adaptation of Ramistic dialectic. Prefatory material (letter) in Latin, but text is in English. Begins "Logike (a) is a greeke word, and signifieth speech, whether grammatical, or rhetoricall, (b) specially the art of discoursing well" (p. 1). In five books. Could be compared to MacIlmaine's much shorter version.

3.30 1625. THOMAS FARNABY. Index Rhetoricus. London. In Latin.
    A Ciceronian textbook designed for use in the schools. Quite popular. Has generated considerable amount of secondary material. See also Nadeau, 3.161, for the most visible discussion of the work and its history.

3.31 1626. ANTHONY WOTTON. The Art of Logick. London, 204 pp.
    A translation of Ramus. Compare MacIlmaine's (3.14), which is shorter and less developed. Wotton's work is about 200 pp. Title page bears the interesting inscription: "Published for the Instruction of the unlearned," which can be taken to mean those who do not read Latin.

126

3.32   1637. THOMAS HOBBES. <u>A Briefe of the Art of Rhetorique</u>.
       London.
           Hobbes's rhetoric is an adaptation of Aristotle's rhet-
       oric, and is interesting to the student of seventeenth-
       century views of Aristotle. For example, the distinction
       between the enthymeme and syllogism does not center on the
       concept of probability but on the missing first premise:
       "an example is a short induction, and an enthymeme a short
       syllogism; out of which are left, as superfluous, that
       which is supposed to be necessarily understood by the
       hearer; to avoid prolixity, and not to consume the time
       of public business needlessly" (3.32a, p. 425). Does dis-
       cuss the fallacies that are omitted resolutely from Ramist
       rhetorics.

3.32a   MOLESWORTH, SIR WILLIAM. <u>The Whole Art of Rhetoric</u>, in
       <u>The English Works of Thomas Hobbes of Malmesbury</u>. London:
       John Bohn, 1840, pp. 419-510.
           Still the most widely available collection of Hobbes's
       work, at least in libraries. Also contains <u>The Art of</u>
       <u>Rhetoric</u>, which is an adaptation by Dudley Fenner of Talon's
       rhetoric (3.8). Talon was Ramus's disciple. <u>See</u> Ong,
       3.166, and Howell, 3.118, who pointed this out in the same
       year.

3.33   1644. JOHN BULWER. <u>Chirologia: or the Naturall Language of</u>
       <u>the Hand . . . Whereunto is added Chironomia: Or, the Art</u>
       <u>of Manuall Rhetoricke</u>. London.
           Gesture is included under delivery and is generally
       slighted. Describes how to gesture with the hands. Dis-
       cusses <u>passim</u> Cicero, Tacitus, <u>et al.</u>, in connection with
       the subject. The first essay is descriptive, the second
       prescriptive. Reprinted in 1648. Excerpt from 3.33a,
       p. 204 below: "the right index if it marshall-like go
       from finger to finger (to note them with a light touch),
       it doth fit their purpose who would <u>number their arguments</u>
       and, by a visible distinction, set them all on a row upon
       their fingers." Supports and illustrates from Hortensius,
       Cicero, Quintilian, Cresollius, and Chrisippus (pp. 204-5).

3.33a   <u>Chirologia: or the Natural Language of the Hand (and)</u>
       <u>Chironomia: or the Art of Manual Rhetoric, by John Bulwer</u>.
       Edited by James W. Cleary. Carbondale and Edwardsville,
       Ill.: Southern Illinois University Press, 1974, 380 pp.
           The only edition of these two rare works, published as
       one volume. <u>See also</u> Cleary, 3.67.

3.34   1656. WILLIAM CHAPPELL. <u>The Preacher, or the Art and Method</u>
       <u>of Preaching</u>. London.
           By Milton's tutor. Included as an example of the enor-
       mous amount of rhetorics written for the pulpit or

preachers. Essentially an adaptation of Ramism to pulpit oratory; indeed, the term "method" in the title indicates that Chappell considered the work as such.

3.35 1657. JOHN SMITH. The Mysterie of Rhetorique Unvail'd. London: E. Cotes. Reprinted in facsimile: K[arl] S[chneider], ed. New York and Hildesheim: Georg Olms Verlag, 1973, 308 pp.
    Usually attacked for its rather obvious and blatant plagiarism of Hoskins. Also plagiarized Farnaby, although he is given credit in the margins. Smith, however, acknowledges his debt rather generously by Renaissance standards: "It is very true, that many learned Worthies have done exceeding well herein; yet to use the expression of one of them [?]: That a child upon a Gyants shoulders can see further then the Gyant: So I, having the help of their labours, and of other Books . . . (without ostentation be it mentioned) used a more distinct and easie method. . . ." (A5-A6). Furthermore, his method is more distinct and easy: adds table of contents in alphabetical order, with definitions, and page references for definitions and examples. Clearly printed and well organized. A good starting point for the study of primary materials. Facsimile edition is extremely clear copy. The scholarly apparatus of the facsimile is as follows: "The present facsimile is reproduced from a copy in the possession of the British Museum, London Shelfmark: 11805. e. 38. K.S." Then follows the text and numbered pages.

3.36 1659. JOHN PRIDEAUX. Sacred Eloquence. London, 138 pp.
    Subtitle of special interest: "The Art of Rhetorick As it is layd down in Scripture." In contrast to the Ramist practice of bisection, this divides elements into sevens. Defines thus: "Sacred Eloquence in a Logicall kind of Rhetorick, to be used in Prayer, Preaching, or Conference; to the glory of God, and the convincing, instructing, and strengthening our brethren" (A2r). Treats schemes and tropes.

3.37 1667. THO.[MAS] SPRAT. The History of the Royal-Society of London. London, 455 pp. Reprinted in facsimile: Jackson I. Cope and Harold Whitmore Jones, eds. St. Louis: Washington University Press; and London: Routledge and Kegan Paul, 1958. Third printing, 1966, 565 pp.
    Obviously not a rhetoric, but valuable as a statement of deliberate policy concerning prose style and rhetoric during the seventeenth century. The society maintained "a constant Resolution, to reject all the amplifications, digressions, and swellings of style: to return back to the primitive purity, and shortness, when man deliver'd so many things, almost in an equal number of words" (p. 113).

The members of the society preferred "the language of
Artizans, Countrymen, and Merchants, before that, of
Wits, or Scholars" (p. 113). This is relevant to Morris W.
Croll's thesis (3.75) concerning the rise of Anti-
Ciceronianism. Still, argues that "the Greeks spoke best,
when they were in their glory of conquest" (p. 41), which
statement is open to a number of interpretations. Facsimile edition contains an introduction (27 pp.), notes, and
appendixes (78 pp.). See also Cope, 3.69.

3.38 1668. JOHN WILKINS. An Essay Toward a Real Character, And a
Philosophical Language. London, 471 pp.
    A Royal Society publication. Date of composition should
be somewhat earlier as Wilkins complains about losing much
of the work in the London fire. Extensive tables. An
attempt to construct a new universal language. About this,
Wilkins confidently claims that "a man of ordinary capacity
may more easily learn to express himself this [new] way in
one Month, than he can by the Latin in fourty Months"
(p. 454). Next to Spratt (3.37), the most popular example
of Royal Society experiments with language.

3.39 1672. JOHN MILTON. Artis Logicae Plenior Institutio.
London.
    Begins with the standard Ramist definition, "Logica est
ars bene ratiocinandi" (3.39a, p. 18), except in the word
Logica which replaces Dialectica. Differs from Ramist
texts in that there is considerable explication linking
precept and example. Contains "An analytic praxis and a
life of Peter Ramus," which is based on Friege. See Ong,
3.170.

3.39a   A fuller institution of the Art of Logic, arranged after
the method of Peter Ramus, by John Milton, an Englishman,
in The Works of John Milton. Edited and translated by
Allan H. Gilbert. Vol. 2. New York: Columbia University
Press, 1935, 553 pp.
    Contains the complete 1672 text in the original Latin
with English translation on facing pages. Contains notes
on the text (17 pp.).

3.40 1676. BERNARD LAMY, trans. The Art of Speaking. London.
    The first English version of what was mistakenly
attributed to the "Messieurs Du Port Royal." The original
(Paris, 1675) was really a compromise between the Ramist
and the Port Royal points of view (Howell, 3.114, pp. 379-80).
In discussing style, Lamy says that "Poets are desirious
[sic] to delight and surprise us by things that are great,
wonderful, extraordinary: they cannot arrive at their
designed end, unless they maintain the grandeur of things
by the grandeur of words. All that they say being

extraordinary, their expressions . . . ought likewise to be extraordinary; for this cause in Poetry we say nothing without Hyberboles and metaphors" (p. 24). Orators, philosophers, and historians, on the other hand, should remember that "excess of Ornaments keeps the mind of the hearer from being intent upon the substance" (p. 257). Discourse is divided into the five traditional parts. Even though Lamy was not a Port Royalist, this work represents what Englishmen considered to be the Port Royal view of rhetoric.

3.41 1678. JOSEPH GLANVILLE. An Essay Concerning Preaching. London, 113 pp.

Not a rhetoric, but an essay on rhetorical theory. Howell (3.114, p. 394) indicates that the four major rules Glanville has for rhetoric prescribe that it be plain, practical, methodical, and affectionate, but plainness of style is of major importance to Glanville. He argues against the use of figurative language in preaching, especially because "our ends are far greater, and nobler, and so should we speak not as pleasing men, but God" (p. 23). In part, a religious or theological argument against eloquence.

Secondary Works

3.42 ADOLPH, ROBERT. The Rise of the Modern Prose Style.
Cambridge, Mass. and London, England: The MIT Press,
Massachusetts Institute of Technology, 1968, 384 pp.
    Examines shift in English prose style during the Restora-
tion. Argues that "the evidence suggests strongly that the
ultimate influence on the new prose is neither 'science'
nor 'Anti-Ciceronianism' but the new utilitarianism around
which the values of the age are integrated" (p. 6). Concentrates on Bacon, Browne, Glanville, Sprat, and Wilkins
to provide support (p. 6). Compares translations by suc-
cessive translators of identical passages. Appendix: "The
Style of Tacitus." Index.

3.43 ALTMAN, JOEL B. The Tudor Play of Mind: Rhetorical Inquiry
and the Development of Elizabethan Drama. Berkeley:
University of California Press, 1978, 416 pp.
    An attempt to consider rhetoric's "deeper resonances
in the minds which were fashioned by it, and to come to
some better understanding of what this meant for the
dramatic literature such minds produced" (p. 3). Discusses drama in the period as dialectic, or "as a medium
of liberal inquiry, in both the sociological and the cognitive sense" (p. 389). Makes an interesting distinction
that: "While it is true that logic, rhetoric, and poetry
may be applied to both good and evil ends, nonetheless as
arts they may be cultivated without immediate and obvious
reference to external cultural values" (p. 389). A recent
example of application of rhetorical theory to literary
research and analysis. Some illustrative chapter titles:
"Demonstrative and Explorative: Two Paradigms," "The
Method Staged: Debate Plays by Heywood and Rastell," and
"Quaestiones Copiosae: Pastoral and Courtly in John Lyly."
The introduction (11 pp.) provides overview. Index.

3.44 ANDERSON, FLOYD DOUGLAS. "Dispositio in the Preaching of Hugh
Latimer." SM, 35 (1968), 451-61.

Argues that although Latimer's sermons are generally
discussed in terms of their extemporaneous quality, they
are structured: "In this paper I shall endeavor to show
the extent to which Latimer's methods of sermon arrangement
were influenced by the notions of sermon construction that
were prevalent in the Middle Ages" (p. 452). The structure
consisted of the following: "theme, protheme, prayer,
division, and discussion" (p. 461). An indication of how
medieval rhetorical notions persisted into the Renaissance.

3.45 ASHWORTH, E. J. Language and Logic in the Post-Medieval
Period. Dordrech, Holland and Boston, Mass.: D. Reidel
Publishing Company, 1974, 325 pp.
Included here as an illustration of why this bibliography
is of rhetoric and not logic. The first 185 pages are significant in coming to terms with Renaissance logic from the
viewpoint of a twentieth century logician. Gives note-
worthy attention to Walter J. Ong (3.170). Extensive, but
not annotated, bibliography of primary sources includes
Agricola, Averroes, Blundeville, and Ramus--all names familiar to rhetoricians; it excludes Fraunce, Wilson, and
Erasmus. Furthermore, includes important figures in the
field of Renaissance logic that a rhetorician would rightly
consider obscure: Menghus Blanchellus (1542), Richard
Crakanthorpe (London, 1622), and Petrus Tartaretus (Basel,
1515?). It should be noted that the majority of dates indicated are either remarkably close to Ramus's first edition (1543), or later.

3.46 BALDWIN, CHARLES SEARS. Renaissance Literary Theory and
Practice: Classicism in the Rhetoric and Poetic of Italy,
France, and England, 1400-1600. Edited with Introduction
by Donald Lemen Clark. Morningside Heights, N.Y.: Columbia
University Press, 1939, 266 pp.
Concentrates on literary use of Aristotelian and
Ciceronian rhetoric and of classical poetic in general.
Poetic is emphasized; yet "even to the end of the six-
teenth century, Renaissance Poetic was largely rhetoric"
(p. 189). No mention of Ramism as this work concentrates
on traditional rhetoric.

3.47 BALDWIN, T. W. William Shakespere's Small Latine and Lesse
Greeke. 2 vols. Urbana: University of Illinois Press,
1944, 1549 pp.
Massive and lively contribution to rhetorical as well as
to intellectual history. Argues that Shakespeare's Latin
was considerable. "Evolution of the Grammar School"
(vol. 1, 75-463) discusses Erasmus, education of Tudor
monarchs, and the schools under Elizabeth I. "Shakespere's
Grammar School Training" discusses those schools in minute
detail, including the rent schoolmasters paid (vol. 1, 474).

No record that Shakespeare attended any of these schools,
but his familiarity with at least one is evident (vol. 1,
464). Rhetorics described, esp. Ad Herennium, Cicero,
Susenbrotus, Erasmus, Quintilian (vol. 2, 1-238). Discusses pedagogy involved in composition. Closes with discussion of Latin and Greek. Appendixes (vol. 2, 681-720).
Indexes to footnotes (vol. 2, 721-37). General index
(vol. 2, 737-72). Frequently cited--basis for Sister
Miriam Joseph's work (3.133) which says that Baldwin
"adduced evidence to prove not only that Shakespeare had
a thorough and systematic knowledge of rhetoric and logic,
but also that he gained this knowledge from the Latin
textbooks" (p. ix).

3.48 BARISH, JONAS A. "Prose as Prose," in his Ben Jonson and the
      Language of Prose Comedy. Cambridge: Harvard University
      Press, 1967, pp. 41-89.
          Discusses Jonson's use of prose in connection with
      Morris W. Croll's (3.75) use of the term "Baroque."
      Disjunctive nature of Jonson's prose. "The asymmetrical
      tactics that pervade his writing form a rhetoric distinct
      from, and as distinct as, any of the more orthodox rhet-
      orics, an antirhetorical rhetoric that seeks to disguise
      itself almost as a nonrhetoric" (p. 76). See also Wallace,
      3.219, and Jardine, 3.122.

3.49 BARNARD, H[OWARD] C. The French Tradition in Education:
      Ramus to Mme Necker De Saussure. 1922; Reprinted:
      Cambridge, England: Cambridge University Press, 1970,
      333 pp.
          Often cited. Two chapters of special relevance: "The
      University of Paris (1)--Ramus" (pp. 1-38), and "The Ora-
      torian Schools" (pp. 145-83). On Ramus: "In Ramus perished
      the greatest French thinker of the sixteenth century. He
      inevitably invites contrast with his contemporary Montaigne"
      (p. 29). Argues that Ramus is more "serious" than Montaigne.
      Surveys education and rhetoric through the eighteenth cen-
      tury. Bibliography. Index.

3.50 BARNER, WILFRIED. Barockrhetorik: Untersuchungen zu ihren
      geschichtlichen Grundlagen. Tübingen: Max Niemeyer Verlag,
      1970, 557 pp.
          Contains fairly extensive (33 pp.) bibliography of
      secondary material, chiefly in German. Also, somewhat
      annotated bibliography (31 pp.) of primary sources.
      Nominally a survey of the rhetorical influence behind
      German baroque literature, but also a detailed survey of
      rhetorical traditions and practices in Germany during the
      Renaissance. Topics discussed include Nietzsche's role in
      the discussion of baroque style and rhetoric; also, baroque
      rhetoric and the rhetorical tradition, theater and rhetoric,

controversies in the schools concerning rhetoric, and the role of the Jesuits. Index.

3.51 BARON, HANS. "Leonardo Bruni: 'Professional Rhetorician' or 'Civic Humanist'?" Past and Present, 36 (1967), 21-37.
      The final installment in a controversy that involved Hans Baron and Jerrold Seigel directly and Paul O. Kristeller indirectly. Baron had argued in The Crisis of the Early Italian Renaissance: Civic Humanism and Republican Liberty in an Age of Classicism and Tyranny (2 vols. [Princeton, N.J.: Princeton University Press, 1955]), that Bruni was a humanist whose writings changed in tone and focus after 1402. Seigel argued in his "'Civic Humanism' or Ciceronian Rhetoric? The Culture of Petrarch and Bruni," (Past and Present, 34 [1966], 3-48), that Bruni was properly described by Kristeller as a rhetorician and that the works in question were written before 1402. Baron supplies additional support for his dating. Acerbic debate, but Baron's additional bibliographical information was substantial. See Siegel, 3.188.

3.52 BENNETT, A. L. "The Principal Rhetorical Conventions in the Renaissance Personal Elegy." SP, 51 (1954), 107-26.
      Discusses elegies with reference to the six places as discussed by Wilson, Cox, Rainolde, and Day. "The evidence of rhetorical influence rests chiefly upon three features of the personal lament: (1) the biographical method of praise; (2) the emphasis upon the cardinal virtues, and (3) the conventional themes of consolation" (p. 110).

3.53 BLENCH, J. W. Preaching in England in the Late Fifteenth and Sixteenth Centuries: A Study of English Sermons 1450-c. 1600. New York: Barnes and Noble, 1964, 394 pp.
      Extremely detailed, systematic, and extended study of preaching in general during the period, with rhetorical aspects of the subject dominant. Heavily documented (in a representative chapter of 41 pp., there are 328 footnotes) chiefly with primary sources, many in manuscript. Discusses two types of form, the "ancient" and the "modern," with the modern representing the "influence of Aristotelian logic rather than that of the form of the ancient classical oration" (p. 72). Distinguishes three levels of style: the plain, the colloquial, and the ornate. The second of these "uses a racy and pungent speech idiom, and avoids the schemata, but is enriched by frequent homely exempla" (p. 113). Also discusses literary influence of the sermon themes. Eleven-part bibliography (pp. 350-68). Index.

3.54 BOLGAR, R. R. The Classical Heritage and Its Beneficiaries. Cambridge, England: Cambridge University Press, 1954, 600 pp.

A history of classical education that discusses rhetoric
passim, but extensively. Discusses contemporary application of classical learning. Traces influence and use of
classics from ancients through the twentieth century.
Renaissance discussed (pp. 239-379). Often cited as
valuable background. Concentrates on Latin and, to a
lesser extent, Greek. Discusses the vernacular primarily
to illustrate that, through it, "humanism was no longer the
esoteric possession of a few" (pp. 328-29). Ramism discussed very briefly and in terms of Platonic influence.
Appendixes: "Greek MSS. in Italy during the Fifteenth
Century," and "The Translations of Greek and Roman Classics before 1600." Extended (57 pp.) notes. Index (49 pp.).

3.55 BOYLE, MARJORIE O'ROURKE. Erasmus on Language and Method in
Theology. Toronto: University of Toronto Press, 1977,
231 pp.
"This book is a grammar, an exposition of the parts of
speech and the syntax of Erasmus' theological methodology"
(p. xiii). Nevertheless, chapter on "Oratio" (pp. 33-57)
states that, according to Erasmus, "oratory persuades men
sympathetically, directing their lives to faith and concord.
Dialectic traps the intellect in snarls of argumentation"
(p. 55). Extensive notes (106 pp.). Bibliography. Index.

3.56 BREDVOLD, LOUIS I. "Dryden, Hobbes, and the Royal Society,"
MP, 25 (1928), 417-38.
Although Dryden's skeptical nature was not acquired when
he was a member of the Royal Society, he agreed with many
of its ideals and goals. He was "interested in the Royal
Society . . . and recognized that he was like minded with
it; he understood the new philosophy of motion, . . . and
he rejected the dogmatic materialism of Hobbes and
Lucretius" (p. 438). Often cited, but more important for
a study of Dryden than of rhetoric or even the Royal
Society.

3.57 BREEN, QUIRINUS. "Three Renaissance Humanists on the Relation
of Philosophy and Rhetoric," in Christianity and Humanism:
Studies in the History of Ideas. Grand Rapids, Mich.:
William B. Eerdmans, 1968, pp. 1-68.
A translation from the Latin, with introduction, of The
Correspondence of G. Pico Mirandola and Ermolao Barbaro concerning the Relation of Philosophy and Rhetoric. Translates Melanchthon's Reply to Pico. Essentially, Pico found
philosophy superior to rhetoric, Ermalco felt the two were
potentially harmonious, and Melanchthon found rhetoric
superior to philosophy (pp. 1-2).

3.58 BROADBENT, J. B. "Milton's Rhetoric," MP, 56 (1959), 224-42.
"I am mainly concerned with schemes: that is, non-
tropical arrangements of words and syntax having a prosodic

and therefore often a semantic effect" (p. 226). After
listing and defining what "branches of rhetoric" he omits
(including forensic figures and prose schemes), he discusses Milton's use of eloquence, defining terms as he
proceeds. Indicates that "Milton was writing at a time
when rhetoric had overripened and was about to fall away
altogether for a long time" (p. 240).

3.59 BUSH, DOUGLAS. "Bibliography," in his English Literature in
the Earlier Seventeenth Century, 1600-1660. Second edition,
revised. New York and Oxford: Oxford University Press,
1962, pp. 461-668.
An extended bibliographical essay that covers many relevant works not included in this bibliography, and Bush
indicates that "a great deal of more or less important
material is necessarily omitted" (p. 461). The first edition was published in 1945 as the first of this well-known
series, but was extensively revised for this second edition.

3.60 CAMDEN, CARROLL. "Memory, The Warder of the Brain." PQ, 18
(1939), 52-72.
Discusses natural and artificial memory, various theories
as to the exact location of the memory in the brain, and
theories of how memory works. Discusses theories concerning
poor memory and loss of memory current during the Renaissance,
including phlegm and melancholy, physiological cures, and
memory aids. Describes systems of Simonides, Quintilian,
Lull, and Peter of Ravenna. Describes some Elizabethan
versions including William Fulwood's The Castle of Memory
(1562), and Copland's Phoenix. Other authors: Alexander
Dickson, Giordano Bruno, Thomas Nashe, Henry Cornelius
Agrippa, and Francis Bacon. Memory systems popular as a
"short cut to knowledge" (p. 72).

3.61 CARPENTER, FREDERIC IVES, ed. "Introduction," in Leonard Cox:
The Arte or Crafte of Rhetoryke. Chicago: The University
of Chicago Press, 1899, pp. 7-34.
Carpenter's introduction (21 pp.) gives a biography,
dates work, discusses work, places work in historical context, gives Melanchthon's outline. Includes the invention
portion of Melanchthon's Institutiones Rhetoricae, in Latin.
Contains notes to Cox (pp. 103-12). Glossarial index.

3.62 CLARK, DONALD LEMEN. "Ancient Rhetoric and English Renaissance
Literature." SQ, 2 (1951), 195-204.
Indicates the scope of rhetorical studies with a list of
full-length works dealing primarily with rhetorical principles. Discusses pervasiveness of rhetoric in the English
Renaissance. Offers a one-paragraph definition of rhetoric
as understood during the period (p. 197). Surveys parts of
rhetoric, parts of an oration. Discussion of influence

of Shakespeare and Milton among others. Discusses declama-
tion and argument. Authors discussed include Cicero,
Quintilian, William Chappell, Fletcher and Massinger, and
Spenser. A brief introduction to, or summary of, the field.

3.63   CLARK, DONALD LEMEN. John Milton at St. Paul's School: A
       Study of Ancient Rhetoric in English Renaissance Education.
       New York: Columbia University Press, 1948, 283 pp.
          Describes St. Paul's, its statutes, schoolmasters, and
       curriculum. Discusses textbooks. Rhetorics surmised to be
       Talaeus's, Butler's, or Farnaby's. Compares them. De-
       scribes "Latin Epistle" (pp. 131-51). Surveys Progymnasmata
       with examples from Milton and constant reference to Lorich.
       Gives rhetoric a broad definition: grammar, rhetoric, and
       logic "are all arts of communication in language" (p. 5).
       Emphasis on Milton as a Ramist.

3.64   CLARK, DONALD LEMEN. Rhetoric and Poetry in the Renaissance:
       A Study of Rhetorical Terms in English Literary Criticism.
       New York: Columbia University Press, 1922, 174 pp.
          "In view of . . . modern efforts to make a more scien-
       tific differentiation between kinds of literature than is
       possible on the basis of the traditional distinction be-
       tween prose and poetry, the present historical study of
       the distinction made by Aristotle and other Greek writers
       between rhetoric and poetic may be suggestive" (p. 9). Con-
       tains author index and chapter called "Logic and Rhetoric
       in the English Renaissance" (19 pp.).

3.65   CLARK, DONALD LEMEN. "The Rise and Fall of Progymnasmata in
       Sixteenth and Seventeenth Century Grammar Schools." SM,
       19 (1952), 259-63.
          Background on Progymnasmata, especially Apthonius's
       (cf. Rainolde, 3.12). Points out that Latin versions of
       Apthonius's Greek work were popular because of the graded
       series of examples. Describes examples by type. Describes
       popularity of Mosellanus, Cantanaeus, and Agricola. Lists
       editions and dates. Indicates 1681 (which Howell, 3.114,
       gives as the termination date of Ramus's domination) as the
       "end of the Apthonian epoch" (p. 263). Lists editions of
       Lorich.

3.66   CLARKE, M. L. Classical Education in Britain, 1500-1900.
       Cambridge: Cambridge University Press, 1959, 242 pp.
          Survey of textbooks, statutes, teachers, and students in
       England--the first 84 pp. most relevant. General back-
       ground of humanism. Colet's statutes. Argues that while
       most theory preferred use of Christian writers, in practice
       the pagan writers dominated. Describes Ascham and Erasmus
       as early influences. Discusses importance of Ad Herennium,
       Progymnasmata, and De Copia, and also John Fisher and the

introduction of Greek in the curriculum (p. 24). Describes
debate over Greek pronunciation (pp. 24-28); also
Elizabeth I and humanist progress. States that "the
seventeenth century was on the whole a period of steady
progress on the lines already laid down in the previous
century" (p. 34). Milton's approach to education
(pp. 37-38). Discusses conversation books and Latin. In
the seventeenth century, even though "logic and moral philosophy" were most important, "academic occasions were
adorned with ornate Latin speeches which showed the wit
and classical learning of the orator and his hearers"
(p. 66). Eighteenth century covered in six pages.

3.67 CLEARY, JAMES W., ed. "Editor's Introduction," in Chirologia:
      or the Natural Language of the Hand (and) Chironomia: or
      the Art of Manual Rhetoric, by John Bulwer. Carbondale
      and Edwardsville, Ill.: Southern Illinois University Press,
      1974, pp. xiii-xxxix.
          Cleary's preface (pp. ix-xii) states that "the present
      edition consists of a modernized text accompanied by a set
      of general notes. While the text derives from the 1644
      editio princeps of the Chirologia . . . Chironomia printed
      by Tho. Harper, the new edition is complete save for
      the frontispieces which have been deleted. The general
      notes are both editorial and exegetical in nature, and,
      basically, serve either to identify textual alterations or
      to clarify obscure terms or statements" (pp. ix-x).

3.68 COHEN, MURRAY. "Language and the Grammar of Things, 1640-
      1700," in his Sensible Words: Linguistic Practice in
      England, 1640-1785. Baltimore: The Johns Hopkins Univer-
      sity Press, 1977, pp. 1-42.
          Argues from the perspective of the eighteenth century
      and finds fault with Richard Foster Jones's work (3.127
      and 3.131) for overlooking the strength of the scientific
      spirit through the eighteenth century (esp. pp. xiv-xv).
      Discusses the various attempts made at reformation of
      language. Emphasis is on a linguistic approach. Includes
      some facsimile pages from texts.

3.69 COPE, JACKSON I. "Introduction," in History of the Royal
      Society by Thomas Sprat. Edited by Jackson I. Cope and
      Harold Whitmore Jones. St. Louis: Washington University
      Press; London: Routledge and Kegan Paul, 1958,
      pp. xii-xxxii.
          Indicates that this edition is prepared because Sprat's
      work is not easily available otherwise and because misquota-
      tions from it have "resulted in more than one startling
      conclusion in print" (p. v). Discusses Sprat in historical
      context. Points to Sprat's patriotic intentions. Dis-
      cusses Sprat's views on language (pp. xxv-xxx). Appendixes

include "Origins of the Royal Society" (pp. 65-67), "After-
math: Stubbe's Attacks on the Royal Society" (pp. 68-74),
and, by H. W. Jones, "Archives Version of Hooke's 'Method
for Making a History of the Weather,'" (pp. 75-78). Pref-
atory material in Roman numerals, text in original pagination, notes and appendices in Arabic numerals.

3.70 COPE, JACKSON I. "Ramist Implications," in The Metaphoric
Structure of Paradise Lost. Baltimore: The Johns Hopkins
Press, 1962, pp. 27-49.
    Summarizes the debate over Ramism's impact on seventeenth-
century thought: Rosemond Tuve (3.208) excluded Milton
from Ramus's influence (p. 29), and George Watson (3.224)
countered that Sidney, Jonson, and Milton were the sole
English Ramist poets (p. 29). Perry Miller (3.158)
avoided Ramism's "more profound literary implications,"
but Charles Feidelson, Jr. in his Symbolism and American
Literature (Chicago: University of Chicago Press, 1953),
indicated that Ramism "prevents" metaphysical poetry (p. 31).
Walter J. Ong's (3.170, 3.172, et al.) thesis is that
"Ramism was the Renaissance manifestation in which Europe
saw the Scholastic revolution completed, the revolution
converting the ancient aural world into the spatial world
of the printed book, into the mechanistic Newtonian uni-
verse, into a pattern of dichotomizing diagrams. . . ."
(p. 32). Discusses Sprat, Hobbes, Hall, Bacon, George Fox
(the Quaker), Locke, and Milton.
    Remainder of book (in all, 192 pp.) discusses Milton,
especially Paradise Lost, which he considers to be spatially
structured. Also summarizes Milton criticism (pp. 1-26).

3.71 COSTELLO, WILLIAM T., S. J. The Scholastic Curriculum at Early
Seventeenth-Century Cambridge. Cambridge: Harvard University Press, 1958, 231 pp.
    Relies heavily on seventeenth-century manuscripts to
reconstruct instructional procedure at Cambridge University.
Discusses general background, undergraduate curriculum of
the arts and the sciences, and the graduate curriculum
(i.e., the trivium and quadrivium). Points out that the
study of logic was "genuinely Aristotelian" (p. 45), and
argues that rhetoric was closely related to ethics, and
involved copying, required memorization, and fostered close
analysis of poetry (pp. 55-65). Emphasizes commonplace
books. Summary and Conclusion states that "the primary aim
at Cambridge was the acquisition of a classical, well-
rounded Latin style, with the particular purpose of success
in the public and private disputations and declamations on
which a student's preferment depended" (p. 148). Bibliography, chiefly manuscripts (17 pp.). Notes. Index (18 pp.).
Ramism discounted as an influence on the curriculum.

3.72 CRAIG, HARDIN. The Enchanted Glass: The Elizabethan Mind in
      Literature. New York: Oxford University Press, 1936,
      307 pp.
          Discusses rhetoric and its influence on Renaissance
      authors passim, but two chapters concentrate on the sub-
      ject. Chapter 6, "The Well of Democritus," (pp. 139-59)
      concentrates on logic and Ramist influence: "Ramist
      logic . . . became one of the principal channels through
      which school learning manifested itself in literature"
      (p. 142). Indicates that medieval rhetoric had "narrowed
      its ground to mere ornamentation" (p. 142). Chapter 7,
      "The Eloquence of Persuasion" (pp. 160-81), concentrates
      on persuasion and stresses the wide currency and influence
      that rhetoric had in the period. Aristotle and Quintilian,
      as well as Wilson, discussed as forces in eloquence and
      persuasion. Index. P. A. Duhamel (3.83) says Craig sug-
      gests that Ramus "thought of himself as a friend of Aris-
      totle, simplifying and clarifying the logic and rhetoric
      which had become obscured" (p. 163).

3.73 CRANE, WILLIAM G[ARRETT]. Wit and Rhetoric in the Renaissance:
      The Formal Basis of Elizabethan Prose Style. Morningside
      Heights, N.Y.: Columbia University Press, 1937, 291 pp.
          An early general survey of rhetoric in the sixteenth and
      seventeenth centuries with an emphasis on amplification.
      "According to . . . [Ramus's] view, the rhetorical devices
      of chief interest to this [Crane's] study, those most used
      for amplifying and adorning themes, fall under the heading
      'logic'" (p. 55). Originally intended as a study relating
      to Donne's use of the word "wit." Appendixes (44 pp.) of
      "passages cited" throughout--almost exclusively in English
      or English translation. Discussion of rhetoric as it
      appears and is used in courtesy books, essays, the "Sen-
      timental Novel and Romance" (pp. 102-78), and elsewhere.
      T. W. Baldwin (3.47), in reference to Crane's discussion
      of Sherry, says "he does not give the evidence on which his
      conclusions are based" (p. 37), but treats Crane's discus-
      sion as valuable throughout.

3.74 CROLL, MORRIS W. "Attic Prose: Lipsius, Montaigne, Bacon,"
      in "Attic" and Baroque Prose Style: The Anti-Ciceronian
      Movement (Essays by Morris W. Croll). Edited by J. Max
      Patrick and Robert O. Evans, with John M. Wallace.
      Princeton, N.J.: Princeton University Press, 1969,
      pp. 167-206.
          Essay first published in Schelling Anniversary Papers by
      His Former Students (New York: The Century Company, 1923),
      pp. 117-50. Collection first published 1966, first paper-
      back 1969.
          Justus Lipsius "provided the model of a Stoic style"
      (p. 177) that became standard during the seventeenth century

even though he wrote in Latin. Montaigne's impact is "due in large measure to the fact that he was the first of the Anti-Ciceronian leaders to use a vernacular language in his writings, and this is so great a point of difference that it cannot be passed over in a discussion of seventeenth-century prose style" (p. 181). States that: "Bacon's great service to English prose was that he naturalized a style in which ingenious obscurity and acute significance are the appropriate garb of the mysteries of empire, and by means of his example the Tacitean strain became familiar to many English writers . . ." (p. 195). In short, "the Anti-Ciceronian leaders--Montaigne, Charron, Pasquier in France, Bacon, Hall, Jonson, Wotton in England--are the actual founders of modern prose style in their respective languages" (p. 184).

3.75 CROLL, MORRIS W. "'Attic Prose' in the Seventeenth Century." SP, 18 (1921), 79-128.
Bulk of discussion is on classical authors, especially the Greeks. Distinguishes between "Attic" and "Asiatic" style: "in the controversies of the Anti-Ciceronians 'Attic style' means . . . the genus humile or subtile, 'Asiatic' describes the florid, oratorical style of Cicero's early orations or any style ancient or modern distinguished by the same copious periodic form and the Gorgianic figures that attend upon it" (p. 96).

3.76 CROSS, MORRIS W. "The Baroque Style in Prose," in "Attic" and Baroque Prose Style: The Anti-Ciceronian Movement (Essays by Morris W. Croll). Edited by J. Max Patrick and Robert O. Evans, with John Wallace. Princeton, N.J.: Princeton University Press, 1969, pp. 207-33.
Discusses the two forms of the "Attic" or "baroque" (the two terms are synonyms; "baroque" replacing "Attic" in later works by Croll) prose style: "the first we will call, by a well-known seventeenth-century name, the période coupée, or, in an English equivalent, the 'curt period' (so also the stile coupé, or the 'curt style'); the other by the name of the 'loose period' (and the 'loose style'); though several other appropriate titles suggest themselves in each case" (p. 211). Quotes and analyzes Montaigne, Burton, Browne, as examples of the curt style.

3.77 CROLL, MORRIS W. "Justus Lipsius and the Anti-Ciceronian Movement at the End of the 16th and the Beginning of the 17th Century." Translated and summarized by J. Max Patrick, in "Attic" and Baroque Prose Style: The Anti-Ciceronian Movement (Essays by Morris W. Croll). Edited by J. Max Patrick and Robert O. Evans, with John Wallace. Princeton, N.J.: Princeton University Press, 1969, pp. 1-44.

Pagination corresponds with that in French in an earlier
(1966) edition; actually 14 pages. English summary of this
influential early essay. Patrick's note: "Revue du
Seizième Siècle, II (July, 1914), 200-242; reprinted in
Style, Rhetoric, and Rhythm, pp. 7-44 (in French), ed.
John M. Wallace" (pp. 7-8). Patrick's foreword reads:
"Essentially, Croll's idea here is that instead of sub-
ordinating ideas, spontaneity, and feelings to Ciceronian
externals, forms, and dictates, men like Lipsius, Muret,
and Bacon imitated Latin authors of the Silver Age, especially Seneca and Tacitus, who adjusted, manipulated, and
subordinated form to make it answer the fire and feeling of
a mind in the process of thinking" (p. 6). See also
Patrick, 3.175.

3.78 CROSS, MORRIS W. "Muret and the History of 'Attic' Prose."
      PMLA, 39 (1924), 254-309.
          Discusses Ciceronianism and Anti-Ciceronianism in the
      sixteenth century. Argues that in 1572, Marc-Antoine
      Muret "had reached the climax of a long development"
      (p. 291) as an Anti-Ciceronian. Various of Croll's works
      are often cited.

3.79 DAVIDSON, HUGH M. Audience, Words and Art: Studies in
      Seventeenth-Century French Rhetoric. Columbus: Ohio
      State University Press, 1965, 201 pp.
          Seven independent but related essays with a summary
      chapter. Author states in his preface that "I have tried
      to do four things: (1) to recover the crucial steps in
      the attempt to reconstitute rhetoric as a discipline for
      France and for the French Language in the seventeenth cen-
      tury (Chapters I-II); (2) to analyze the opposition to that
      attempt as it appears in the Logique of Port-Royal (Chap-
      ters III-IV); (3) to show how Pascal . . . invented an art
      of persuasion which is reflected in the Lettres provinciales
      especially, but also in the Pensées (Chapter V); and (4) to
      compare and contrast the ways in which . . . the audi-
      ence . . . becomes specified in the minds of Corneille,
      Racine and Molière as they write and defend their dramatic
      works (Chapter VI)" (p. vii). Elocution slighted by Port-
      Royalists. Bibliography. Index.

3.80 DENEEF, A. LEIGH. "Epideictic Rhetoric and the Renaissance
      Lyric." JMRS, 3 (1973), 203-31.
          Begins with Aristotle and surveys types of epideictic
      literature. Compares Wilson and Cox. Discusses Farnaby,
      giving special importance to his synoptic charts. Dis-
      cusses Puttenham. Concludes that "a fuller understanding
      of the development of the epideictic tradition may provide
      the historical framework within which that ceremonial nature
      can be more carefully and profitably defined. There is

still much to be learned about this rhetorical genre, but
the material available seems fruitful indeed" (p. 231).
Emphasis is significantly on epideictic rhetoric.

3.81 DODD, MARY C. "The Rhetorics in Molesworth's Edition of
      Hobbes." MP, 50 (1952), 36-42.
          Another discussion of Fenner's work in the Molesworth
      edition. Dodd was anticipated by Walter J. Ong (3.166)
      and Wilbur Samuel Howell (3.166), in print at least, in
      pointing this out. Claims, however, that her recognition
      of the fact is documented in 1948 (p. 36). For Molesworth,
      see also 3.32a.

3.82 DOUGLAS, DONALD G., ed. Philosophers on Rhetoric: Traditional
      and Emerging Views. Skokie, Ill.: National Textbook Com-
      pany, 1973, 273 pp.
          A casebook on philosophical approaches to rhetoric with
      Bacon as the earliest figure discussed. Contains relevant
      articles by Karl R. Wallace (3.219), Lester W. Thonssen
      (3.205), and Otis Munroe Walter, Jr. (3.222).

3.83 DUHAMEL, PIERRE ALBERT. "The Logic and Rhetoric of Peter
      Ramus." MP, 46 (1948-49), 163-71.
          Argues that Ramus felt his "natural method" was what
      Aristotle intended and that Cicero and Quintilian confused
      matters. Explains division between logic and rhetoric as
      logical consequences of certain principles: "that nothing
      should be included in an art unless it is universally true,
      unless it is homogenous with all of the art, unless it is
      proper to that art only, and unless it is primarily and
      naturally located in this art" (p. 163). Homogeneity most
      often violated in previous practice. Discusses Milton's
      Logic (3.39). Quotes Ramus (3.7) in notes. Concludes
      that "Ramus' contribution was not to the theory of rhetoric
      or of logic" but "by his translations and use of the ver-
      nacular, plus his reduction of the arts to a few principles,
      he made logic readily available to, and employed by, a
      large group of people and filled the world with logic-
      choppers" (p. 171).

3.84 DUHAMEL, P. ALBERT. "Milton's Alleged Ramism." PMLA, 67
      (1952), 1035-53.
          Surveys Milton's prose works and indicates where they
      reflect Ramist influence and where Aristotelian. Dis-
      cusses Milton's logical work and illustrates how, unlike
      Ramus's, it relates precept and example. Concludes that
      "everywhere we turn in Milton's prose we find evidence of
      his disagreement with the Ramistic belief that the mind
      reacted spontaneously when truth was presented to it be-
      cause of a point-for-point correspondence between idea and
      reality. Milton did not share the incredible optimism of

the Ramists as he did not accept the pessimism of Aristotle
in hedging the mind about in all its operations with in-
numerable safeguards against error. Taking a position
somewhere between the two, he synthesized a system of logic
and wrote in the traditional patterns of humanistic expression" (p. 1053).

3.85 DUHAMEL, P. A. "Sidney's Arcadia and Elizabethan Rhetoric."
SP, 45 (1948), 134-50.
"This paper rests on the assumption that rhetoric occu-
pies a peculiar position among the arts deriving its matter
and purpose from the more fundamental philosophical premises of the system of which it is a part and affecting the
style of a particular author" (p. 134). Compares and contrasts passages from Sidney and Lyly to Sidney's advantage.
See also King, 3.135.

3.86 DUNN, E. CATHERINE. "Lipsius and the Art of Letter-writing."
SR, 3 (1956), 145-56.
A reading of Justus Lipsius's Epistolica institutio as
intending to separate the art of letter writing from that
of oratory. Indicates three types of letters: (1) grave,
(2) learned or technical, and (3) the "genuine" or familiar
letter (pp. 151-52). Indicates that Lipsius eliminated invention and disposition from consideration (p. 152).
"Lipsius withdrew the letter from complication with the
oration and associated it with the dialogue, offering then
a consistent pattern of style in the conversational manner
of spoken discourse, and suggesting the great comic drama-
tists as models of a Latin prose at once simple, familiar,
and graceful, with the urbanity and sprightliness of truly
'Attic' speech" (p. 156). A reaction to Croll (3.74).

3.87 DUNN, CATHERINE M., ed. "Introduction," in The Logike of the
Moste Excellent Philosopher P. Ramus, Martyr: Translated
by Roland MacIlmaine (1574). Northridge, Calif.: San
Fernando Valley State College, 1969, 120 pp.
Introduction (24 pp.) provides brief but concise and
accurate overview of logic in Europe. Covers classical,
medieval, and Renaissance periods, with attention to Ramism
in England. Extensive (35 pp.) notes which identify sources
of illustrations. Bibliography.

3.88 EHNINGER, DOUGLAS. "Bernard Lami's L'Art de Parler: A Critical Analysis." QJS, 32 (1946), 429-34.
On the "Port Royal Rhetoric." Examines its influence
and publishing history. First English version in 1676, one
year after first published in France. Lami not a member of
the Port Royal. "The text of L'Art de Parler may conveniently be divided into two parts. The larger portion of it
consists of discussions which relate to the following:

(1) the physiological bases of speech, (2) functional grammar, (3) the science of poetic, (4) style, and (5) pronunciation. Appended to these discussions is a discourse on the art of persuasion" (p. 431).

3.89   FISCH, HAROLD. "The Puritans and the Reform of Prose Style." ELH, 19 (1952), 229-48.
        Supplements Perry Miller (3.158). Points out that Puritan reform of prose begins with Lawrence Chaderton in 1578. Indicates that most Puritans did not publish their sermons, but that Chaderton and Rainolde did. Indicates that their remarks should be considered relatively mild. Influence of Ramism. Argues that Puritans were opposed to imagination in theory, but not always in practice. Argues that the Royal Society was closely associated with the Puritans (p. 246), and its influence on prose style was well known (p. 246). See Jones, 3.131.

3.90   FISH, STANLEY EUGENE. "The Milk of the Pure Word," in his Surprised by Sin: The Reader in Paradise Lost. New York: St. Martin's Press, 1967, pp. 57-91.
        The two most relevant subheadings to this chapter are "(i) The Formal Defence" and "(ii) the Rhetorical Defence." An example: "The formal proof of deity, rigorously non-rhetorical, becomes part of the rhetorical proof (in Stoic-Ramus theory the oratorical and philosophical ideals tend to merge)" (p. 80). Emphasis in these early sections on Paradise Lost, but the rhetorical background is significant. Discusses Milton's theories on rhetoric and logic passim.

3.91   FISHER, PETER F. "Milton's Logic." JHI, 23 (1962), 37-60.
        Argues against "the suggestion that Milton's early rationalism was fundamentally at odds with the prophetic spirit of Ramist logic and its reliance on the intuitive perception of logical relations" (p. 37). In other words, "Milton gives every indication of having moved from an earlier rationalist to a later voluntarist position" (p. 37). Nowhere mentions Walter J. Ong (3.170), yet refers to Milton's Life of Ramus (p. 39). A discussion of Milton's Ramist logic which "sought to restore invention to argument and emphasize discovery as the primary basis upon which logical method depended, not only for its material but for its direction" (p. 60).

3.92   FLETCHER, HARRIS FRANCIS. The Intellectual Development of John Milton: Volume I: The Institution to 1625: From the Beginnings Through Grammar School. Urbana, Ill.: University of Illinois Press, 1956, 479 pp.
        Focus of study is Milton, but is relevant to the entire educational system of the time. This volume concentrates on the early years, that is, grammar school education, and

also as far back as the petty schools (preschool). Chapter
discussions on these languages: English, Latin, Greek,
Hebrew, Italian, French, Spanish. "There is therefore much
suggestive information concerning Milton's grammar school
period, though no documented and precise account of what
happened to the particular boy in whom we are most interested" (p. 428). Some other figures discussed are Ascham,
Bacon, D. L. Clark (3.64), Colet, Erasmus, John Florio,
Fenner, Mulcaster, Ramus, and Wilson. Bibliography. Index.

3.93 FLETCHER, HARRIS FRANCIS. The Intellectual Development of
      John Milton: Volume II: The Cambridge University Period,
      1625-32. Urbana, Ill.: University of Illinois Press,
      1961, 701 pp.
         This is a continuation of volume 1 (3.92) through
      Milton's university years. Argues that the real reason
      for the furor over Ramus's logic was its brevity (p. 143f.).
      On rhetoric: "No longer the blind following of rigid rules
      as in grammar school, nevertheless rhetoric was peculiar
      because it was always pervasively applied rather than
      taught as a theory, a treatment that resulted in more use
      of it, not less" (p. 201). Contains "The Surviving Written
      Pieces from the Cambridge years, 1625-32" (pp. 391-552).
      Other authors not mentioned in my annotation to volume 1
      (3.92) include Agricola, Sir John Cheke, Cicero, Farnaby,
      Talon. Contains edition of "Holdsworth's 'Directions for
      a Student in the Universitie'" (pp. 623-64), written by a
      contemporary pedagogue. Bibliography of works used.
      Index.

3.94 FRANCE, PETER. Rhetoric and Truth in France: Descartes to
      Diderot. Oxford: Oxford University Press, 1972, 290 pp.
         Focus is on rhetoric in France in the seventeenth and
      eighteenth centuries, but much of the work also applies
      to England. Chapter "Theory: Rhetoric in the ancien
      regime," discusses general theory and also acts as a sum-
      mary. Bibliographical Essay. Index.

3.95 FRENCH, J. MILTON. "Milton, Ramus, and Edward Philips." MP,
      47 (1949-50), 82-87.
         Asserts that Edward Philips's Mysteries of love and
      eloquence (1658) is plagiarized from Robert Fage's transla-
      tion of Ramus.

3.96 GILBERT, ALLAN H. "Logic in the Elizabethan Drama." SP, 32
      (1935), 527-45.
         Early study of the use of logic as a literary device in
      Elizabethan drama. Logic often indicates "a man of educa-
      tion" (p. 528). Indicates that logic was also used to por-
      tray a comic pedant (p. 545). Concludes that "the genius
      of the age favored logical expression and must be invoked

by any one who will appreciate the appearance in drama of the terms of the schools" (p. 545).

3.97 GILBERT, NEAL W. Renaissance Concepts of Method. New York: Columbia University Press, 1969, 263 pp.
      A history of method both as a word and as a concept. Begins with discussion of Plato, Aristotle, and the Stoics, and their transmission through the medieval period (pp. 3-115). Part two (pp. 119-220) concentrates on the Renaissance, but seldom ranges past 1600. Emphasizes the Greek origin of method. Argues that the Humanists (especially Vives and Ramus) favored the single method whereas the traditionalists opposed this as rhetorical logic. Traditionalists favored the scientific method as more effective in developing knowledge. Bibliography. Index.

3.98 GILMAN, WILBUR ELWYN. "Milton's Rhetoric: Studies in His Defense of Liberty." University of Missouri Studies, 14, 3 (1939), 1-193.
      Discusses Milton's rhetoric in six of his pamphlets: Areopagitica, Of Education, Of Reformation, Of Civil Power in Ecclesiastical Causes, The Tenure of Kings and Magistrates, and The Readie and Easie Way to Establish a Free Commonwealth. The general drift of Gilman's argument is that Milton was not primarily a Ramist: index does not even mention the name.

3.99 GRAVES, FRANK PIERREPONT. Peter Ramus and the Educational Reformation of the Sixteenth Century. New York: The Macmillan Co., 1912, 238 pp.
      An early biography and analysis. Biography subscribes to the legend that Charpentier ordered Ramus's assassination and accepts most of Freigius's statements as factual (cf. Ong, 3.170). Discussion of Ramus's work and influence (pp. 108-218) includes charts in English translation. Covers Ramus's reforms in all areas, including grammar and mathematics. Index.

3.100 HALLAM, GEORGE W. "Sidney's Supposed Ramism," in Renaissance Papers, 1963. Japan: The Southeastern Renaissance Conference, Charles E. Tuttle Company, 1964, pp. 11-20.
       "Sidney may have believed Peter Ramus to be the best writer on the art of logic, but so long as he had any of the poetic in him, he parted company with the Ramists themselves" (p. 20). Discussion of the Defence in connection with Temple's Analysis tractionis de poesie contextae a nobilissimo viro Phillipo Sidneio Equite Aurato. Highly indebted to J. P. Thorne (3.206).

3.101 HAMILTON, K. G. The Two Harmonies: Poetry and Prose in the Seventeenth Century. Oxford: At the Clarendon Press, 1963, 226 pp.

Discusses rhetoric as background to seventeenth-century
poets, especially Dryden. Discusses "The Proper Style in
Poetry and Prose" (pp. 1-44): concern is with development
of the "plain style." From 1575, prose was characterized
by Euphuism, then became Senecan, and by the end of the seventeenth century became simple and plain. Poetry moved from
Spenserian in style through Metaphysical to simple and
plain (6-7). Discusses "Poetry and Rhetoric" (pp. 45-94)
and traces "the origins of this association of poetry with
the subjects of the classical trivium" (p. 46). States
that "in the later years of the sixteenth century the
rhetorical texts were almost without exception" Ramist
(p. 86). The basic thesis is that "the prevailing concept
of verbal utility" changed from verbal to spatial "analogies" (p. 196). Accepts, in other words, Walter J. Ong's
(3.170) thesis. Bibliography. Index.

3.102 HANNA, ROBERT. "Francis Bacon, The Political Orator," in
       Studies in Rhetoric and Public Speaking in Honor of James
       Albert Winans by Pupils and Colleagues. Edited by A. M.
       Drummond. New York: Russell and Russell, 1962, pp. 91-132.
       Relates Bacon's rhetorical theory to his practice.
       Argues that Bacon constructed his rhetorical theory using
       the classical rhetoricians as a basis, "but his theory was
       constructed, essentially, to meet his own needs as a speaker.
       With Bacon, theory and practice were never completely dis-
       sociated. It is the intimate connection of theory and
       practice which . . . accounts in large part, we [Hanna]
       believe, for his great success as a speaker" (p. 132).
       Supported with discussions of Bacon's speeches. Argues
       for Aristotle's influence, while conceding Cicero's.

3.103 HARDISON, O. B., JR. "The Orator and the Poet: The Dilemma
       of Humanist Literature." JMRS, 1 (1971), 33-44.
       "What the humanists symbolize by their near identifica-
       tion of the orator and the poet is an ideal harmony of
       power and beauty. It is a seductive ideal which retained
       its force throughout the Renaissance" (p. 38). Discusses
       briefly Petrarch, Spenser, and Milton; relates the distinc-
       tion between poetry and oratory to the distinction between
       the contemplative and active lives, respectively. Suggests
       Kant freed art from its practical obligations (pp. 43-44).

3.104 HARDISON, O. B., JR. The Enduring Monument: A Study of the
       Idea of Praise in Renaissance Literary Theory and Practice.
       Chapel Hill: The University of North Carolina Press, 1962,
       254 pp.
       Emphasis is on poetry in the Renaissance, but with per-
       vasive attention to rhetorical influence, especially Aris-
       totle's. Discusses Renaissance theories of Epideictic
       poetry. Most relevant is the second chapter, "Rhetoric,

Poetics, and the Theory of Praise." Discusses
Progymnasmata, Puttenham, Scalinger (esp. 109 ff.).
Appendix: lists of "Epideictic Types" from Menander and
Scalinger. Index.

3.105 HARRIER, RICHARD. "Invention in Tudor Literature: Historical
Perspectives," in Philosophy and Humanism: Renaissance
Essays in Honor of Paul Oskar Kristeller. Edited by
Edward P. Mahoney. New York: Columbia University Press,
1976, pp. 370-86.
"Our [Harrier's] aim will be two-fold: first, to consider the inability and reluctance of literary historians
to meet the challenge presented by a rhetorical literature;
and second, to outline some evidence of qualitative change
within the unbroken continuity of Tudor rhetorical practice" (p. 371). This volume contains the relevant "Bibliography of the Publications of Paul Oskar Kristeller for
the Years 1929-1974," (pp. 543-89). Also: "Paul Oskar
Kristeller and His Contribution to Scholarship" (pp. 1-18).

3.106 HARRISON, JOHN L. "Bacon's View of Rhetoric, Poetry, and the
Imagination." HLQ, 20 (1957), 107-25. Reprinted in
Essential Articles for the Study of Francis Bacon. Edited
by Brian Vickers. Hamden, Conn.: 1968, pp. 253-71.
Makes three main points: "(a) Bacon's interest in
allegory and myth tended to preserve . . . imagination
whereby poetry could still bind, by an idealistic verisi-
militude, images of things . . . (b) his linking of divine
illumination and poetry [etc.] . . .; and (c) his acknowl-
edgment of the large role Imagination played in both poetry
and rhetoric, authorized its importance in matters political
and ethical . . . no matter what the vehicle" (p. 108).
Charts Bacon's system (p. 109). Feels that Karl R. Wallace
in his Communication and Rhetoric (3.219) denigrates Bacon's
estimation of poetry.

3.107 HEATH, TERRENCE. "Logical Grammar, Grammatical Logic, and
Humanism in Three German Universities." SR, 18 (1971),
9-64.
Frequently cited for its detailed commentary on grammar
and logic, but not focused on rhetoric. Considers "the
question of late medieval grammar and logic and examine[s]
the influence of humanistic thought and activity within the
traditional course of studies in these subjects. For this
purpose, I have chosen the three southern German universities of Freiburg-im-Breisgau, Ingolstadt, and Tübingen"
(p. 10), and indicates that these were typical of the period. "Positive grammar . . . supplied logic with significant terms, but was itself completed through disputation,
in which the arbiter of true and false was logic" (p. 49).
Concludes that the "formal analysis of terms and

propositions had already been weakened in the later Middle
Ages, when the determination of the suitability of a statement for use in argumentation was reassigned to the logico-
grammatical speculations of the modistae" (p. 64).
Concludes that the humanists preferred dialectic because
they felt that such rigorous logic did not apply to language. In general, relates grammar and logic in the way
that many entries relate rhetoric and poetic or rhetoric
and logic.

3.108   HERRICK, MARVIN T.   Comic Theory in the Sixteenth Century.
        1950; Reprinted: Urbana, Ill.: University of Illinois
        Press, 1964, 256 pp.
           Perhaps Herrick's central work. Reprints or restates
        some material in "The Place of Rhetoric in Poetic Theory"
        (3.110). Central argument is that rhetoricians, especially
        Donatus, were the central force at work in shaping Renais-
        sance comedy. Discusses Terence as his comedy provided the
        basis for the theories of these rhetoricians. Discounts
        Aristotle's influence, especially that of the Poetics.

3.109   HERRICK, MARVIN T.   "The Early History of Aristotle's Rhetoric
        in England." PQ, 5 (1926), 242-57.
           A survey of Aristotle's influence as seen in the work of
        Leonard Cox, Thomas Wilson, Roger Ascham, Gabriel Harvey,
        Frances Bacon, George Jewel. "By 1620 there was no excuse
        for any educated Englishman's not knowing the Rhetoric"
        (p. 257). Ignores Harvey's Ramism, and offers quotes as
        referring to Aristotle that probably refer to Ramus (p. 252).

3.110   HERRICK, MARVIN T.   "The Place of Rhetoric in Poetic Theory."
        QJS, 31 (1948), 1-22.
           Emphasis is on rhetoric and drama, in that order. Dis-
        cusses Willichius's (Zurich, 1550) commentaries on Terence,
        which commentaries were directly rhetorical. Discusses
        types of oration, parts of rhetoric, parts of an oration,
        Scalinger, Aristotle, and the like. Concludes that "clas-
        sical rhetoric was, after all, the solid basis of literary
        criticism in the sixteenth century, and classical rhetoric
        laid the foundation of the literary criticism of succeeding
        centuries" (p. 22).

3.111   HORNBEAK, KATHERINE GEE.   The Complete Letter Writer in Eng-
        lish (1568-1800), in Smith College Studies in Modern Lan-
        guages, 15. Northhampton, Mass.: The Collegiate Press,
        1934, 160 pp.
           Chapter 1 is especially relevant, discussing Day, among
        others. A fairly complete survey of collections of letters.
        Relevant to Morris W. Croll's study of Lipsius (3.74). Dis-
        cusses letter writing as a rhetorical genre. The entire
        work extends well beyond our scope (the last chapter is on

Richardson). Appendix 2 (128 ff.) is a bibliography of collections of sample letters including works by Fulwood, Abraham Fleming, Nicholas Breton, and Thomas Gainsford. Important or relevant primary material not included here. Index.

3.112   HOWARD, LEON. "'The Invention' of Milton's 'Great Argument': A Study of the Logic of 'God's Ways to Men.'" HLQ, 9 (1946), 149-73.

Deals with "(1) the general character of Milton's logic and its possible relationship to his statement of his theme and purpose in Paradise Lost, with (2) his particular analysis of the logic of causation in his treatise, and with his apparent use of that analysis in Paradise Lost in connection with (3) the 'efficient' cause, (4) cause as 'matter' and 'form,' and (5) the 'final' cause or 'end'" (p. 150). Argues that there is greater logical consistency in the poem than generally believed.

3.113   HOWELL, WILBUR SAMUEL. "The Arts of Literary Criticism in Renaissance Britain: A Comprehensive View," in his Poetics, Rhetoric, and Logic: Studies in the Basic Disciplines of Criticism. Ithaca and London: Cornell University Press, 1975, pp. 71-122.

Attacks Brian Vickers's work (3.210) as a misunderstanding of logic, and a misinterpretation of rhetoric. Suspects Vickers's Ramist sympathies at fault. Quotes Wilson and Bacon in support of Aristotle: "with Aristotle's teachings in mind, Bacon made logic the art of addressing the world of scholars, and rhetoric, the world of laymen" (p. 78). Quotes Donne as further support. Fable, or fiction, distinguishes poetry from logic and rhetoric (p. 87); supports with Sidney's Defense, Bacon, Jonson. Discusses oratory in Milton, especially Paradise Lost. Argues that to appreciate the role of rhetoric in the English Renaissance totally, one must recognize the traditionalist inclusion of invention and disposition within the area or province of rhetoric.

3.114   HOWELL, WILBUR SAMUEL. Logic and Rhetoric in England, 1500-1700. Princeton, N.J.: Princeton University Press, 1956, 421 pp.

Extended, authoritative, and detailed history of logic and rhetoric in England. Indicates that scholastic logic, through the work of John Seton and Thomas Wilson, dominated in England until 1570 when Ramism began to spread. Divides traditional or pre-Ramist rhetoric into Ciceronian, stylistic, and formulary. Ciceronian rhetorics considered all five operations, stylistic the figures, and formulary the five operations through examples. Seventeenth-century rhetorical movements included the systematics as a compromise between

scholastic and Ramist rhetoric, the Port Royal Logic, and
Bacon's Advancement of Learning. Quotes extensively from,
and gives full titles of, all chief rhetorics of the period.
Translates from Latin works passim. Index (12 pp.).

3.115 HOWELL, WILBUR SAMUEL. "Nathaniel Carpenter's Place in the
Controversy between Dialectic and Rhetoric." SM, 1 (1934),
20-41.
"Carpenter's view is of considerable interest, both for
its own sake and for other reasons. This paper presents a
translation of his essay [Logica pugno, Rhetorica palmae,
non recte a Zenone comparatur]. . . . A brief review of
his life and a comment on his interest in rhetoric precede
the translation, and the concluding part of this study discusses his argument in the light of other significant views
on the same subject" (p. 21). Carpenter opposes Zeno's
distinction of the closed fist and open palm to represent
logic and rhetoric respectively, rhetoric often being more
compact. Other authors discussed: Agricola, Ramus, Talon,
Fenner, Fraunce, Wilson (briefly), and Bacon (5 pp.).

3.116 HOWELL, WILBUR SAMUEL. "Oratory and Poetry in Fénelon's
Literary Theory," in his Poetics, Rhetoric, and Logic:
Studies in the Basic Disciplines of Criticism. Ithaca and
London: Cornell University Press, 1975, pp. 123-40. Originally published in QJS, 37 (1951), 1-10. Reprinted in
Readings in Rhetoric. Edited by Lionel Crocker and Paul A.
Carmack. Springfield, Ill.: C. C. Thomas, 1965,
pp. 242-56.
Fénelon sees oratory and poetry as "instruments of similar value in human affairs" (p. 125), and he insists that
each of them at its best teaches as well as delights
(p. 127). But he differentiates between them, nevertheless,
by allowing portraiture (the building of word pictures) to
be the essential ingredient in each, and by going on to say
that portraiture "is still more lively and stronger among
the poets than among the orators" (p. 135). "Poetry" he
adds, "differs from simple eloquence only in this: that
she paints with ecstacy and with bolder strokes." What
this distinction seems finally to mean is that the word
pictures of poetry gain their added power by virtue of
their being the lifelike representations of imagined or
fictional situations, whereas word pictures in oratory
(or in history or biography) must go no further than to be
lifelike representations of realities (p. 140). If this is
Fénelon's basic thesis, and indeed it appears to be no less
within the context of his literary theory, his distinction
between oratory and poetry is recognizably, though perhaps
somewhat reluctantly, Aristotelian.

3.117 HOWELL, WILBUR SAMUEL. "Poetics, Rhetoric, and Logic in
Renaissance Criticism," in Classical Influences on European

Culture, A.D. 1500-1700. Proceedings of an International
Conference held at King's College, Cambridge, April 1974.
Edited by R. R. Bolgar. Cambridge, England: Cambridge
University Press, 1976, pp. 155-62.
Argues that "there was in the Renaissance a literature
which owed its primary allegiance to what critics of that
time called dialectic or logic; there was a literature
which owed its primary allegiance to rhetoric, in the full
classical sense of that term; and there was a literature,
the most remarkable of all, which owed its primary allegiance to poetical theory, or to poetics" (p. 155). Argues
the importance of understanding all three allegiances.

3.118 HOWELL, WILBUR SAMUEL. "Ramus and English Rhetoric: 1574-
       1681." QJS, 37 (1951), 299-310.
       Material later included in his major work (3.114).
       Reviews Ramus's status with scholars and critics. Argues
       that 1574-1681 marks the period of Ramus's vogue and influ-
       ence in Great Britain. Describes Ramism (pp. 300-302),
       MacIlmaine (p. 303), Sherry (p. 304), Fenner (pp. 304-305),
       and Fraunce (pp. 305-306). First points to the fact that
       Hobbes's The Arte of Rhetoric (1681) was really by Fenner
       (3.18). Walter J. Ong (3.166) published the same insight
       in the same year. Discusses Royal Society (p. 310).

3.119 HOWELL, WILBUR SAMUEL. "Renaissance Rhetoric and Modern
       Rhetoric: A Study in Change," in his Poetics, Rhetoric and
       Logic: Studies in the Basic Disciplines of Criticism.
       Ithaca and London: Cornell University Press, 1975,
       pp. 141-62. First published in The Rhetorical Idiom.
       Edited by Donald C. Bryant. Ithaca: Cornell University
       Press, 1958. Reprinted in The Province of Rhetoric.
       Edited by Joseph Schwartz and John A. Rycenga. New York:
       The Ronald Press Company, 1965, pp. 292-308.
       Compares and contrasts present status and quality of
       contemporary theory and practice of oral and written com-
       munication arts and skills with those of the Renaissance,
       to the advantage of the Renaissance. Speculates that per-
       haps rhetoric "can recover some of the ground it has lost
       in the last four hundred years, if it endeavors always to
       see its present problems in the light of its long and
       illustrious history" (p. 162).

3.120 HUDSON, HOYT H. "Jewel's Oration Against Rhetoric: A Trans-
       lation." QJS, 14 (1928), 374-92.
       In his Oration: Jewel denounces rhetoric vehemently
       after announcing that he will turn his attention hereafter
       to the poets. Rhetoric is "void of dignity and reward, it
       is wholly idle, inane, futile, and trivial" (p. 379).
       Hudson suggests that the oration may be a "tour de force
       of mingled irony, burlesque, and rhetorical display, with

perhaps a modicum of serious intent" (p. 375). [Ong,
(3.172) does not list Jewel, but the attack is against
eloquence and the figures, and Jewel does oppose rhetoric
to reason (p. 387).]

3.121 JAMIESON, KATHLEEN. "Pascal vs. Descartes: A Clash Over
Rhetoric in the Seventeenth Century." CM, 43 (1976),
44-50.
Article about a resistance against the revolution in
prose style: "at the beginning of the modern scientific
age . . . Pascal . . . defended the art of persuasion from
the extinction implied by Descarte's method" (p. 44). Furthermore, "the clash between Pascal and Descartes is
arbitrated in rhetoric's favor in the influential rhetoric
text, L' Art de Parler" (p. 44). States that "Pascal set
down, in fragmentary form, a concept of persuasion which
rejected Descartes's method in favor of an enthymematic,
audience-centered, psychologically based concept. This
concept of persuasion dominates our view of rhetoric today"
(p. 50). See also Sprat (3.37).

3.122 JARDINE, LISA. Francis Bacon: Discovery and the Art of Discourse. London, New York: Cambridge University Press,
1974, 275 pp.
Provides survey of dialectic. Discusses controversy
between Temple (Ramist) and Digby (traditionalist) to
Temple's advantage. Maintains that although Bacon separated dialectic and rhetoric as did Agricola and Ramus
before Bacon, he found both to be only persuasion and,
hence, inferior to discovery (the finding of new truths).
Discusses induction, memory, and observation. Points to
and illustrates copiously Bacon's use and modification of
Aristotle. Extensive quotation from Bacon. Charts. Index.
Bibliography. Appendix on terminology.

3.123 JARDINE, LISA. "Humanism and Dialectic in Sixteenth-Century
Cambridge: A Preliminary Investigation," in Classical
Influences on European Culture, A.D. 1500-1700. Edited
by R. R. Bolgar. Cambridge, England: Cambridge University
Press, 1976, pp. 141-54.
Discusses Lorenzo Valla's Dialecticae Disputationes.
Translates passages with Latin in footnotes. Argues against
traditional thesis that Valla's intention was "to subordi-
nate dialectic to rhetoric" (p. 144). Discusses Gabriel
Harvey's orations: Ciceronianus, and Rhetor. Maintains
that Harvey felt dialectic was important and "singles out"
Agricola "as having recognised and reconstructed the Roman
view of dialectic" (p. 147). Discusses Harvey's annotation
of Quintilian as showing his debt to "Valla's Dialecticae
Disputationes and Agricola's De Inventione Dialectica"
(p. 149). States that reformed dialectic "of Valla and

Agricola modelled on Cicero and Quintilian, retained its
central position . . . in Cambridge" and that this "goes
a considerable way towards justifying the claim that this
was essentially a humanist programme of study" (p. 154).

3.124 JARDINE, LISA. "The Place of Dialectic Teaching in Sixteenth-
Century Cambridge." SRen, 21 (1974), 31-62.
    Argues that the teaching program at Cambridge was far
more flexible during the sixteenth century than generally
thought. Discusses scholastic approach and Peter of Spain.
Indicates that the trivium gradually gained in importance
so that in the period in question (1560-1590), it dominated.
Reprints student book lists and outlines of study, and
states there were "five times more dialectic handbooks as
rhetoric handbooks" (p. 46), which indicates the university's emphasis on dialectic. Agricola and then Melanchthon
were the most popular authors in this area. Agricola presented a "direct challenge" to the scholastic approach in
pedagogy (pp. 51-53). Dialectic becomes more concerned with
eloquence (p. 53). Temple and Harvey, English Ramists, further simplify dialectic (p. 59).

3.125 JOHNSON, FRANCIS R. "Introduction." The Foundacion of
Rhetorike by Richard Rainolde. New York: Scholars'
Facsimiles and Reprints, 1945, pp. iii-xxii.
    Traces briefly the influence of rhetoric on Elizabethan
literature. Describes Apthonius's Progymnasmata and indicates that Rainolde's work is an adaptation of it. Indicates Cicero was "beyond the capacity" of Elizabethan
students (p. v). Describes Renaissance views on commonplace
books. Provides brief (3 pp.) history of progymnasmata
manuals, especially Reinhard Lorich (3 pp.). Indicates
Foundacion "typical" of Elizabethan taste, but examples
are "far from literary masterpieces" (p. xvi). Brief
biography of Rainolde (2 pp.). Discusses influence of
The Foundacion.

3.126 JOHNSON, F[RANCIS] R. "Two Renaissance Textbooks of Rhetoric."
HLQ, 6 (1943), 427-44.
    Published here because World War II delayed publication
of his edition (3.12), in which it appeared as an
introduction.

3.127 JONES, RICHARD FOSTER. Ancients and Moderns: A Study of the
Battle of the Books. Washington University Studies--New
Series. Language and Literature--No. 6. St. Louis:
1936, 370 pp.
    "The present treatise aims at being a history not of
science but of the idea of science in the seventeenth century. I am interested in tracing the rise and progress of
this idea, the attitudes which supported, accompanied, or

sprang from it, and the forces which opposed it" (p. vii).
Calls those forces humanism. Focus is on primary material
in England. An expansion of earlier ideas concerning the
change in prose style in the century, but devotes considerable space to sixteenth century as well. Extensive (71 pp.)
and detailed notes discuss primary sources. No Index. A
second edition in 1961.

3.128 JONES, RICHARD F. "The Attack of Pulpit Eloquence in the
Restoration: An Episode in the Development of the Neo-
Classical Standard for Prose." JEGP, 30 (1931), 188-217.
    "It is the purpose of the present article . . . to dis-
cuss the many and earnest efforts made to impose upon sermons the same style that had been found most serviceable to
science" (p. 189). Uses 1660 as the turning point from
ornate to direct prose. Some authors involved in this
shift and discussed here include John Wilkins, Robert Boyle,
Robert South, Samuel Parker, John Eachard, Joseph Glanville,
and Robert Ferguson. An early study which lists several
primary works not included in this bibliography. Quotations
from these works serve also as annotations.

3.129 JONES, RICHARD F. "Science and English Prose Style in the
Third Quarter of the Seventeenth Century." PMLA, 45 (1930),
977-1009.
    "It is the purpose of this article to show that the
attacks on the old, as well as the formulation of a new,
style find consistent expression in those associated with
the new science" (p. 978). Discusses Bacon's influence.
Uses parallel passages from Glanville to illustrate the
brevity of his later, in contrast to his earlier, style.
Indicates this change is typical of the Royal Society's
influence: "the extent to which Glanville's style changed
under their discipline is a fair gauge of the influence
that must have been exerted upon all the members of the
society, and, through them, upon the outside world"
(p. 1009).

3.130 JONES, RICHARD F. "Science and Language in England of the
Mid-Seventeenth Century." JEGP, 31 (1932), 315-31.
    Attempts to "furnish a more substantial basis for the
theory that in the attitude of science toward language is
to be discovered the most important origin of the stylistic
reformation with which the scientists were enthusiastically
concerned" (p. 315). Also defends his theories against
Croll and Crane (pp. 328-29).

3.131 JONES, RICHARD FOSTER. The Triumph of the English Language:
A Survey of Opinions Concerning the Vernacular from the
Introduction of Printing to the Restoration. Stanford:
Stanford University Press, 1953, 353 pp.

Subtitle very descriptive; the vernacular movement
needed to contend with the issue of whether eloquence was
possible in languages other than the classical ones. Emphasis is on English. Chapter headings include "The Unelo-
quent Language," "The Misspelled Language," "The Eloquent
Language," and "The Useful Language." Extensive quotations
from primary sources; translations of Latin passages provided. Figures discussed and analyzed include Ascham,
Bacon, Blount, Cox, Day, Elyot, Harvey, John Jewel, Lever,
Lipsius, Milton, Mulcaster, Puttenham, Ramus, Sprat, Wilson
and other less important rhetoricians and grammarians.
Work "aims at being a history of ideas concerning the
English tongue--its nature, use, and improvement--during
the period 1476-1660" (p. viii). Neologizing discussed
passim and at length by primary sources. Index (15 pp.).

3.132   JONES, WILLIAM M., ed.   The Present State of Scholarship in
         Sixteenth-Century Literature. Columbia, Mo.: The Univer-
         sity of Missouri Press, 1978, 271 pp.
            Six essays concerning opportunities for further research
         in Italian, French, Spanish, English, German, and Neo-Latin
         literature. Remarks on the importance of rhetorical research
         made passim. Jones indicates that "the bibliographies,
         while making no effort at completeness, do provide the major
         tools for research and examples of current types of criti-
         cism" (p. v).

3.133   JOSEPH, SISTER MIRIAM, C. S. C.   Rhetoric in Shakespeare's
         Time: Literary Theory of Renaissance Europe.   1947;
         Reprinted: New York: Harcourt, Brace & World, Inc., A
         Harbinger Book, 1962, 432 pp.
            Reprint omits Part 2 which is a study of Shakespeare's
         use of rhetorical principles. Retains original pagination,
         however.
            "This study undertakes to establish four points: First,
         that the general theory of composition . . . in Shakespeare's
         time is to be found in one form in the contemporary works on
         logic and rhetoric combined; second, that it is to be found
         in another form in the work of the figurists . . . ; third,
         that these two forms . . . are fundamentally alike" and
         that Shakespeare's work is an illustration (p. 4). Chart
         of traditionalists, figurists, and Ramists, chiefly in
         English vernacular. Definitions of figures arranged under
         the headings of Invention, Argumentation, pathos, and ethos.
         Definitions from vernacular rhetorics. Bibliography.
         Index.

3.134   KENNEDY, WILLIAM J.   Rhetorical Norms in Renaissance Literature.
         New Haven and London: Yale University Press, 1978, 237 pp.
            Argues that critical attention should shift from its
         focus on ornamentation to consideration of the strategy

employed by the speaker on his audience. Argues that
linguists and structural critics "forget that each literary
utterance adds up to more than the sum of its linguistic
parts" (p. 15). Then applies strategic theories to the
poetry of Petrarch, Ronsard, Sidney, Erasmus, More,
Rabelais, Ariosto, D'Aubigne, and Milton in subsequent
chapters: "The . . . chapters demonstrate the comple-
mentarity of these rhetorical norms in generating larger
systems of genre, style, and mode on the one hand and in
lending some relief to the course of literary history on
the other" (p. 18).

3.135 KING, WALTER N. "John Lyly and Elizabethan Rhetoric." SP,
52 (1955), 149-61.
Replies to P. A. Duhamel (3.85): "I question . . .
whether Lyly flirts with logic quite as cavalierly as
Duhamel insists" (p. 150). Argues against reading "set
pieces" out of context. Agrees with Duhamel's central
points concerning rhetoric, but attempts to defend Lyly
within that context. Argues that Lyly was as concerned
with logic and reason as he was with eloquence. Extracts
syllogisms, disjunctive and otherwise, from Euphues. Points
out that Lyly's major work has as its subtitle "The Anatomy
of Wit" (p. 153).

3.136 KOLLER, KATHRINE. "Abraham Fraunce and Edmund Spenser." ELH,
7 (1940), 108-20.
Indicates that Fraunce's reputation was quite strong in
his own time. After discussing briefly the use Fraunce
made of Spenser and Sidney in his Shepheardes Logike,
Lawiers Logike, and The Arcadian Rhetorike, discusses
Fraunce as a poet and translator of the school of Sidney
and Spenser.

3.137 KRANIDAS, THOMAS. "Milton and the Rhetoric of Zeal." TSLL,
6 (1965), 423-32.
Related to Puritan impact on rhetorical theory: "I
should like to examine Puritan fervor and its 'rhetoric
of zeal' as it relates to its antithesis, the Anglican
via media and its claims for moderation" (p. 423). Surveys
and discusses many Puritan figures involved in the controversy. Argues Revelation 3: 16 (p. 432) the root of such
"language of zeal."

3.138 KRAPP, GEORGE PHILIP. The Rise of English Literary Prose.
New York: Oxford University Press, 1915, 566 pp.
One of the earliest studies of style (or eloquence).
Frequently cited. Remains a fair introduction to many of
the authors and titles of the English Renaissance.

3.139 KRISTELLER, PAUL OSKAR. Eight Philosophers of the Italian
Renaissance. Stanford, Calif.: Stanford University Press,
1964, 208 pp.
Contains chapters on Valla, Petrarch, Ficino, Pico,
Pomponazzi, Telesio, Patrizi, and Bruno. Of importance:
an appendix titled "The Medieval Antecedents of Renaissance Humanism" (22 pp.). Includes bibliographical survey
(10 pp.). Index. Based on the Arensberg Lectures given at
Stanford University.

3.140 KRISTELLER, PAUL OSKAR. Renaissance Thought: The Classic,
Scholastic, and Humanist Strains. 1955; New York: Harper
Torchbooks, Harper and Row, 1961, 179 pp.
A collection of lectures by Kristeller, with additions
and revisions. Background which traces humanism, Aristotelianism, Platonism, religion, scholasticism, and philosophy in the European Renaissance. Emphasis is on importance
of rhetoricians, and also explains the relationship between
Aristotelianism and Platonism. Argues that Platonism did
not supplant Aristotelianism, but that humanism redirected
it. Most humanists were rhetoricians. Discusses Arabic
influence, Augustianism, Bruni, Aquinas. Importance of
rhetoric extensive, discussed passim. Index.

3.141 KUSPIT, DONALD B. "Melanchthon and Dürer: The Search for the
Simple Style." JMRS, 3 (1973), 177-202.
"What this study offers in an account of Melanchthon's
consciousness of art understood in terms of his belief that
the 'simplicity of Dürer's art conveyed religious truth,
had the power or [sic] revelation'" (p. 179). Argues at
Melanchthon "appropriated classical categories of literary
rhetoric to explain German Renaissance style" (p. 184).
Footnote 34 (pp. 195-96) discusses eloquence.

3.142 LANG, ROBERT A. "The Teaching of Rhetoric in French Jesuit
Colleges, 1556-1762." SM, 19 (1952), 286-98.
Agrees with William P. Sandford (3.183, 184) that French
rhetorical influence of seventeenth-century England was
great and argues that French Jesuit colleges were an important part of that rhetorical tradition. Concludes that
"the importance of rhetoric in this program is clear, for,
together with the pervasive aim of instilling Christian
virtue, the main objective of the lower classes [in school]
was to attain 'perfect eloquence.' Rhetorical doctrine was
based upon classical theory with Cicero being the model of
style and Quintilian furnishing the pedagogical method.
One notes, however, tendencies toward overemphasis of style,
formalism, separation of logical proof from invention, and
a mechanical use of topoi or loci in place of a really
virile doctrine of invention" (p. 298).

3.143 LANG, ROBERT A. "Rhetoric at the University of Paris, 1550–
       1789." SM, 23 (1956), 216–28.
           Subheadings are descriptive and they include "History of
       the University" (p. 216), "The Organization of the Univer-
       sity" (p. 217), "The Place of Rhetoric in the Arts Curric-
       ulum" (p. 217), and "The Method of Teaching" (p. 220). All
       of this information is admittedly a rehash, but the point
       is that "although the professors claimed to be following
       classical doctrine, they were actually teaching a mixture
       of written composition and sophistic rhetoric during most
       of the period from 1550 to 1789" (p. 228).

3.144 LANHAM, RICHARD A. A Handlist of Rhetorical Terms: A Guide
       for Students of English Literature. 1968; Paperback re-
       print: Berkeley: University of California Press, 1969,
       160 pp.
           Contents: "Alphabetical List of Terms," "Terms Classi-
       fied According to Divisions of Rhetoric," "The Terms by
       Type," "Terms Classified as Ornaments," "Terms Especially
       Useful in Literary Criticism," "Some Important Dates,"
       "Works Cited." Uses terms chiefly from classical sources,
       but also includes Puttenham's English versions of same.
       Gives pronunciation, examples and illustrations, definitions.

3.145 LANHAM, RICHARD A. The Motives of Eloquence: Literary Rhet-
       oric in The Renaissance. New Haven: Yale University Press,
       1966, 246 pp.
           Argues that criticism has concentrated on the "serious"
       nature of man to the exclusion of the rhetorical. These
       two natures existed in harmony through the Renaissance,
       and most literature had thus a dual purpose. Defines the
       "rhetorical view of life" as conceiving of "reality as
       fundamentally dramatic, man as fundamentally a role player"
       (p. 5). Discusses in connection with Shakespeare,
       Castiglione, Rabelais, and also Plato and Ovid. Points
       out that scholarship "on classical and Renaissance rhetoric
       [is] nearly endless" (p. 225). Bibliography. Index.

3.146 LECHNER, SISTER JOAN MARIE, O.S.U. Renaissance Concepts of
       the Commonplaces: An Historical Investigation of the Gen-
       eral and Universal Ideas Used in All Argumentation and Per-
       suasion With Special Emphasis on the Educational and
       Literary Tradition of the Sixteenth and Seventeenth Cen-
       turies. New York: Pageant Press, 1962, 286 pp.
           An attempt to define commonplace as it was understood
       in the English Renaissance. Argues that the term had a
       wide variety of meanings and "was used synonymously with
       topic (topos, locus)--its most general meaning--thesis,
       passage, oration, and a multitude of other things" (p. 227).
       Consequently, "the [Renaissance] student was never quite
       sure which he had found, the 'subject topic' with its

storehouse of material or the 'analytic topic' with its
single argument" (p. 68). Discusses the traditional subject matter of rhetoric with commonplace as the central
focus. No index. Bibliography, annotated in places.
Brief (3 pp.) preface by Walter J. Ong, S.J.

3.147 LEECH, G. N. "Linguistics and the Figures of Rhetoric," in
Essays on Style and Language: Linguistic and Critical
Approaches to Literary Style. Edited by Roger Fowler.
London: Routledge and Kegan Paul, 1966, pp. 135-56.
"My primary aim . . . will be to suggest how linguistic
theory can be accommodated to the task of describing such
recurrent phenomena in literature as metaphor, parallelism,
alliteration and antithesis" (p. 136). However, "rhetoric
only enters into the discussion in so far as it has provided us with most of our terminology for talking about
these features" (p. 136). Figures are considered "devia-
tions," but without negative connotations.

3.148 LESSENICH, ROLF P. Elements of Pulpit Oratory in Eighteenth-
Century England (1660-1800). Kölm: Böhlau-Verlag, 1972,
277 pp.
Of more relevance for the years (1700-1800), but does
discuss the change in the late seventeenth-century attitude
toward prose style. Chapter 2 is titled "Text, Subject,
Exordium, Explication, Proposition, and Partition"
(pp. 43-81). The purpose of the work is to furnish "an
elementary groundwork in the form of a rhetorical and theological handbook which will considerably facilitate and
fertilize further contributions toward the historiography
of one of the most important, and most neglected, kinds of
English literature" (p. xi).

3.149 MacDONALD, HUGH. "Another Aspect of Seventeenth-Century
Prose." RES, 19 (1943), 33-43.
Argues against a radical change in prose style during
the last part of the seventeenth century, indicating that
"there had existed throughout the first half of the century, as there had existed from the days of Chaucer, or
for that matter King Alfred, a straightforward prose"
(p. 34). Argues also that political pamphleteering, which
was quite evident before the Royal Society, contributed to
the more direct nature of English prose. Discussion in-
volves Hoskins, Wilkins, Bacon, Sprat, Walton, and others.

3.150 NO ENTRY

3.151 McGREW, J. FRED. "A Bibliography of the Works on Speech Composition in England During the 16th and 17th Centuries."
QJS, 15 (1929), 381-412.

Secondary Works

A convenient and less selective listing of many primary
works of historical significance published, for the most
part, in England. Chronological (pp. 381-99). Alphabetical
(pp. 399-410). Reprints (pp. 410-12). Includes works not
strictly rhetorics or logics but which have rhetorical im-
port (e.g., Hoby's translation of Castiglione's Courtier).

3.152 McLUHAN, MARSHALL. "Francis Bacon: Ancient or Modern?"
Renaissance and Reformation, 10 (1974), 93-98.
Walter J. Ong frequently acknowledges a debt to McLuhan,
and his Ramus and Talon Inventory (3.172) is dedicated to
him. Argues that "systems analysis today is avant garde
in much the same way that in the sixteenth century Peter
Ramus was regarded as contemporary in his application of
the old scholastic methods to the new humanist materials
of history and poetry and oratory" (p. 93). Discusses
Bacon.

3.153 McNALLY, J. R. "Recor et Dux Populi: Italian Humanists and
the Relationship between Rhetoric and Logic." MP, 67
(1969), 168-76.
Considers the relationship between rhetoric and logic.
Discusses "the range of meanings latent in the notion of
'rhetorical logic'" (p. 169). Considers rhetoric as opposed
to dialectic in the works of Petrarch, Valla, Pico della
Mirandola, and Ermalao Barbaro (pp. 169ff.). Quotes extensively these important figures, in translation, and gives
Latin originals in notes. Rhetoric seen as favored over
dialectic (passim, and p. 176).

3.154 MAIR, G. H. "Introduction," in Thomas Wilson: Wilson's Arte
of Rhetorique. Edited by G. H. Mair. Oxford: At the
Clarendon Press, 1909, pp. i-xxxiv.
Provides brief biography. Points out that Wilson's Rule
of Reason and Arte of Rhetorique are based on Aristotle.
Quotes Wilson extensively. Calls Book I preliminary
(p. xx). Wilson's examples "are of not great worth"
(p. xxi). Summarizes Book II. Book III "commended"
(p. xxii). Indicates that Wilson, a pre-Elizabethan, avoids
"language," unlike Mulcaster. Wilson influenced Shakespeare
(p. xxiii). The Arte of Rhetorique of "historical interest"
(p. xxxiv). Note on collation. Early work.

3.155 MAJOR, JOHN M. "Milton's View of Rhetoric." SP, 64 (1967),
685-711.
Attributes Milton's eventual distrust of eloquence to
his view that Milton was finally disillusioned "with all
things temporal, including human knowledge and the arts"
(p. 711). Argues that Milton distrusted eloquence, and
that Ramism added to his distrust. Still, Milton's attitude
remained ambivalent: "to explain it is as difficult as it

is to account satisfactorily for the longer ambivalence of
Milton's attitude toward human learning itself" (p. 696).

3.156 MATTHIESSEN, FRANCIS OTTO. Translation: An Elizabethan
Art. Cambridge: Harvard University Press, 1931, 242 pp.
Analyzes the merits and qualities of five translations:
Hoby's Courtier, North's Plutarch, Florio's Montaigne, and
Holland's Livy and Suetonius. Discusses how Elizabethan
translations were translated for the times, and not for the
purpose of scholarship. A study of how the Elizabethans
viewed their language as opposed to the others, where and
when they did well or failed. For example: "in general
Hoby stays even too close to the Italian" (p. 33).

3.157 MEAD, WILLIAM EDWARD. The Pastime of Pleasure by Stephan
Hawes. London: Oxford University Press, 1928 (for 1927),
376 pp.
Introduction and preface total 116 pp. Subheadings include "Hawes and His Time," "Analysis," "Editions,"
"Sources," "Grammar," "Metre," and "Literary Traits." Contains woodcuts. Textual notes. Notes. Glossary. Pre-
serves original spelling generally.

3.158 MILLER, PERRY. The New England Mind: The Seventeenth Century.
New York: The Macmillan Co., 1939; Cambridge: Harvard
University Press, 1954, 539 pp.
Describes considerable influence of Ramus on seventeenth-
century New England. Discussion of dichotomic charts--ex-
plains how to read them (pp. 126-7). Explains that Ramism
became an effective tool against nominalists, and that it
"posits the existence of an objective truth, to which it
asserts man has access" (p. 151). Natural method, hence,
refers to its ability to reveal truth about nature. Nature
is "a natural framework in which arbitrary power was confined within inviolable order, yet in which the order was
so marvelously contrived that all divinely avowed ends
were swiftly accomplished" (pp. 207-8). Discusses rhetoric
in sermons--Puritans called for a plain style while at the
same time making copious use of figures. Describes Talon's
work. Discusses Perkins's debt to Ramus and influence of
Puritans. Appendixes, one a bibliographical essay on
Ramism now superseded by Walter J. Ong (3.172). Index.

3.159 MULDER, JOHN R. The Temple of the Mind: Education and Literary
Taste in Seventeenth-Century England. New York: Western
Publishing Company, Pegasus, 1969, 165 pp.
General study. Introductory. Three chapters are par-
ticularly relevant: "Schoolmasters and college tutors
trained their students in language, logic, and rhetoric
(Chapter one). This emphasis nurtured a particular kind
of literary taste: a fondness for logical, often

dialectical structure (Chapter two) and a delight in word
play (Chapter three)" (p. vii).

3.160 MURRIN, MICHAEL. The Veil of Allegory: Some Notes Toward a
Theory of Allegorical Rhetoric in the English Renaissance.
Chicago and London: The University of Chicago Press, 1969,
234 pp.
Argues that a study of sixteenth-century rhetoricial
texts will not facilitate understanding of allegorical
poetry unless the different purposes of oratory and allegory
are properly understood. Allegory veils truth, he argues,
for the twofold purpose of shielding truth from the unin-
itiated and revealing it to the elite. Oratory has as its
primary purpose communication to the greatest possible number. Drama fills a niche between the two. Speaks of the
"Renaissance identification of poetry with allegory" (p. 3).
Although focus is on Spenser, Murrin attempts to derive
"a comprehensive theory of allegorical rhetoric" (p. ix).

3.161 NADEAU, RAY. "Talaeus Versus Farnaby on Style." SM, 21
(1954), 59-63.
Nadeau's summary: "It is, indeed, an ironic twist of
fortune that Thomas Farnaby's very popular and classical
[traditionalist] Index rhetoricus, almost completely
stripped of its classicism by later writers and editors,
became as exclusively Ramian a rhetoric of tropes and
schemes as all of the Talaen rhetorics against which it
was initially arrayed" (p. 63). Documents Smith's (3.35)
plagiarism from Farnaby and mentions "the effrontery of his
[Smith's] title" (p. 62).

3.162 NELSON, NORMAN E. Peter Ramus and the Confusion of Logic,
Rhetoric, and Poetry. University of Michigan Contributions in Modern Philology, No. 2. Ann Arbor: University
of Michigan Press, April, 1947, 22 pp.
Anti-Ramist. Argues that Ramus was a very minor figure
in logic, but an important although wrong headed educator.
Hopes this article, or pamphlet, will call "attention to
the serious danger of mistaking historical influence for
intrinsic importance or every neologist for a champion of
progress" (p. 22). Attacks Tuve (p. 22). Walter J. Ong
(3.170) says this article "warns against making too much
of the inner consistency of Ramus' thought" (p. 385).

3.163 NELSON, WILLIAM. "The Teaching of English in Tudor Grammar
Schools." SP, 59 (1952), 119-43.
In spite of the "weight of scholarly opinion, I propose
to argue that the grammar masters of the sixteenth century
conceived it an essential part of their duty to train their
students in the correct and comely use of the vernacular"
(p. 119). Carefully documented and respected study of the

issue, but the "weight of scholarly opinion" remains where it was.

3.164 ONG, WALTER J., S.J. "Commonplace Rhapsody: Ravisius Textor, Zwinger and Shakespeare," in Classical Influences on European Culture, A.D. 1500-1700. Edited by R. R. Bolgar. Cambridge, England: Cambridge University Press, 1976, pp. 91-126.

Commonplaces "related to the evolving noetic economy" of the period (p. 92). Commonplaces describes as "assemblages in writing or print of cumulative commonplaces, these latter being understood to include both lengthy passages and briefer expressions, down to mere modus dicendi, as in Erasmus's De Copia, stocked in formulaic fashion out of the extant store of knowledge for further exploitation as occasion might demand" (p. 94). Ioannes Ravisius Textor (Jean Tisier, 1470?-1524) described as neglected today but "familiar" to Shakespeare (p. 95). Describes Textor's commonplaces, including 185 suicides. Zwinger discussed with Textor as "typographical equivalents of Homer" as collectors of tales (p. 119). Shakespeare's sonnet 129 printed with Textor's Latin interlinear (p. 122-23) to show Shakespeare's familiarity.

3.165 ONG, WALTER J., S. J. "Fouquelin's French Rhetoric and the Ramist Vernacular Tradition." SP, 51 (1954), 127-42.

Central point is that "Fouquelin's work has apparently never been recognized for what it is: not simply an incidental work in which Talon had some hand, but nothing less than the companion piece to the keystone in the Ramist structure, the famous French Dialectique by Ramus" (p. 129). Describes the work. Only difference between Talon's Latin work and Fouquelin's French one is "in the matter of French verse" (p. 133). Points out that the work was not very popular (pp. 141-42).

3.166 ONG, WALTER J., S. J. "Hobbes and Talon's Ramist Rhetoric in English." TCBS, 1, part 3 (1951), 260-69.

Establishes that The Art of Rhetorick Plainly Set Forth, commonly attributed to Thomas Hobbes, is nothing more than a reprint of an English-language adaptation of the Ramist Rhetorica of Audomarus Talaeus done by Dudley Fenner. Cf. Howell, 3.118.

3.167 ONG, WALTER J., S. J. "Memory as Art." RQ, 20 (1967), 253-60.

Essentially a laudatory review but also a detailed description of Frances A. Yates (3.232). Makes suggestions for further study, chiefly on the relation between the Renaissance memory systems and oral memory.

3.168   ONG, WALTER J., S. J.   "Oral Residue in Tudor Prose Style."
        <u>PMLA</u> (1965), 145-54.
        "By oral residue I mean habits of thought and expression
        tracing back to preliterate situations or practice, or de-
        riving from the dominance of the oral as a medium in a
        given culture, or indicating a reluctance or inability to
        dissociate the written medium from the spoken" (p. 146).
        Argues that since rhetoric was originally an oral discipline,
        and since the writers of the Renaissance were strongly in-
        fluenced by rhetoric, the oral tradition continues to make
        itself felt in their writings. Discusses parts of an ora-
        tion, Erasmus, Cicero, and Quintilian. Explains the rhap-
        sodic aspects of Nashe, Lyly, Greene, and Lodge, and
        relates them to classical training. Indicates that this
        oral quality or "residue" is different from that found in
        more modern writers, who consciously attempt to mimic oral
        communication for artistic purposes.

3.169   ONG, WALTER J., S. J.   "Ramist Method and the Commercial
        Mind." <u>SRen</u>, 8 (1961), 155-72.
        Argues that the Ramist method of dichotomization has an
        appeal to the commercial mind because the commercial mind
        is characterized by a propensity to view the world con-
        cretely and mechanistically, and Ramism's spatial dia-
        gramming of knowledge gave "bits" of information definite
        places in space. It also made this diagramming rather
        mechanical.

3.170   ONG, WALTER J., S.J. <u>Ramus, Method, and the Decay of Dialogue:</u>
        <u>From the Art of Discourse to the Art of Reason</u>. 1958;
        Reprinted: New York: Octagon Books, Farrar, Strauss &
        Giroux, 1974, 427 pp.
        Authoritative survey and analysis of Peter Ramus. Shows
        influence of the new invention of print on Ramus's reorgani-
        zation of knowledge: Ramus took space as the sensory situs
        of intellectual knowledge rather than sound, as preprint
        ages had commonly done. Background on Scholasticism with
        emphasis on logic. Describes Rudolph Agricola as a popu-
        larizer and as a precursor of Ramus as well as Peter of
        Spain's debt to and departures from Aristotle. Renaissance
        universities described as analogous to teaching guilds.
        Discusses Ramus's debt to and attacks on Aristotle. Main-
        tains that Ramus mentions Plato chiefly to annoy Peripatetics.
        Reprints several Ramist dichotomic charts in their various
        stages of evolution. Treats attacks on Ramus by Gonveia
        and Charpentier. Quotes and translates Ramus, Talon, and
        other influential Latin writers (works not always available
        in convenient translation). "Talon was Ramus' man"
        (p. 271), and Ramus often wrote under his name. "Plain
        style, which is really nonrhetorical style, alone is accept-
        able to reasonable man" (p. 284). Ramist dialectic

suffered in Paris because of Ramus's poor defense of it against his critics, but his rhetoric flourished. His influence on seventeenth century was profound, but not generally acknowledged. Index, extensive on primary sources. Bibliography to supplement his Ramus and Talon Inventory (3.172).

3.171 ONG, WALTER J., S. J. "Ramus: Rhetoric and the Pre-Newtonian Mind," in English Institute Essays 1952. Edited by Alan S. Downer. New York: Columbia University Press, 1954, pp. 138-70.

Ramus's pedagogical reforms utilized visual, quasi-geometric, quantitative illustrations involving units of knowledge, and this was made possible by the uniform positioning of words on a surface of paper as a result of the printing press. The concept of quantification, therefore, is not unique with Newton and the physical and mathematical sciences, but also extends into quite diverse regions of the mind of this period. Significant for intellectual history as well as rhetoric.

3.172 ONG, WALTER J., S. J. Ramus and Talon Inventory. Cambridge: Harvard University Press, 1958, 658 pp.

The full subtitle is descriptive: A Short-Title Inventory of the Published Works of Peter Ramus (1515-1572) and of Omer Talon (ca. 1510-1562) In their Original and in their Variously Altered Forms with Related Material: 1. The Ramist Controversies: A Descriptive Catalogue 2. Agricola Check List: A Short-Title Inventory of Some Printed Editions and Printed Compendia of Rudolph Agricola's Dialectical Invention (De Inventione Dialectica). Fully annotated in English. Companion Study to Ramus, Method, and the Decay of Dialogue (3.170). "This Inventory is to provide elementary documentation for the study of Ramism and its milieu. It furnishes a list of all editions which I have been able to discover of works by Peter Ramus (1515-72) and . . . Omer Talon . . . , together with subsidiary lists of materials and authors involved in Ramism, and locates copies of editions" (p. 1).

3.173 ONG, WALTER J., S. J. Rhetoric, Romance, and Technology: Studies in the Interaction of Expression and Culture. Ithaca and London: Cornell University Press, 1971, 359 pp.

A collection of Ong's essays and articles which includes "Oral Residue in Tudor Prose Style," "Tudor Writings on Rhetoric, Poetic, and Literary Theory," "Memory as Art," and "Ramist Method and the Commercial Mind," which are annotated here. Also includes essays dealing with other periods. The essays "focus individually on periods or persons from the Renaissance through the present age, but they also reach far back beyond the Renaissance into antiquity

and even into prehistory, where rhetoric had its beginnings
in the primal oral, preliterate culture of mankind" (p. viii).

3.174   ONG, WALTER J., S. J.   "Tudor Writings on Rhetoric."   SRen,
        15 (1968), 39-69.
        A relatively general but compact survey of Renaissance
        rhetoric, "much indebted" to Wilbur Samuel Howell (3.114),
        arguing that the importance of rhetoric during the English
        Renaissance has been underestimated. Surveys kinds of
        orations, parts of orations, letter writing, progymnasmata,
        invention, topics, and so on. Section on English rhetoric
        with attention to commonplaces. Section on Ramism dis-
        cusses debate between Ramists and traditionalists. Closes
        with discussion of Bacon.

3.175   PATRICK, J. MAX and ROBERT O. EVANS with JOHN M. WALLACE, eds.
        "Attic" and Baroque Prose Style: The Anti-Ciceronian Move-
        ment (Essays by Morris W. Croll). Princeton, N.J.:
        Princeton University Press, 1969.
        A collection of influential pioneer essays by Croll,
        first printed in 1966. The back cover of the paperback
        edition states that "J. Max Patrick . . . worked more than
        twelve years on Style, Rhetoric, and Rhythm: Essays by
        Morris W. Croll, the clothbound edition from which the four
        essays in the present volume are extracted." His associ-
        ates for that book were Robert O. Evans, John M. Wallace,
        and R. J. Schoeck. Provides forewords to each essay, ex-
        pands the footnotes and brings them up to date, and includes
        an index. The index can serve as a bibliography as it lists
        key terms and authors which appear in the notes as well as
        the essays. Contains biographical note on Croll by
        Thomas H. English. Essays not included which appeared
        in the earlier edition are not particularly relevant here.
        This edition is to be preferred over the original publica-
        tions of the essays because of the notes and apparatus.

3.176   PATTERSON, ANNABEL M.   Hermogenes and the Renaissance: Seven
        Ideas of Style. Princeton, N.J.: Princeton University
        Press, 1970, 256 pp.
        Contends the pervasiveness of Hermogenes' influence in
        Renaissance through his seven Ideas of Clarity, Grandeur,
        Beauty, Speed, Ethos, Verity, and Gravity. N.B.: [This
        is "Hermogenes of Tarsus, who flourished in the second cen-
        tury A.D." (p. xi)]. Argues that Gravity was the source of
        the concept of Decorum, especially as Sturm amplified both.
        Application of these Ideas deals "only with those ideas
        which seem to have been of most value to Renaissance writers,
        and they are organized according to the major nondramatic
        genres of poetry" (p. xii). In her terms, "Gravity, which
        is both the climax of the scheme and the acid test of its
        flexibility, is seen as the stylistic principle of renais-
        sance epic" (p. xii).

3.177 PETERSON, DOUGLAS L. The English Lyric from Wyatt to Donne:
A History of the Plain and Eloquent Styles. Princeton,
N.J.: Princeton University Press, 1967, 399 pp.
    A study of the influence rhetoric exerted on the English
lyric. An attempt to show that the influence of Petrarch
was colored by the English poets' awareness of stylistic
concerns. Indicates he is extending the work of Tuve
(p. 8).

3.178 RINGLER, WILLIAM. "The Immediate Source of Euphuism." PMLA,
53 (1938), 678-86.
    Argues that John Rainolds, through his lectures at
Oxford, is the source of the style for which John Lyly is
best known, and for which Gabriel Harvey invented the term.
Indicates that this article "supplements" Croll's work
(p. 686).

3.179 RINGLER, WILLIAM. "Introduction" in his edition of Oratio in
Laudem Artis Poeticae [Circa 1672] by John Rainolds.
Princeton Studies in English, 20. Edited by G. H. Gerould.
Princeton, N.J.: Princeton University Press, 1940, pp. 1-23.
    Points out that Rainolds "was in his own time a person
of exceptional importance and influence" (p. 2). Dates
presentation of Oratio 14 July 1572. Analyzes it as a
classical oration and discusses its style. Lists sources.
States that "the surprising thing about Rainold's sources
is that, with the exception of Cicero's Pro Archia, no
essays on poetry are included among them" (p. 19). In
short, "the prime sources of Rainold's ideas are not treatises on poetic, but treatises on rhetoric" (p. 19). Lists
other editions in 1619, 1628. The commentary (pp. 63-87)
indicates sources and influence, especially on Sidney:
"The following commentary, in addition to being exegetical,
is designed to show the sources of the Praise of Poetry and
to indicate the appearance of the ideas and illustrations
contained in it in the writings of other sixteenth-century
Englishmen" (p. 63).

3.180 RIX, HERBERT DAVID. Rhetoric in Spenser's Poetry. Pennsylvania State College Studies, no. 7. State College,
Pennsylvania: The Pennsylvania State College, 1940, 88 pp.
    Despite title, this work emphasizes, and is related to,
rhetoric. Outlines several sixteenth century rhetorics including Cox (3.5), Rainolde (3.12), Peacham (3.16), and
Fraunce (3.20). Provides a list of figures with definitions adapted from Susenbrotus (3.66) and Peacham. Gives
illustrations from Spenser, and discusses Spenser in connection with rhetoric. One of only twenty-five modern works
listed in Lanham (3.144, p. 148).

3.181   ROSSI, PACLO.   Francis Bacon: From Magic to Science.
         Translated by Sacha Rabinovitch.   London: Routledge
         and Kegan Paul, 1968, 298 pp.
              Revision of the Italian version with minor changes.
         "In his 'new' scientific logic, Bacon incorporated some
         typical concepts of traditional rhetoric.   He substituted
         the collection of natural places for that of rhetorical
         places.   He adapted the art of memory to other than tradi-
         tional ends.   He devised the tables or instruments of clas-
         sification to organise reality and thus enable the memory
         to assist intellectual operations.   And he used the Ramistic
         rules for defining forms" (p. 219).   Relevant chapters are
         titled "The Classical Fable," "Logic, Rhetoric, and Method,"
         "Language and Communication," and "Rhetorical Tradition and
         the Method of Science."   Index.

3.182   SACKTON, ALEXANDER H.   Rhetoric as a Dramatic Language in Ben
         Jonson.   New York: Columbia University Press, 1948, 192 pp.
              Two of eight chapters are directly relevant: "The Tradi-
         tion of Rhetoric in the Age of Jonson," and "Some Uses of
         Rhetoric in Literature."   Concentration in other chapters
         is on Jonson's use of hyperbole and jargon.   Stresses ironic
         or indirect methods of communicating with an audience.   Bib-
         liography.   Index.

3.183   SANDFORD, WILLIAM P[HILLIPS].   "English Rhetoric Reverts to
         Classicism, 1600-1650."   QJS, 15 (1929), 503-25.
              Argues that "practically all of the English works on the
         subject until 1600 dealt with style and delivery" (p. 504).
         Still, many "scholars and teachers" were "laying stress
         upon the importance of inventio and dispositio" (p. 504).
         Discusses Harvey as a Ciceronian.   Short discussion of
         classical elements in Dresser, Keckerman, Soarez, Cresol,
         Caussin, Vossius, Farnaby, Butler, Pemble, Bacon, Bulwer,
         Vicar, Farnaby (in greater detail), and Pemble (again).
         Mentions the "school of Talaeus, Fraunce, et al." in
         passing (p. 519) and omits Ramus.   An early work.

3.184   SANDFORD, WILLIAM PHILLIPS.   English Theories of Public Address,
         1530-1828.   Columbus, Ohio: H. L. Hedrick, 1931, 212 pp.
              Included here because it is frequently cited, but the
         author's own statement is to be carefully noted: "the
         dissertation herewith presented in mimeographed form has
         been of service to a number of graduate students in speech
         and rhetoric.   To make it available to a larger number, it
         is now (1931) published.   Some minor corrections have been
         made, but it is probable that further investigation will
         reveal other desireable changes" (p. 6).

3.185 SCHOECK, R. J. "Rhetoric and Law in Sixteenth-Century England."
       SP, 50 (1953), 110-27.
           Title descriptive. Discusses relationship between Eng-
       lish common law and rhetoric: Lincoln's Inn, Gray's Inn,
       and the Inner and Middle Temple. Quotes Elyot at length
       on how the parts of rhetoric relate to the lawyer's pro-
       fession. Discusses Wilson and analyzes the Arte of
       Rhetorique, especially with reference to judicial orations.
       Discusses Fraunce's Lawiers Logike. Indicates that "during
       the sixteenth century the education of many of the common
       lawyers was not so strictly and severely professional as it
       had been in the Middle Ages" (p. 123). Suggests lines of
       further study and then says "I myself hope in future stud-
       ies to extend some of the lines which have been suggested
       here" (p. 127).

3.186 SCREECH, M. A. "Commonplaces of Law, Proverbial Wisdom and
       Philosophy: Their Importance in Renaissance Scholarship
       (Rabelais, Joachim Du Bellay, Montaigne)," in Classical
       Influences on European Culture, A.D. 1500-1700. Edited by
       R. R. Bolgar. Cambridge, England: Cambridge University
       Press, 1976, pp. 127-34.
           Title is descriptive. Explains how references to common-
       place books can help recover meanings in Renaissance authors
       using Rabelais and Montaigne in connection with several
       commonplace books.

3.187 SEATON, ETHEL. "Introduction." In Abraham Fraunce: The
       Arcadian Rhetorike. Edited from the Edition of 1588 by
       Ethel Seaton. Oxford: Published for the Luttrell Society
       by Basil Blackwood, 1950, pp. vii-lv.
           Dates Fraunce's work 1588. Contains brief biography
       (2 pp.) and history of Ramism (3 pp.). Contains summary
       of Fraunce's adaptations from Talon. Points out that
       Fraunce's contribution was to add examples from Philip
       Sidney as illustrations of the figures. Fraunce used
       illustrations from Homer, Virgil, Petrarch, Tasso (Fraunce
       knew complete Gerusalemme Liberata), Sieur du Bartas,
       Denisot, Scalinger, Boscan, Garcilassa, and ignored Ariosto.
       Discusses Sidney, Edmund Spenser, and Richard Willey, usu-
       ally in relation to Fraunce. Discusses the book's influ-
       ence. Explains collation and gives list of corrections.

3.188 SEIGEL, JERROLD E. Rhetoric and Philosophy in Renaissance
       Humanism. Princeton, N.J.: Princeton University Press,
       1968, 268 pp.
           Argues that Cicero is the model for Renaissance rhetoric,
       and Cicero felt that eloquence helped the philosopher com-
       municate truth and wisdom. The fact that eloquence could
       be used to further evil made philosophy superior to rhetoric.
       Peripatetic philosophy was more worldly and thus consistent

with the needs of the time, but stoic philosophy was more
logical and consistent. Petrarch fought against the physi-
cians who dominated the universities and attempted to con-
trol rhetoric. Salutati drifted from supporting eloquence
to emphasizing Christian truth. Bruni emphasized Aristotle
as opposed to Cicero. Valla asserted the rhetor's superior-
ity to all philosophers. While medieval philosophers studied rhetoric, their main concern was how it related to
truth, ethics, and Christianity. With the four mentioned,
we see rhetoric again studied as an end in itself. From
Petrarch to Valla we see a gradual movement from a union of
rhetoric and philosophy to the exaltation of rhetoric over
all disciplines.

3.189 SLOAN, THOMAS O. "Introduction," in his edition of The Pas-
       sions of the Minde in General by Thomas Wright. Urbana,
       Ill.: The University of Illinois Press, 1971, pp. xi-xlix.
          Discusses "the non-Ramistic integrity of Wright's view
       of rhetoric, the nature of his Ramistic marks, and finally
       the Thomist imprint upon his discussion of persuasion"
       (pp. xxxii-xxxiii). Lists five extant editions of Wright's
       work: 1601, 1604, 1620, 1621, and 1630. "Although the
       present edition reproduces the text from the 1630 edition,
       it is . . . modeled on the 1604 edition. The differences
       between the last four editions are insignificant compared
       with the differences between any one of them and the 1601
       edition" (p. xlvi).

3.190 SLOAN, THOMAS O. "The Crossing of Rhetoric and Poetry in the
       English Renaissance." The Rhetoric of Renaissance Poetry
       from Wyatt to Milton. Edited by Thomas O. Sloan and
       Raymond B. Waddington. Berkeley: University of California
       Press, 1974, pp. 212-42.
          Concentrates on "two radical transformations," Ramism
       and when "rhetorical theory converged with devotional theory
       and once more established common ground . . . between orators
       and poets" (p. 214). Discusses Thomas Wilson and Ramism
       (pp. 217-25). Contends poetry lingered behind rhetorical
       theory during Ramist period, but devotional theory moved
       poetry forward--Donne is an example. Discusses Thomas
       Wright's The Passions of the Minde in General (1604) and
       then Obadiah Walker's Some Instructions Concerning the Art
       of Oratory (1659) to support his contention (pp. 231-42).
          The entire collection of ten essays by different authors
       discusses rhetorical theory as it applies to specific poets
       or poems. "The tone of the collection is a contentious one,
       sometimes bordering on the outright polemical" (p. 1).

3.191 SLOAN, THOMAS O. "Rhetoric and Meditation: Three Case Stud-
       ies." JMRS, 1 (1971), 45-58.
          "One is struck by the gap between practice and theory.
       English prose in particular flourished, but rhetorical

theories were thin and relatively impoverished. In this
essay I shall argue that the art of meditation provided
much that was missing in seventeenth-century rhetoric, so
much in fact that rhetoric and meditation taken together
constitute the true rhetorical theory of the age" (p. 45).
Relies much on Obadiah Walker's Some Instructions concerning the Art of Oratory, and discusses nontraditional exclusion of passion from his theory (pp. 55-58).

3.192   SMITH, A. J. "An Examination of Some Claims Made for Ramism."
        RES, 7 (1956), 348-59.
        Asserts quite correctly, if one assumes he means the
        vernacular, that "one has to search hard in sixteenth-
        century English literature to find any considerable mention
        of Ramus and Ramism" (p. 349), but Nash, Harvey, and Ascham
        are obvious exceptions. Discusses Fraunce. "The conclusion
        is that altogether too much has been made of the attempt at
        reform in teaching method called Ramism, in itself as an
        influence" (p. 359). Suggests the term "wit" is more apt
        for discussions of Metaphysical poetry. But see also Ong,
        3.170; Tuve, 3.208; and Crane, 3.73. Cope, 3.70 discusses
        this problem of Ramism and its importance in scholarship.

3.193   SMITH, G. C. MOORE. "A Note on Milton's Art of Logic." RES,
        13 (1937), 335-40.
        A note on the dating of Milton's logic. Concludes that
        "either, then, the treatise was written later than the
        thirties or it was added to after it was originally drafted"
        (p. 336).

3.194   SONNINO, LEE A. A Handbook to Sixteenth-Century Rhetoric.
        New York: Barnes and Noble, Inc., 1968, 288 pp.
        Emphasizes the figures of eloquence, but includes defini-
        tions of all known rhetorical terms used by the Renaissance
        scholars. Representative definitions given from classical
        authors as well. Collates examples under definitions.
        Separates those known by Greek names from those (a majority)
        in Latin. Index of figures by types such as addition, ad-
        mission, amplification, etc. Index of terms "of Greek ori-
        gin and regularly used in Latinate form" (p. 272). Lists
        kinds of oratory, divisions of rhetoric, parts of a speech,
        and the divisions of eloquence (p. 243). Charts of sub-
        divisions. "Critical Bibliography of Important Renaissance
        Texts" (pp. 236-38). Bibliography of vernacular texts
        (pp. 238-40).

3.195   SOUTHERN, A. C. Elizabethan Recusant Prose, 1559-1582: A
        Historical and Critical Account of the Books of the Refugees
        Printed and Published Abroad and at Secret Presses in England
        Together with an Annotated Bibliography of the Same. London
        and Glasgow: Sands and Co., 1950, 589 pp.

Subtitle accurate. General thesis is that the prose
works of the recusants emphasized invention and disposition
(or, together, composition) while the protestant rhetoricians under Elizabeth I ignored or paid less attention to
this than to elocution (eloquence) (p. xii). Authors, publishers, works too numerous to mention--annotated bibliography alone runs 149 pp., much in small type. Also arranges
works in chronological order (p. 542 ff.). Argues that
these authors have been given far too little attention both
for their quality and their impact upon the English vernacular, even though their primary purpose was to fight for a
cause.

3.196   SPRAGUE, RICHARD S., ed. "Introduction," in The Rule of Rea-
        son Conteinying The Arte of Logique by Thomas Wilson.
        Northridge, Calif.: San Fernando Valley State College
        Foundation, 1972, pp. xi-xxv.
            Discusses Wilson's revisions in subsequent editions.
        Calls attention to "Wilson's carefully wrought and reworked
        structure and style of presentation" (p. xx).

3.197   STATON, WALTER F., JR. "The Characters of Style in Elizabethan
        Prose." JEGP, 57 (1958), 197-207.
            Provides definitions of the high, middle, and low styles
        and then discusses them as used by Sidney, Lyly, Nash, and
        Greene. All three styles used whenever appropriate to the
        authors' subject matter and the circumstances. All three
        styles used ornamentation. Indicates that the "plain style
        employs ordinary diction, proverbs, and humor and avoids
        elaborate figures of sound and thought; it is used for un-
        important subjects before small audiences and for logical
        proof rather than emotional persuasion" (p. 198).

3.198   STEADMAN, JOHN M. "Ethos and Dianoia: Character and Rhetoric
        in Paradise Lost," in Language and Style in Milton: A
        Symposium in Honor of the Tercentenary of Paradise Lost.
        Edited by Ronald David Emma and John T. Shawcross. New
        York: Frederick Ungar Publishing Co., 1967, pp. 193-232.
            Argues that "no analysis of Milton's rhetoric can dis-
        pense with his Ars Logica. Like other Ramists, he believed
        that the rhetorician should derive his arguments from the
        commonplaces of logic; and in practice (though not in theory)
        the technical differences between the Ramist and Aristotelian
        classifications tended to disappear" (p. 194). Supports his
        argument with an analysis of Paradise Lost.

3.199   STEPHENS, JAMES. "Bacon's New English Rhetoric and the Debt
        to Aristotle." SM, 39 (1972), 248-59.
            An attempt to determine the character of Bacon's debt to
        or use of Aristotle. Argues that Bacon senses in Aristotle
        "the kind of hypocrisy and left-handed [sic] advice which

has caused philosophy to be separated from rhetoric for
many centuries" (p. 259). (Cf. Seigel, 3.188.) "Bacon's
primary concern is to make rhetoric respectable again for
a new age and for the purposes of a new Philosophy" (p. 259).
"Bacon returns to Aristotle and works to accomplish three
things: 1) correction of inconsistencies and gaps in Aristotle's logic, 2) revision and enrichment of the system of
topics, and 3) preparation of the syllogism and enthymeme
for . . . social and moral research" (p. 252).

3.200   STEPHENS, JAMES. <u>Francis Bacon and the Style of Science</u>.
        Chicago: The University of Chicago Press, 1975, 200 pp.
           Discusses Bacon's ambivalent attitude toward rhetoric
        in terms of his dual audience: a learned and obscure but
        precise style for the learned and a more attractive one for
        the acolyte. Discusses the acroamatic style (<u>passim</u>) for
        the learned which consists of "secret alphabets, hiero-
        glyphs, codes and tables" (p. ix). Discusses all of Bacon's
        works since Bacon's concern with rhetoric was not confined
        to any one work or period of time. Indicates Bacon most
        indebted to Aristotle, but not slavishly so. Chapter
        titles: "The Philosopher, His Audience, and Popular Rhet-
        oric," "Science and Style," "A Theory of the Philosophical
        Style," and "Fable-Making as a Strategy of Style." Index.

3.201   STEPHENS, JAMES. "Rhetorical Problems in Renaissance Science."
        <u>PR</u>, 8 (1975), 213-29.
           "So serious was the question of how best to dress and
        present the new philosophy, that not one of the major fig-
        ures in Renaissance science fails to discuss it at some
        length or to justify his own solution to the problem"
        (p. 213). The overriding concern was the question of how
        to attract and inform the select while simultaneously ob-
        scuring the message to the uninitiated. Bacon suggests
        figurative language (p. 216). Copernicus supported clarity
        for all (p. 217). Discusses Kepler at some length, dwelling
        on his sense of humor (pp. 223 ff.).

3.202   STRUEVER, NANCY S. <u>The Language of History in the Renaissance:</u>
        <u>Rhetoric and Historical Consciousness in Florentine Humanism</u>.
        Princeton, N.J.: Princeton University Press, 1970, 222 pp.
           Points out that "the rehabilitation of the Sophists which
        finds its source in Nietzsche entails a rehabilitation of
        rhetoric as the historical vehicle of Sophistic insight"
        (p. 3) and develops throughout. Descriptive chapter head-
        ings include "Rhetoric, Poetics, and History--Coluccio
        Salutati," "Rhetoric, Politics, and History--Leonardo Bruni,"
        and "Rhetoric, Ethics, and History--Poggio Bracciolini."
        Index (11 pp.). Gives significant attention to relation
        between speaker and audience (cf. Kennedy, 3.134).

3.203 SWEETING, ELIZABETH J[ANE]. Early Tudor Criticism: Linguistic
and Literary. Oxford: Basil Blackwell, 1940, 193 pp.
A general and relatively early study of pre-Elizabethan
Tudor criticism that deals with the following rhetoricians
(among others): Bacon, Cox, Elyot, Jewel, Melanchthon,
Quintilian, Ramus, Sherry, and Wilson. Chapter titled
"Rhetoric and Literary Criticism." Discussion of rhetoric
concentrates on practical applications.

3.204 TAYLOR, WARREN. Tudor Figures of Rhetoric. Whitewater, Wis.:
1972, 188 pp.
Reprint of Taylor's 1937 dissertation. The most relevant
chapters are entitled "A Dictionary of Tudor Figures of
Rhetoric," "Tudor Classifications of Figures," and "The
First Occurrence in English of the Names of Figures."
Bibliography in this work is of editions used by Taylor,
not necessarily the earliest or most influential ones.

3.205 THONSSEN, LESTER W. "Thomas Hobbes' Philosophy of Speech," in
Philosophers on Rhetoric: Traditional and Emerging Views.
Edited by Donald G. Douglas. Skokie, Ill.: National Textbook Company, 1973, pp. 50-55.
An early (1932) attempt to establish the importance of
Hobbes to rhetoric: "the purpose of this paper is to present the name of a great thinker who, though infrequently
referred to in our professional circle [(Speech)], made a
philosophical discursion the character of which it may be
worthwhile to investigate" (p. 50). Considers Hobbes "a
contributor of no mean distinction" (p. 54). Originally
published as "Thomas Hobbes' Philosophy of Speech," QJS,
18 (1932), 200-206. See also Douglas, 3.82.

3.206 THORNE, J. P. "A Ramistical Commentary on Sidney's 'An
Apologie for Poetry.'" MP (1956-57), 158-64.
An outline of Ramism which "is not a logical system in
the full sense of the term at all. It has one concern
only--the normative problem of language" (p. 159). Argues
that Ramus returns to the earlier view, as old as Plato,
that rhetoric is "a means mainly to misrepresent and mis-
lead" (p. 160). For a Ramist, then, the only distinction
between poetry and other forms of writing is that poetry is
written in verse. Discusses Sidney's Defense in connection
with "Analysis tractationis de poesi contextae a nobilissimo
viro Philippo Sidneio Equite Aurato," a commentary thereon
written by William Temple (1555-1627), Sidney's secretary.
Temple, a leading Ramist, had his differences with Sidney
concerning poetic theory.

3.207 TOPLISS, PATRICA. The Rhetoric of Pascal: A Study of His Art
of Persuasion in the Provinciales and the Pensées.
Amsterdam: Leicester University Press, 1966, 342 pp.

Pascal was apparently a strong influence on <u>Port-Royal</u>
(p. 9), and this is an attempt to see what sort of rhetoric
Pascal would have written. Contains bibliography of sources,
chiefly in French, which relate to the subject of rhetoric
(see pp. 327-28).

3.208   TUVE, ROSEMOND. <u>Elizabethan and Metaphysical Imagery: Renais-</u>
        <u>sance Poetic and Twentieth-Century Critics</u>. Chicago: The
        University of Chicago Press, 1947, 448 pp.
             Landmark study. Discusses nearly every rhetorical issue
        and relates them to the practice of Renaissance
        poets. The figures and principles of elocution and thought
        become images in the poetry of Chaucer, Spenser, Sidney,
        Marlowe, and Donne among many others. Gives much attention
        to figures of amplification. Earlier poets (before <u>c</u>. 1500-
        1600) favored amplification and the later ones (i.e., the
        Metaphysicals) those of logic. Sidney "a known Ramist"
        (p. 351). Mentions Ramus's thesis, but fails to define
        <u>commentitia</u>, a problem discussed by Walter J. Ong (3.170).
        Ramism emphasizes disjunctive syllogism. Replete with de-
        tail and reference to English rhetorics. Not yet supplanted,
        but subject of some attack (<u>see</u> Smith, 3.192 and Watson,
        3.224). Appendix. Index. Bibliography.

3.209   TUVE, ROSEMOND. "Imagery and Logic: Ramus and the Metaphys-
        ical Poets." <u>JHI</u>, 3 (1942), 365-400.
             Author's book (3.208) is a more detailed and widely
        available presentation of the same theses. First, that
        images must be understood in the context of their function.
        Second, that there is a "definite connection between logical
        training and the methods of forming and using images, with
        a considerable relationship between the Ramistic re-
        organization of logic and the lines of development taken
        by imagery in the first half of the seventeenth century"
        (p. 370).

3.210   VICKERS, BRIAN. <u>Classical Rhetoric in English Poetry</u>. London,
        New York: Macmillan, St. Martin's Press, 1970, 180 pp.
             Argues Ramism's chief innovation is in use of vernacular
        for illustrations, and this attribute is shared by some tra-
        ditionalists such as Sir John Cheke and Ascham. Argues that
        use of figures becomes increasingly important during the
        Renaissance. "Tropes" refers to a shift in meaning, and
        "figures" to a shift in structure. Refutes belief that
        Renaissance rhetoric is an extension of Medieval rhetoric.
        Surveys the history of the figures from classical times,
        but places emphasis on Renaissance theory and usage.
        Ramists neglected emotional impact of figures, but not
        Sidney whose Ramism is dubiously established (pp. 109-10).
        Hoskins akin to Longinus, Puttenham to Quintilian. Chapter
        4 emulates Fraunce--figures defined with examples from clas-
        sics through Alexander Pope. Closes with rhetorical

analysis of popular short works by Sidney, Shakespeare, and
Herbert. Bibliography. Index to authors, figures used.

3.211 VICKERS, BRIAN. Francis Bacon and Renaissance Prose.
Cambridge, England: Cambridge University Press, 1968,
329 pp.
    Discusses Bacon's theory and practice of organization
or partitio. Examines aphorisms in the Renaissance sense
of conveying authority, and use of them by Machiavelli and
Bacon. Discusses Senecan and Ciceronian influence on English Renaissance prose style--concludes that Bacon used
Ciceronian "symmetrical syntax" (p. 117), discusses, concludes it is poetic. Examines metaphor in Renaissance
prose and analyzes Bacon's use of imagery as part of his
thought. Analogy of great importance in Bacon. Bacon's
revisions confirm conclusions. Surveys Renaissance opinions of Bacon as "supreme" (p. 237). Includes opinions of
Charleton, Osborn, Jonson, Sprat, Glanville. Eighteenth-
century opinion negative. Reputation revives in nineteenth
century. Discusses. Appendix. Notes. Bibliography.
Index.

3.212 WAGNER, RUSSELL H. "Thomas Wilson's Arte of Rhetorique."
SM, 27 (1960), 1-32.
    Compares Wilson to Cox (3.5), and Sherry (3.9). Provides
brief biography of Wilson. Discusses Ascham and Cheke.
Pages 11-32 concentrate on Arte of Rhetorique. States that
for Wilson "rhetoric is the art of discourse; . . . it
implies knowledge and premeditation; it is that which
enables the orator to deal fully (largely) with any suit-
able subject" (p. 13). Traces Cicero's and Quintilian's
influence. Points out that Wilson's division of his work
into three books is not as important as his division of
rhetoric into five parts. Argues that between 1551 and
1553, his definition of rhetoric expanded to include some
logic. "Wilson's book, as a whole, treats rhetoric as a
practical art consisting not of absolute rules but of precepts for application and adaptation" (p. 31).

3.213 WAGNER, RUSSELL H. "Thomas Wilson's Contributions to Rhetoric,"
in Historical Studies of Rhetoric and Rhetoricians. Edited
by Raymond F. Howes. Ithaca, New York: Cornell University
Press, 1961, pp. 107-13.
    Argues strongly for the originality and influence of
Wilson. Credits Wilson with making rhetoric move "from the
museum to the market-place" (p. 113) and having a profound
effect on current rhetorical practice and theory. Editor
of work: "reprinted, by permission, from Papers in Rhetoric,
edited by Donald C. Bryant and privately printed in St.
Louis in 1940" (p. 444).

3.214 WAGNER, RUSSELL H. "Thomas Wilson's Speech Against Usury,"
       in Historical Studies of Rhetoric and Rhetoricians. Edited
       by Raymond F. Howes. Ithaca, N.Y.: Cornell University
       Press, 1961, pp. 225-38.
           Included here because studies of Wilson's practice are
       extremely rare. On his speech, Wagner argues that "the
       fact that this [19 April 1571] was his only attempt in the
       House at defending an unpopular cause in rough-and-tumble
       debate, give[s] it some importance. Moreover, its subject
       and purpose, together with the long dialogue of usury which
       he had already written and which he published the next year,
       conspire to justify attention to this speech" (p. 225).
       Does not make a very strenuous attempt to relate the speech
       to his Arte of Rhetorique. Editor's note: "reprinted, by
       permission, from the Quarterly Journal of Speech, February
       1952" (p. 444).

3.215 WAGNER, RUSSELL H. "Wilson and His Sources." QJS, 15 (1929),
       525-37.
           Finds Wilson's debt to Aristotle small. Wilson "relies
       on Quintilian for demonstrative oratory, on Erasmus for
       deliberative, and on the Ad Herennium for judicial" (p. 533).
       Juxtaposes passages from the latter to Wilson. Wilson made
       good use of his sources and "gave to his English rhetoric
       an English flavor" (p. 537).

3.216 WALLACE, KARL R. "Aspects of Modern Rhetoric in Francis
       Bacon." QJS, 42 (1956), 398-406.
           An attempt to show how far ahead of his time Bacon
       actually was: "Bacon is not merely modern; he is ultra-
       modern" (p. 406). Wallace states that he is "suggesting
       that Bacon's interests in the nature and processes of oral
       communication coincide with the interests of modern students
       of communication" (p. 398). Major support seems to be
       Bacon's intense interest in psychology: "Bacon has satu-
       rated communication with psychology. Communication must
       rely upon all the faculties of the mind. It engages the
       whole man" (p. 405). Short, general article.

3.217 WALLACE, KARL R. "Bacon's Conception of Rhetoric," in
       Philosophers on Rhetoric: Traditional and Emerging Views.
       Edited by Donald G. Douglas. Skokie, Ill.: National Text-
       book Company, 1973, pp. 25-49.
           An earlier (1936) and briefer version of ideas more
       fully developed and supported in his book (3.219). "To
       set out in detail Bacon's views on rhetorical address would
       require a volume; the present study aims to be merely an
       introductory chapter" (p. 25). Indicates that The Advance-
       ment of Learning is most appropriate for study of Bacon's
       rhetorical theories, but that throughout Bacon's works
       Bacon offers practical "suggestions which I shall group

under the heads of invention, disposition, memory and
delivery" (p. 37). Originally published as "Bacon's Conception of Rhetoric," SM, 3 (1936), 21-48.

3.218 WALLACE, KARL R. "Francis Bacon and Method: Theory and
Practice." SM, 40 (1973), 243-72.
Published posthumously. States that "it is evident that
Francis Bacon not only understood the nature of method, but
that he applied his knowledge of method, disposition, and
order with intent and point. Yet in selecting the purpose
and determining the organizational plan of a communication
he never allowed the strict principles of Ramean method to
obstruct the principle of utility and the requirements of
a subject matter and audience" (p. 272). Summary of Bacon's
views on method (pp. 244-55), mentioning Wilson. Compares
to Ramus, especially McIlmaine's version (3.14), and
Granger--also Wilson's Rule of Reason and Hobbes. See also
Gilbert, 3.97.

3.219 WALLACE, KARL R. Francis Bacon on Communication and Rhetoric
or: The Art of Applying Reason to Imagination for the
Better Moving of the Will. Chapel Hill, N.C.: The University of North Carolina Press, 1943, 291 pp.
"The purpose of this study is to set forth and to evaluate Francis Bacon's theory of public discourse" (p. 1).
Discusses Bacon's corpus in connection with the five parts
of rhetoric, including memory, as well as psychology and
the classical and Renaissance rhetoricians. Surveys
Bacon's influence. "In final judgment, it may be said
that Francis Bacon, viewing rhetoric in its relation to
all learning, saw public address with greater perspective
than his English kin. Yet his perspective did not keep him
from offering new and practical suggestions that would help
both speaker and writer to discover content and to estimate
the soundness of his inferences, particularly in the deliberative address" (p. 218). Argues that "most important of
all, he was the first to work out the central function of
rhetoric on psychological grounds" (p. 218). Extensive
(39 pp.) bibliography with helpful section titled "Books
on Rhetorical Theory, 1500-1700" (pp. 231-39). Remains a
standard and authoritative work on Bacon's rhetorical
theory, although Wilbur Samuel Howell (3.114) supplanted
the chapters on Bacon's contemporaries. See also Stephens,
3.200.

3.220 WALLACE, KARL R. "Imagination and Francis Bacon's View of
Rhetoric," in Dimensions of Rhetorical Scholarship. Edited
by Roger Nebergall. Norman, Okla.: A Publication of the
Department of Speech, University of Oklahoma, 1963,
pp. 65-81.

Concludes that, for Bacon, "reason renders the product plausible, imagination renders it sensible. In the kind of union that Bacon has envisaged, neither reason nor imagination works independently . . . there is a sort of transmutation of transsubstantiation going on between reason and imagination" (p. 81). Reason and Imagination, Bacon thinks, are two of the four faculties of rhetoric. "We shall proceed, first, to see what imaginative activity was held to consist of and, second, to see what Bacon meant when he linked imagination with rhetoric" (p. 66).

3.221 WALLACE, KARL R. "Rhetorical Exercises in Tudor Education." QJS, 22 (1936), 28-51.
An early study. "For the most part, my observations are based on school statutes of the period, and on Tudor biography, history, books of manners, and letters and treatises on education" (p. 29). He has not used rhetorics because they do not reflect what "actually happened in the grammar school" (p. 29), except for Rainolde (3.12). After some detail, concludes that "together with the theme, the declamation, and other rhetorical devices, it [the disposition] was supposed to produce . . . readiness and elegance of expression" (p. 51).

3.222 WALTER, OTIS MUNROE, JR. "Descartes on Reasoning," in Philosophers on Rhetoric: Traditional and Emerging Views. Edited by Donald G. Douglas. Skokie, Ill.: National Textbook Company, 1973, pp. 56-64.
Publishing in 1951, Walter says that "in a survey of thirty-five bibliographies, journals, and text-books in speech no significant reference to Descartes was found by the writer" (p. 56). Decides when Descartes was right or wrong: "Descartes believed that he had made clarity the sole test of truth" (p. 60), but "clarity is not the essence of reasoning, but the byproduct of reasoning" (p. 60). First published as "Descartes on Reasoning," SM, (1951), 47-53. See also Douglas, 3.82.

3.223 WARNICK, BARBARA. "Fénelon's Recommendations to the French Academy Concerning Rhetoric." CM, 45 (1978), 75-84.
"The Letter to the Academy was a protest against the rhetorical practice of Fénelon's time" (p. 77), and was a reaction to Ramist rhetoric (p. 77). Argues that Fénelon thought that art should communicate without calling attention to itself as art. Discusses Fénelon's three "styles of speaking" (pp. 80-81). States that "Fénelon's ideal orator . . . was an incorruptible man committed to the welfare of his country and determined to expose the truth and, along with it, the justice of his cause" (p. 84).

3.224 WATSON, GEORGE. "Ramus, Miss Tuve, and the New Petromachia."
MP, 55 (1958), 259-62.
    A lively summary of Ramist criticism. Discusses and
attempts to refute A. J. Smith (3.192) and Rosemond Tuve
(3.208). Concludes that "it is still not clear that
there is any need to seek a connection between Ramism and
English poetry; but, if one must be sought at all, the neo-
Ramists might surely have found a happier hunting-ground
than the poems of men as unPuritanical and unsimple as the
English metaphysicals" (p. 262). That is to say, if Ramism
appealed to the Puritans as Perry Miller (3.158) says, and
believed in simplification as most critics believe, how
could Donne be a Ramist?

3.225 WEBBER, JOAN. The Eloquent "I": Style and Self in Seventeenth-
Century Prose. Madison, Wis.: The University of Wisconsin
Press, 1968, 312 pp.
    "Seventeenth-century literature contains a number of
works of prose nonfiction in which the self-conscious first
person singular is so important that it can be employed by
the critic as a central means to a definition of the nature
of the style" (p. 3). Compares and contrasts Anglican and
Puritan prose styles, with the Anglican more likely to be
interested in art as art and the Puritan's prose "less
volatile and less resonant than that of the Anglican" (p. 8).
Discusses Donne, Bunyan, Lilburne, Burton, Richard Baxter,
Sir Thomas Browne, Milton, and Thomas Traherne. Contains a
bibliographical essay, notes (22 pp.), and index (5 pp.).

3.226 WILLCOCK, GLADYS DOIDGE and ALICE WALKER. "Introduction," in
The Arte of English Poesie by George Puttenham. Edited by
Gladys Doidge Willcock and Alice Walker. Cambridge, England: Cambridge University Press, 1936, pp. xi-cx.
    First to authoritatively establish George Puttenham as
author. Dates composition in mid-1560s. Discusses all
three books of Puttenham's work, but is apologetic concerning Book III. Speaks of "the rhetorical cult (now
deadest of all) a sort of religious industry in language
that soon enabled it [English verse? language?] to throw
away its crutches of schemes and tropes" (p. xi).

3.227 WILLIAMSON, GEORGE. The Senecan Amble: A Study in Prose Form
from Bacon to Collier. 1951; Chicago: The University of
Chicago Press, Phoenix Books, 1966, 377 pp.
    "This is not a history of prose style in the seventeenth
century, but an account of its most incisive pattern. Yet,
as it deals with one of the extremes that serve to define
contemporary styles, it becomes more than the story of a
fashion" (p. 7). Deals with Anti-Ciceronian movement
during the seventeenth century. Discusses Lipsius, Bacon,
and the Royal Society. Builds on the work of Morris Croll.

Traces a shift from Cicero to Seneca as prose model of the
age. Often cited. "Index of Authors" (6 pp.).

3.228 WILLIAMSON, GEORGE [E.]. "Senecan Style in the Seventeenth
Century." PQ, 15 (1936), 321-51.
Early article on the role of Seneca in the change in
prose style during the seventeenth century. Related to
Morris W. Croll and Richard Foster Jones. Thesis is that
"the separation or opposition of the curt style and the
loose style distinguishes the Restoration from the first
half of the century" (p. 325). Discusses Lipsius, Bacon,
Owen Feltham, and Milton, among numerous others.

3.229 WILSON, H. S. "Gabriel Harvey's Orations on Rhetoric." ELH,
12 (1945), 167-82.
Describes three orations: Ciceronianus and Rhetor
(which is composed of two orations). Ciceronianus "extrava-
gant," but not in "bad taste" (p. 170). Points out that
this is Harvey's declaration of his devotion to Ramus
(171-72). Dates Harvey's rhetorical conversion at 1568-
1569. Harvey attacks Ascham (p. 173). The Rhetor "even
more ardently Ramist" (p. 175). The second oration therein
uses the "allegorical figure" of Exercitatio (p. 178).
"Harvey is the earliest English advocate of Ramus I can
identify; and it is plain that it took more than a fair
share of initiative to be a Ramist advocate in England when
Harvey delivered" these orations (pp. 180-81).

3.230 WILSON, HAROLD S. "Introduction," in Gabriel Harvey's
Ciceronianus, With an Introduction and Notes by Harold S.
Wilson, And an English Translation by Clarence A. Forbes.
University of Nebraska Studies, November 1945; Studies in
the Humanities No. 4. Lincoln, Nebr.: 1945, pp. 1-34.
Discusses Harvey's reputation, university career, and
dates lecture as near May, 1576. Only one edition (1577)
of Ciceronianus. Describes work as deliberative oratory
concerning the best Latin style (p. 14). Discusses Harvey's
Ramism. Points to and illustrates the high quality of
Harvey's Latin.

3.231 WRIGHT, LOUIS B. "William Perkins: Elizabethan Apostle of
'Practical Divinity.'" HLQ, 3 (1939-40), 171-96.
Surveys and discusses many of Perkins's works. Points
out that Perkins was extremely popular during the seventeenth century, but has been relatively ignored since.
Discusses The Arte of Prophecying briefly (p. 188), and
then examines his influence on New England (pp. 194-95).
Sees Perkins as anti-eloquence. Perkins was a realist
who was "helping to shape the whole social, ethical, and
even literary outlook of the masses of Englishmen"
(p. 196).

3.232 YATES, FRANCES A. <u>The Art of Memory</u>. Chicago: The University of Chicago Press, 1966, 416 pp.

Traces and discusses memory as a part of rhetoric from Simonides of Ceos through Leibnitz. Concentrates on Renaissance. Points out that fifteenth- and sixteenth-century memory treatises are abundant. Indicates that most medieval treatises follow <u>Ad Herennium</u>, but many of the Renaissance treatises follow Aristotle's principles of memory through association. Artificial memory systems described: Rossellius and places, Romberch and visual alphabet, Peter of Revenna, Lullism as art of memory, discussed at length. Several chapters on Giordano Bruno who stirred some controversy in England: "Giordano Bruno: The Secret of Shadows," "Giordano Bruno: The Secret of <u>Seals</u>," "Giordano Bruno: Last Works on Memory," and "The Art of Memory and Bruno's Italian Dialogues." Bruno's system described in conflict with the natural method of "Ramism as an Art of Memory." Bruno's death by Inquisition for practicing magic described as well as those magical elements. Robert Fludd's theater stage method and possible diagram of actual reconstructed Globe Theatre presented. Diagrams and illustrations (facsimile), some quite obscure but relevant. Index.

3.233 YATES, FRANCES A. <u>Giordano Bruno and the Hermetic Tradition</u>. Chicago: The University of Chicago Press, 1964, 480 pp.

Development of concepts the author deems necessary for full understanding of her book (3.232). Background on Hermes Trismegistus who influenced Bruno through Cornelius Agrippa. Summarizes five Hermetic writings (pp. 22-40) with Ficino's commentary interspersed. Does discuss memory (esp. pp. 190-204). Uses "Hermes Trismegistus" as a term to "cover the whole movement studied in this book" (p. 455). Hermes, of course, never existed, but during the Renaissance he was considered to have been an ancient.

Part 4

The Eighteenth Century

WINIFRED BRYAN HORNER

Introduction

In looking over the eighteenth-century authors of works on rhetoric, one is struck by the familiarity of the names: Joseph Priestley, man of science who discovered oxygen; Adam Smith, author of the <u>Wealth of Nations</u>; Thomas Sheridan, son of Richard Sheridan and himself a well-known actor; Lord Kames, lawyer and literary critic; and David Hume, eminent philosopher. Few of these men would have considered themselves only rhetoricians, but all of them were deeply concerned with human discourse and the discovery and communication of ideas. In their lifetimes, all of them developed rhetorical theories as they pursued other interests or taught moral philosophy, moral science, or rhetoric and belles lettres at their universities.

Such men indicate the nature of eighteenth-century rhetoric, which is characterized by its close connection with the philosophic, psychological, and epistemological movements of the day. The eighteenth century was a period of great concern with the nature of knowledge, its relation to experience, and the ways in which knowledge is discovered, organized, and disseminated. Out of these concerns came the rhetoricians and the rhetorical theories of the period. For the eighteenth century, rhetoric was central to all intellectual life.

Just as modern theorists view rhetoric as closely connected with twentieth-century cognitive theory and language philosophy, so for eighteenth-century theorists, it was closely allied with empiricism, faculty psychology, the doctrine of association, the philosophy of common sense, and the study of belles lettres. These close connections present obvious problems for the bibliographer who must make appropriate choices about what to include and exclude. For example, David Hume's rhetorical theory is distributed throughout many of his philosophical essays, and thus his collected essays must be included. Also, Thomas Reid's epistemological system, although technically not a rhetoric, is basic to so many important rhetorical theories that it cannot reasonably be excluded.

Rhetoric's close connection with education is also apparent in the eighteenth century, when mastery of "correct" written and spoken language was important for an emerging middle class. Many handbooks

and school books of the time demonstrate the continuing connection
between rhetorical theory and education. Such works, whose number is
legion, represent applied theory and are only minimally represented
here. The ones included, such as James Burgh's The Art of Speaking,
are meant to serve as examples of many others like them.

Rhetoric's alliance with logic is still very much in evidence in
the eighteenth century in spite of the earlier attempt by Peter Ramus
to separate the disciplines. Isaac Watts defines logic as "the art
of using reason well in our inquiries after Truth, and the Communication of it to others" (4.8, p. 13). Such a concept shared by other
eighteenth-century logicians and rhetoricians makes it virtually impossible to separate logic and rhetoric.

As the century draws to a close, the scholar sees the philosophical
and rhetorical concern with belles lettres and the concept of "taste"
and with the beginnings of the great interest in literary criticism and
aesthetics. There is a shift during the century from the early concern
with the generation of a text to the later concern with its reception
by a reader. The works represented here show the roots of that shift
within the rhetorical theories of such men as Adam Smith, Hugh Blair,
and Lord Kames, and their works necessarily lead the scholar to the
vast literature on "taste" and aesthetics. Such subjects, however,
are represented in this study only while still incorporated within
the rhetorical theory out of which they were born. Thus Hugh Blair's
work on "taste" in his famous Lectures is still within the province
of a rhetorical theory and is included, while Alexander Gerard's well-
known "Essay on Taste," published in 1759, is exclusively concerned
with aesthetics and is therefore omitted. In the final analysis, any
attempt to separate literary criticism, aesthetics, philosophy, logic,
or psychology from the system of rhetorical thought distorts and reduces the true picture, since in the eighteenth century, before the
age of high specialization, many thinking men in different fields of
endeavor considered themselves rhetoricians and rhetorical theory, in
turn, permeated the intellectual climate.

It is important at some point to designate lines of difference
among the primary works in eighteenth-century rhetoric since the differences are not always apparent in the titles, which can, in fact,
be misleading. Thus, Dominique Bouhours's La Manière de bien Penser
dans les Ouvrages d'Esprit appears in two English translations, the
first entitled The Art of Criticism and the second entitled The Arts
of Logick and Rhetoric. Not only are the terms--logic, rhetoric,
criticism, and style--used interchangeably, but, over and over again,
the term rhetoric is used for texts having widely variant subject
matter. For the purpose of delineating real substantive differences,
the primary rhetorical works can be divided into several broad
categories.

The first category would include those rhetorics in the neoclassical tradition. Of paramount importance in this group are John

Holmes's <u>The Art of Rhetoric Made Easy</u>, John Lawson's <u>Lectures</u>, and John Ward's <u>A System of Oratory</u>. The third work, published in 1759, is probably the fullest restatement of the classical canon in the English language. All of these texts preserve Ciceronian doctrine largely intact.

In a second category are the stylistic texts of the eighteenth century that saw rhetoric as confined to stylistic ornamentation. Included here are the works of John Brightland, Anthony Blackwall and Thomas Gibbons, typical of others that were current at the time.

An important third category would include those works that concentrate on the fifth office of rhetoric, elocution, an important and popular movement in the eighteenth century. John Mason's <u>An Essay on Elocution</u>, published in 1748, is one of the early elocutionary treatises and was followed in 1761 by James Burgh's <u>The Art of Speaking</u>, written for younger students, a widely circulated and popular text in both England and the United States. John Herries's later work, <u>The Elements of Speech</u>, was an attempt to popularize the movement while the works of the well-known actors Thomas Sheridan and John Walker demonstrate the close connection between elocution and the stage. Joshua Steele, a member of the mechanical school of elocution, attempts, in his work, to record the intonational patterns and rhythms of speech by means of an intricate symbol system roughly based on musical terminology. Elocutionary manuals were popular in the eighteenth century and those included in this bibliography such as the anonymous <u>An Essay on the Action Proper for the Pulpit</u>, 1753, and Thomas Leland's <u>A Dissertation on the Principles of Human Eloquence</u>, 1764, are examples of many others like them.

A fourth group of works includes those treatises on logic by Isaac Watts and William Duncan, and the translation by John Henley of de Crousaz's <u>A New Treatise of the Art of Thinking</u>. These authors still consider logic to be a theory of learned communication. In the latter part of the century, in the works of Thomas Reid, George Campbell and Lord Kames, there emerges a new logic of scientific enquiry. The syllogism comes under serious attack, particularly by Reid and Campbell, and deduction and scientific experimentation become the way of discovering truth. Thus, although logic is still connected with communication in many earlier works, in the latter half of the century it becomes increasingly separate from rhetorical theory.

A final category of primary works included here deals with aesthetics and literary criticism, emphasizing standards of judgment and taste. Faculty psychology, the doctrine of associationism, and the philosophy of common sense were influential in this development. One of the early works on the art of criticism was that of Dominique Bouhours, but Lord Kames's <u>Elements of Criticism</u>, published in 1762, was the first of its kind to suggest taste and a moral sense as a basis for critical standards of judgment. His work was influential

on Adam Smith, Thomas Reid, Joseph Priestley, and Hugh Blair, and it
is from this group of authors that the principles of aesthetics and
English literary criticism developed in the nineteenth century.

Although the great lectures published at the English and Scottish
universities during the period cannot be confined to any single subject category, no overview of eighteenth-century rhetoric would be
complete without mention of them. John Lawson initiated the custom
in 1758 with the publication of the lectures that he delivered at
Trinity College, Dublin. Others like John Ward, Thomas Leland,
George Campbell, and Hugh Blair followed suit, and many of these
lectures were used in British and American colleges well into the
nineteenth century. Hugh Blair's Lectures went through at least 130
editions, the last in 1911. Their influence on eighteenth- and
nineteenth-century letters is impossible to measure, but it was
obviously great.

Ultimately, it is in these lectures that the large issues can be
traced; it is in these lectures that rhetoric shows its connection
not only with classical doctrine, but also with eighteenth-century
philosophy, psychology, education, and literary criticism. It is in
these lectures that the best of eighteenth-century rhetoric can be
most clearly divined as it evolves out of the classical canon, is
altered by Cartesian, Baconian and Ramistic rhetoric, or by the
epistemology of its own age, and moves into the rhetorical and aesthetic concerns that mark subsequent developments in the discipline
of English letters. Finally, it is through these lectures that the
voice of eighteenth-century rhetoric speaks most eloquently.

The secondary scholarship in the field of eighteenth-century
rhetoric has been led by a small but active group of scholars. Wilbur
Samuel Howell's work, Eighteenth-Century British Logic and Rhetoric,
published in 1971, furnishes a comprehensive overview through close
analyses of the texts of the period. The scholarship is thorough and
accurate and any serious study of eighteenth-century rhetoric must
begin with that work as well as his articles. The introduction to
James Golden and Edward P. J. Corbett's The Rhetoric of Blair,
Campbell, and Whately, first published in 1968 and reissued in 1980,
provides a brief survey of eighteenth-century rhetoric with an examination of its roots in classical doctrine. The work of Vincent
Bevilacqua covers a range of eighteenth-century rhetorical figures
including Adam Smith, John Lawson, Alexander Gerard, James Beattie,
Joseph Priestley, George Campbell, and Hugh Blair, but, unfortunately,
his work in eighteenth-century rhetoric does not appear to extend beyond 1968. Douglas Ehninger's work is primarily concerned with
eighteenth-century theories of invention in connection with Campbell,
Blair, and Ward, while Warren Guthrie's dissertation and the articles
derived from that study provide a full picture of rhetorical practices in the United States during the period.

Introduction

In addition to these scholars, during the late fifties and sixties the names of Lloyd Bitzer, Adelbert E. Bradley, Jr., Herman Cohen, Clarence Edney, and G. P. Mohrmann appear prominently in the study of historical rhetoric as that subject became one of concern in the discipline of speech. After this period of interest, with the outstanding exception of Wilbur Samuel Howell, the scholarship diminishes and virtually disappears in the seventies.

With the current revival of interest in applied rhetoric and its historical tradition, it is to be hoped that young scholars will take up that work once again. There is still much to be done and such studies would greatly enhance our understanding of not only eighteenth-century life and letters but our own times as well.

No work of this kind can be accomplished without the help of librarians. I am grateful for the support of the librarians at the National Library of Scotland, the universities of London and Edinburgh, the British Library, and my own library at the University of Missouri-Columbia.

I should also like to express my appreciation to a number of scholars for their assistance in reviewing the manuscript and suggesting changes and additions and, most of all, for supporting me and this work from its inception. I include among these, Edward P. J. Corbett, Haskell Hinnant, Wilbur Samuel Howell, James J. Murphy, Walter J. Ong, John R. Roberts, and Richard Young.

Acknowledgement is also due to the Research Council of the Graduate School at the University of Missouri, Columbia, for providing funds for travel and typing assistance.

WINIFRED BRYAN HORNER
University of Missouri-Columbia

Primary Works

*4.1   1702. ANON. <u>An Essay upon the Action of an Orator; As to his</u>
<u>Pronunciation and Gesture, Useful both for Divines and Law-</u>
<u>yers, and necessary for all Young Gentlemen, that study how</u>
<u>to Speak well in Publick</u>. London, 268 pp.
     English translation of Michel Le Faucheur's <u>Traicté de</u>
<u>l'action de l'orateur</u>, printed in 1657 at Paris from an un-
published treatise. The Latin version of Melchior Schmidt
and the English translations were influential in England
in the early elocutionary movement of the eighteenth century. An anonymous pamphlet, <u>Some Rules for Speaking and</u>
<u>Action</u>, published in London in 1715 and based on this trans-
lation, had five English editions.

4.1a   ANON. <u>The Art of Speaking in Public or an Essay on the</u>
<u>Action of an Orator</u>. London, 1727, 265 pp.
     Second edition of the English translation of Le Faucheur's
<u>Traicté</u> with an "Introduction relating to the Famous Mr.
Henly's present Oratory." The anonymous editor asserts
that he is responding to "great Demands" for this second
edition, "The town having been of late very much alarm'd
at the <u>Reverend</u> and <u>ingenious</u> Mr. Henly's extraordinary
Performances and Attempts, to revive the ancient Manner of
Speaking in Public" (p. xiv). (Annotation based on microfilm. BCRE Reel no. 4, Item 42.)

*4.1b   ANON. <u>An Essay upon Pronunciation and Gesture, Founded</u>
<u>upon the Best Rules and Authorities of the Ancients</u>.
London, 1750.
     Third edition of English translation of Le Faucheur's
<u>Traicté</u>. For a discussion of these translations, <u>see</u>
Howell, 4.103, pp. 164-81.

4.2   1705. DOMINIQUE BOUHOURS. <u>The Art of Criticism; or The Method</u>
<u>of Making a Right Judgment Upon Subjects of Wit and Learning.</u>
<u>In four dialogues</u>. London, 315 pp.
     First edition in English of Bouhours's <u>La Manière de bien</u>
<u>Penser dans les Ouvrages d'Esprit</u>, Paris, 1687, 482 pp.
"Translated from the best edition of the French, of the

famous Father Bouhours, by a person of quality" (from the
title page). Four dialogues between Eudoxe and Philanthe.
The first deals with truth, the second with agreeableness,
delicacy, and grandeur, and the third and fourth with the
necessity for clearness and intelligibility. The NUC lists
sixteen French editions between 1687 and 1771. (Annotation
based on Nouvelle Edition, Paris, 1768.)

4.2a   The Arts of Logick and Rhetorick, illustrated by examples
        taken out of the best authors, antient and modern. London,
        1728, 473 pp.
            The second English edition of Bouhours's La Manière,
        freely edited by J. Oldmixon whose name does not appear on
        the title page but does appear at the end of the dedication.
        Adds English examples. One of the early movements in the
        development of criticism. Oldmixon explains in the preface:
        "The Design of Père Bouhours is to form the judgment not by
        dry and rigid Rules only, but by the Beauties and Blemishes
        of the most celebrated Writers, ancient and modern"
        (Sig. A.1.r).

*4.3 1706. RENE RAPIN. The Whole Critical Works of Monsieur Rapin,
        In Two Volumes . . . Newly Translated into English by Sev-
        eral Hands. 2 vols. London, 590 pp.
            The publication of the first English translation of
        Rapin's collected works, "established in learned circles
        in Britain the idea that the belles lettres had four prin-
        cipal branches and eight preeminent authors, so far as the
        literature of ancient Greece and Rome was concerned"
        (Howell, 4.103, p. 524). Includes his Réflexions sur
        l'Usage de l'Eloquence de ce Temps and his Discours sur la
        Comparaison de l'Eloquence de Démosthène et de Cicéron.

4.4 1712. JOHN BRIGHTLAND. A Grammar of the English Tongue.
        London, 266 pp.
            In the Ciceronian tradition, the author "endeavors to
        open the Doore to all Englishmen, to learn the Arts in
        their own Mother-Tongue; as did the Greeks, and the Romans
        did of old, and the French Nation does at present"
        (Sig. A.2.v.). Part 1 (130 pp.) is devoted to "Grammar,"
        Part 2 to the "Art of Poetry," and Part 3 (23 pp.) to
        "Rhetoric or the Art of Persuasion." A traditional Aris-
        totelian approach to rhetoric is followed by a listing of
        tropes. He identifies trope as "a Word . . . known almost
        to the very Fishwives" (p. 183). Concludes with a section
        on logic. (Annotation based on microfilm. BCRE Reel no. 1,
        Item 10.)

4.5 1718. ANTHONY BLACKWALL. An Introduction to the Classics.
        London, 256 pp. Reprinted with revisions and additions in
        Robert Dodsley, The Preceptor, London, 1748. Extracted

from The Preceptor and reprinted for the "Use of the University in Cambridge," Boston, 1796.

A collection of essays "designed for the Use and Instruction of Younger Scholars; and Gentlemen who have for some Years neglected the Advantages of Their Education, and have a mind to resume those pleasant and useful Studies" (Sig. A.2.r.). An attempt to "reform Rhetorick from the Rubbish and Barbarism which it lies under in the common books; those dry and trifling Systems in some Schools" (Sig. A.3.r.). Limits rhetoric to stylistic ornamentation. Chapter 1 of the second part defines the concept of tropes and figures. Chapters 2, 3, and 4 treat the chief tropes and figures in some detail. Widely circulated and influential in the neoclassic tradition. (Annotation based on microfilm. BCRE Reel no. 1, Item 7.)

4.6 1722. WILLIAM STEVENSON. Dialogues Concerning Eloquence. London. 342 pp.

The first English translation of Fénelon, Archbishop of Cambrai's Dialogues sur L'Eloquence en General first published in Amsterdam in 1717. Using the dialectic mode, Fénelon inveighs against the old stylistic rhetoric and argues for a new style of preaching based on simplicity, naturalness, and conviction. Later English translations by Alfred Jenour and Samuel J. Eales appeared in London in 1847 and 1897. For a modern translation, see Wilbur Samuel Howell's Fénelon's Dialogues on Eloquence (Princeton, N.J.: Princeton University Press, 1951, 160 pp.).

4.7 1724. JEAN PIERRE DE CROUSAZ. A New Treatise of the Art of Thinking; Or, a Compleat System of Reflections, Concerning the Conduct and Improvement of the Mind. 2 vols. London, 919 pp.

A translation by John Henley of Crousaz's La Logique which sees logic as learned communication. Crousaz defines logic as a "System of such Principles, Observations, and Maxims, as are able to furnish the human Understanding with a greater Degree of Penetration . . . either to discover Truth of itself, or to comprehend it when proposed to it by others, or lastly, to communicate it to them in its Turn upon its own Discovery" (vol. 1, p. 2). At least five editions or abridgments in Europe in the eighteenth century, although this is the only edition of the English translation.

4.8 1725. ISAAC WATTS. Logick; Or the Right Use of Reason in the Enquiry after Truth. London. 543 pp.

Defines logic as the "art of using reason well in our inquiries after Truth, and the Communication of it to others" (p. 13). Demonstrates the close connection between a theory of enquiry and a theory of communication. Divided

into four parts: "Of Perception and Ideas," "Of Judgment
and Proposition," "Of Reasoning and Syllogism," and "Of
Method." (Annotation based on Early American Imprints:
Evans no. 22246, microprint of sixteenth edition, Philadelphia, 1789, 371 pp.)

4.9 1739. JOHN HOLMES. The Art of Rhetoric Made Easy: In Two
     Books. London, 95 pp.
         "The Elements of Oratory, Briefly stated, and fitted for
     the Practice of the Studious Youth of Great-Britain and
     Ireland" (from the title page). Written primarily for
     youth in grammar schools, it follows the classical canon.
     Book 1 divides rhetoric into invention or "the finding of
     Arguments" (p. 1), disposition or "the right placing of
     arguments" (p. 15), elocution or "the adornment of our Ex-
     pression with Tropes, Figures, and Beautiful Turns" (p. 24),
     and pronunciation or "the Ornaments of Utterance and Action"
     (p. 73). Book 2 is a summary of Longinus's On the Sublime.
     In 1786, combined with John Stirling's A System of Rhetoric,
     first published in London, 1733. (Annotation based on
     microfilm. BCRE Reel no. 5, Item 45.)

4.10 1741. DAVID HUME. Essays Moral, Political and Literary.
      Reprinted in The World's Classics, 33. London: William
      Clowes and Sons, Limited, 1904, 616 pp.
          Hume's attitudes toward rhetoric, together with his con-
      cept of taste, are reflected in many of these essays, but
      of special importance are "Of the Delicacy of Taste and
      Passion" (p. 3), "Of Eloquence" (p. 98), "Of Simplicity
      and Refinement in Writing" (p. 196), "Of Tragedy" (p. 221),
      and "Of the Standard of Taste" (p. 231). In "Of Eloquence,"
      Hume asserts that there has been a serious decline in modern
      eloquence compared with that of the ancients. An endorse-
      ment of ancient principles of rhetoric and a rejection of
      modern. Although a member of the empirical school of
      philosophy and an eighteenth-century literary stylist,
      Hume's attitudes toward eloquence are "curiously static,
      curiously unhistorical, and curiously antiquarian" (Howell,
      4.103, p. 616).

4.11 1748. WILLIAM DUNCAN. "The Elements of Logick." London.

4.11a   WILLIAM DUNCAN. The Elements of Logic. Philadelphia,
      1792, 240 pp.
          First printed anonymously in Robert Dodsley's The Pre-
      ceptor, London, 1748, this is the first American edition.
      Sees logic as the ability of the mind to form ideas, to see
      relations between ideas, and to demonstrate those relations
      through discourse. Book 2 deals with the grounds of judg-
      ment and the doctrine of propositions, Book 3 with reason-
      ing and demonstration.

4.12 1748. JOHN MASON. <u>An Essay on Elocution or Pronunciation</u>.
London, 39 pp.
   One of the earliest treatises on elocution. Asserts
that "Elocution is a Branch of Oratory, the Power and Importance of which is greater than is generally thought;
insomuch that Eloquence takes it's Name from it" (p. 3).
Concentrates on the fifth part of rhetoric: "Pronunciation;
or the Art of managing the Voice, and Gesture in speaking"
(p. 4). (Annotation based on microfilm. Eighteenth-
Century Sources for the Study of English Literature and
Culture, Roll 87.)

4.13 1753. ANON. <u>An Essay on the Action Proper for the Pulpit</u>.
London, 87 pp.
   One of the elocutionary manuals popular in the eighteenth-
century often credited to John Mason. Treats <u>actio</u> alone
and divides it into voice and gesture. Offers practical
suggestions to the preacher for cultivating voice and gesture appropriate for the pulpit.

4.14 1758. JOHN LAWSON. <u>Lectures Concerning Oratory Delivered in
Trinity College, Dublin</u>. London, 486 pp. Reprinted in
facsimile: E. Neal Claussen and Karl R. Wallace, eds.
Southern Illinois University Series, Landmarks in Rhetoric
and Public Address. Edited by David Potter. Carbondale:
Southern Illinois University Press, 1972, 510 pp.
   These lectures and those of Thomas Leland (4.20) are the
only known lectures extant from the Erasmus Smith Foundation
at Trinity College, Dublin. The twenty-three lectures fall
within the Ciceronian tradition and reflect a reaction
against rhetoric as merely stylistic ornamentation. Lectures 1-7 are on the "History of Eloquence," lectures 8 and
9 on "Address to Reason," lectures 10 and 11 on "Address to
the Passions," lecture 12 on "Style," 13 on "Ornament," 14
on "Composition," 15 on "Figures," 16 and 17 are on "Reading the Poets," 18 on "Style," 19 through 22 on "Eloquence
of the Pulpit," and lecture 23 is on "Modern Latin Poesy."
Lawson established a new custom for the publication of lectures followed by other eighteenth-century rhetoricians.
Four printings in the eighteenth century.

4.15 1759. JOHN WARD. <u>A System of Oratory, Delivered in a Course
of Lectures Publicly read at Gresham College</u>. 2 vols.
London, 879 pp.
   Published a year after Ward's death, these lectures in
the neoclassical tradition were delivered at Gresham College where Ward taught for 38 years. Fifty-four lectures,
nearly 900 pages. Probably the fullest restatement of
classical doctrine in the English language.

4.16 1761. JAMES BURGH. The Art of Speaking. London. Reprinted:
Boston, 1795, 335 pp.
    Contains "An Essay; in which are given Rules for express-
ing properly the principal Passions and Humours, which occur
in Reading or public Speaking;" and, second, "Lessons taken
from the Ancients and Moderns" (from the title page). Concludes with "An Index of the Passions." Written for younger
students, it was a widely circulated and popular example of
an elocutionary text. The NUC lists eighteen editions, with
eleven American ones.

4.17 1762. THOMAS SHERIDAN. A Course of Lectures on Elocution
Together With Two Dissertations on Language. London.
Reissued: New York: Benjamin Blom, Inc., 1968, 290 pp.
    One of the most popular elocutionary texts of the
eighteenth century, written by an actor and showing the
close connection between the stage and the elocutionary
movement. After two preliminary sections, there are five
sections on articulation, accent, emphasis, pauses and
stops, tones, and gestures. The two dissertations are the
"Heads for a Plan for the Improvement of Elocution and For
Promoting the Study of the English Language in order to the
Refining, Ascertaining, and Reducing it to a Standard; together with Some Arguments, to enforce the Necessity of
Carrying such a Plan into Execution." Eleven eighteenth-
century editions listed in NUC. Sheridan also published
two other popular elocutionary texts: Lectures on the Art
of Reading in 1775 and A Rhetorical Grammar of the English
Language in 1781. (Annotation based on microfilm. BCRE
Reel no. 7, Item 67.)

4.18 1762. HENRY HOME, LORD KAMES. Elements of Criticism.
Edinburgh. 3 vols. Reprinted in facsimile: Anglistica
and Americana, A Series of Reprints Selected by Bernhard
Fabian, et al. Hildesheim and New York: George Olms
Verlag, 1970, 3 vols., 1241 pp.
    Demonstrates the shift in rhetoric from emphasis on the
creative act to an emphasis on reader reaction and the development of critical standards for judgment. Taste and a
moral sense are the principles of Kames's criticism and
both "are rooted in human nature, and are governed by principles common to all men" (p. 7). Twenty-five chapters in
three volumes. The first sixteen chapters deal with his
psychological tenets, the following six with language, and
Chapter 25 with a "Standard of Taste." The NUC lists sixteen English editions and forty-six American ones.

4.19 1762-63. ADAM SMITH. Lectures on Rhetoric and Belles Lettres
Delivered in the University of Glasgow by Adam Smith Re-
ported by a Student in 1762-63. Edited by John M. Lothian.
Southern Illinois University Series, Landmarks in Rhetoric

and Public Address. Edited by David Potter. Carbondale: Southern Illinois University Press, 1971, 245 pp.

At the urging of Lord Kames and others, Adam Smith presented a series of lectures on rhetoric and belles lettres at local halls and clubs as well as at the universities in Edinburgh and Glasgow. These student notes are all that survive of the twenty-nine lectures. The first ten concern the nature of language and style with a brief consideration of figures of speech. The next six deal with narrative, didactic, and rhetorical prose followed by several lectures on historical and descriptive writing. Concludes with lecture on demonstrative, deliberative, and judicial eloquence. Interspersed with examples, some modern and many ancient. Smith saw rhetoric as a theory for all language--historical, poetic, scientific, and oratorical. Index added by editor.

4.20 1764. THOMAS LELAND. A Dissertation on the Principles of Human Eloquence. London, 106 pp.

The substance of lectures read in the Oratory School of Trinity College, Dublin. A reply to a treatise on the Doctrine of Grace by the Lord Bishop of Gloucester, who argued that pulpit oratory must be divinely inspired. Leland questions "Whether an inspired Language must be a language of perfect Eloquence" (p. vi). Leland held the Erasmus Smith lectureship at Trinity College and his and John Lawson's (4.14) are the only extant lectures from that Foundation. (Annotation based on microfilm. BCRE Reel no. 5, Item 49.)

4.21 1764. THOMAS REID. An Inquiry into the Human Mind, on the Principles of Common Sense. London and Edinburgh, 557 pp.

Widely read in the early part of the eighteenth century both in England and Scotland and considered influential in the development of later eighteenth-century rhetorical theory. Editions in 1765, 1769, 1785, 1801, 1810, 1817, 1822 and 1823. Reid's answer to Hume's philosophy in particular and to skepticism in general. States that skepticism has triumphed over all the dictates of common sense, and that all philosophy must be rooted finally in common sense. Treats all of the sensations in order--a chapter for each: "Smelling," "Tasting," "Hearing," "Touch," and "Seeing"--interspersing them with his inquiry into the nature of the human mind. Concludes that ideas in the mind are formed by reflection or analogy, and common sense. These principles largely replaced the concepts of classical invention in later eighteenth-century rhetorical doctrine.

4.22 1767. THOMAS GIBBONS. Rhetoric. London, 482 pp.

A stylistic rhetoric typical of others which were current in the eighteenth century. Gibbons asserts that he is adding to the work of the Reverend Mr. Anthony Blackwall

(4.5), and Dr. John Ward (4.15) by drawing not only from
the ancients but also from the moderns. Draws examples
from "writers ancient and modern" as well as from the
"sacred Scriptures" (Sig. A.6.r.). Discusses the general
nature of tropes in Part 1 and the figures in Part 2, followed by examples. (Annotation based on microfilm. BCRE
Reel no. 4, Item 38.)

4.23 1773. JOHN HERRIES. The Elements of Speech. London, 275 pp.
      An attempt to popularize the elocutionary movement. "We
intend to conduct the young speaker from lower degrees of
perfection, to higher, till at last he is enabled to dis-
play to the best advantage, all the riches of language,
the charms of voice, the powers of understanding, of the
imagination, and of the passions" (p. 8). Part 1 contains
eight chapters that treat the sounds of language in terms
of the organs of speech and the way that sounds are produced, with chapters 5 and 6 devoted to speech impediments
and teaching the deaf and dumb to speak. The eight chapters of Part 2 are on the qualities and command of speech.

4.24 1774. THOMAS REID. "A Brief Account of Aristotle's Logic,"
      in vol. 2, Appendix of Henry Home, Lord Kames's Sketches
of the History of Man. 2 vols. Edinburgh and London.
Reprinted: Thomas Reid. Philosophical Works. 2 vols.
Hildesheim: George Olms Verlag, 1967, 2, 681-714.
      Six chapters in which Reid explains and evaluates Aris-
totle's logic. A leader of the new logic, Reid attacks the
syllogism saying that it is the use of a proposition to
prove itself--a petitio principii. Acknowledges debt to
Locke: "The state of logic is much altered since Locke
wrote. Logic has been much improved" (p. 230).

4.25 1774. THOMAS REID. "Lectures on the Fine Arts," in Thomas
      Reid's Lectures on the Fine Arts. Edited by Peter Kivy.
Martinus Nijhoff, 1973, pp. 19-57.
      Edited from a manuscript in the Edinburgh University
Library (La.III, 176), comprised of a title page and
ninety-seven pages. Reid's plan is to consider (1) the
connection between mind and body, (2) taste, (3) fine arts,
(4) eloquence, and (5) how these powers might be improved.
Although these lectures are labeled Volume 1, there is no
second volume.

4.26 1775. JOSHUA STEELE. An Essay Towards Establishing the
      Melody and Measure of Speech to be Expressed and Perpetuated
by Peculiar Symbols. Piccadilly, 215 pp.
      Dedicated to the president and fellows of the Royal
Society, this work belongs to the mechanical school of
elocution. Presents an intricate system of recording the
intonation and rhythm patterns of speech. Roughly based

on musical terminology. (Annotation based on microfilm. BCRE Reel no. 7, Item 73.)

4.27 1776. GEORGE CAMPBELL. The Philosophy of Rhetoric. London. Reprinted: New Edition, London, 1850, 429 pp. New Edition reprinted in facsimile: Lloyd Bitzer, ed. Southern Illinois University Series, Landmarks in Rhetoric and Public Address. Edited by David Potter. Carbondale: Southern Illinois University Press, 1963, 476 pp.

Used as a textbook in American colleges, this work had at least ten editions in the nineteenth century. Campbell asserts that "all the ends of speaking are reducible to four: every speech being intended to enlighten the understanding, to please the imagination, to move the passions, or to influence the will" (p. 1). Chapter 6 of Book 1 contains Campbell's attack on the syllogism. Campbell's rhetoric is grounded in eighteenth-century philosophy and faculty psychology, and his approach is the one commonly used in twentieth-century rhetoric texts.

4.28 1777. JOSEPH PRIESTLEY. A Course of Lectures on Oratory and Criticism. London, 322 pp. Reprinted in facsimile: Vincent M. Bevilacqua and Richard Murphy, eds. Southern Illinois University Series, Landmarks in Rhetoric and Public Address. Edited by David Potter. Carbondale: Southern Illinois University Press, 1965, 391 pp.

Delivered at Warrington Academy, one of the important dissenting academies. Influenced by the doctrine of the association of ideas. Acknowledges debt to Lord Kames and Dr. Ward's Oratory (4.15). Reduces all composition to narration and argumentation, in which we "relate facts . . . or we lay down some proposition, and endeavor to prove or explain it" (p. 6). Part 3, "Of Style," starts with lecture 1, "Of Taste," and the "Nature of Figurative Language" (p. 71), and introduces the section on criticism--a shift from theory of practice to a theory of criticism. Widely influential. Facsimile edition contains a "Catalogue of Books written by Joseph Priestley" (pp. 314-16).

4.29 1781. JOHN WALKER. Elements of Elocution. Being the Substance of a Course of Lectures on the Art of Reading: Delivered at several Colleges in the University of Oxford. London, 379 pp.

A full elocutionary text widely circulated. Part 1 covers Walker's doctrine of punctuation and voice inflection. Part 2 covers accent, emphasis, gesture and some seventy-five passions. Detailed directions for expressing such passions by placement of the hands and feet as well as by eye, nose, head, and eyebrow movements. Students interested in Walker's part in the elocutionary movement should also see his A Rhetorical Grammar or Course in Elocution

(London, 1785, 385 pp.), a text designed for youth, and his
The Melody of Speaking Delineated; or, Elocution Taught Like
Music, By Visible Signs (London, 1787, 78 pp.). The second
text takes account of the sounds of the language and attempts to form a system of marks to indicate proper voice
inflection and emphasis. (Annotation based on microfilm.
BCRE Reel no. 8, Item 81.)

4.30 1783. HUGH BLAIR. Lectures on Rhetoric and Belles Lettres.
2 vols. London and Edinburgh, 1064 pp. Reprinted in
facsimile: Harold F. Harding, ed. 2 vols. Southern
Illinois University Series, Landmarks in Rhetoric and
Public Address. Edited by David Potter. Carbondale:
Southern Illinois University Press, 1965, 1086 pp.
"At least one hundred and thirty editions were issued,
the last in 1911. Scores of thousands of copies were
printed over scores of years" (Editor's Foreword,
p. v.). Widely used in both England and the United
States. Volume 1 contains four lectures on taste, four on
language, and four on figurative language. Volume 2 contains lectures on different kinds of eloquence: for popular assemblies, the Bar, and the Pulpit. Concludes with a
consideration of historical and philosophical writing and
poetry. Blair follows the classical tradition, especially
Quintilian, but adds to it the tenets of the eighteenth-
century philosophy of common sense wherein the senses become a series of topoi.

4.31 1785. NOAH WEBSTER. An American Selection of Lessons in
Reading and Speaking. Philadelphia. Reprinted: Third
Edition Greatly Enlarged. Philadelphia, 1787, 372 pp.
Contains a section on the rules of elocution and direc-
tions for expressing the principal passions of the mind.
There are forty editions listed in Evans.

4.32 1792-94. JAMES BEATTIE. Elements of Moral Science. 2 vols.
Philadelphia, 572 pp.
An abridgment of lectures delivered at Marischal College
on moral philosophy and logic. Volume 1 treats briefly the
faculty of speech and the essentials of language. Shows
strong influence of faculty psychology. Chapter 1 of part
4 of volume 2 treats rhetoric, concentrating on style and
the general nature of poetry. (Annotation based on Early
American Imprints: Evans microprint nos. 24081 and 26630.)

Secondary Works

4.33 BACON, WALLACE A. "The Elocutionary Career of Thomas Sheridan
(1719-1788)." _SM_, 31 (March 1964), 1-53.
    An account of Sheridan's life and theatrical career with
    discussions of his lectures on elocution and reading. Bib-
    liography of Sheridan's works (pp. 52-53).

4.34 BATE, WALTER JACKSON. From Classic to Romantic: Premises of
    Taste in Eighteenth-Century England. Cambridge: Harvard
    University Press, 1946, 205 pp.
    Traces the classic and neoclassic background for the
    theory of taste as well as its effects on Romanticism.
    Chapters 4 and 5 are concerned with the "Association of
    Ideas" and the "Premise of Feeling."

4.35 BENSON, FRANK THOMAS. "A Comparative Analysis of George
    Campbell's 'Philosophy of Rhetoric.'" Ph.D. dissertation,
    University of Minnesota, 1962, 239 pp.
    Argues that Campbell, in his Philosophy of Rhetoric,
    attempted to substitute David Hume's logic for the Aris-
    totelian system. Concludes that Campbell's view of rhetoric
    and logic is, nevertheless, essentially Aristotelian. (An-
    notation based on Dissertation Abstracts 24/04, p. 1745.)

4.36 BENZIE, W. The Dublin Orator: Thomas Sheridan's Influence on
    Eighteenth-Century Rhetoric and Belles Lettres. Menston
    and Yorkshire, England: Scolar Press, Ltd., 1972, 118 pp.
    Argues that it was Sheridan's "determination to 'revive
    the ancient art of oratory' that led him to attack the 18th
    century system of education and propose a program of studies
    which was so progressive it looked forward nearly two hun-
    dred years to British education in the early twentieth cen-
    tury" (p. v). Chapter 1 is on Sheridan's British Education,
    2 and 3 are on his Lectures on Elocution, 5 is on his Lec-
    tures on the Art of Reading, and 6 is on Sheridan's
    Dictionary.

4.37 BEVILACQUA, VINCENT M. "Adam Smith and Some Philosophical
      Origins of Eighteenth-Century Rhetorical Theory." <u>MLR</u>,
      63 (1968), 559-68.
          Asserts that Smith's lectures were shaped by eighteenth-
      century philosophic thought and that his rejection of tra-
      ditional rhetoric and his emphasis on stylistic and
      belletristic rhetoric were typical of his period. Traces
      influence of Smith on Hugh Blair and Henry Home, Lord Kames.

4.38 BEVILACQUA, VINCENT M. "Adam Smith's Lectures on Rhetoric and
      Belles Lettres." <u>Studies in Scottish Literature</u>, 3
      (July 1965), 41-60.
          Argues that Smith's lectures reflect prevailing
      eighteenth-century philosophical and literary ideas rather
      than classical theory. Also argues the strong influence of
      Smith in "anticipating in mood and precept the works of
      Kames and Blair" (p. 60).

4.39 BEVILACQUA, VINCENT M. "Alexander Gerard's Lectures on Rhet-
      oric: Edinburgh University Library MS. Dc. 5.61." <u>SM</u>,
      34 (August 1967), 384-88.
          A report of notes taken by a student at Marischal Col-
      lege, Aberdeen in 1758-59, purportedly from the lectures
      of Alexander Gerard who was a professor at the college from
      1750 to 1760. Asserts that the lectures "foreshadow a
      union of traditional and Baconian rhetorical theory later
      evident in James Beattie, Hugh Blair, and George Campbell"
      (p. 388).

4.40 BEVILACQUA, VINCENT M. "Campbell, Priestley, and the Contro-
      versy Concerning Common Sense." <u>SSJ</u>, 30 (Winter 1964),
      79-98.
          Outlines the controversy between the schools of common
      sense and associationism and the effect of these opposing
      points of view on George Campbell and Joseph Priestley.
      "The conflict is noteworthy to students of rhetoric because
      it points up a conflict of fundamental psychological con-
      cepts underlying a variety of rhetorical principles in
      Campbell's <u>Rhetoric</u> and Priestley's <u>Lectures</u>" (p. 98).

4.41 BEVILACQUA, VINCENT M. "James Beattie's Theory of Rhetoric."
      <u>SM</u>, 34 (June 1967), 109-24.
          Asserts that Beattie's rhetoric was primarily "a sty-
      listic and epistemological one, founded on the related
      premises that verbal expression is a natural capacity of
      the mind whose improvement is promoted by direct examina-
      tion of the phenomena of human nature." Beattie's rhetoric,
      according to Bevilacqua, is illustrative of "rhetorical
      theory as it was taught in eighteenth-century Scottish
      universities" (p. 124).

4.42 BEVILACQUA, VINCENT M. "Philosophical Assumptions Underlying Hugh Blair's <u>Lectures on Rhetoric and Belles Lettres</u>." <u>WS</u>, 31 (Summer 1967), 150-64.

Maintains that two assumptions underlie Blair's <u>Lectures</u>. First, Blair believes that rhetoric, as well as belles lettres, is the verbal expression of the mental powers of the human mind as they are evidenced in language. He also assumes that such powers comprise "man's fundamental rational, emotional, and imaginative capacities" (p. 159).

4.43 BEVILACQUA, VINCENT M. "Philosophical Influences in the Development of English Rhetorical Theory: 1748 to 1783." <u>Proceedings of the Leeds Philosophical and Literary Society, Literary and Historical Section</u>, 12 (April 1968), 191-215.

Argues that the view of rhetoric held by Adam Smith, Lord Kames, George Campbell, Joseph Priestley, and Hugh Blair is a direct result of the scientific reformation in philosophy, and that this view "altered classical theories of rhetoric by limiting rhetorical invention to a non-investigative function, by restricting rhetoric to an exclusively communicative capacity, and by placing renewed emphasis on style" (p. 207).

4.44 BEVILACQUA, VINCENT M. "Philosophical Origins of George Campbell's <u>Philosophy of Rhetoric</u>." <u>SM</u>, 32 (March 1965), 1-12.

A study of three influences on Campbell's <u>Philosophy of Rhetoric</u>: (1) the influence of Bacon; (2) the influence of scientific analysis from Bacon, Descartes, and Newton; and (3) the influence of moral and aesthetic theory from David Hume and Adam Smith.

4.45 BEVILACQUA, VINCENT MICHAEL. "The Rhetorical Theory of Henry Home, Lord Kames." Ph.D. dissertation, University of Illinois at Urbana-Champaign, 1961, 219 pp.

Asserts that Kames's rhetoric is an attempt "to formulate a 'Newtonian rhetoric'; to find, that is, a rhetorical counterpart to gravitation, a principle which would unify the world of rhetoric as 'attraction' had unified the physical world" (p. 2). Asserts that Kames saw human nature as the unifying principle of his rhetoric. Sees Kames's emphasis on style, drawn from the writings of Demetrius, Dionysius, and Longinus, as characteristic of the interest during the later eighteenth century in belles lettres and in the concept of taste. Draws Kames's theory from the <u>Elements of Criticism</u>, 1762, as well as from the five other relevant works of Kames. Separate chapters deal with Kames's theories of <u>inventio</u>, <u>dispositio</u>, <u>elocutio</u>, and <u>actio</u>.

4.46 BEVILACQUA, VINCENT M. "Two Newtonian Arguments Concerning 'Taste.'" <u>PQ</u>, 47 (October 1968), 585-90.

Argues that both John Lawson and Edmund Burke "employ Sir Isaac Newton's <u>regulae philosophandi</u> as arguments against viewing 'taste' as a distinct or a variable capacity of the mind" (p. 585). Also asserts that both men applied the scientific premises of the British empirical tradition to aesthetics.

4.47 BEVILACQUA, VINCENT and RICHARD MURPHY. "Editors' Introduction" and "Index," in <u>A Course of Lectures on Oratory and Criticism by Joseph Priestley</u>. <u>See</u> 4.28, pp. ix-lviii and pp. lix-lxix.

Biographical background of Priestley as well as a description of the philosophical and cultural climate of the eighteenth century as dominated by faculty psychology and the doctrine of association. Analyzes the lectures in their two main parts: oratory and criticism. Concludes that Priestley's theory of rhetoric is that of a man of science who was an "index scholar" rather than an original thinker. Selected bibliography and index.

4.48 BITZER, LLOYD F. "Editor's Introduction," in <u>The Philosophy of Rhetoric by George Campbell</u>. <u>See</u> 4.27, pp. ix-xxxvii.

Asserts that Campbell's work is an important contribution to rhetorical theory and that Campbell wrote as a philosopher rather than as a practical rhetorician and so "permitted fundamental issues of metaphysics and epistemology to spill over into the theory of rhetoric" (p. x). Outlines Campbell's theory of human nature as well as his responses to phenomenology, empiricism, skepticism, sensation, and naturalism. Bibliography of editions (pp. xix-xxi) and selected bibliography on Campbell, David Hume and the period (pp. xxvi-xxvii).

4.49 BITZER, LLOYD. "Hume's Philosophy in George Campbell's <u>Philosophy of Rhetoric</u>." <u>PR</u>, 2 (Summer 1969), 139-66.

Shows that Campbell's rhetoric depended upon David Hume's views on the "primacy of imagination and feeling, on empiricism and skepticism, on the doctrine of the association of ideas, on the process of experience and, above all, on the analysis of belief" (p. 140). Concludes that Hume's quality of "vivacity" dominates Campbell's rhetoric.

4.50 BITZER, LLOYD F. "A Re-Evaluation of Campbell's Doctrine of Evidence." <u>QJS</u>, 46 (April 1960), 135-40.

Asserts that Campbell's Doctrine of Evidence in Chapter 5 of his <u>Philosophy of Rhetoric</u> (4.27) is an attempt to define the nature of knowledge by answering the question: "Precisely what are the legitimate kinds of evidence?" (p. 134). Campbell finds them in the "common-sense

principles which are intuitively certain and which provide
the underpinnings for a multitude of other truths" (p. 140).

4.51　BOHMAN, GEORGE V.　"Rhetorical Practice in Colonial America,"
in History of Speech Education in America.　Edited by
Karl R. Wallace.　New York:　Appleton-Century-Crofts, Inc.,
1954, pp. 60-79.
　　　Describes the types of speaking exercises in which students participated and the development of rhetorical training in early American colleges.

4.52　BORMANN, D. ROBERT.　"A Rhetoric of the German Enlightenment:
Johann C. Gottsched's Ausfuhrliche Redekunst."　SM, 38
(June 1971), 92-108.
　　　A description of one of the most "complete, popular, and
'modern' of the many eighteenth-century German rhetorics"
(p. 108).　Adapted the faculty psychology of Christian Wolff
to persuasion with the guiding principle being not the mes-
sage but the mind of the hearer.　An English version appeared in London in 1770.

4.53　BOWERS, JOHN WAITE.　"A Comparative Criticism of Hugh Blair's
Essay on Taste."　QJS, 47 (December 1961), 384-89.
　　　Explains that the inclusion of an essay on taste in
Blair's volume on rhetoric and belles lettres was dictated
by late eighteenth-century philosophical and critical
thought.　Compares Blair's concept of taste with those of
Edmund Burke and Immanuel Kant and points out that Blair's
standard of taste, unlike those of Burke and Kant, is use-
less, because it is unstable and shifts with every nation
in every age.

4.54　BRADLEY, ADELBERT EDWARD, JR.　"John Ward's Theory of Rhetoric."
Ph.D. dissertation, The Florida State University, 1955,
447 pp.
　　　Argues for the importance of Ward's theory since it was
influential in both England and America.　Compares Ward's
theory with those that preceded it, with special emphasis
on its relation to classical theory.　Concludes that "it
emerges as the best representative of the English neoclassical movement in rhetoric" (p. 428).　Treats, in
separate chapters, Ward's concepts of invention, disposition, elocution, and pronunciation.

4.55　BRADLEY, BERT E., JR.　"The Inventio of John Ward."　SM, 26
(March 1959), 56-63.
　　　A summary of Ward's approach to inventio.　Asserts that
Ward based his lectures on ancient doctrine and that "the
whole fabric of Ward's inventio retains the texture of the
classical theories" (p. 63).　A greatly abridged version of
Chapter 3 of his dissertation (4.54).

4.56 BRADLEY, BERT E., JR. "John Ward's Concept of Dispositio."
      SM, 24 (November 1957), 258-63.
          An analysis of Ward's approach to dispositio, particu-
      larly in comparison to classical theory. Asserts that "Ward
      presents, on the whole, a faithful reflection of the clas-
      sical theory" (p. 263). A greatly abridged version of
      Chapter 4 of his dissertation (4.54).

4.57 BURWICK, FREDERICK. "Associationist Rhetoric and Scottish
      Prose Style." SM, 34 (March 1967), 21-34.
          Points out the close agreement among the "associationist
      rhetoricians"--Joseph Priestley, George Campbell, and Hugh
      Blair--on the sense of psychological order in prose style.
      Traces the evidence of this style through "controlling word
      order, tightening clausal sequences, repeating key ideas"
      in the works of several nineteenth-century Scottish writers.

4.58 BUSHNELL, NELSON S. "Lord Kames and Eighteenth Century
      Scotland." Studies in Scottish Literature, 10 (April 1973),
      241-54.
          A review of Ian Simpson Ross's Lord Kames and the
      Scotland of His Day (Oxford: At the Clarendon Press, 1972).
      Bushnell describes Kames as having a "finger in every bowl
      of porridge in Scotland" (p. 252).

4.59 CLAUSSEN, E. NEAL and KARL R. WALLACE. "Editors' Introduction,"
      in Lectures Concerning Oratory by John Lawson. See 4.14,
      pp. ix-liii.
          Points out that Lawson, in publishing his lectures,
      established a new custom that would be followed by other
      British university lecturers in the eighteenth century.
      A short biography of Lawson together with a description of
      the events following the publication of the lectures as
      well as their reception and influence. Bibliography.

4.60 COHEN, HERMAN. "Hugh Blair on Speech Education." SSJ, 29
      (Fall 1963), 1-11.
          Discusses Blair's concluding lecture, no. 34, as "one
      of the systematically developed statements on speech educa-
      tion by an eighteenth-century rhetorical theorist" (p. 1).

4.61 COHEN, HERMAN. "Hugh Blair's Theory of Taste." QJS, 44
      (October 1958), 265-74. Reprinted in Lionel Crocker and
      Paul A. Carmack, eds. Readings in Rhetoric. Springfield,
      Ill.: Charles C. Thomas, 1965, pp. 333-49.
          A summary of Blair's theory of taste from his Lectures.
      Relates Blair's concept of taste to that of Lord Kames,
      David Hume, Edmund Burke, and Sir Joshua Reynolds.

4.62 COHEN, HERMAN. "The Mirror Image: Eighteenth Century
      Elocutio and the New Philosophy." WS, 26 (Winter 1962),
      22-27.

Discusses the influence of Thomas Hobbes and John Locke
on the theories of elocutio held by eighteenth-century
British rhetoricians.

4.63 COHEN, HERMAN. "The Rhetorical Theory of Hugh Blair." Ph.D.
      dissertation, State University of Iowa, 1954, 480 pp.
      Asserts that Blair rewrote for his eighteenth-century
      audience the rhetorical principles of the Greek and Roman
      writers, adding material from his contemporaries; notably,
      Thomas Sheridan, Lord Kames, David Hume, and Sir Joshua
      Reynolds. (Annotation based on Dissertation Abstracts,
      14/06, p. 1004.)

4.64 COHEN, HERMAN. "William Leechman's Anticipation of Campbell."
      WS, 32 (Spring 1968), 92-99.
      A description of a student's notes of the lectures of
      William Leechman who held the position of Professor of
      Divinity in the University of Glasgow from 1743 to 1766.
      Points out similarities between the rhetorical theories of
      Leechman and George Campbell and argues that both men re-
      flected the changing intellectual climate and the cultural
      reawakening of eighteenth-century Edinburgh.

4.65 COHEN, RALPH. "The Rationale of Hume's Literary Inquiries,"
      in David Hume, Many-Sided Genius. Edited by Kenneth R.
      Merrill and Robert W. Shahan. Norman, Okla.: University
      of Oklahoma Press, 1976, pp. 97-117.
      Explores the rationale of David Hume's literary inquiries
      from remarks in a number of his works including "Of Elo-
      quence." Concludes that "the value of art . . . for the
      critical reader and for society" constituted that rationale
      (p. 115).

4.66 CORBETT, EDWARD P. J. "Hugh Blair as an Analyzer of English
      Prose Style." CCC, 9 (May 1958), 98-103.
      Suggests that instructors of English might well look for
      help in their teaching to Blair's Lectures and particularly
      to his method of analyzing prose style in Lectures 20-24.

4.67 CORBETT, EDWARD P. J. "Hugh Blair: A Study of His Rhetorical
      Theory." Ph.D. dissertation, Loyola University--Chicago,
      1956.
      Analyzes the key rhetorical concepts in Blair's Lectures
      on Rhetoric and Belles Lettres and relates them not only to
      those of his contemporaries but also to the classical tra-
      dition, which Blair either adopts or modifies.

4.68 CORBETT, EDWARD P. J. "Hugh Blair's Three (?) Critical Dis-
      sertations." Notes and Queries, 199 (November 1954),
      478-80.

A discussion of the authorship of the three critical
dissertations in the Macpherson editions of Ossian. Maintains that Blair wrote only one of the dissertations.

4.69 DOLPH, PHIL. "Taste and The Philosophy of Rhetoric." WS, 32
(Spring 1968), 104-13.
Traces George Campbell's attitude toward taste and concludes that Campbell's notion of rhetoric is dual "wherein
utility and beauty have almost equal influence" (Campbell,
4.27, p. xliii). Shows Campbell's involvement in the
eighteenth-century school of taste and compares his idea
of taste with those of Edmund Burke, Francis Hutcheson,
Alexander Gerard, and Lord Shaftesbury.

4.70 EDNEY, CLARENCE W. "Campbell's Lectures on Pulpit Eloquence."
SM, 19 (March 1952), 1-10.
Presents nine reasons why Campbell's lectures on pulpit
eloquence deserve the attention of students of rhetoric.

4.71 EDNEY, CLARENCE W. "English Sources of Rhetorical Theory in
Nineteenth-Century America," in History of Speech Education
in America. Edited by Karl R. Wallace. New York:
Appleton-Century-Crofts, Inc., 1954, pp. 80-104.
Traces influence of eighteenth-century English rhetori-
cians (George Campbell, Hugh Blair, Richard Whately, and
Joseph Priestley) on nineteenth-century American theory.

4.72 EDNEY, C[LARENCE] W. "George Campbell's Theory of Logical
Truth." SM, 15 (1948), 19-32.
Discusses Campbell and the representative theory of
ideas as well as his theories of verbal-logical processes,
intuitive evidence, deductive evidence, and his attitude
toward the syllogism. Concludes that Campbell was relatively unacquainted with Aristotelian logic and that his
theory of evidence was "transitional."

4.73 EDNEY, CLARENCE W. "Hugh Blair's Theory of Dispositio." SM
23 (March 1956), 38-45.
Equates Blair's concept of dispositio with the classical
parts of speech. "To get to such fundamental matters as
the discovery, selection, and adaptation of proofs, he
[Blair] makes use of the various divisions of a speech"
(p. 39). Cites Blair's failure to explore audience analysis, logical proof, and the "elusive subject of feeling-
motive-emotion" (p. 45).

4.74 EHNINGER, DOUGLAS. "Campbell, Blair, and Whately: Old Friends
in a New Light." WS, 19 (October 1955), 263-69.
Argues that, contrary to most scholarly opinion, George
Campbell, Hugh Blair, and Richard Whately were actually
anticlassicist and introduced the new eighteenth-century

psychology and epistemology of the British empiricists into
their rhetorical theories.

4.75 EHNINGER, DOUGLAS. "Campbell, Blair, and Whately Revisited."
SSJ, 28 (Spring 1963), 169-82. Reprinted in Lionel Crocker
and Paul A. Carmack, eds. Readings in Rhetoric. Springfield, Ill.: Charles C. Thomas, 1965, pp. 359-73.
   Holds that George Campbell, Hugh Blair, and Richard
Whately reversed the return to classicism initiated by
John Lawson and John Ward and, in fact, were a major influence in setting a trend that has persisted for two
centuries.

4.76 EHNINGER, DOUGLAS. "Dominant Trends in English Rhetorical
Thought, 1750-1800." SSB, 18 (September 1952), 3-12.
Reprinted in Lionel Crocker and Paul A. Carmack, eds.
Readings in Rhetoric. Springfield, Ill.: Charles C.
Thomas, 1965, pp. 297-307.
   Traces four movements in the latter half of the eight-
eenth century: classicism, psychological-epistemological
theories of discourse, elocutionism, and belletristic rhet-
oric. Notes briefly the principal exponents of each.

4.77 EHNINGER, DOUGLAS. "George Campbell and the Revolution in
Inventional Theory." SSB, 15 (May 1950), 270-76.
   Contends that "the classical notion of inventio as a
technique of search and discovery gives way to a more comprehensive concept, and that the familiar eighteenth-
century doctrine of the 'management' or 'conduct' of a
discourse is born" (p. 257). Consequently, the idea of
inventio is enlarged with a subsequent narrowing of
dispositio. See La Russo, 4.117.

4.78 EHNINGER, DOUGLAS. "George Campbell and the Rhetorical Tradition: A Reply to La Russo." WS, 32 (Fall, 1968), 276-79.
   Answer to La Russo (4.117). Reaffirms his original position by asserting that Campbell was "revolutionary" in using
"as his 'starting point' certain assumptions concerning how
men come to know and to believe" (p. 279). Argues that
this "starting point" distinguishes post-Lockean rhetoric
from classical rhetoric.

4.79 EHNINGER, DOUGLAS. "John Ward and His Rhetoric." SM, 18
(March 1951), 1-16.
   After a short biography of Ward and an analysis of his
two-volume System of Oratory (4.15), Ehninger concludes
with a summary evaluation of the man and his work.

4.80 EHNINGER, DOUGLAS. "Selected Theories of Inventio in English
Rhetoric: 1759-1828." Ph.D. dissertation, The Ohio State
University, 1949.

A study of the inventional doctrines between 1759-1828 with emphasis on the various changes in the doctrine during that period and the influences responsible for those changes. Asserts that the period demonstrates a "conveniently telescoped revolution in doctrine" that "culminates in a type of rhetorical theory which is in many ways similar to that current at the present time" (p. 6). The inventional systems of John Ward, George Campbell, Joseph Priestley, Hugh Blair, and Richard Whately are selected for special study.

4.81 EHNINGER, DOUGLAS and JAMES GOLDEN. "The Intrinsic Sources of Blair's Popularity." SSB, 21 (Fall 1955), 12-30.
Blair's lectures were delivered for twenty-four years at the University of Edinburgh and, when published in 1783, went through more than seventy editions and were translated into French, Italian, Spanish, and German. Lists five reasons for this popularity and wide acceptance. Argues that Blair's approach was pedagogically attractive, and while adopting many of the theories popular in the eighteenth century, Blair also provided a sane approach toward invention and style and presented his rhetoric in a "simple, straightforward, and attractive" written form (p. 21). See also, Golden, 4.86.

4.82 ETTLICH, ERNEST [EARL], DOMINIC LA RUSSO, HERMAN COHEN, G. P. MOHRMANN, and PHIL DOLPH. "Symposium: The Rhetorical Theory of George Campbell." WS, 32 (Spring 1968), 84-113.
Four papers on Campbell's theory with introduction by Ettlich. See also La Russo, 4.117; Cohen, 4.64; Mohrmann, 4.126; Dolph, 4.69.

4.83 FRANDSEN, KENNETH D. "Ward, Adams, and Classical Rhetoric." SSJ, 34 (Winter 1968), 108-15.
A comparison between two classicists, the Englishman John Ward and the American John Quincy Adams. Traces the influence of Ward and notes the innovations of Adams.

4.84 FRITZ, CHARLES A. "From Sheridan to Rush: The Beginnings of English Elocution." QJS, 16 (February-November 1930), 75-88. Reprinted in Lionel Crocker and Paul A. Carmack, eds. Readings in Rhetoric. Springfield, Ill.: Charles C. Thomas, 1965, pp. 319-32.
Maintains that elocution, as taught in American schools, had its roots in eighteenth-century England. Notes the influence of Joshua Steele and Thomas Sheridan and discusses the work of John Walker at some length.

4.85 GOLDEN, JAMES L. "Hugh Blair: Minister of St. Giles." QJS, 38 (April 1952), 155-60.
Attributes Hugh Blair's effectiveness as a sermon writer and preacher to his "strong ethical qualities, his choice

of practical subjects adapted to the needs of his audience, and his pleasing style" (p. 160).

4.86 GOLDEN, JAMES and DOUGLAS EHNINGER. "The Extrinsic Sources of Blair's Popularity." SSB, 22 (Fall 1956), 16–32.
        Argues that the two main cultural reasons for the success of Blair's lectures were his own immense reputation and the social/educational climate of the time. See also Ehninger, 4.81.

4.87 GOLDEN, JAMES L. and EDWARD P. J. CORBETT. The Rhetoric of Blair, Campbell, and Whately. New York: Holt, Rinehart and Winston, Inc., 1968, 399 pp.
        Reprints of "the most significant portions" of Hugh Blair's Lectures on Rhetoric and Belles Lettres (1783), George Campbell's The Philosophy of Rhetoric (1776), and Richard Whately's Elements of Rhetoric (1828). Each section accompanied by a bibliography. General introduction (17 pp.) includes an historical overview of rhetoric prior to the eighteenth century. Also traces four responses to classical tradition in the eighteenth century and then, in turn, the individual responses of Campbell, Blair, and Whately.

4.88 GRAVE, S. A. The Scottish Philosophy of Common Sense. Oxford: At the Clarendon Press, 1960, 262 pp.
        Extensive background on the common–sense school of philosophy, a major force in later eighteenth–century rhetoric. Discusses the chief exponents of that school: Thomas Reid, James Beattie, and Donald Stewart and their association with George Campbell.

4.89 GRAVLEE, G. JACK and JAMES R. IRVINE. "Watt's Dissenting Rhetoric of Prayer." QJS, 59 (December 1973), 463–73.
        The authors maintain that Isaac Watts develops a theory of prayer grounded in traditional rhetorical precepts in his Guide to Prayer, published in 1715.

4.90 GRAY, GILES WILKESON. "What was Elocution?" QJS, 46 (February 1960), 1–7.
        Defends the basic principles of the eighteenth–century elocutionists. Attributes elocution's "fall from grace" to its subsequent association with reading aloud, to its development into an art form divorced from content, and finally to its degeneration into mere "statue–posing, bird calls, and imitations of children" (p. 7).

4.91 GROVER, DAVID H. "John Walker: The 'Mechanical' Man Revisited." SSJ, 34 (Summer 1969), 288–97.
        Commonly considered the founder of the elocutionary school, Walker, according to Grover, acting as a "compiler

or synthesizer," borrowed heavily from James Burgh, Joshua
Steele, Thomas Betterton, and others. See also Lamb, 4.115.

4.92 GUTHRIE, WARREN ALAN. "The Development of Rhetorical Theory
in America, 1635-1850." Ph.D. dissertation, Northwestern
University, 1940, 260 pp.
      A comprehensive study of the development of rhetorical
theory in America. Partially reprinted with revisions in
4.94. Appendix includes a list of rhetorical works published in the United States during the period and a chart
showing relative use of certain rhetorical works in American colleges. Bibliography.

4.93 GUTHRIE, WARREN. "The Development of Rhetorical Theory in
America: The Dominance of the Rhetoric of Style, 1635-
1730." SM, 13 (1946), 14-22.
      Asserts that the rhetoric taught in the American col-
leges before 1730 was almost wholly concerned with style
to the exclusion of everything else. Based in part on
Chapter 1 of his dissertation (4.92).

4.94 GUTHRIE, WARREN. "The Development of Rhetorical Theory in
America, 1635-1850: Domination of the English Rhetorics."
SM, 15 (1948), 61-71.
      Asserts that during the last part of the eighteenth
century American rhetoric was dominated by the "great
English works" of George Campbell, Hugh Blair, and Richard
Whately. Describes the beginnings of an American rhetorical
tradition "influenced by, but distinct from, contemporary
English doctrines" (p. 67). Based in part on Chapter 3 of
his dissertation (4.92).

4.95 GUTHRIE, WARREN. "The Development of Rhetorical Theory in
America 1635-1850-V: The Elocution Movement--England."
SM, 18 (March 1951), 17-30. Reprinted in Joseph Schwartz
and John A Rycenga, eds. The Province of Rhetoric. New
York: The Ronald Press Company, 1965, pp. 255-74.
      Traces the beginnings of the elocutionary movement in
England with its origins in the criticism of oratory and
education. Mentions briefly the most popular exponents of
the elocutionary school: John Mason, Thomas Sheridan,
James Burgh, Joshua Steele, John Walker, and Gilbert Austin.
Based in part on Chapter 4 of his dissertation (4.92).

4.96 GUTHRIE, WARREN. "The Development of Rhetorical Theory in
America, 1635-1850: The Growth of the Classical Tradition,
1730-1785." SM, 14 (1947), 38-54.
      Asserts that although Aristotle's works were not widely
read, Cicero's De Oratore became one of the most popular
works in the American colonies. Discusses influence of the
British neoclassical rhetorics of John Brightland, Francois

Fénelon, John Lawson, Thomas Leland, John Holmes, Joseph Priestley, and John Ward, as well as the stylistic rhetoric of Anthony Blackwall, and the works on elocution of John Mason and Thomas Sheridan. Concludes with the place of rhetoric in the curricula of six American colleges. Based in part on Chapter 2 of his dissertation (4.92).

4.97 HARDING, HAROLD F. "Editor's Introduction," in Lectures on Rhetoric and Belles Lettres by Hugh Blair. See 4.30, pp. viii-xl.
A review of Blair's life and a summary of each lecture. A section entitled "The Value of Blair's Lectures" treats Blair's sources and the relation of his lectures to those of Adam Smith. "List of references" (pp. xxvii-xxxv).

4.98 HARDING, HAROLD F. "English Rhetorical Theory, 1750-1800." Ph.D. dissertation, Cornell University, 1937, 379 pp.
Part 1 is an overview of the school textbooks, essays, lectures, and treatises on rhetoric from 1750 to 1800. Discusses popular ideas on eloquence for the same period in Part 2. In Part 3, treats the connections between rhetoric and psychology and literary criticism. Concludes that "eighteenth-century rhetorical writers as a group were not very original" or "alert to the full implications of the philosophic and aesthetic theorizing that was going on about them" (p. 371). Bibliography includes the main rhetorical works of the period listed both chronologically and alphabetically by author.

4.99 HARGIS, DONALD E. "James Burgh and The Art of Speaking." SM, 24 (November 1957), 275-84.
A detailed summary and discussion of The Art of Speaking. Asserts that in this work "elocution became an automatic process based upon set stereotypes devoid of thought and feeling." Emphasis is on "the details of the mechanics of delivery" (p. 284).

4.100 HORN, ANDRAS. "Kames and the Anthropological Approach to Criticism." PQ, 44 (1965), 211-33.
Examines the assumptions underlying the fundamental questions posed by Kames of "what it is in man that makes a given phenomenon aesthetically pleasing" (p. 211).

4.101 HOWELL, WILBUR SAMUEL. "Adam Smith's Lectures on Rhetoric: An Historical Assessment." SM, 36 (November 1969), 393-418. Reprinted with revisions in Essays on Adam Smith. Edited by Andrew S. Skinner and Thomas Wilson. Oxford: At the Clarendon Press, 1975, pp. 11-43.
Describes Lothian's discovery in 1961 of a student's notebook containing a transcript of Adam Smith's lectures on rhetoric. Asserts that "rhetorical theory in the

nineteenth century might have taken a better turn . . .
had Adam Smith's lectures been available" (p. 396). Asserts
that Adam Smith selected what he wished from older theories
while adding insights of his own.

4.102   HOWELL, WILBUR SAMUEL. "The Declaration of Independence
and Eighteenth-Century Logic." WMQ, 3rd ser., 18
(October 1961), 463-84. Reprinted in A Casebook
on the Declaration of Independence. Edited by Robert
Ginsberg. New York, 1967, pp. 194-215. Also reprinted in
Wilbur Samuel Howell, Poetics, Rhetoric, and Logic: Studies
in the Basic Disciplines of Criticism. Ithaca and London:
Cornell University Press, 1975, pp. 163-90.
Discusses the influence on Thomas Jefferson of William
Duncan's Elements of Logic (4.11). Maintains that the
Declaration of Independence is "a perfect example of the
method of science as described so convincingly by Duncan"
(p. 478). See also Howell's "The Declaration of Indepen-
dence: Some Adventures with America's Political Masterpiece"
(QJS, 62 [October 1976], 221-33).

4.103   HOWELL, WILBUR SAMUEL. Eighteenth-Century British Logic and
Rhetoric. Princeton, N.J.: Princeton University Press,
1971, 751 pp.
A full overview of eighteenth-century thought. Traces
the classical influences in eighteenth-century logic and
rhetoric in Chapters 2 and 3, and outlines the new logic
and rhetoric which emerges later in the century in Chapters 5 and 6. Chapter 4 treats the British elocutionary
movement. Considered to be the definitive work on
eighteenth-century British logic and rhetoric.

4.104   HOWELL, WILBUR SAMUEL. "Introduction," in his Fénelon's Dialogues on Eloquence. Princeton, N.J.: Princeton University
Press, 1951, pp. 1-53.
Asserts that "in the long perspective of history,
Fénelon's Dialogues on Eloquence appear not only as an
effective counterstand against Ramus's neo-scholastic theory
of communication but also as the first modern rhetoric
(p. 44). Maintains that Fénelon thought of "oral delivery
as the outward and visible sign of an inward state of conviction and feeling" (p. 45).

4.105   HOWELL, WILBUR SAMUEL. "John Locke and the New Rhetoric."
QJS, 53 (December 1967), 319-33.
Points out Locke's similarity to Bacon and Descartes in
temper and attitude and describes his twofold influence on
the eighteenth-century new rhetoric. Locke pointed out the
inadequacy of the topics and urged the procedures of science
and scholarship in their place. He also added the concept
of expository or didactic writing to the province

of rhetoric. Discusses Locke's influence on John Holmes, John Ward, Joseph Priestley, Hugh Blair, Adam Smith, and George Campbell.

4.106 HOWELL, WILBUR SAMUEL. "Oratory and Poetry in Fénelon's Literary Theory." QJS, 37 (February 1951), 1-10. Reprinted in Lionel Crocker and Paul A. Carmack, eds. Readings in Rhetoric. Springfield, Ill.: Charles C. Thomas, 1965, pp. 242-56. Reprinted in Wilbur Samuel Howell, Poetics, Rhetoric, and Logic: Studies in the Basic Disciplines of Criticism. Ithaca and London: Cornell University Press, 1975, pp. 123-40.

Discusses Fénelon's analysis of oratory and poetry in the Dialogues and the Letter to the Academy. Maintains that Fénelon sees delight and persuasiveness as the object of both.

4.107 HOWELL, WILBUR SAMUEL. "The Plough and the Flail: The Ordeal of Eighteenth-Century Logic." HLQ, 28 (1964-65), 63-78.

Argues that modern man tends to think of rhetoric and logic as mutually exclusive and has, in fact, forgotten the "creative relationship" that once existed between the two. Describes the ordeal of eighteenth-century logic as deriving from two opposing viewpoints: the first saw logic in Aristotelian terms as a method of inquiry, the second saw logic "no longer as an instrument of communication in the world of learning but as the tool of the empirical scientist in his quest for verifiable truths about the physical world" (p. 64).

4.108 HOWELL, WILBUR SAMUEL. "Sources of the Elocutionary Movement in England: 1700-1748." QJS, 45 (February 1959), 1-18. (Reprinted with considerable expansion in Howell, 4.103, pp. 143-203.)

Sketches the history of the elocutionary movement between 1700 and 1748. Detailed discussions of Le Faucheur's Traitté; the anonymous pamphlet, Some Rules for Speaking and Action; and John Henley as direct forerunners of John Mason and Thomas Sheridan.

4.109 IRVINE, JAMES R. "James Beattie's Psychology of Taste." WS, 34 (Winter 1970), 21-28.

Maintains that Beattie was not a major figure in eighteenth-century rhetoric, but that because of his use of "faculty psychology, his rather extensive description of Imagination as the primary faculty of Taste, and his use of specific psychological elements," his views illuminate those of the stylists, particularly George Campbell and Hugh Blair, who follow him (p. 28).

4.110 JEFFERSON, D. W. "Theories of Taste in the Eighteenth Century." Proceedings of the Leeds Philosophical and Literary
Society, Literary and Historical Section, 5 (1938-43), 1-9.
Outlines three theories of "taste," the eighteenth-
century word for the faculty of artistic appreciation: the
"sensationalist" theory, the "internal sense" theory, and
the theory of the doctrine of the association of ideas.

4.111 KEESEY, RAY E. "John Lawson's Lectures Concerning Oratory."
SM, 20 (March 1953), 49-57. Reprinted in Lionel Crocker
and Paul A. Carmack, eds. Readings in Rhetoric. Springfield, Ill.: Charles C. Thomas, 1965, pp. 283-96.
Examines Lawson's Lectures under the headings of invention, disposition, style, and delivery and concludes that
Lawson's adaptation of classical rhetoric to pulpit oratory
offers little that is new. His objections to "mechanical
systems" of speech, however, mark him as one of the first
to object to the precepts of the elocutionary movement.

4.112 KELLEY, WILLIAM G., JR. "Thomas Reid on Common Sense: A
Meta-Rational Approach to Truth." SSJ, 39 (Fall 1973),
40-54.
Asserts that Reid believes "common sense to be the
irreducible atom of intellectual substance of which all
rationality is made--a process which lies antecedent to
rationality and presents irresistible truths to the mind"
(p. 54). This view was widely influential in later
eighteenth-century rhetorical theory.

4.113 KING, E. H. "James Beattie's Literary Essays (1776, 1783) and
the Evolution of Romanticism." Studies in Scottish Literature, 11 (April 1974), 199-216.
Finds precedents for Romantic criticism in the similarities between the theories of Beattie and Wordsworth. "One
of the clearest indications of the value and representative
quality of Beattie's criticism is the extent to which it
anticipates Wordsworth" (p. 212).

4.114 KIVY, PETER. "Introduction," in his Thomas Reid's Lectures on
the Fine Arts. The Hague: Martinus Nijhoff, 1973,
pp. 1-18.
Asserts that "the content of the Lectures was not adequate to its design," but argues that Thomas Reid has "with
a few brief remarks, deepened the epistemological significance of the fine arts" (p. 17).

4.115 LAMB, JACK HALL. "John Walker and Joshua Steele." SM, 32
(November 1965), 411-19.
Discusses the close similarity between the theory of
inflections of Walker and Steele and argues against the
charges of plagiarism made against Walker. Asserts that

"the idea of inflections occurred to John Walker spontane-
ously" (p. 419). See also Grover, 4.91.

4.116 LAND, STEPHEN K. "James Beattie on Language." PQ, 51
(October 1972), 887-904.
Maintains that James Beattie's theories of language
"although philosophically inconsiderable, are of importance
to the history of ideas and particularly to the history of
aesthetics," when viewed as a bridge between the linguistic
philosophies of Thomas Reid and the Romantics (p. 904).

4.117 LA RUSSO, DOMINIC. "Root or Branch? A Re-examination of
Campbell's 'Rhetoric.'" WS, 32 (Spring 1968), 85-91.
Takes up the controversy between Douglas Ehninger
(4.77) and Douglas McDermott (4.121) and argues against
George Campbell's "originality" as supported by Ehninger.
Asserts that "the Philosophy of Rhetoric, as part of the
general spirit of the times and as an offspring of common
progenitors, assumes a place next to similar works of that
period" (p. 91).

4.118 LEHMANN, WILLIAM C. Henry Home, Lord Kames, and the Scottish
Enlightenment: A Study in National Character and in the
History of Ideas. The Hague: Martinus Nijhoff, 1971,
384 pp.
Chapter 14, "Literary Criticism and the Question of
Style in Writing," is a summary of Elements of Criticism
(4.18) and a discussion of its public reception in England,
France, Germany, as well as in Scotland. Concludes with a
brief discussion of "The Progress of Taste and of the Fine
Arts" in Kames's Sketches of the History of Man.
Bibliography.

4.119 LESSENICH, ROLF P. Elements of Pulpit Oratory in Eighteenth-
Century England (1660-1800). Koln: Böhlau-Verlag, 1972,
276 pp.
States that his purpose is to provide "a rhetorical and
theological handbook which will considerably facilitate and
fertilize further contributions" to eighteenth-century sermon literature, "an important subject in its time, but one
that has been seriously neglected by modern scholars"
(pp. x-xi). Selected bibliography of primary sources
(pp. 237-57).

4.120 LOTHIAN, JOHN M. "Introduction" in Lectures on Rhetoric and
Belles Lettres Delivered in the University of Glasgow by
Adam Smith Reported by a Student in 1762-63. See 4.19,
pp. xi-xl.
Describes the procurement of the manuscript and offers
biographical background on Smith, outline of contents of
lectures, their influence, and the role of the literary

societies and periodicals in eighteenth-century Scottish culture. Asserts that the culture was marked by a strong desire for self improvement which was the climate out of which Smith's lectures came.

4.121 McDERMOTT, DOUGLAS. "George Campbell and the Classical Tradition." QJS, 49 (December 1963), 403-409. Reprinted in Lionel Crocker and Paul A. Carmack, eds. Readings in Rhetoric. Springfield, Ill.: Charles C. Thomas, 1965, pp. 349-58.

Argues that the "heart of classical rhetoric was an understanding of man's mind as he operated in society" (p. 408). Asserts that the revolutionary aspect of Campbell's work is in his "attempt to link rhetoric with the psychological principles of the human mind," and that, in this respect, Campbell "may, indeed, be said to bring us into a new country" (p. 409).

4.122 McGUINNESS, ARTHUR E. Henry Home, Lord Kames. New York: Twayne Publishers, Inc., 1970, 160 pp.

Chapters 3 and 4 provide a summary of Elements of Criticism. Chapter 3, "Psychology and Art," demonstrates the close relation that Kames saw between philosophy and aesthetics; Chapter 4, "Style," considers the changes which Kames made in traditional theory. Bibliography.

4.123 McKENZIE, GORDON. Critical Responsiveness: A Study of the Psychological Current in Later Eighteenth-Century Criticism. University of California Publications in English, 20 (1949), 311 pp.

Describes the psychological approach to literary criticism that became current in the eighteenth century. Asserts that the shift from "an examination on a neoclassical basis of the external work of art to an attempt to understand and evaluate literary experience on the basis of the reactions of talented readers" represents an important transition in literary criticism (p. 5). Includes close analyses of works of Lord Kames and Hugh Blair among others.

4.124 McKENZIE, GORDON. "Lord Kames and the Mechanist Tradition." Essays and Studies. University of California Publications in English, 14 (1943), 93-121.

Traces the mechanistic or associationist tradition in literary criticism from Thomas Hobbes, John Locke, George Berkeley, and David Hume. Terms Kames a "common-sense mechanist" as evidenced in the Elements of Criticism. Argues that Kames was able to "think ingeniously and at times fruitfully either as a theologian or a mechanist, but he was never able successfully to bring the two kinds of thinking together" (p. 95).

4.125 MEERSMAN, ROGER. "Père René Rapin's Eloquence des Belles
　　　　Lettres." SM, 38 (November 1971), 290-301.
　　　　　　Maintains that René Rapin is "largely ignored by
　　　　scholars even though he was one of the first and most
　　　　successful critics to combine the study of rhetoric, poetry,
　　　　history, and philosophy under the single controlling fac-
　　　　tor of eloquence" (p. 290).

4.126 MOHRMANN, G. P. "George Campbell: The Psychological Back-
　　　　ground." WS, 32 (Spring 1968), 99-104.
　　　　　　States that empiricism exerted a double influence on
　　　　Campbell. On the one hand, his rhetoric was a response to
　　　　the skepticism that came out of Cartesian doubt and, on the
　　　　other, it utilized empirical methodology. Argues that asso-
　　　　ciationist principles were basic to Campbell's rhetoric, but
　　　　that the influence of faculty psychology has been overrated.

4.127 MOHRMANN, G. P. "Kames and Elocution." SM, 32 (June 1965),
　　　　198-206.
　　　　　　Argues that Kames "verbalized assumptions that can be
　　　　seen operating in varied aspects of eighteenth-century
　　　　thought," and, further, that he "established a funded source
　　　　from which the elocutionary movement drew directly, and
　　　　sketched a critical posture that was to support its posi-
　　　　tion for decades" (p. 206).

4.128 MOHRMANN, G. P. "The Language of Nature and Elocutionary
　　　　Theory." QJS, 52 (April 1966), 116-24.
　　　　　　Demonstrates that the elocutionary movement arose out of
　　　　the advance of science with its emphasis on empirical ob-
　　　　servation, the fascination with sentiment and feeling, and
　　　　finally out of the rhetorical tradition itself.

4.129 MONK, SAMUEL H. "The Seventeen-Sixties: Sublimity, Psychol-
　　　　ogy, and Original Genius" in his The Sublime: A Study of
　　　　Critical Theories in XVIII-Century England. New York:
　　　　Modern Language Association of America, 1935, pp. 101-33.
　　　　　　Discusses the views of Lord Kames on the emotions of
　　　　grandeur and sublimity and the defense of Ossian by Hugh
　　　　Blair. Outlines the connection of the eighteenth-century
　　　　rhetoricians to the concept of the sublime.

4.130 MORGAN, FRANK, JR. "Adam Smith and Belles Lettres." Ph.D.
　　　　dissertation, The University of Mississippi, 1966, 374 pp.
　　　　　　"An attempt to establish the philosophical basis and to
　　　　formulate the central tenets of his belletristic thought"
　　　　(from the title page). Draws on all of Smith's philosoph-
　　　　ical and rhetorical works including the Dissertation on the
　　　　Origin of Languages, Essays on Philosophical Subjects, and
　　　　the student's class notes of his lectures on rhetoric and
　　　　belles lettres delivered at the University of Glasgow.

4.131 MURPHY, MARY C. "Detection of the Burglarizing of Burgh: A
Sequel." CM (formerly SM), 43 (June 1976), 140-41.
Refutes Wayland Parrish's 1952 article (4.134) which
maintained that Thomas Sheridan's essay "On Public Speaking" is an exact copy of James Burgh's forty-six page
essay, "The Art of Speaking." Maintains that Parrish er-
roneously attributed the theft to an American who published
A Rhetorical Grammar of the English Language in Philadelphia
in 1783. Murphy asserts that Sheridan, himself, plagiarized
Burgh's Essay and published it with A Rhetorical Grammar in
1781.

4.132 NEWMAN, JOHN B. "The Role of Joshua Steele in the Development
of Speech Education in America." SM, 20 (March 1953),
65-73.
Argues that Steele's quasimusical prosody evolved into
a pedagogy that culminated in the Walker-Rush tradition of
elocution, and his study of speech as a "physical entity"
contributed to the evolution of the later scientific study
of speech.

4.133 NORTH, ROSS STAFFORD. "Joseph Priestley on Language, Oratory,
and Criticism." Ph.D. dissertation, The University of
Florida, 1957, 360 pp.
Examines Priestley's views of language, oratory, and
criticism within the framework of later eighteenth-century
English rhetorical thought. Chapter 4 identifies four
trends: classical, belletristic, elocutionary, and
psychological-epistemological. After a discussion of
Priestley's Lectures on Oratory and Criticism, North examines Priestley's connections with the four trends and
concludes that his system reflected the current trends in
eighteenth-century English rhetorical doctrine.

4.134 PARRISH, W[AYLAND] M. "The Burglarizing of Burgh, or the
Case of the Purloined Passions." QJS, 38 (December 1952),
431-34.
Maintains that John Walker, in his Elements of Elocution
(London, 1781) only reprinted with slight revisions most of
James Burgh's descriptions of the passions. But see also
Murphy, 4.131.

4.135 PERRIN, PORTER GALE. "The Teaching of Rhetoric in the American Colleges before 1750." Ph.D. dissertation, University
of Chicago, 1936, 225 pp.
Examines the place of rhetoric in the curricula of
Harvard College, the College of William and Mary, and Yale
College before 1750. Asserts that rhetoric became an increasingly important discipline after 1720. A study of the
rhetorical theses of the period shows an increasing interest
in persuasion and delivery and is "evidence of a more

active rhetoric . . . closer to the ancient teaching"
(p. 107).

4.136 RANDALL, HELEN WHITCOMB. "The Critical Theory of Lord Kames."
       Smith College Studies in Modern Languages, 22 (1940-41),
       154 pp.
            Explains how "Kames shaped a critical position according
       to methods adapted from contemporary moral philosophy, and
       how he helped to turn the stream of criticism into new
       channels" (p. v). Kames was instrumental in initiating
       the shift from traditional rhetoric to a concern with
       literary criticism.

4.137 RASMUSSEN, KAREN. "Inconsistency in Campbell's Rhetoric:
       Explanation and Implications." QJS, 60 (April 1974),
       190-200.
            Points out the inconsistency between George Campbell's
       epistemology and his methodology. Campbell, in his intro-
       duction to the Philosophy of Rhetoric (1776), appears to
       endorse empirical observation and comparison as the basis
       of knowledge, which explains his indictment of the syllogism.
       Rasmussen points out, however, that in his reliance on in-
       stinctive, intuitive propositions of common sense, Campbell
       accepts absolutes in contrast to true empirical methodology,
       which honors only empirical tests for premises. Concludes
       that Campbell "operated under absolutist assumptions simi-
       lar to those of determinism" because of "an inability to
       reject fundamental tenets of his era, to broaden the per-
       spective common to the time in which he lived" (p. 195).

4.138 REID, RONALD F. "Research Notes: John Ward's Influence in
       America: Joseph McKean and the Boylston Lectures on Rhet-
       oric and Oratory." SM, 27 (November 1960), 340-44.
            Argues that the statutes governing the Boylston Profes-
       sorship at Harvard University were based on John Ward's
       System of Oratory. Traces the direct influence of Ward
       on Joseph McKean, one of the Boylston professors.

4.139 ROSS, IAN SIMPSON. Lord Kames and the Scotland of His Day.
       Oxford: At the Clarendon Press, 1972, 435 pp.
            A biography of Kames, primarily concerned with his legal
       career. Chapter 14 is an analysis of the Elements of Criti-
       cism (4.18), its precursors and successors, and its place
       in eighteenth-century Scottish legal and philosophical
       thought. Bibliography of manuscripts and publications of
       Lord Kames and bibliography of secondary articles, books,
       and pamphlets (pp. 378-402).

4.140 SANDFORD, WILLIAM P. English Theories of Public Address, 1530-
       1828. Columbus, Ohio: H. L. Hedrick, 1931, 212 pp.

Chapter 3 is "The Eighteenth Century: Classicism, Elocution" (pp. 131-90). "Chronological List of the Principal English Works on Public Adress, 1530-1828" (pp. 192-202).

4.141 SCHMITZ, ROBERT M. Hugh Blair. New York: King's Crown Press, 1948, 174 pp.
A history of the life and writings of Hugh Blair. Chapter 6 is a summary of the Lectures. Bibliographies of Blair's works with lists of editions, adaptations, anthologies, etc. (pp. 139-45) and reference bibliography (145-58).

4.142 SCOTT, WILLIAM ROBERT. Adam Smith As Student and Professor. Glasgow: Jackson, Son and Company, 1937, 470 pp.
A full biography. Part 2 contains Adam Smith's documents, many published here for the first time.

4.143 SKOPEC, E[RIC] W. "Thomas Reid's Fundamental Rules of Eloquence." QJS, 64 (October 1978), 400-408.
Based on a study of Thomas Reid's unpublished lectures on rhetoric, Skopec reports that Reid's rhetoric includes three principles: "the claim that eloquence is a fine art, the use of art to express mental phenomenon, and the examination of natural signs of mental activity" (p. 407).

4.144 SKOPEC, ERIC. "Thomas Reid's Rhetorical Theory; a Manuscript Report." CM, 45 (August 1978), 258-64.
A report on a manuscript of Reid's unpublished lectures on eloquence delivered at Glasgow. Asserts that Reid's desire to ground rhetoric on the interaction between mind and body is related to the development of psychologically oriented rhetorics, but that the distinctive character of Reid's rhetoric results from his attention to fundamental philosophical problems.

4.145 SPENCE, PATRICIA. "Sympathy and Propriety in Adam Smith's Rhetoric." QJS, 60 (February 1974), 92-99.
Examines Adam Smith's Lectures in relation to his major work on ethics, Theory of Moral Sentiments. Argues that "Smith's 'sentimental' tenets provide the philosophical assumptions for his rhetoric," and that "this ethical theory, when applied to his rhetorical theory, transforms moral judgment into aesthetic judgment--a transformation which abetted the development of 18th century belletristic definitions of discourse" (p. 92). Presents the major tenets of the Theory of Moral Sentiments and then explicates Smith's rhetorical principles as they are related to his moral sense theory.

4.146 THOMAS, OTA. "The Teaching of Rhetoric in the United States During the Classical Period of Education," in A History and Criticism of American Public Address. Edited by William

Norwood Brigance. New York: Russell and Russell, 1960, vol. 1, 193-212.

A general review of the place of rhetoric in the curricula of American colleges. Also includes the literary societies and a list of the principal texts used from 1700 to 1850.

4.147 THOMAS, OTA. "The Theory and Practice of Disputation at Yale, Harvard, and Dartmouth from 1750 to 1800." Ph.D. dissertation, University of Iowa, 1942, 314 pp.

Outlines the development of undergraduate disputation exercises at Yale, Harvard, and Dartmouth during the second half of the eighteenth century. Chapter 3 contains a discussion of the rhetorical texts and reference books used in the schools at the time.

4.148 THOMPSON, WAYNE N. "Aristotle as a Predecessor to Reid's 'Common Sense.'" SM, 42 (August 1975), 209-20.

Points out the similarities and differences between Reid's Common Sense and Aristotle's First Principles. On deduction, Reid is anti-Aristotelian. Concludes that "much in Reid, including several key ideas . . . is Aristotelian, but the major concepts are his own" (p. 220).

4.149 VANDRAEGEN, DANIEL. "Thomas Sheridan and the Natural School." SM, 20 (March 1953), 58-64. Reprinted in Lionel Crocker and Paul A. Carmack, eds. Readings in Rhetoric. Springfield, Ill.: Charles C. Thomas, 1965, pp. 308-18.

Discusses the question of whether Sheridan belonged to the "natural" or "mechanical" school. Concludes that if one must apply either label that "existing evidence justifies identifying him as a member in good standing of the Natural School" (p. 64).

4.150 VOITLE, ROBERT. "Introduction" in Henry Home, Lord Kames's Elements of Criticism. See 4.18, vol. 1, i-xiv.

Argues that aspects of Kames's critical thought seem "to anticipate tendencies in Romantic critical theory; his insistence on essential simplicity in preference to the flimsily complex and ornate; on a mature approach to metrics and sound values; on poetic imagery which is vivid, evocative, and particular; and on a sophisticated concept of the nature of reality and illusion in literature. Of these, some are, in fact, universal, and all have a validity which transcends particular literary movements" (vol. 1, xiv).

4.151 WARNICK, BARBARA. "Fénelon's Recommendations to the French Academy Concerning Rhetoric." CM, 45 (March 1978), 75-84.

Fénelon, according to Warnick, departed from views of rhetoric commonly held in the seventeenth century and foreshadowed modern rhetorical theory in his emphasis on content rather than form.

Secondary Works

4.152 WENZEL, JOSEPH. "Rhetoric and Anti-Rhetoric in Early American
       Scientific Societies." QJS, 60 (October 1974), 328-36.
          Traces the concern for the problems of scientific com-
       munication in America, which were similar to those in England.
       The American Philosophical Society founded by Benjamin
       Franklin in 1743, and the American Academy of Arts and
       Sciences founded by James Bowdoin in 1780 grew out of the
       ideological tenets of the Royal Society. Both American
       societies, like the Royal Society, showed an interest in
       language in general and in scientific communication in par-
       ticular. Concludes that "in the first century and a half
       of their existence, American scientific societies came to
       grips with their special problems of communication, and
       evolved a set of precepts which may, in a loose sense only,
       be called a rhetoric of science" (p. 336).

Part 5
The Nineteenth Century

DONALD C. STEWART

Introduction

Nineteenth-century American and English rhetoric is something like
the terrain west of the Appalachians immediately after the American
Revolution. It contains a great deal of territory, diverse and at
times surprising inhabitants, numerous problems for the scholar-
traveler who ventures there, and few reliable interpreters to report
on what it is really like. This essay is a brief account of one
scholar-traveler's tentative and unfinished journey into that un-
charted region.

Two problems stand out immediately: sorting out the various
strands of activity that can be called "rhetorical" throughout the
century, and accounting for the decline of that which can legitimately
be called rhetoric into that which cannot: specifically, English composition as it was shaped by Harvard's program in the late nineteenth
century and as it persisted in the twentieth century for nearly sixty
years. The latter became primarily a school activity that emphasized
superficial mechanical correctness and extremely conservative concepts of usage.

At least four kinds of legitimate "rhetorical activity" existed
in the nineteenth century. (By "rhetorical activity" I refer to any
activity that unites theory and practice in the art, or science as
some prefer, of discourse.)

(1) The classical tradition, descended from the works of Plato,
Aristotle, Cicero, and Quintilian, persisted throughout the century,
at times more visibly than at others. It surfaces most noticeably in
the lectures of the first two holders of the Boylston Chair at Harvard,
John Quincy Adams and Joseph McKean. Their work, however, was not
much imitated by either their peers or their successors.

(2) Belletristic rhetorical criticism emerged as a force to be
reckoned with in the work of Hugh Blair, late eighteenth-century
Scottish rhetorician, who had enormous influence in the nineteenth
century. Blair's Lectures on Rhetoric and Belles Lettres was the
principal text in nearly half of the American college rhetoric programs for nearly fifty years. Although he acknowledges the influence

229

of Quintilian, Blair was much less interested in invention and arrangement than he was in style and belles lettres in general. This is an emphasis found in the work of Thomas De Quincey, Alexander Jamieson, and James Boyd, all of them authors of works that were widely read.

(3) Blair's contemporary, George Campbell, had been trying to do something very different from Blair or the classical rhetoricians. Because of his close association with Scottish intellectuals, particularly groups that were knowledgeable about David Hume's work, he sought to develop a rhetorical theory that would fit the prevailing conceptions of mind. This wedding of early psychology and rhetoric was theoretically sound, but Campbell's theories were vulnerable to the investigations of empirical science and they eventually lost their influence.

(4) Finally, one is struck most of all in the nineteenth century by the force and vigor of the elocutionary movement. Gilbert Austin's Chironomia and James Rush's Philosophy of the Human Voice gave the whole study of delivery, one that had been neglected for centuries, some solid scientific respectability. The interest in elocution also contributed to public awareness of and interest in preaching, as well as in public speech making and debate. I have not cited many works about great American orators of the nineteenth century, however, preferring to focus on works on elocution as a branch of rhetoric, but the period had some of the great names in American oratorical history, among them Edward Everett, Daniel Webster, Henry Ward Beecher, Robert Green Ingersoll, and a lanky bearded man from Illinois who, in two and one-half minutes in November of 1863, gave what may well be the most famous speech in American history.

Unfortunately, classical, belletristic, psychological, and even elocutionary rhetoric gave way in the latter half of the century to what can only be called, charitably, "practical" rhetoric.* The concern with forms of discourse (narration, description, exposition, and argument), with unity, coherence, and emphasis, as well as with paragraph construction, usage, and mechanical correctness which began to dominate the textbooks of the era, was generated by increased enrollments in the colleges and particularly by Harvard's decision to become a training ground for leaders in American society. Into what

---

*Opinion is not unanimous on this subject. Richard Young of Carnegie-Mellon says he vacillates between contempt for late nineteenth-century composition/rhetoric and a sense that what developed served genuine educational and social needs at that time. James Berlin of Wichita State and I are inclined to be less charitable that Professor Young is. I would argue that late nineteenth-century composition theory and practice was less a response to the social and educational needs of the time and more a reflection of a select class's wrong-headed attitudes about the importance of usage and superficial editorial accuracy and their conviction that rhetoric lacked any serious intellectual or philosophical depth.

had been somewhat of a New England finishing school came raw country
boys who, despite their natural intellectual gifts, needed to be
taught to speak and write like Harvard gentlemen. A. S. Hill and
his colleagues were happy to oblige. Reinforcing this unfortunate
trend were the reports of the Committee on Composition to the Harvard
Board of Overseers in 1892, 1895, and 1897. They generated the "back-
to-basics" movement of the 1890s and set the study of composition in
a direction that had most unfortunate consequences for it. Only Fred
Scott of the University of Michigan and Gertrude Buck of Vassar attempted to turn back the tide and enrich rhetorical theory by making
it theoretically and philosophically interdisciplinary and by restoring to rhetoric its primary social funtion--meaningful communication
between citizens in a free society--but they were unable to resist
the Harvard movement.

Generally, then, one can say that rhetoric, which was branching
at the beginning of the century into a number of potentially interesting fruitful subdisciplines, instead degenerated into the most
superficial study of written composition. As a consequence, rhetoric,
or English composition, became the poor but economically sustaining
force behind graduate literature programs of English departments;
oratory became the property of speech teachers who eventually found
their own professional identity in the Speech Association of America
in 1912; and serious linguistic study became the province of specialists whose work has become, in many instances, divorced from and un-
intelligible to many teachers of literature and composition today.

That, at least, is what I have been able to make of the amorphous
mass of material that one loosely calls "nineteenth-century rhetoric."
Much work still needs to be done. A good start would be to address
several textual problems that are annoying to one doing serious work
in this field. John Witherspoon's lectures, given in the eighteenth
century but published in the early nineteenth, are a case in point.
What has become of the apparently incomplete or spurious edition of
1794? How complete are the first and second Woodward editions of
1801 and 1802, and are they Woodward's justification for calling their
printing of the Lectures on Moral Philosophy and Eloquence in 1810
"Woodward's Third Edition"?

De Quincey's chaotic literary legacy is another problem. The
three principal essays on rhetoric are scattered--"Rhetoric," in
Blackwood's in 1828, four separate essays on "Style" in Blackwood's
in 1840 and 1841, and "Language," which has no date but was apparently
collected in De Quincey's complete edition of his works in 1853. An
additional problem is that at the same time De Quincey was working on
an English edition of his works, Ticknor and Fields in Boston were
trying to put together a complete American edition.

Herbert Spencer's essay on style and Whately's Elements of Rhetoric are bibliographical curiosities. Spencer's essay appears to have
developed from a now unlocatable piece written around 1843 or 1844.

Eventually, it went through a number of separate editions. Whately's essay on rhetoric was first a collection of notes developed into an encyclopedia article. This was then printed as a book and modified and enlarged several times before becoming the seventh edition of Whately's Elements of Rhetoric.

Even dating can present occasional problems. Alexander Bain's 1866 work on rhetoric gives 1866 on the title page but 1867 on the copyright page, right after the title page. A number of books, later in the century, show differing copyright and publication dates. I do not know the reasons for the phenomenon, but an editor of the period would. For the sake of this bibliography, I have used the earliest date, usually the date of copyright, for each work.

Two other problems in assembling a bibliography of this kind are worth mentioning. First, it would be impossible to cite all the editions of several of the primary works listed here because some, Alexander Jamieson's Grammar of Rhetoric and Polite Literature, and Samuel P. Newman's A Practical System of Rhetoric, for example, went through as many as fifty or sixty editions! Each work of this kind is a potentially fruitful editorial and textual problem. Studies of these editions might reflect the extent to which the authors of the books were sensitive to changing emphases in rhetorical theory and practice throughout the century.

A second problem, one probably peculiar to the nineteenth century, is the paucity of secondary material on the period. The list of scholars who have made a significant contribution to our understanding of nineteenth-century rhetoric is very small: Albert Kitzhaber, Warren Guthrie, Ronald Reid, Paul Ried, Lionel Crocker, Douglas Ehninger, Wayland M. Parrish, Virgil Baker, Clarence Edney, and Hoyt Hudson are the most obvious. But there has been no Wilbur Samuel Howell or James Murphy for this period. I cannot speculate why such a person did not emerge in departments of speech, but there is good reason why no one in English departments did. From about 1900, at which time the English department model developing at Harvard was establishing itself, composition and rhetoric were poor sisters to literary scholarship and criticism. Those who specialized in composition or rhetoric survived only as directors of freshman programs and writers of textbooks. Kitzhaber is nearly unique in his generation in having made a commitment to rhetoric, staying with it for ten years or more, and still surviving professionally. Wayland Parrish's remark in the late 1940s that English departments had abandoned rhetoric and that the field belonged entirely to speech teachers was literally true. But the times are changing. The job market, more than anything else, has made rhetoric respectable, for a while at least, and serious scholarship in rhetorical history and theory is experiencing unprecedented vigor in a number of departments. It is hoped that this activity will generate more studies that will increase our understanding of modern composition's immediate past: the theory and practice of rhetoric in the nineteenth century.

Introduction

Some acknowledgments are due. To Professors Edward P. J. Corbett of Ohio State University, Richard Young of Carnegie-Mellon, and James Berlin of Wichita State for reading preliminary copy and pointing out my errors and omissions; to Ellyn Taylor and Kim Cunningham of Kansas State University's Interlibrary Loan Program for prompt responses on books I requested and for patient OCLC searches that turned up so many details necessary for the completion of this bibliography. My thanks, many times, to all of them.

DONALD C. STEWART
Kansas State University

Primary Works

5.1   1806.   GILBERT AUSTIN.   Chironomia, or a Treatise on Rhetorical
       Delivery.   London: T. Cadell and W. Davies, 608 pp.   Re-
       printed in facsimile: Mary Margaret Robb and Lester
       Thonssen, eds.   Southern Illinois University Series,
       Landmarks in Rhetoric and Public Address.   Edited by
       David Potter.   Carbondale: Southern Illinois University
       Press, 1966, 657 pp.
           The first exhaustive treatment on action.   Together with
       James Rush's Philosophy of the Human Voice (5.9), it formed
       the basis for subsequent studies and teaching in elocution
       in the nineteenth century.

5.2   1810.   JOHN QUINCY ADAMS.   Lectures on Rhetoric and Oratory,
       Delivered to the Classes of Senior and Junior Sophisters
       in Harvard University.   2 vols.   Cambridge: Hilliard and
       Metcalf, 837 pp.
           Lectures by the first Boylston Professor of Rhetoric at
       Harvard who attempted to unite classical doctrines and the
       rhetorical theory of his era.

5.3   1810.   JOHN THELWALL.   The Vestibule of Eloquence; Original
       Articles, Oratorical and Poetical.   London: J. M. Creery,
       168 pp.
           Lectures on the school of elocution founded in 1800 by
       Thelwall and on his theory of elocution.

5.4   1810.   JOHN WITHERSPOON.   Lectures on Moral Philosophy and
       Eloquence.   Philadelphia: Woodward's 3rd ed., 304 pp.
           Lectures given between 1768 and 1794 at the College of
       New Jersey (later Princeton) and published posthumously.
       Publication history reveals a 1794 incomplete edition of
       the complete works of Witherspoon (not generally available
       now) and an 1804-5 ten-volume edition of the complete works
       by Ogle and Aikman; J. Pillans; J. Ritchie and J. Turnbull
       of Edinburgh in which Volume 7 contains the lectures on
       eloquence.   Woodward's published incomplete editions in
       1801 and 1802 before printing the Lectures on Moral

Philosophy and Eloquence separately in 1810, hence "Woodward's 3rd" edition.

5.5   1816. [EDWARD T. CHANNING]. "On Models in Literature." North American Review, 3 (July 1816), 202-209.
      Details Channing's objection to the doctrine of imitation, particularly the use of models for prose composition.

5.6   1820. ALEXANDER JAMIESON. Grammar of Rhetoric and Polite Literature. First American from last London edition. New Haven: A. H. Maltby, 361 pp.
      An essentially belletristic rhetoric, largely derivative from Hugh Blair, George Campbell, and Lord Kames (Henry Home), which went through fifty-three editions in the nineteenth century.

5.7   1825. JONATHAN BARBER. Exercises in Reading and Recitation Reduced to a System of Notation. York, Pennsylvania: J. Barber and C. Mason, 251 pp.
      This work and Barber's Grammar of Elocution (5.12) and A Practical Treatise on Gesture (5.13) were attempts to arrange and adapt for teaching at Yale and Harvard the principles of elocution set out in Gilbert Austin's Chironomia (5.1) and James Rush's Philosophy of the Human Voice (5.9).

5.8   1827. SAMUEL P. NEWMAN. A Practical System of Rhetoric. Portland: Shirley and Hyde, 252 pp.
      The first American rhetoric designed for classroom use. Largely derivative from the works of Hugh Blair and George Campbell, it went through sixty editions in the nineteenth century.

5.9   1827. JAMES RUSH. The Philosophy of the Human Voice. Philadelphia: J. Maxwell, 620 pp.
      A doctor of medicine's attempt to study voice scientifically. Together with Gilbert Austin's Chironomia (5.1), it formed the basis for elocutionary studies in the nineteenth century.

5.10 1828. [THOMAS DE QUINCEY]. "Elements of Rhetoric." Blackwood's Magazine, 34, no. 167 (December 1828), Part 2, 885-908.
      Begun as a review of Richard Whately's Elements of Rhetoric (5.11), the essay becomes De Quincey's attempt at "correcting the popular misconceptions of rhetoric and basing his own definition on an interpretation of Aristotle that counters much scholarly opinion." See Burwick, 5.61, p. xii.

5.11 1828. RICHARD WHATELY. Elements of Rhetoric. London, Oxford: John Murry and J. F. Parker, 405 pp.

First published (with The Elements of Logic) in 1822 as
a monograph for Coleridge's Encyclopedia Metropolitana, it
was printed as a separate book in 1828 and went through
seven editions to 1846. The final edition contained 162
pages more, in Parts 1 and 2, than were in the Metropolitana
article. The work essentially rejected invention as discovery, converting that to invention as management. It
also represented a reaction against the belletristic, elocutionary, or psychological-epistemological rhetorical positions of many of Whately's contemporaries. For discussion
of dating problems with the encyclopedia article and the
first edition, see Howell, 5.124 and Parrish, 5.148.

5.11a   WHATELY, RICHARD. Elements of Rhetoric. Edited by
Douglas Ehninger. Southern Illinois University Press
Series, Landmarks in Rhetoric and Public Address. Edited
by David Potter. Carbondale: Southern Illinois University
Press, 1963, 509 pp.
A reprint of the seventh edition of Whately's Elements
of Rhetoric.

5.12 1830. JONATHAN BARBER. A Grammar of Elocution. New Haven:
A. H. Maltby, 344 pp.
A scientific treatise on voice that acknowledges
Quintilian as the most thorough of classical writers on
elocution but expresses heavy indebtedness to James Rush
and his scientific analysis of voice and its application
to the whole subject of delivery.

5.13 1831. JONATHAN BARBER. A Practical Treatise of Gesture.
Cambridge: Hilliard and Brown, 131 pp.
A practical work on gesture, chiefly abstracted from
Gilbert Austin's Chironomia (5.1), by E. T. Channing's
assistant at Harvard.

5.14 1836. EBENEZER PORTER. Lectures on Eloquence and Style
(revised by Lyman Matthews). Andover: Gould and Newman,
186 pp.
Lectures published posthumously by the Bartlett Professor
of Sacred Rhetoric at Andover Academy. Influence of this
work generally limited to the academy.

5.15 1840-41. [THOMAS DE QUINCEY]. "Style." Blackwood's Magazine,
48, No. 297 (July 1840), 1-17; 48, No. 299 (September 1840),
387-98; 48, No. 300 (October 1840), 508-21; 49, No. 304
(February 1841), 219-28.
A four-part essay that begins by developing the argument
of the separation of manner and matter in style. It is an
argument continued in the essay on language (5.27).

5.16   1844. JAMES R. BOYD. <u>Elements of Rhetoric and Literary</u>
       <u>Criticism</u>. New York: Harper and Brothers, 306 pp.
            A work by the principal of Black River Institute. Em-
       phasis on style with heavy indebtedness to Hugh Blair,
       George Campbell, Richard Whately, and Isaac Watts. A sup-
       plementary part containing material on definition and de-
       scription, <u>dispositio</u>, belletristic criticism, and the
       origin of language was added in the fifth edition of 1846.

5.17   1844. RICHARD GREEN PARKER. <u>Aids to English Composition,</u>
       <u>Prepared for Students of All Grades</u>. Boston: R. S. Davis,
       418 pp.
            Deals only with written composition. Subjects are gram-
       mar, poetry, narration, letter writing, themes, orations,
       and sermons. Virgil Baker (5.49) calls this book the cul-
       mination of a period in which textbook writers were clas-
       sifying types of discourse. Parker has six: Narrative,
       Descriptive, Didactic, Persuasive, Pathetic, and Argumenta-
       tive. Baker also sees the book as representing a point of
       transition from focus on the listener or reader to focus on
       the nature of subject matter.

5.18   1845. HENRY MANDEVILLE. <u>Elements of Reading and Oratory</u>.
       Utica: R. Northway and Co., 460 pp.
            For fifty years a standard text for first term freshmen
       at Hamilton College New York where the author taught from
       1841 to 1849.

5.19   1850. FRANZ THEREMIN. <u>Eloquence a Virtue; or Outline of a</u>
       <u>Systematic Rhetoric</u>. Translated by William G. T. Shedd.
       New York: John Wiley, 181 pp.
            Warren Guthrie (5.101, p. 107) states: "The essential
       contribution of this work is its conception of rhetoric as
       a 'virtue' and its attempt to provide an ethical critique
       for public address." The work is a translation of Theremin's
       "Die beredsamke eine tugend; oder Grundlinient einer
       systematischen rhetoric," originally published in 1814.

5.20   1852. CHAUNCEY ALLEN GOODRICH. <u>Select British Eloquence</u>.
       New York: Harper and Brothers, 947 pp.
            A collection of speeches by eminent British orators
       dating from a speech delivered by Sir John Eliot June 3,
       1628, to Lord Brougham's inaugural at the University of
       Glasgow, April 6, 1825. Brief biographical sketches and
       rhetorical analyses are provided.

5.21   1852. [HERBERT SPENCER]. "The Philosophy of Style." <u>West-</u>
       <u>minster Review</u>, 114 (October 1852), 234-47.
            States Spencer's principle of economy and attempts to
       discover a conceptual link between the major rhetorical
       works of Hugh Blair, George Campbell, Richard Whately, and

Lord Kames (Henry Home). The essay may derive from an
earlier work, "Force of Expression," whose date, 1843 or
1844, and place of publication, have not been verified.

5.22   1856. EDWARD T. CHANNING. Lectures (on Rhetoric and Oratory)
Read to Seniors at Harvard College. Boston: Ticknor and
Fields, 314 pp. Reprinted: Dorothy Anderson and Waldo
Braden, eds. Southern Illinois Press Series, Landmarks
in Rhetoric and Public Address. Edited by David Potter.
Carbondale: Southern Illinois University Press, 1968,
377 pp.
     Twenty lectures "upon subjects suggested by rhetoric" by
the third Boylston Professor of Rhetoric at Harvard. The
view of rhetoric is classical, not sophistic; the subjects
covered include "the relationship between public address
and society; the general nature of rhetoric; the four types
of oratory; special problems of preaching; and several matters pertaining to style and to literary criticism." See
review of this work, Hance, 5.111.

5.23   1859. M. B. HOPE. The Princeton Text-Book in Rhetoric.
Princeton, N.J.: John T. Robinson, 293 pp.
     The principal text at Princeton in the mid-nineteenth
century. Despite assertions of originality by the author,
it draws considerably on the work of Richard Whately, James
Rush, Gilbert Austin, Franz Theremin, and classical authors.

5.24   1866. ALEXANDER BAIN. English Composition and Rhetoric.
New York: D. Appleton and Co., 343 pp.
     An attempt "to methodize instruction in English Composi-
tion" (p. 3) by dividing the study of it into two parts:
(1) composition in general, which is mainly a discussion of
style, and (2) division of composition into Narration,
Description, Exposition, Argument, and Poetry. The latter
part continues to influence modern textbooks that are organized around the forms of discourse. Two dates of publication are given: 1866 and 1867. Subsequent editions of the
work were enlarged to two volumes.

5.25   1867. HENRY N. DAY. The Art of Discourse. New York:
Charles Scribner and Co., 359 pp.
     A new work developed from Day's Elements of the Art of
Rhetoric, 1850. Discussion of Invention in four categories--
Explanation, Confirmation, Excitation, and Persuasion--and
Style as oral, suggestive, or grammatical properties.
Widely used during the middle of the nineteenth century.

5.26   1870. JOHN A. BROADUS. A Treatise on the Preparation and
Delivery of Sermons. New York: A. C. Armstrong and Son,
514 pp.

A popular treatise for ministers that had gone through
forty-two editions by 1926. Aristotle, Cicero, Quintilian,
Richard Whately, and Alexandre Vinet the greatest influences on the work, particularly in its discussion of the
rhetorical strategies. Eventually translated into Chinese,
Japanese, and Portuguese.

5.27 1876. [THOMAS DE QUINCEY]. "Language," in Works of Thomas
De Quincey, vol. 2, Boston: Houghton Mifflin and Co.,
373-93.
Together with "Elements of Rhetoric" (5.10), and "Style"
(5.15), this essay contains De Quincey's principal remarks
on the subject of rhetoric. Unlike the two earlier essays,
"Language" has no verifiable date or place of first publication. It was collected in De Quincey's collection of his
own works in 1853 and has been subsequently linked with the
other two essays in other editions of De Quincey's work.
In all these essays, the emphasis is primarily belletristic,
expressing the author's concern with creativity and style,
not with the whole range of rhetorical issues in the classical canon.

5.27a DE QUINCEY, THOMAS. Essays on Rhetoric. Edited by
Frederick Burwick. Southern Illinois University Press
Series, Landmarks in Rhetoric and Public Address. Edited
by David Potter. Carbondale: Southern Illinois University
Press, 1967, 352 pp.
A collection of five essays by De Quincey, the major
emphasis being on the three that comprise his basic posi-
tion on rhetoric: "Rhetoric," "Style," and "Language."

5.28 1877. DAVID J. HILL. The Science of Rhetoric. New York:
Sheldon and Co., 304 pp.
"A systematic presentation of the laws of discourse for
advanced classes" (p. 3). Attempts to overcome what the
author perceives as limitations in the work of Hugh Blair,
Franz Theremin, Richard Whately, and others by developing
a comprehensive, inductively arrived at theory of discourse.
Codifier of the four forms of discourse.

5.29 1878. ADAMS SHERMAN HILL. The Principles of Rhetoric and
Their Application. New York: Harper and Brothers, 313 pp.
The principal textbook for Harvard's English A, the
progenitor of modern freshman composition courses. Prin-
cipal emphases of the author, fifth Boylston Professor of
Rhetoric, on style and correct usage.

5.29a 1895. ADAMS SHERMAN HILL. The Principles of Rhetoric
and Their Application. New York: American Book Co.,
441 pp.

Amplification of the concepts in the 1878 edition with addition of material on the forms of discourse.

5.30   1885. JOHN FRANKLIN GENUNG. The Practical Elements of Rhetoric. Amherst: J. E. Williams, 230 pp.
        The principal work on rhetoric, the emphasis primarily on style, by Amherst's Professor of Rhetoric and English Literature.

5.30a   1886. GENUNG, JOHN FRANKLIN. The Practical Elements of Rhetoric. 2nd ed. Boston: Ginn and Co., 488 pp.
        Emphases the same as those of the first edition, but greatly amplified in this and succeeding editions.

5.31   1889. WALTER PATER. "Style," in Appreciations; with an Essay on Style. New York: The Macmillan Co., pp. 1-36.
        Sets forth Pater's theory of the necessity of precision in choice of words and sentences, and form so adapted to matter that form is finally indistinguishable from matter.

5.32   1891. FRED NEWTON SCOTT and JOSEPH VILLIERS DENNEY. Paragraph Writing. Ann Arbor: Register Publishing Co., 114 pp.
        Presentation of the paragraph as a theme in miniature together with a discussion of the theory of the paragraph.

5.33   1891. BARRETT WENDELL. English Composition: Eight Lectures Given at the Lowell Institute. New York: Charles Scribner's Sons, 316 pp.
        Lectures on style, words, sentences, paragraphs, whole compositions, clearness, force, and elegance, which set forth Wendell's principal contribution to rhetorical theory: the concepts of Unity, Coherence, and Mass (Emphasis).

5.34   1894. EDWIN H. LEWIS. The History of the English Paragraph. Chicago: University of Chicago Press, 199 pp.
        Lewis's doctoral dissertation at Chicago. Studies the form and history of the English paragraph from the time of Alfred to that of Oliver Wendell Holmes.

5.35   1896. HIRAM CORSON. The Voice and Spiritual Education. New York: The Macmillan Co., 198 pp.
        One of the earliest works in the field of oral interpretation.

5.36   1897. FRED NEWTON SCOTT and JOSEPH VILLIERS DENNEY. Composition-Rhetoric, Designed for Use in Secondary Schools. Boston: Allyn & Bacon, 416 pp.
        Stresses three of Scott and Denney's major concepts about rhetoric: "rhetoric as the informing discipline for composition; the paragraph as the central unit of composition; and the composition, whatever its length and nature, as an

organic form." (Edward P. J. Corbett and Virginia Burke, Preface to The New Century Composition-Rhetoric. New York: Appleton-Century-Crofts, 1971, p. xv.)

5.37   1898. HENRY G. PEARSON. The Principles of Composition, with an Introduction by Arlo Bates. Boston: D. C. Heath and Co., 155 pp.
       Written for the English Composition course at Massachusetts Institute of Technology, it was the first text to invert the order in which parts of an essay were to be studied. Barrett Wendell and followers had moved as follows: word, sentence, paragraph, entire essay. Pearson started with the entire essay and worked back to the word.

5.38   1899. GERTRUDE BUCK. The Metaphor--A Study in the Psychology of Rhetoric. Contributions to Rhetorical Theory, No. 5. Edited by Fred Newton Scott. Ann Arbor: Inland Press, 78 pp.
       The first doctoral dissertation in rhetoric prepared under the direction of Fred Newton Scott. Drawing on the data of the psychology of the day, it attempts to establish the case for metaphor as organic, not mechanical.

Secondary Works

5.39 ABERNATHY, ELTON. "Trends in American Homiletic Theory Since 1860." SM, 10 (1943), 68-74.
    Notes that rhetoricians of the pulpit, prior to 1900, regarded a sermon as the work of one divinely inspired by God to interpret the Bible. Tenets from classical rhetoric dominated conceptions of the structure of such sermons. In recent years changes in the conception of the preacher's role have also affected his perception of the rhetoric he employs.

5.40 ANDERSON, DOROTHY I. "Edward T. Channing's Definitions of Rhetoric." SM, 14 (1947), 81-93.
    Argues that Channing "attempted to establish rhetoric as a fundamental communicative art including all skills used in common by speakers and writers and excluding all skills peculiar to the different departments of Belles Lettres" (p. 92).

5.41 ANDERSON, DOROTHY I. "Edward T. Channing's Teaching of Rhetoric." SM, 16 (August 1949), 69-81.
    Argues that Channing's method--lectures, attempts to help students comprehend their textbooks, encouragement of declamation in a natural manner--contributed significantly to Channing's apparent success as a teacher.

5.42 ANDERSON, DOROTHY I. and WALDO W. BRADEN. "Introduction," in Lectures Read to the Seniors at Harvard College. Southern Illinois University, Landmarks in Rhetoric and Public Address. Edited by David Potter. Carbondale: Southern Illinois University Press, 1968, pp. ix-lii.
    Provides background on Channing and the Boylston Chair at Harvard. Analysis of the contents of the lectures and some judgment on the extent of their influence.

5.43 ANDERSON, ROBERT. "James Rush--His Legacy to Interpretation." SSJ, 33 (Fall 1967), 20-28.

Argues for a return to the principles, not the excesses, of delivery that Rush advocated, thus restoring delivery to an honorable place in rhetorical studies.

5.44 ARMOUR, RICHARD and RAYMOND F. HOWES. "Addenda to Coleridge the Talker." QJS, 32 (October 1946), 298-303.
Further amplification of the thesis of the book published in 1940: "that Coleridge the talker was the essential Coleridge, of whom Coleridge the writer of prose, Coleridge the poet, and Coleridge the lecturer were somewhat distorted reflections" (p. 303).

5.45 ARMOUR, RICHARD and RAYMOND HOWES. Coleridge the Talker. Ithaca, New York: Cornell University Press, 1940, 496 pp.
A collection and analysis of then available material on Coleridge's talk.

5.46 AUER, J. JEFFREY and JERALD L. BANNINGA. "The Genesis of John Quincy Adams's Lectures on Rhetoric and Oratory." QJS, 49 (April 1963), 119-32.
A study of Adams's general background in rhetoric, the sources he consulted and utilized in preparing his lectures, the circumstances of the lectures' composition and delivery, and their reception by contemporaries.

5.47 AUER, J. JEFFREY and JERALD L. BANNINGA. "Introduction," in John Quincy Adams's Lectures on Rhetoric and Oratory. New York: Russell and Russell, 1969, 7 pp., not numbered.
Brief note on the circumstances surrounding the preparation of these lectures, their critical reception, and their influence.

5.48 AZARNOFF, RAY S. "Walt Whitman's Concept of the Oratorical Ideal." QJS, 47 (April 1961), 169-72.
Argues that Whitman found a common ground in the activity and social purposes of both poets and orators.

5.49 BAKER, VIRGIL L. "Development of Forms of Discourse in American Rhetorical Theory." SSJ, 18 (May 1953), 207-15.
Traces the development of the forms of discourse from the work of John Witherspoon to D. J. Hill whose Science of Rhetoric (5.28) codifies these trends and establishes the four forms in contemporary theory.

5.50 BAKER, VIRGIL L. Review of Samuel Kirkham's An Essay on Elocution (1833) and Henry Mandeville's Elements of Reading and Oratory (1849). QJS, 16 (February 1930), 133-37.
Argues that these two books reveal the "persistence of the grammatical approach to elocution long after the introduction of the physiological approach instituted by James Rush in 1827" (p. 133).

5.51 BAKER, VIRGIL L. Review of William Russell's The American
Elocutionist (1844); Orthophany; or The Cultivation of
the Voice in Elocution (1845); Pulpit Elocution (1846).
QJS, 19 (February 1933), 109-10.
Says The American Elocutionist was more influenced by
John Walker than by James Rush but that The Orthophany, a
collaboration with James E. Murdock, was developed as practical application of Rush's theory. The Pulpit Elocution
applies the principles developed in the two other books to
preaching.

5.52 BANNINGA, JERALD L. "John Quincy Adams as a Contemporary
Critic." CSSJ, 16 (August 1965), 173-78.
Calls attention to the length and scope of Adams's remarks on the orators of his time and discusses Adams's
qualifications as a critic of oratory.

5.53 BARTON, FRED J. "The Significance of 'Extempore Speech' in
English and American Rhetorics." QJS, 27 (April 1941),
236-51.
Suggests that the term "extempore" shifts meaning as one
follows it from period to period. References to its use
in the work of Whately, John Quincy Adams, E. T. Channing,
and other nineteenth-century rhetoricians.

5.54 BAXTER, BATSELL B. The Heart of the Yale Lectures. New York:
The Macmillan Co., 1947, 345 pp.
Study of the contributions of preachers to the theory of
public address. Reviewed by Lionel Crocker (QJS, 34
[February 1948], 98-99), who calls it a "splendid contribu-
tion to the field of rhetorical theory."

5.55 BERLIN, JAMES. "Richard Whately and Current-Traditional
Rhetoric." Forthcoming in CE, 1980.
Notes a shocking lack of knowledge about Whately among
modern composition teachers, an irony since "Whately's
Elements [of Rhetoric] served as a prototype for the textbooks written by Genung and Hill, works which in turn shaped
our modern college rhetorics" (p. 3, manuscript).

5.56 BORMANN, ERNEST G. "The Rhetorical Theory of William Henry
Milburn." SM, 36 (March 1969), 28-37.
A brief study of the subjects and themes of the "natural"
preacher/orator of the nineteenth-century American frontier,
and of their subsequent appearance in later American history
and culture.

5.57 BRIGANCE, W. N., ed. A History and Criticism of American Public Address. New York: McGraw-Hill, 1943, 2 vols., 1948 pp.
Deals with the influence of public speaking on American.
history.

5.57a   HOCHMUTH, MARIE, ed. A History and Criticism of American Public Address. Vol. 3. New York, London, Toronto: Longmans, Green, and Co., 1955, 554 pp.

    A continuation of the earlier work edited by Brigance.

5.58   BROCKRIEDE, WAYNE. "Bentham's Criticism of Rhetoric and Rhetoricians." QJS, 41 (December 1955), 377-82.

    Concludes that Bentham distinguished between "classical and truncated rhetoric" and that he was particularly harsh in his criticisms of the latter. Accused it of being shallow, excessively ornamental, confused, and deceptive. He censured, among others, Plato, Aristotle, Cicero, the Apostle Paul, and others of similar stature. Only George Campbell escaped his scorn.

5.59   BROCKRIEDE, WAYNE E. "Bentham's Philosophy of Rhetoric." SM, 23 (November 1956), 235-47.

    Analyzes the function of utilitarian logic and language and argues that Bentham believed that "speakers should support and listeners accept, propositions on the basis of the utilitarian standard: good reasons, supported by specific and abundant evidence, free from fallacies, expressed in clear language, and showing that the given proposal will probably promote the greatest happiness of the greatest number of people" (p. 245).

5.60   BURKE, REBECCA J. "Gertrude Buck's Rhetorical Theory." Occasional Papers in the History and Theory of Composition, No. 1. Edited by Donald C. Stewart. Kansas State University, 1978, 26 pp.

    A study of Buck's essays on grammar and rhetoric with emphasis on her perception of grammar's origin and growth as being organic, not mechanical, and of the social importance of rhetoric.

5.61   BURWICK, FREDERICK. "Introduction," in De Quincey's Essays on Rhetoric. Southern Illinois University Series, Landmarks in Rhetoric and Public Address. Edited by David Potter. Carbondale: Southern Illinois University Press, 1967, pp. xi-xlviii.

    Argues that "De Quincey's signal contribution to the history of rhetoric is that he brought together, for the first time, the principal elements of Scottish associationism and German aesthetics" (p. xiii).

5.62   CAMPBELL, JOHN ANGUS. "Darwin and The Origin of Species: The Rhetorical Ancestry of an Idea." SM, 37 (March 1970), 1-14.

    Argues that acceptance of Darwin's ideas, even those that in a short time could not withstand rigorous logical examination, occurred not because of their scientific

validity but because of Darwin's ability to synthesize
rhetorically disparate and opposed intellectual traditions.

5.63 CAPLAN, HARRY and HENRY H. KING. "Pulpit Eloquence: A List
of Doctrinal and Historical Studies in English." SM, 22
(Special Issue 1955).
   A comprehensive bibliography of critical and historical
studies on the rhetoric of preaching. Pages 37-92 cover
the nineteenth century.

5.64 CHAMBERS, STEPHEN and G. P. MOHRMANN. "Rhetoric in Some American Periodicals." SM, 37 (June 1970), 111-20.
   Study of "the nature of the rhetorical inheritance for
the period under consideration" (p. 120), and of the way
that inheritance was reflected in magazine articles dealing
with rhetorical theory and practice.

5.65 CHERWITZ, RICHARD A. and JAMES W. HIKINS. "John Stuart Mill's
On Liberty: Implications for the Epistemology of the New
Rhetoric." QJS, 65 (February 1979), 12-25.
   Argues that Mill's is not a rhetoric of the "persuasive
art" but rather "a rhetoric of public discussion broadly
conceived" (p. 12). Furthermore, Mill's rhetoric of public
discussion contains elements of both traditional rhetorical
theory and anticipations of the foundation of modern rhetorical theory.

5.66 COCKERHAN, LOUIS W. "Alexander Bain's Philosophy of Rhetoric."
Ph.D. dissertation, University of Illinois, 1968, 248 pp.
   Discusses the ways in which Bain's associationist concepts of the mind inform his work in logic, grammar, and
rhetoric.

5.67 CORBETT, EDWARD P. J. "What Is Being Revived?" CCC, 18
(October 1967), 166-72.
   A brief examination of nineteenth-century rhetoric and
the persistence of some of its concepts in twentieth-
century rhetorical theory and practice.

5.68 CROCKER, LIONEL. "An Elocutionist Saves Matthew Arnold's
Tour; or The Ungrateful Matthew Arnold." WS, 30
(Summer 1960), 189-94.
   Argues that Arnold's American speaking tour of 1883
would have been a disaster, since Arnold was not accustomed
to speaking before large audiences in large halls, but that
he received help in elocution (which he later scarcely
acknowledged) from John Wesley Churchill of Andover.

5.69 CROCKER, LIONEL. "Charles Haddon Spurgeon's Theory of Preaching." QJS, 25 (April 1939), 214-24.

A study of the career and rhetorical practice of the minister of the Metropolitan Tabernacle in London.

5.70   CROCKER, LIONEL. <u>Henry Ward Beecher's Speaking Art</u>. New York: Fleming H. Revell Co., 1937, 243 pp.
   A study of Beecher's personality, training, art, and influence.

5.71   CROCKER, LIONEL. Review of Samuel Newman's <u>Practical System of Rhetoric</u>. QJS (June 1934), 458-60.
   Contains the following information: that Newman was professor of rhetoric at Bowdoin; that his book was a required text at Amherst; that it went through sixty editions by 1860; that it was primarily a text for writers. The book's subjects were philosophy of rhetoric; cultivation of taste; skill in language use; skill in literary criticism; forming a good style. It was influenced by Aristotle, Quintilian, Cicero, Thomas Wilson, Hugh Blair, George Campbell, and Richard Whately. Newman was not afraid of independent judgments, however, as when he contradicted Blair on taste.

5.72   CROCKER, LIONEL. Review of William Shedd's <u>Literary Essays</u>. QJS, 20 (February 1934), 142-43.
   Notes three essays contained in the work, "The Ethical Theory of Rhetoric and Eloquence," "The Characteristics and Importance of a Natural Rhetoric," and "The Relation of Language and Style," which set forth Shedd's ideas on the distinguishing characteristics of rhetoric and its relationship to Christian character. Shedd was holder of the Chair of Sacred Rhetoric and Pastoral Theology at Auburn.

5.73   CROCKER, LIONEL. "The Rhetorical Influence of Henry Ward Beecher." QJS, 18 (February 1932), 82-87.
   Argues that Beecher was a greater force than Phillips Brooks, that he had skillfully blended his own experience with his knowledge of the classical and eighteenth-century English and Scottish rhetoricians, and that he is "America's only preacher-rhetorician worthy to take his place alongside those great English preacher-rhetoricians, Blair, Campbell, and Whately" (p. 87).

5.74   CROCKER, LIONEL. "The Rhetorical Training of Henry Ward Beecher." QJS, 19 (February 1933), 18-34.
   Supplements Crocker's article (5.73) on Beecher's influence by tracing the classroom training and reading of Beecher (principally in classical works and the dominant late eighteenth-century figures) plus his observation and use of more contemporary figures. Conclusion is the same: Beecher "was partly self-taught and partly a product of textbook teaching" (p. 24).

5.75   CROCKER, LIONEL. "Robert Green Ingersoll's Influence on
       American Oratory." QJS, 24 (April 1938), 299-312.
          Develops the influence of Ingersoll on rank-and-file
       public speakers represented in textbooks and on major
       orators of the late nineteenth and early twentieth cen-
       turies: Albert Beveridge, Robert LaFollette, William
       Jennings Bryan, William Borah, and Eugene Debs.

5.76   CROCKER, LIONEL. "Walt Whitman's Interest in Public Speaking."
       QJS, 26 (December 1940), 657-67.
          Discussion of Whitman's interest in declamation and con-
       versation. Principal influences seem to have been Robert
       Ingersoll and Henry Ward Beecher.

5.77   DAVIDSON, WILLIAM L. "Professor Bain's Philosophy." Mind,
       N.S., 13 (1904), 161-79.
          Argues that Bain was instrumental in overturning meta-
       physical conceptions of mind in favor of those that are
       more modern or can be empirically tested.

5.78   DAVIS, RICHARD BEALE. "James Ogilvie, An Early American
       Teacher of Rhetoric." QJS, 28 (October 1942), 289-97.
          Discussion of an influential Scottish rhetorician during
       the first quarter of the nineteenth century.

5.79   DENTON, GEORGE B. "Herbert Spencer and the Rhetoricians."
       PMLA, 34 (March 1919), 89-111.
          A study of Spencer's borrowings from Hugh Blair, George
       Campbell, Richard Whately, and Lord Kames (Henry Home) with
       special emphasis on his use of Campbell's idea of the econ-
       omy of attention.

5.80   DENTON, GEORGE B. "Origin and Development of Herbert
       Spencer's Principle of Economy," in The Fred Newton Scott
       Anniversary Papers. Chicago: University of Chicago Press,
       1929, pp. 55-92.
          Attempts to deal with a problem noted by Scott in his
       introduction to Spencer's essay on The Philosophy of Style
       (5.21): "The cause of this obscurity is to be found . . .
       in the sudden change and enlargement of meaning which, at
       the very close of the essay, is given to the conception of
       economy" (p. 55).

5.81   DOUGLAS, WALLACE. "Rhetoric for the Meritocracy," in English
       in America. Edited by Richard Ohmann. New York: Oxford
       University Press, 1976, pp. 97-132.
          Examines the philosophy of rhetoric (and composition)
       that accompanied the development of the Boylston Chair at
       Harvard and the decision of Harvard to become a training
       ground for American leaders.

5.82 DURHAM, WELDON B. "The Elements of Thomas De Quincey's Rhetoric." SM, 37 (November 1970), 240-48.
   A reexamination of De Quincey's "Rhetoric" (5.10) which
raises questions about the relationship of De Quincey's
ideas on rhetoric to Whately's, to his (De Quincey's) own
literary ideas, and to the rhetorical tradition.

5.83 EDNEY, C. W. "George Campbell's Theory of Public Address."
Ph.D. dissertation, University of Iowa, 1946.
   At the time, the most detailed analysis of Campbell's
theory of public address.

5.84 EDNEY, CLARENCE. "Richard Whately on Dispositio." SM, 21
(August 1954), 227-34.
   Study of Parts 1 and 2 in The Elements of Rhetoric
(5.11) together with excerpts from The Elements of Logic,
leading to eight generalizations characterizing Whately's
conception of arrangement.

5.85 EHNINGER, DOUGLAS. "Campbell, Blair, and Whately: Old Friends
in a New Light." WS, 19 (October 1955), 263-69.
   Argues that Hugh Blair, George Campbell, and Richard
Whately did not restate ancient rhetorical doctrines but
were instead at the center of a revolution against classicism. Thus, one finds them much closer to current rhetorical theory than was hitherto believed.

5.86 EHNINGER, DOUGLAS. "Campbell, Blair, and Whately Revisited."
SSJ, 28 (Spring 1963), 169-82.
   Amplification of positions taken in the article in
Western Speech, 1955 (5.85). Argues that the influence of
Blair, Campbell, and Whately on modern rhetoric has been
great and that it has not been classical (derivative of
Aristotle, Cicero, Quintilian). Instead, "it was the new
psychology and epistemology of the great British empiricists
as expressed by George Campbell, the new critical system of
the belletristic school as interpreted and applied by Hugh
Blair, and the Copplestonian logico-rhetoric of early
nineteenth-century Oxford as developed by Richard Whately
that put the rhetoric of style and of Ramism once and for
all to rest" (p. 181).

5.87 EHNINGER, DOUGLAS. "Introduction," in Richard Whately's Elements of Rhetoric. Southern Illinois University Series,
Landmarks in Rhetoric and Public Address. Edited by David
Potter. Carbondale: Southern Illinois University Press,
1963, pp. ix-xxx.
   Cites extremes of critical judgment on the work, by
Sir Richard Jebb and by I. A. Richards, and asserts "the
importance of approaching the work armed with some knowledge of its intended character and purpose, of the

intellectual environment in which it was written, and of the rhetorical tradition to which it adheres" (p. ix).

5.88 EHNINGER, DOUGLAS. "Selected Theories of *Inventio* in English Rhetoric, 1759-1828." Ph.D. dissertation, Ohio State University, 1949.

Provides background on the classical rhetoricians' concepts of invention, then discusses the particular "inventional systems" of John Ward, Hugh Blair, George Campbell, Joseph Priestley, and Richard Whately.

5.89 EHNINGER, DOUGLAS. "Whately on *Dispositio*." QJS, 40 (December 1954), 439-41.

Wishes to correct what he sees as a misunderstanding of Whately's meaning interpreted by Clarence Edney in the August, 1954, Speech Monographs (5.84). Says Edney is wrong in thinking that Whately limits himself to argumentative composition. Rather, Whately says that argument and invention are the only provinces that belong exclusively to rhetoric.

5.90 ETTLICH, ERNEST EARL. "John Franklin Genung and the Nineteenth Century Definition of Rhetoric." CSSJ, 17 (November 1966), 283-88.

Evaluates Genung's contributions to rhetorical theory, his work in relation to that of other late nineteenth-century rhetoricians, and the extent to which his work helped to effect the transition in rhetoric from the late nineteenth to the twentieth century.

5.91 ETTLICH, ERNEST E. "Theories of Invention in Late Nineteenth Century American Rhetorics." WS, 30 (Fall 1966), 233-41.

A survey and evaluation of conflicting theories of invention in the work of G. P. Quackenbos, John Hart, Brainerd Kellog, Henry Day, John Genung, A. S. Hill, and D. J. Hill.

5.92 FREEMAN, WILLIAM. "Whately and Stanislavski: Complementary Paradigms of Naturalness." QJS, 56 (February 1970), 61-66.

Argues that "naturalness is the philosophic core of both Richard Whately's system of delivery and Konstantin Stanislavski's system of acting, and it is this concept of naturalness common to both Stanislavski and Whately that has caused them to be the target of critical abuse and shallow interpretation" (p. 61). This article studies the naturalism common to both Whately and Stanislavski and works toward a more accurate understanding of them.

5.93 FRITZ, CHARLES A. "From Sheridan to Rush: The Beginnings of English Elocution." QJS, 16 (February 1930), 75-88.

Argues that elocution as taught in American schools had
its roots in the work of eighteenth-century English writers.
Does cite significant nineteenth-century American books on
elocution: The Pious Instructor by Daniel Cooledge;
Ebenezer Porter's Analysis and Rhetorical Reader (5.14);
Gilbert Austin's Chironomia (5.1).

5.94 GATES, LEWIS E. "Newman as a Prose Writer," in Three Studies
      in Literature. New York: The Macmillan Co., 1899,
      pp. 64-123.
          Analysis of several famous Newman pieces, particularly
      the Apologia Pro Vita Sua, with emphasis on Newman's rhe-
      torical strategies. Argues that Copplestone and Whately
      were the principal influences on his rhetorical art.

5.95 GOLDEN, JAMES L. and EDWARD P. J. CORBETT. The Rhetoric of
      Blair, Campbell, and Whately. New York: Holt, Rinehart,
      and Winston, 1968, 410 pp.
          Contains seven chapters (on invention, arrangement,
      argumentation, elocution) from the seventh edition of
      Richard Whately's Elements of Rhetoric (5.11a) plus analy-
      sis of eighteenth-century responses to classical rhetoric
      and the responses of Whately (and George Campbell and Hugh
      Blair) to those trends.

5.96 GOODFELLOW, DONALD M. "The First Boylston Professor of Rhet-
      oric and Oratory." NEQ, 19 (September 1946), 372-89.
          Contains a detailed account of the history of the form-
      ing of the Chair and a discussion with some analysis of
      the work of the first occupant: John Quincy Adams.

5.97 GOULDING, DANIEL J. "The Role of Debate in Parliament: A
      Nineteenth Century View." WS, 33 (Summer 1969), 192-98.
          Cites Thomas Babington Macauley who found that from the
      seventeenth to the early nineteenth century "parliamentary
      deliberation . . . was frequently less exacting than the
      political exigencies and needs of the state required"
      (p. 148) and that those who were skilled in rhetoric but
      often not well qualified in other necessary areas acquired
      political power and influence they should not have had.

5.98 GRAY, GILES W. and LESTER HALE. "James Rush, Dramatist."
      QJS, 29 (February 1943), 55-61.
          Discussion of the work of a man who laid the theoretical,
      philosophical, and scientific bases for speaking in the
      nineteenth century.

5.99 GRONBECK, BRUCE E. "Archbishop Richard Whately's Doctrine of
      'Presumption' and 'Burden of Proof': An Historico-Critical
      Analysis." Master's thesis, University of Iowa, 1966.

Contains detailed analysis of Whately's doctrine of
'presumption' and 'burden of proof' followed by discussion
of the workability of the doctrine and a judgment on
Whately's contributions to argumentation.

5.100   GROVER, DAVID H.   "Elocution at Harvard: The Saga of Jonathan
        Barber."   QJS, 51 (February 1965) 62-67.
            An account of Jonathan Barber's tenure as assistant to
        E. T. Channing at Harvard; of his linking of "the oral tra-
        dition of [Joshua] Steele and [James] Rush to the physical
        tradition of [Gilbert] Austin . . . [and] the possibil-
        ity . . . that Barber may have introduced into elocution
        the dichotomies of phrenology . . . thus paving the way for
        the pseudoscientific 'systems' which were so evident later
        in the century" (p. 66).

5.101   GUTHRIE, WARREN.   "The Development of Rhetorical Theory in
        America, 1635-1850."   SM, 13 (1946), 14-22; 14 (1947),
        38-54; 15 (1948), 61-71; 16 (August 1949), 98-113; 18
        (March 1951), 17-30.
            A comprehensive review of significant authors and trends
        in rhetorical theory in the period cited.

5.102   HABERMAN, FREDERICK.   "De Quincey's Theory of Rhetoric."
        Eastern Public Speaking Conference, 1940, Papers and
        Addresses.   New York: The H. W. Wilson Co., 1940,
        pp. 191-203.
            Purpose is to "discuss chiefly De Quincey's first essay
        on the subject [Rhetoric] in order to understand his theory;
        secondly, to show his inconsistency with later works; and
        finally, to explain the reason for the inconsistency"
        (p. 192).

5.103   HABERMAN, FREDERICK W.   "The Elocution Movement in England:
        1750-1850."   Ph.D. dissertation, Cornell University, 1947.
            "Focuses upon the movement [elocutionary] itself, its
        teachers and lecturers, its books and treatises, its laws
        and principles. . . . treats of the genesis, the develop-
        ment, and the terminology of the movement; of the founders
        and their theories; of the contributions made to the move-
        ment over a period of a hundred years . . . is a history
        of the theory and philosophy of elocution, not of its im-
        pact on education or on society . . . study is designed
        then, as a contribution to a history of elocution and
        ultimately to a history of rhetoric" (Preface, p. 1).

5.104   HABERMAN, FREDERICK W.   "English Sources of American Elocu-
        tion," in A History of Speech Education in America.
        Edited by Karl Wallace.   New York: Appleton-Century-
        Crofts, 1954, pp. 105-26.

Concerned with "the phenomenon of elocution in England:
with the genesis of the movement; with the characteristics
of the movement--its scope, methodology, divisions, and
terminology; with the authors and books which were the substance of the elocutionary ideas; and with the host of
other elocutionary books which followed in the train of
the movement" (p. 105).

5.105   HABERMAN, FREDERICK W.   "John Thelwall: His Life, His School
        and His Theory of Elocution."   QJS, 33 (October 1947),
        292-98.
            Discusses Thelwall's school of elocution and his attempt
        to make elocution a science.

5.106   HALE, LESTER L.   "Dr. James Rush," in A History of Speech Edu-
        cation in America.   Edited by Karl Wallace.   New York:
        Appleton-Century-Crofts, 1954, pp. 219-37.   Reprinted in
        Lionel Crocker and Paul A. Carmack, eds. Readings in Rhet-
        oric.   Springfield, Ill.:   Charles C. Thomas, 1965,
        pp. 529-41.
            Asserts that Rush's Philosophy of the Human Voice (5.9)
        is an intelligent and scholarly book, an "attempt to apply
        medical science, as it was known to him, to the analysis of
        human behavior and the processes of neurological control.
        In Rush, medical science and speech come together" (p. 219).

5.107   HALE, LESTER L.   "Dr. James Rush--Psychologist and Voice Scien-
        tist."   QJS, 35 (December 1949), 448-55.
            Argues that Rush was, first, a physician, whose interest
        in the functioning of the mind led to his taking the posi-
        tion that it was a physiological phenomenon that manifested
        itself eventually in verbalization.   He thus became "one of
        the early contributors to the modern concept of speech as
        the index to the total personality.   He was a speech psy-
        chologist, and probably America's first voice scientist"
        (p. 455).

5.108   HALE, LESTER L.   "Principles of James Rush as Applied to
        Interpretation."   SSB, 7 (November 1941), 43-45.
            Attempts to correct inflexible and mistaken interpreta-
        tions of Rush's work and to clarify some of the general
        tenets upon which it was founded.

5.109   HALE, LESTER L.   "A Re-Evaluation of the Vocal Philosophy of
        Dr. James Rush as Based on a Study of His Sources."   Ph.D.
        dissertation, Louisiana State University, 1942.
            Studies Rush's reactions to previous treatises on voice
        and tries to determine Rush's basic philosophy on the sub-
        ject, the extent of his originality, and the degree to which
        he adapted previous work.   Concludes that Rush's work is not
        well understood, that his originality lies in areas in

which he has merely adapted precepts from previous work. General conclusion is that Rush's "system," in 1942, was not well understood.

5.110 HANCE, KENNETH G. "The Elements of the Rhetorical Theory of Phillips Brooks." SM, 5 (December 1938), 16-39.
Discussion of Invention, Arrangement, Style, Memory, and Delivery in Lectures on Preaching, The Bohlen Lectures, and other documents by the pastor of Trinity Church, Boston.

5.111 HANCE, KENNETH. Review of Edward T. Channing's Lectures [on Rhetoric and Oratory] Read to the Seniors in Harvard College. QJS, 30 (October 1944), 364-65.
Asks and attempts, briefly, to answer two questions: "(1) In what tradition of rhetoric are these lectures? (2) Of what interest or value are they?"

5.112 HARGIS, DONALD E. "Hiram Corson and Oral Interpretation." WS, 29 (Winter 1965), 37-49.
Brief review of Corson's career, primarily at Cornell, and of his anticipation of modern theories of oral interpretation.

5.113 HARRINGTON, ELBERT. "Rhetoric and the Scientific Method of Inquiry." University of Colorado Studies, Series in Language and Literature, No. 1 (December 1948), 1-64.
Study of invention that attempts to answer these questions: "(1) To what extent as a problem of rhetoric were [past writers on the subject] concerned with sound thought for the speaker? (2) What methods did they propose to achieve it? (3) To what extent were they concerned with modes of proof extraneous to the subject-matter?" Of special interest to nineteenth-century specialists is the discussion of Whately's rhetoric, pp. 52-64.

5.114 HAYWORTH, DONALD. Review of Whately's Elements of Rhetoric. QJS, 14 (November 1928), 594-96.
Argues that Whately's book was used twice as much between 1830 and 1880 as were those of Blair and Campbell and that knowledge of it is indispensable for knowledge of rhetorical theory in academic circles during this time. Notes that Whately anticipated Theodore Roosevelt in maintaining that it is unethical to debate the side of an issue that is opposed to what one really believes.

5.115 HIGGINSON, THOMAS WENTWORTH. Cheerful Yesterdays. Boston and New York: Houghton Mifflin Co., 1898, 361 pp.
Notes that Edward Channing was highly regarded as a teacher of composition. Among his pupils were Ralph Waldo Emerson, Charles Francis Adams, Oliver Wendell Holmes, James Russell Lowell, Francis Child, Henry David Thoreau,

and others. "It will be seen that the classic portion of
our literature came largely into existence under him" (p. 53).

5.116   HOCHMUTH, MARIE. "Phillips Brooks." QJS, 27 (April 1941),
        227-36.
            Assessment of the historical, sociological, and personal
        reasons that enabled Brooks to achieve the eminence he did.

5.117   HOCHMUTH, MARIE and RICHARD MURPHY. "Rhetorical and Elocu-
        tionary Training in Nineteenth-Century Colleges," in A
        History of Speech Education in America. Edited by Karl
        Wallace. New York: Appleton-Century-Crofts, 1954,
        pp. 153-177.
            Studies nineteenth-century elocutionary training in
        quarter centuries and argues that classical rhetoric was
        at the heart of it despite occasional emphases on "the
        science of voice, the quasi-scientific elocutionary system,
        the combination of muscle and vocal rhythm in Delsartian
        systems" (p. 156). Out of this movement, however, the
        modern speech department emerged.

5.118   HOLLOWAY, JOHN. The Victorian Sage. London: Macmillan and
        Co., 1953, 309 pp.
            Studies of Thomas Carlyle, Benjamin Disraeli, George
        Eliot, John Henry Newman, Matthew Arnold, and Thomas Hardy,
        Victorian "sages." Attempts to reach a fuller understanding
        of what each said and the manner in which he or she said it.
        The manner appears to be a kind of argument that goes be-
        yond formal logic; it is intuitive and concerned with the
        ability to gain fresh perceptions about things already
        apparently known.

5.119   HOOSER, GERARD A. Review of SIU Landmark's edition of
        Edward T. Channing's Lectures Read to the Seniors of Harvard
        College. PR, 3 (Winter 1970), 59-62.
            A review of Channing's contribution to rhetorical theory
        and philosophy. Finds Channing contributing to the percep-
        tion of rhetoric as stylistics and little else.

5.120   HOSHOR, JOHN P. "American Contributions to Rhetorical Theory
        and Homiletics" in A History of Speech Education in America.
        Edited by Karl Wallace. New York: Appleton-Century-Crofts,
        1954, pp. 129-52.
            Notes that at the beginning of the nineteenth century,
        British rhetorics, particularly those of Hugh Blair and
        George Campbell and later that of Richard Whately, domi-
        nated the field, but that a number of American works were
        produced and proved to be significant influences on their
        times. Books by John Witherspoon, Samuel Newman, Ebenezer
        Porter, Chauncey Allen Goodrich, E. T. Channing, J. R. Boyd,
        Franz Theremin (in William Shedd's translation), Henry Day,

M. B. Hope, A. S. Hill, and John Genung, among others, are cited.

5.121   HOSHOR, JOHN P.   "Lectures on Rhetoric and Public Speaking, by Chauncey Allen Goodrich." SM, 14 (1947), 1-38. Reprinted in Lionel Crocker and Paul A. Carmack, eds. Readings in Rhetoric. Springfield, Ill.: Charles C. Thomas, 1965, pp. 474-528.
    A biographical note on Goodrich, an account of the history of Goodrich's lectures, and some excerpts on a variety of topics from them.

5.122   HOSHOR, JOHN P.   "The Rhetorical Theory of Chauncey Allen Goodrich." Ph.D. dissertation, University of Iowa, 1947.
    Studies Goodrich's rhetorical theory as it emerges in his unpublished lectures, letters, articles, and criticism contained in Select British Eloquence (5.20). Also examines the extent to which he applies his theory and attempts to discover the rationale for his rhetorical criticism.

5.123   HOWELL, WILBUR S.   "De Quincey on Science, Rhetoric, and Poetry." SM, 13 (1946), 1-13.
    Examines "the propriety of Baldwin's remark [reference to C. S. Baldwin, Ancient Rhetoric and Poetic] that De Quincey's distinction between the literature of knowledge and the literature of power supports and strengthens Aristotle's distinction between rhetoric and poetry" (p. 2). Concludes that Baldwin is not justified in making this assertion.

5.124   HOWELL, WILBUR S.   Eighteenth Century British Logic and Rhetoric. Princeton, N.J.: Princeton University Press, 1971, 742 pp.
    Brief discussion of the problems in dating Whately's articles on logic and rhetoric in the Encyclopedia Metropolitana (p. 700).

5.125   HOWELL, WILBUR S.   "John Locke and the New Rhetoric." QJS, 53 (December 1967), 319-33.
    Traces the influences of Locke's work on Part 1 of Whately's Elements of Rhetoric and Elements of Logic (5.11).

5.126   HOWELL, WILBUR S.   Review of Lionel Crocker's Henry Ward Beecher's Speaking Art. QJS, 24 (February 1938), 153-55.
    Argues that Crocker's book, while useful, should have given fuller treatment to the character of Beecher's audience and should have been edited more carefully.

5.127   HOWES, RAYMOND F.   "Coleridge and Rhetoric." QJS, 12 (June 1926), 145-56.

Draws together Coleridge's thinking on "the power of the
spoken word . . . the value of unity of thought and feeling . . . the relation of ideas to style and diction . . .
definition of the imagination . . . the distinction between
persuasion and conviction . . . rhetorical figures . . .
and suggestions for argumentation" (p. 155).

5.128 HUDSON, HOYT. "De Quincey on Rhetoric and Public Speaking,"
in Historical Studies of Rhetoric and Rhetoricians. Edited
by Raymond F. Howes. Ithaca: Cornell University Press,
1961, pp. 198-214. Reprinted in Studies in Rhetoric and
Public Speaking in Honor of James A. Winans. New York:
Russell and Russell, 1962, pp. 132-51.
Discussion of a few of De Quincey's ideas "which appear
specially significant, considered in relation to rhetorical
tradition and recent stylistic theory and practice; and
illustrations from [De Quincey's] own practice of the
salient points of this theory" (p. 199). Discussion also
of additional miscellaneous observations by De Quincey.
Emphasis continually on the range and fertility of
De Quincey's ideas.

5.129 HUDSON, HOYT. Review of Ebenezer Porter's Lectures on Eloquence and Style (1836) and listing of Porter's Lecture on
the Analysis of Vocal Inflections (1824) and An Analysis of
the Principles of Rhetorical Delivery (1827). QJS, 13
(June 1927), 337-40.
Analysis of the principal features of The Lectures on
Eloquence (5.14) by the professor of sacred rhetoric, later
president, of Andover Theological Seminary. The reviewer
notes the other two titles for the record since he was unable to locate them.

5.130 HUDSON, HOYT. Review of The Fred Newton Scott Anniversary
Papers, by Former Students and Colleagues. Chicago: University of Chicago Press, 1929. QJS, 16 (April 1930),
237-38.
Contains a note of praise for Scott and takes special
mention of George B. Denton's paper on Herbert Spencer.
See Denton, 5.80.

5.131 HUDSON, HOYT. Review of Austin Phelps's Theory of Preaching
and John Broadus's Treatise on Sermons. QJS, 15
(June 1929), 444-45.
A portion of the review is a study of the influence of
the Broadus book (it had gone through forty-two editions
by 1926), one adopting a scientific approach to preaching
and drawing heavily on the classical rhetoricians as well
as on contemporary writers on rhetoric and preaching.

5.132   HUNT, EVERETT LEE. Review of The Copeland Reader: An Anthology of English Poetry and Prose. Edited by Charles Townsend
Copeland. New York: Charles Scribner's Sons, 1926, 1687
pp. QJS, 13 (April 1927), 202-206.
A capsule history of the Boylston Chair at Harvard, a
note that Copeland was its seventh occupant, and a review
of the book.

5.133   HUNT, EVERETT L. Review of Fred Newton Scott's The Standard
of American Speech and Other Papers, Boston: Allyn & Bacon,
1926. QJS, 12 (November 1926), 384-85.
Says the collection is "distinguished by scholarship,
urbanity, and humor," and takes special note of certain
papers in it: "The Congress of Letters"; "The Standard of
American Speech"; "The Genesis of Speech"; and "Two Ideals
of Composition." Notes that C. S. Baldwin would not agree
with Scott's interpretation of Aristotelian or sophistic
rhetoric.

5.134   JENSEN, J. VERNON. "The Rhetorical Influence of Thomas Henry
Huxley on the United States." WS, 31 (Winter 1967), 29-36.
Points out Huxley's obvious contributions to the cause
of Darwinism, but makes a further case for Huxley as a
gifted rhetorician and as a symbol in England and the
United States of "courageous, free, responsible expression"
(p. 36).

5.135   JORDAN, HAROLD M. "Rhetorical Education in American Colleges
and Universities, 1850-1915." Ph.D. dissertation, Northwestern University, 1952.
A study of the history and nature of rhetorical training
in American colleges from 1850, the "final year covered in
[Warren] Guthrie's study," (which see, 5.101, p. 5) and
1915, the year which marked the founding of the National
Association of Academic Teachers of Public Speaking. Topics
covered include the organization of departments which of-
fered training in rhetoric, rhetoric textbooks, elocution,
and the kind of training students received from activities
and public exhibitions.

5.136   KING, ANDREW A. "Thomas De Quincey on Rhetoric and National
Character." CSSJ, 24 (Summer 1974), 128-34.
Discusses "the concept of national character . . . De
Quincey's concept of national character, and . . . the
meaning of these foundations for contemporary scholars"
(p. 129).

5.137   KITZHABER, ALBERT R. "Rhetoric in American Colleges: 1850-
1900." Ph.D. dissertation, University of Washington, 1953.
An analysis of persons, events, and trends that shaped
the teaching of rhetoric in America during the latter half
of the nineteenth century.

5.138　LAMBERTSON, FLOYD WESLEY. "A Survey and Analysis of American Homiletics Prior to 1860." Ph.D. dissertation, University of Iowa, 1930.

　　　　A study of the purposes, content, arrangement, style, and delivery of sermons prior to 1860, with numerous observations about contrasts in attitude and theory that occurred between earlier periods and the nineteenth century. Attention also given to the speaker and the audience.

5.139　LEATHERS, DALE G. "Whately's Logically Derived Rhetoric: A Stranger in Its Time." WS, 33 (Winter 1969), 48-58.

　　　　Contrasts the positions of John Stuart Mill and Whately to argue that Whately was intellectually isolated from the dominant thinkers of his time in being anti-empirical.

5.140　LINDSLEY, CHARLES F. "George William Curtis: A Study in the Style of Oral Discourse." QJS, 5 (March 1919), 79-100.

　　　　Study and appreciation of the oratorical style of Curtis with emphasis upon the theme that his discourse was his personality.

5.141　McKERROW, RAY E. "'Method of Composition': Whately's Earliest 'Rhetoric.'" PR, 11 (Winter 1978), 43-58.

　　　　Discussion of the stages of composition preceding Whateley's Elements of Rhetoric (5.11) for the Encyclopedia Metropolitana. Article contains the "brief" outline of 1822 (edited version of John Henry Newman's copy), which helps establish the probable dates of the encyclopedia article, assists scholars studying the development of the Rhetoric, and "offers an important clarification of [Whately's] conception of the role of 'management' in rhetoric" (p. 43).

5.142　McKERROW, RAY E. "Probable Argument and Proof in Whately's Theory of Rhetoric." CSSJ, 36 (Winter 1975), 259-66.

　　　　Discusses three aspects of Whately's theory of rhetoric: "(1) The meaning of 'argument,' (2) the nature of probable argument, and (3) the methods by which probable arguments are constructed" (p. 259).

5.143　McKERROW, RAY E. "Whately's Theory of Rhetoric." Ph.D. dissertation, University of Iowa, 1974.

　　　　Argues that Whately's rhetoric departs from classical conceptions, from Campbell and associationism, and breaks new ground, in the era, in the philosophy and practice of rhetoric.

5.144　MOHRMANN, G. P. "The Real Chironomia." SSJ, 34 (Fall 1968), 17-27.

　　　　Argues that Austin's conception of gesture was neither so mechanical nor so limited as popularly believed and that

Chironomia (5.1) is an excellent introduction to the elocutionary movement.

5.145 MURPHY, RICHARD. "Goodrich's Select British Eloquence:
       Microcard Edition." CSSJ, 9 (Fall 1957), 37-42.
           An adaptation of Murphy's introduction to a microcard
       edition of Goodrich's work, which is quite rare. Contains
       information about the date of publication, size, and scope
       of Goodrich's work.

5.146 PARRISH, WAYLAND M[AXFIELD]. "Richard Whately's Elements of
       Rhetoric, Parts 1 and 2: A Critical Edition." Ph.D. dis-
       sertation, Cornell University, 1929.
           Studies Parts 1 and 2 of the seventh edition of Whately's
       Elements of Rhetoric (5.11a) (with references to earlier
       editions) as part of an effort to examine "the sources,
       background, development . . . scope" (p. 1) and place in
       the rhetorical tradition to which the work belongs.

5.147 PARRISH, WAYLAND MAXFIELD. "The Tradition of Rhetoric." QJS,
       33 (December 1947), 464-67.
           Discussion of the absence of rhetorical tradition from
       contemporary texts, the age-old conflict between rhetoric
       as a mode of discovering truth and sophistic, and a now
       famous quotation: "English teachers . . . have abandoned
       the very name of rhetoric, and the classical tradition is
       now completely in our [speech teachers'] hands" (p. 467).

5.148 PARRISH, WAYLAND MAXFIELD. "Whately and His Rhetoric." QJS,
       15 (February 1929), 58-79. Reprinted in Lionel Crocker and
       Paul A. Carmack, eds. Readings in Rhetoric. Springfield,
       Ill.: Charles C. Thomas, 1965, pp. 374-96.
           Study of Parts 1 and 2 of Whately's Rhetoric (5.11).
       Argues that it is essentially a textbook on argumentation.
       Contains discussion of formative influences, particularly
       Copplestone's, on Whately, history of the work's composi-
       tion, sources for the Rhetoric, and Whately's original
       contributions.

5.149 PARRISH, WAYLAND MAXFIELD. "Whately on Elocution," in The
       Rhetorical Idiom: Essays in Rhetoric, Oratory, Language,
       and Drama, Presented to Herbert A. Wichelns. Edited by
       Donald C. Bryant. Ithaca: Cornell University Press, 1958,
       pp. 43-52.
           Argues that Whately would have done better had he left
       the subject of elocution alone because he was not suffi-
       ciently prepared to deal with it.

5.150 PAUL, WILSON B. "John Witherspoon's Theory and Practice of
       Public Speaking." SM, 16 (November 1949), 272-90.

Says that Witherspoon, who was unique in American rhetorical history because he both taught a college course in
rhetorical theory and practiced that theory in the pulpit
and in public assemblies, derived his ideas primarily from
Quintilian and Cicero. He was the bridge between the colonial orator and the American statesman of the nineteenth
century.

5.151 PENCE, ORVILLE. "The Concept and Function of Logical Proof in
the Rhetorical System of Richard Whately." SM, 20
(March 1953), 23-39.
Study of Part 1 of The Elements of Rhetoric (5.11), and
selected portions of The Elements of Logic (5.11), which
deal with the application of logic to rhetoric.

5.152 POMEROY, RALPH S. "Whately's Historic Doubts: Argument and
Origin." QJS, 49 (February 1963), 62-74.
A study of one of Whately's smallest but most popular
works, which argues that, disclaimers aside, he was a con-
troversialist. It attempts to show by "an examination of
its argument and origin, how The Historic Doubts produces
a 'lively idea' of the evidential value of testimony . . . ;
how it combines an exercise in historical imagination with
the development of a specific rhetorical intention; and how
it illustrates the remark . . . that 'truth, when witty, is
the wittiest of all things'" (p. 74).

5.153 RAHSKOPF, HORACE. "John Quincy Adams' Theory and Practice of
Public Speaking." Archives of Speech, 1 (September 1936),
7-98.
An abridgment of Rahskopf's dissertation on Adams. See
Rahskopf, 5.155.

5.154 RAHSKOPF, HORACE G. "John Quincy Adams: Speaker and Rhetorician." QJS, 32 (December 1946), 435-41. Reprinted in
Lionel Crocker and Paul A. Carmack, eds. Readings in
Rhetoric. Springfield, Ill.: Charles C. Thomas, 1965,
pp. 463-73.
Argues that Adams summarized and adapted classical
rhetoric for his era (when the elocutionary movement was
predominant) and that his speeches were solid and courageous
efforts on such subjects as state's rights and Jacksonian
democracy, constitutional rights, and slavery.

5.155 RAHSKOPF, HORACE G. "John Quincy Adams' Theory and Practice
of Public Speaking." Ph.D. dissertation, University of
Iowa, 1935.
Observes that although Adams made no original contribution to rhetorical theory, he did organize, summarize, and
intelligently critique both classical rhetoric and that of
his own era. As a speaker, he lacked charisma, but he was

widely respected for the energy, integrity, and intelligence
with which he argued for those causes in which he most
strongly believed: "intense patriotism . . . strong central government . . . [and] opposition to slavery" (p. 132).

5.156   RAY, JOHN W.   "The Moral Rhetoric of Franz Theremin." SSJ,
          40 (Fall 1974), 33-49.
               Argues the originality and significance of Theremin's
          work on three counts: (1) the book made "moral commands
          intrinsic to the practice of persuasive discourse"; (2) it
          made "a unique attempt to maintain the dominance of logical
          appeal while at the same time reserving a vital place for
          emotional appeal"; (3) "it is a reaction and counterstate-
          ment to the pervasive trends of eighteenth-century rhetorical
          theory in that it seeks to ground rhetorical theory in objec-
          tive realism and rational certitude" (pp. 48-49).

5.157   REID, RONALD F.   "The Boylston Professorship of Rhetoric and
          and Oratory, 1806-1904: A Case Study of Changing Concepts
          of Rhetoric and Pedagogy." QJS, 45 (October 1959), 239-57.
               Studies not only the persons involved in the evolution
          of this chair at Harvard, but also the century-long shift
          in its emphases, from an early concern with the tradition
          of classical rhetoric to concern exclusively for a narrow
          concept of written composition and eventually to an abandon-
          ing of rhetoric and oratory for literature and poetry.

5.158   REID, RONALD F.   "John Ward's Influence in America: Joseph
          McKean and the Boylston Lectures on Rhetoric and Oratory."
          SM, 27 (November 1960), 340-44.
               Brief study of Ward's influence on the second holder of
          the Boylston Chair at Harvard. Comments on his lack of
          qualifications for that chair.

5.159   REIN, IRVING J.   "The New England Transcendentalists: Philoso-
          phy and Rhetoric." PR, 1 (Winter 1968), 103-17.
               Asks whether or not the transcendentalists' philosoph-
          ical premises generated the rhetorical strategies observ-
          able in their discourse. Also identifies four strategies:
          "revelation, transcendence, salvation, and omission"
          (p. 105).

5.160   RIED, PAUL E.   "The Boylston Chair of Rhetoric and Oratory."
          WS, 24 (Spring, 1960), 83-88. Reprinted in Lionel Crocker
          and Paul Carmack, eds. Readings in Rhetoric. Springfield,
          Ill.: Charles C. Thomas, 1965, pp. 456-62.
               Traces the development of the philosophy of speech educa-
          tion as molded by holders of the Boylston Chair and con-
          cludes that this position "has represented at best a neutral
          effect rather than a positive aid to the development of
          speech education" (p. 88).

5.161 RIED, PAUL E. "Joseph McKean: The Second Boylston Professor
       of Rhetoric and Oratory." QJS, 46 (April 1960), 419-24.
       Argues that the second holder of the Boylston Chair,
       although overshadowed by both his predecessor, John Quincy
       Adams, and his successor, Edward T. Channing, made no orig-
       inal contribution to rhetorical theory but "was the first
       of the American rhetoricians to criticize in an organized
       manner a wide diversity of both classical and contemporary
       rhetorical theories" (p. 424).

5.162 RIED, PAUL E. "Francis Child: The Fourth Boylston Professor
       of Rhetoric and Oratory." QJS, 55 (October 1969), 268-75.
       Argues that Child subverted the purposes for which the
       Boylston Chair was created and as a consequence ejected
       speech education from the Harvard curriculum, putting in
       its place, the study of literary criticism.

5.163 RIED, PAUL E. "The Philosophy of American Rhetoric as it
       Developed in the Boylston Chair of Rhetoric and Oratory at
       Harvard University." Ph.D. dissertation, Ohio State, 1959.
       An examination of the ways in which holders of the
       Boylston chair shaped its duties to serve their own atti-
       tudes and interests. Author concludes with the observation
       that recent Boylston Professors have been poets; their in-
       fluence on current rhetorical theory has been negligible.

5.164 ROBB, MARY MARGARET and LESTER THONSSEN. "Introduction" to
       Gilbert Austin's Chironomia. Southern Illinois University
       Series, Landmarks in Rhetoric and Public Address. Edited
       by David Potter. Carbondale: Southern Illinois University
       Press, 1966, pp. ix-xxi.
       Backgrounds on Austin, his book, and the influence of
       his ideas in the nineteenth century.

5.165 RODGERS, PAUL C. "Alexander Bain and the Rise of the Organic
       Paragraph." QJS, 51 (December 1965), 399-408.
       Finds the origin of modern ideas about the paragraph--
       that its unity, coherence, and emphasis arise organically,
       as well as logically, from the amplification of a topic
       idea stated in a single sentence--in Bain's work on rhetoric.

5.166 ROUSSEAU, LOUSENE G. "The Rhetorical Principles of Cicero and
       Adams." QJS, 2 (1916), 397-409.
       Argues that John Adams had perhaps too much respect for
       Cicero, even to the point of copying the great Roman
       wholesale.

5.167 SANDFORD, WILLIAM P. English Theories of Public Address,
       1530-1828. Columbus, Ohio, Harold L. Hedrick, 1931, 212 pp.
       Points to the long, relatively unbroken tradition of
       rhetorical principles and practice originating in classical
       antiquity and continuing to the present and argues that

there is special educational significance now in studying "the development of rhetorical theory . . . in England from the time of the first rhetoric in the vernacular, 1530, to the publication of Richard Whately's monumental rhetoric of 1828" (p. 3).

5.168   SCOTT, FRED NEWTON.   Introduction and notes to De Quincey, Thomas, Essays on Style, Rhetoric, and Language.   Boston: Allyn & Bacon, 1893, pp. iii-v, pp. ix-xxiv.
        An expression of what Scott saw as fundamental in De Quincey's essays on the general subject of rhetoric and language: a suggestion of the notion that form is organic, not mechanical; that the social nature of language is of first priority to any writer; that usage is determined by custom and that a comparative study of languages illuminates one's understanding of his/her own.

5.169   SELF, ROBERT T.   "Barrett Wendell."   Twayne United States Authors Series, No. 261.   Boston: G. K. Hall, 1975.
        A brief biography of Wendell. Of particular interest are pages 130-34 in which the author suggests that Wendell's influence on subsequent composition teaching in America was extensive and beneficial.

5.170   SHAW, WARREN CHOATE.   History of American Oratory.   Indianapolis: Bobbs-Merrill, 1928, 679 pp.
        Draws together background material and selected speeches from great American orators. Sections on Abraham Lincoln, Henry Ward Beecher, Robert Green Ingersoll, Henry Clay, John Calhoun, and Daniel Webster especially interesting to nineteenth-century specialists.

5.171   SHEARER, NED.   "Alexander Bain and the Genesis of Paragraph Theory."   QJS, 58 (December 1972), 408-17.
        Argues that Bain did not originate paragraph theory. Rather, he developed and systematized it by drawing on the work of earlier theorists "as well as [by extrapolating] concepts from established sentence theory which he applied to the paragraph in a manner consistent with several laws of association psychology" (p. 409).

5.172   SHEARER, NED.   "Alexander Bain and the Teaching of Rhetoric." CSSJ, 23 (Spring 1973), 36-43.
        Attempts to "explain Bain's theory of rhetorical pedagogy through an analysis of (1) his psychological principles of learning, (2) his programs for classroom instruction as well as individual study, and (3) his concept of the application of rhetorical principles to the efficacy of the teacher" (p. 36). Concludes with a comparison of Bain's ideas and those of W. Ross Winterowd.

5.173 SHEARER, NED. "The Rhetorical Theory of Alexander Bain."
       Ph.D. dissertation, University of Wisconsin, 1967.
           Concludes that Bain was an eclectic who borrowed from a
       number of sources to construct a rhetorical theory that is,
       in the final analysis, neither original nor innovative.
       Author does recognize Bain's influence on conceptions of
       the paragraph, the forms of discourse, and figures of speech.

5.174 SNODDY, ROWENA. "The Classical Bases of John Quincy Adams'
       Theory of Rhetorical Arrangements." Master's thesis,
       University of Oklahoma, 1948.
           Finds Adams drawing on Cicero for his ideas about the
       exordium, types of subjects, classifications, and defini-
       tion of proof; on Aristotle for concepts about narration,
       the importance of propositions, and conclusions; and on
       Quintilian for kinds of propositions, ideas about
       epicheirema and enthymemes, refutation, and theories
       of digression and transition.

5.175 SPROULE, J. MICHAEL. "The Psychological Burden of Proof: On
       the Development of Richard Whately's Theory of Presumption."
       CM, 43 (June 1976), 115-29.
           "Whately's psychological theory of presumption and bur-
       den of proof recommends itself to argumentation theory for
       two reasons. . . . it is a superior model for the inter-
       pretation of Whately's advanced and diverse thinking on
       presumption. . . . it offers greater utility for the appli-
       cation of psychological factors to logical ones in argu-
       mentation" (p. 129).

5.176 STERN, ARTHUR A. "When Is A Paragraph?" CCC, 27
       (October 1976), 253-57.
           Argues that the modern paragraph, contrary to statements
       in textbooks, which reflect a conception of the paragraph
       developed by Alexander Bain in 1866, are not logical units,
       hence easily identifiable by all who know textbook descrip-
       tions of paragraphs.

5.177 STEWART, DONALD C. "The Barnyard Goose, History, and Fred
       Newton Scott." EJ, 67 (November 1978), 14-17.
           Argues that scholars of English, at large, know
       very little about the modernity of Fred Scott, Professor
       of English and Head of the Department of Rhetoric at
       Michigan from 1903-26.

5.178 STEWART, DONALD C. "Rediscovering Fred Newton Scott." CE, 40
       (January 1979), 539-47.
           An examination of the professional career and the peda-
       gogical, philosophical, and rhetorical ideas of NCTE's
       first president, professor of English and Head of the
       Department of Rhetoric at the University of Michigan from
       1903-26.

5.179   SUMMERS, DOROTHY. "The Classical Bases of John Quincy Adams'
        Theory of Rhetorical Invention." Master's thesis, Univer-
        sity of Oklahoma, 1942.
            Concludes that although Adams knew Aristotle's rhetoric,
        he was more disposed to draw on Cicero and Quintilian for
        his principles of invention. Suggests that the latter were
        less philosophical and more practical.

5.180   TACEY, WILLIAM S. "Emerson on Eloquence." TS, 6
        (September 1958), 23-27.
            A summary of Emerson's ideas on oratory, orators, audi-
        ence, and style and delivery in his two lectures on
        eloquence.

5.181   TALLEY, PAUL M. "De Quincey on Persuasion, Invention, and
        Style." CSSJ, 16 (November 1965), 243-54.
            Argues that De Quincey's essays on rhetoric show that he
        had "a sound, though limited, conception of persuasion which
        illuminated invention as a form of persuasion rather than
        merely as the discovery of persuasive means" (p. 243).

5.182   THONSSEN, LESTER W. Review of Andrew Comstock's A System of
        Elocution (1844). QJS, 19 (February 1933), 105-108.
            Notes that Comstock is in the scientific tradition of
        James Rush, then summarizes the author's "treatment in elo-
        cutionary manner, of voice and gesture" (p. 108), and sug-
        gests that this work is important enough to be included
        among other significant nineteenth-century treatises on
        elocution.

5.183   TOWNE, RALPH L. and FREDERICK J. SPECKEN. "Robert Green
        Ingersoll: A Case Study of Free Speech." TS, 10
        (November 1962), 10-12, 29.
            Brief account of Ingersoll's life and career, which
        argues his influence on his own and subsequent generations
        on the defense of freedom of speech, thought, and expression.

5.184   TYLER, JOHN M. "John Franklin Genung." Amherst Graduates'
        Quarterly, 9 (February 1920), 67-68.
            Brief biographical and appreciatory note on Amherst's
        most famous professor of rhetoric.

5.185   WAGNER, R. H. "Review of Works by John Witherspoon. 10 vols.
        Edinburgh, 1805. QJS, 13 (November 1927), 476-79.
            Discussion of the history of the text of Witherspoon's
        works (1805 was the first complete edition) with emphasis
        on volumes 6 and 7, which contain the lectures on moral
        philosophy and eloquence. Traces Witherspoon's indebtedness
        to Cicero, Quintilian, and Horace but indicates his wide
        reading of contemporary sources. Argues that Witherspoon's
        lectures were just as original as those of John Quincy Adams
        but not as well known.

5.186 WATKINS, LLOYD I. "Lord Brougham's Authorship of Four Rhetorical Articles in The Edinburgh Review." QJS, 42
(February 1956), 55-63.
    Argues that Brougham authored 1810 and 1812 articles on
Lord Erskine, an 1813 article on Cicero, and an 1821 article on Demosthenes. Since the Edinburgh Review was as
influential as it was and a mirror of the intellectual
life of the times, the author suggests that attempts be
made to identify other anonymous authors of articles in
the magazine.

5.187 WATKINS, LLOYD I. "Lord Brougham's Comments on the Education
of an Orator." WS, 29 (Spring 1965), 102-107.
    Identifies Brougham as "the most famous British rhetor-
ical critic in the first half of the nineteenth century"
(p. 102), and then presents Brougham's demanding theory
of education for public speakers.

5.188 WEIDNER, HAL RIVERS. "Three Models of Rhetoric: Traditional,
Mechanical, and Vital." Ph.D. dissertation, University of
Michigan, 1975.
    Argues that in the nineteenth century a vitalistic theory
of rhetoric replaced both traditional (Aristotelian) and
mechanical (Campbellian) theories of rhetoric, but that in
the latter half of this century this theory was not found
to be adequate for teaching written composition. It was
replaced by "practical" rhetoric, which was atheoretical,
which reduced composition teaching to concern with super-
ficialities, but which has continued to dominate the teaching of writing in the twentieth century.

5.189 WELLEK, RENE. "De Quincey's Status in the History of Ideas."
PQ, 23 (July 1944), 248-72.
    Brief note on p. 269, the essence of which is that
Sigmund Proctor's Thomas De Quincey's Theory of Literature
(University of Michigan Publications: Language and Litera-
ture, 19 (1943), 319 pp.) vastly overrates the originality
of De Quincey's remarks on rhetoric.

5.190 WINANS, JAMES A. "Whately on Elocution." QJS, 31
(February 1945), 1-8. Reprinted in Lionel Crocker and
Paul A. Carmack, eds. Readings in Rhetoric. Springfield,
Ill.: Charles C. Thomas, 1965, pp. 397-408.
    Discussion of Richard Whately's working out of a method
for teaching delivery with the author's particular emphasis:
that "delivery should spring from thought and feeling rather
than from rules, and imitation" (p. 1). Discussion also of
Whately's strictures on Thomas Sheridan, John Walker, and
Hugh Blair, all of whom had written on elocution.

5.191 WOLFF, SAMUEL LEE. "Scholars," in The Cambridge History of
       American Literature. Vol. 4. New York: G. P. Putnam's
       Sons, 1921, 472 pp.
              Says that E. T. Channing's lectures on rhetoric were
       "descriptive and practical; he gives a student standards
       by which to judge existing discourse rather than assistance
       in producing his own" (p. 472).

5.192 ZACHARIAS, DONALD W. "Thackeray on 'This Ambulatory Quack
       Business.'" WS, 31 (Winter 1967), 51-58.
              Argues that Thackeray's lecture tour of America in 1852
       was a success in no small part because it combined two im-
       portant elements: a big name and a style that was direct
       and commonsensical.

Index of Authors, Primary Works, and Subjects

Index

Michel, Alain, 1.130
Micken, Ralph A., 1.8b
Middle Ages, 1.7, 132, 153
Middle English literature, 2.49,
    70, 134, 138, 140, 149-150,
    156, 162-163, 173
Migne, Jacques P., 2.40
Milburn, William Henry, 5.56
Mill, John Stuart, 5.65, 139
Miller, Joseph, 2.45
Miller, Perry, 3.18, 70, 158,
    224
Milton, John, 3.7, 39a, 58, 62-
    63, 66, 70, 83-84, 90-93,
    95, 98, 103, 112-113, 131,
    136-137, 155, 190, 193, 198,
    225, 228
--Artis Logicae Plenior
    Institutio, 3.39, 193, 198
--Paradise Lost, 3.198
Mino da Colle, 2.199
Minucian,
--On Epicheiremes, 1.22-22a
Mirandola, Pico, 3.57, 139, 153
modistae, 2.60, 171
Mohrmann, G. P., 4.82, 126-128;
    5.64, 144
Molesworth, Sir William, 3.32a,
    81
Monk, Samuel H., 4.29
Montaigne, Michel Eyquem, 3.49,
    74, 76, 155, 187
More, Sir Thomas, 3.136
Morgan, Frank, Jr., 4.130
Mosellanus, Petrus, 3.6, 65
--Tabulae de schematibus et
    tropis, 3.4
Mosher, Joseph A., 2.137
Moxon, T. A., 1.15b
Mudd, Charles, 1.131
Mulcaster, Richard, 3.17a, 92,
    131
--The First Part of the
    Elementarie, 3.17
Mulder, John R., 3.159
Murdock, James E., 5.51
Murphy, James J., 1.132-134;
    2.44, 89, 138-151
Murphy, Mary C., 4.131
Murphy, Richard, 4.28, 47; 5.117,
    145

Murrin, Michael, 3.160
Myrc, John, 2.157

Nadeau, Ray, 1.6b, 24a, 135-138;
    3.30, 161
narrative, 1.35
Nelson, Norman E., 3.162
Nelson, William, 3.163
neologizing, 3.131, 162
Neoplatonists, 1.26
Nequam, Alexander, 2.61
--Commentary on Martianus Capella's
    De nuptiis, 2.155
Newman, John B., 4.132
Newman, John Henry, 5.94, 118
Newman, Samuel P., 5.8, 71, 120
--A Practical System of Rhetoric,
    5.8, 71
Newton, Sir Isaac, 4.44-46
Nietzsche, Frederick Wilhelm,
    3.50, 202
Nims, Margaret F., 2.152
Nisbet, R. G. M., 1.139
Norden, Eduard, 1.140; 2.153
North, Helen, 1.141
North, Ross Stafford, 4.133
Notker, Labeo, 2.78

Ochs, Donovan J., 1.134, 142
O'Donnell, J. R., 2.154-155
Ogilvie, James, 5.78
Ohmann, Richard, 5.81
Oldmixon, John, 4.2a
omissio, 1.36
Ong, Walter J., 3.7-8, 14, 32a,
    39, 70, 81, 91, 101, 118,
    120, 146, 156, 158, 162,
    164-174, 192, 208
Onulf of Speyer,
--Colores rhetorici, 2.172, 192
oral interpretation, 5.35, 112
Oravec, Thomas, 1.143
Orleans, 2.98, 159, 179
ornament, 3.22, 128, 136, 144,
    152
    See also Eloquence
ornatus, 1.66
orthography, 2.39
Ovid, 3.145
Owst, Gerald R., 2.156-157